Politics and Ideology

Politics
and
Ideology

A Reader edited by
James Donald and Stuart Hall
at the Open University

OPEN UNIVERSITY PRESS

Milton Keynes : Philadelphia

Open University Press
Open University Educational Enterprises Limited
12 Cofferidge Close
Stony Stratford
Milton Keynes MK11 1BY, England

and
242 Cherry Street
Philadelphia, PA 19106, USA

First published 1986

British Library Cataloguing in Publication Data

Politics and ideology.
   1. Ideology   2. Political science
   I. Donald, James   II. Hall, Stuart, 1932–
   320.5   JA71

   ISBN 0-335-15099-3
   ISBN 0-335-15098-5 Pbk

Library of Congress Cataloging-in-Publication Data

Main entry under title:
Politics and ideology.
   Bibliography: p.
   Includes index.
   1. Political science—Addresses, essays, lectures.
2. Ideology—Addresses, essays, lectures.   I. Donald,
James.   II. Hall, Stuart.
JA74.P67 1985   320.5   85-21515

ISBN 0-335-15099-3
ISBN 0-335-15098-5 (pbk.)

Text design by Clarke Williams

Typeset by Gilbert Composing Services, Leighton Buzzard, Bedfordshire.

Printed in Great Britain by St. Edmundsbury Press, Bury St. Edmunds,
Suffolk.

Contents

Preface

Politics and Ideology is one of three readers designed for the Open University course *Beliefs and Ideologies*, the others being *Religion and Ideology* (Bocock and Thompson, 1985) and *Subjectivity and Social Relations* (Beechey and Donald, 1985). The context is important, for the book is not concerned solely with providing accounts of 'political ideologies' in the conventional sense of Conservatism, Liberalism, Socialism and the rest. Instead, it focuses on the variety of ways in which politics and ideology interact.

The reader is therefore divided into four sections. The first, drawing on some of the classic writers on the topic, indicates what is at stake in debates about the relationship between politics and ideology. Specific aspects of this relationship are then explored in more detail in three case studies, each structured around an article specially written for this volume. The second section considers how liberal conceptions form the bedrock of politics in bourgeois democracies; it shows how discursive and ideological elements help to define what constitutes 'the political'. The third section approaches ideology as a mechanism articulating political and cultural spheres, with particular reference to the phenomenon of nationalism and its centrality to British Conservatism. The final section steps outside the context of liberal democracy to look at the attempt of Italian Fascism to create new forms of subjectivity through its organization of popular culture.

In compiling this reader, we have tried to include as comprehensive a range of material as possible. As a result, we have had to shorten many of the articles. We hope that reading them in this form here will encourage readers to return to the original versions to follow through the arguments and debates more fully. Editorial cuts have been marked by three dots in square brackets: [. . .]. Editorial interpolations are placed in square brackets.

Although this book has been designed with the needs of Open University students principally in mind, we hope that it will also prove of value and use to other readers concerned, whether academically or politically, with the vital questions that it addresses.

For their advice and assistance in the preparation of the book, we would like to thank John Eldridge, Ernesto Laclau, Veronica Beechey, Robert Bocock, Gregor

McLennan, Kenneth Thompson, Keith Stribley, Tom Hunter, Joan Higgs, Marie Day, Carol Johns and Jo Mathieson. We are also indebted to the authors of the readings for allowing us to publish their work in abbreviated form.

James Donald

Stuart Hall

References

BEECHEY, V. and DONALD, J. (eds) (1985) *Subjectivity and Social Relations,* Milton Keynes, Open University Press.
BOCOCK, R. and THOMPSON, K. (eds) (1985) *Religion and Ideology,* Manchester, Manchester University Press.

Introduction

This volume is devoted to the analysis of political ideologies. The term 'ideology' has itself undergone considerable redefinition since it was first coined. Destutt Tracy, the French *philosophe*, first employed it during the French Revolution to indicate a new 'science of ideas' which, he hoped, would purge public thought of the taint of false, metaphysical or religious illusions and substitute for them the 'true ideas' of the Revolution. So, even in its earliest form, the concept included the contrast between 'true' and 'false' ideas, and the project of 'unmasking illusory ideas'. Napoleon, who at first supported the project, later abandoned it – and in so doing added a critical, negative or derogatory dimension to the concept. He accused the *savants* of being concerned *only* with ideas and of placing ideal aims above the material interests on which, in his view, post-revolutionary society depended.

Many of the subsequent meanings and connotations of the term, ideology, are therefore already rehearsed in this genealogy. Ideas have social roots and perform a social function. They provide the ideas – 'true' or 'false' – within which men and women 'think' about society and their place in it. There is something critically at stake – this is, ultimately, a *political* question – as to whether the society is using ideas which clarify or mystify their understanding of the social world. Here, also, is the attempt to enlist or recruit ideas for and against crucial political positions; and the critical aspect – the deconstruction or unmasking of ideology. Thinking 'ideologically' comes to mean being led in certain directions by the very concepts we are using; biased or *a priori* thinking; the charge of idealism. These have continued to provide the contested dimensions to the concept of ideology since its earliest appearance.

In this collection, the term ideology is used to indicate the frameworks of thought which are used in society to explain, figure out, make sense of or give meaning to the social and political world. Such ideas do not occur, in social thought, one by one, in an isolated form. They contract links between one another. They define a definite discursive space of meaning which provides us with perspectives on the world, with the particular orientations or frameworks within which we do our thinking. These frameworks both enable us to make sense of perplexing events and relationships – and, inevitably, impose certain 'ways of looking', particular angles of vision, on those events and relationships which we are struggling to make sense of. Without these frameworks, we could not make sense of the world at all. But with them, our perceptions are inevitably structured in a particular direction by the very concepts we are using.

Thus social and political thought is not as open-ended, free-ranging, spontaneous and self-generated as we imagine. We are not, as we imagine, the conscious and intentional authors of our thoughts. Rather we are 'spoken' by the concepts and languages which already exist in our cultural world and which impose their logics on us unconsciously even as we imagine that we enunciate them. Of course, each individual puts together, out of the variety of ideas to which we are exposed, his or her very particular perspective on the world. But when we study these perspectives closely, we find that they tend to fall into broader, shared, collective patterns which are widely diffused throughout society. In formulating political ideas, we frequently locate ourselves within one or other of the great organic views of society already available to us in our culture – of course, imposing on them our own particular inflection. It is not possible to map the enormous variety of individual perspectives, but it is possible to make an inventory of the broad contours of social thought which prevail in any given society at a particular time.

Here, we find the negative and positive aspects of ideology co-existing at any one moment. The *positive* function of ideology is to provide the concepts, categories, images and ideas by means of which people make sense of their social and political world, form projects, come to a certain consciousness of their place in that world and act in it. The *negative* function refers to the fact that all such perspectives are inevitably selective. Thus a perspective positively organizes the 'facts of the case' into *this* and makes sense because it inevitably excludes *that* way of putting things. This is broadly what it means to say that social and political thought always takes place 'within ideology'.

This gives us one important meaning of the term 'political ideologies' and at the same time indicates something of the content of this volume. The collection of articles is concerned with the great range of discursive 'systems of thought' which, in modern societies, confer meaning for their subjects on the contested world of political and social relationships. These are analysed from a variety of perspectives. The volume also deals with some of the major ideological 'formations' which are present in society or which have exercised significant historical influence in the past, like liberalism, or conservatism. We offer various accounts or inventories of their internal structure, content and shape as well as their distinctive logics – how they establish relations between different ideas and concepts. We are also concerned to map their boundaries – the characteristic inflections which they positively impose on what is being thought and hence what they characteristically leave out, omit, suppress or cannot formulate.

The extracts on various aspects of nationalism and the categories used to construct 'other' cultures are particularly relevant here. In these and other cases, we have selected articles which bring out the internal contradictions characteristic of those discourses, which they repeat without being able to resolve. However, as the early history of the term ideology suggests, we cannot only be concerned with the internal structure and logic of different ideologies because the really critical issue arises when we pose questions about the role, function and effect of those frameworks as they actively operate in society. How do ideologies structure political thought? How do they articulate to different political positions? How are they harnessed to conflicting social interests? What perspective on political events do they systematically tend to impose? How are the struggles between competing ideologies resolved and fought through? What are the different forms of consciousness which these competing conceptions of the political world construct? These are some of the key questions which constitute the social analysis of ideology and which surface as soon as we bring the internal analysis of ideology to bear on questions concerning their social and political function, their place in social practice.

At one stage, it was assumed that what mattered most in the study of political ideologies was the great organic 'systems of thought'. These had persisted over long periods of time, become institutionalized within the culture and political life of society, and received, in their time, a high degree of systematization, philosophical reflection and logical elaboration. In Political Science, political ideology has traditionally been taken to mean political thought of this highly systematic or doctrinal form: the great creeds of Liberalism, Conservatism and Socialism for example, which between them have tended to dominate and organize political thought in English society over many centuries. Now, these great 'systems of thought' are indeed of critical importance. Of course, they are not static constructions. They are constantly evolving, being modified and reconstructed in order to be made relevant to changing historical circumstances. We deal in this volume with this evolving historical process within political thought and discourse. Nevertheless, where these doctrinal systems are concerned, we can soon identify a set of core conceptions which define their discursive space of operations and we can recognize the 'family connections' between different variants of these 'systems' which, though not quite the same, clearly belong to the same constellation. The links between classical liberalism and modern neo-liberalism are not direct but they are not difficult to trace. Because these systems of thought have organized political ideas over a long and complex period of history and because they have achieved intensive philosophical elaboration, it is to them that the analysts of political ideologies naturally turn. In this volume we have considered a selection of these grand political constellations – in particular the formations labelled Liberalism, Conservatism, Nationalism and Fascism.

Philosophy and common sense

We were anxious to indicate something of the *range* of political ideologies in this volume. This also influenced our choice of the opening 'classical' extracts. But the general approach has also been influenced by the argument – advanced by, among others, the Italian marxist theorist Antonio Gramsci – that ideology cannot be confined to its 'philosophical' moment. The concept must also include the common sense, everyday conceptions of the world, which do not necessarily carry any of the grand labels, but which form the basis of what has been called 'practical political consciousness'. Ideology also means the often fragmentary, episodic, internally contradictory, and incomplete chains of thought which ordinary people use in everyday social intercourse to figure out and make sense of what is happening in the political and social world. These ubiquitous little frames of thought are the perspectives within which the vast range of everyday political calculation is actually made. Their influence is enormous – altogether incommensurate with what we might imagine to be their logical consistency. People are not very rigorously logical or consistent over long stretches of their political thinking. Yet they are often quite consistent in terms of the basic ideas to which they constantly return – using the same, apparently incomplete and unsatisfactory conceptions and rather ill-defined ideas as the props and supports of critical thought and action.

This terrain of common sense is, we have to acknowledge, profoundly structured by ideology. These two dimensions to political thought – the philosophical and the common sense – are not as separate as they might at first appear. When we look into 'common sense' political thinking we frequently find that it is not what it first appears to be – the obvious, distilled, proverbial wisdom of the ages. Rather, common sense is composed of the historical traces, incomplete borrowings, diluted concepts and prejudices, inherited wisdoms and formulations incorporated from a variety of the 'great systems' of political thought which have sedimented into it. We swing, in our actual thought, from 'liberal' to 'conservative' to 'collectivist' arguments as we move, episodically, from one area of thought or practice to another. We get a kick out of our ancient and revered institutions, believe fervently that every person must be free to maximize his or her self-interest, and see ourselves as responsible and 'caring' members of society – without experiencing much more than a tiny, involuntary hesitation as we shift gears through these conservative, liberal and social-welfarist discourses which consistently 'map out' political thought in British society.

Gramsci argued that there are always two 'floors' to political (or other types of) ideology: 'philosophy' and 'common sense'. The relations between these two levels are extremely complex. They work in both directions. Logically and philosophically elaborated thought leaves its traces in more sporadic and spasmodic everyday common sense. Conversely, the pattern of common-sense beliefs achieves, sometimes, a more rigorous and clarifying philosophical elaboration and consistency. To this, Gramsci added a further argument which touches and expands on the basic theory of the sociological analysis of ideology and social ideas. He argued that the centre of attention *must* be those ideologies which have influenced the thought and action of the great mass of people, which organize thinking about society, which help to form mass consciousness and provide the ideas commonly in use and the categories in which apparently spontaneous practical social thought generally occurs. Such ideologies, he argued, had achieved true historical or 'organic' influence. They are not the occasional, 'willed' ideas which come and go without making any broad historical impact on society. Consequently, by adopting this historical and sociological perspective, we shift the focus of analysis away from highly systematized political doctrine, considered in isolation. We focus, instead, on the way political ideas 'become organic' by being absorbed into the structure of common sense and common practice.

This volume thus adopts a variety of different approaches but, whatever the perspective, the 'great' organic ideologies are analysed in the context of their capacity to form and re-form common sense. This moves the analysis of political ideology from the internal inventory towards the study of the social role of ideas. What matters in the end about ideologies is that they 'organize human masses and create the terrain on which men move, acquire consciousness of their position, struggle etc.' (Gramsci, 1971).

There is another sense in which the object of study in this volume is not so much 'political ideologies', as such, but more the relations between politics and ideology. Again, in conventional Political Science, a clear distinction is usually drawn between these two. Politics has to do with the operation of power and government, in the sphere of the political institutions and the state. Ideology has to do with systems of political and social ideas. In fact, it is difficult to maintain any such clear distinction between the two domains. We have already touched on the political dimension *within* ideology. The relationship between philosophy and common sense, Gramsci argued, is ultimately political. To become effective, ideas must be organized. This relates to the question of how ideas circulate, how thought is produced and who has the principal control over the dissemination and circulation of ideology. It relates also to the structures of thought within the practical consciousness of the mass of the population; and to whom is given, in any society, the specialized function of 'thinking' – i.e. the formation of the intellectual strata and their relations with the masses and mass consciousness. Also, of course, it embraces the relations of power – of force and consent in different combinations – which always accompany the rise to dominance in society of any one distinctive mode of thought, or the contestation between conflicting ideas and conceptions. All these facets of the problem of ideology reflect the fact that the disposition and operation of ideas in society cannot take place outside the interplay of power and interest. All ideology, we may say, operates on the terrain of politics and power and thus poses 'political' questions. The aim here has been to choose a variety of articles which map, from different points of view, these relations between politics and ideology. The 'classic' opening statements, for example, are not statements of particular ideologies so much as statements *about* the relations between politics and ideology.

We can also reverse this order of questions. We have a very clear conception, in our culture, of what constitutes the institutional domain of politics. Its basic elements are elections, political parties, programmes, central and local government, the state apparatus and the operation of *rules* in creating and maintaining ordered socio-economic and political relationships. We do not often acknowledge how culturally specific this definition of politics is–though, on reflection, we know that this is not how many other societies define 'politics', nor does it begin to cover the great range of political forms and relationships known to us historically. What is even more important, we know that 'political relationships' are by no means confined, even in our own society, to the institutional terrain of political parties, elections and voting. In recent years–to roughly illustrate the point–we have become much more aware of the centrality of 'relations of power' to such domains as the family, welfare, health and sexuality, which would not normally have been included under the rubric of conventionally defined 'politics'. What this suggests is that, if all ideological relationships are mediated by power–and hence are in a broad sense 'political'–then there is also a critical sense in which politics itself is *ideologically defined*. What 'politics' is defined as at any one time–what it includes and what it excludes; where its boundaries fall; what concepts are considered legitimate to its analysis and what illegitimate; why at one time politics is confined to the 'public' realm and at another time (as the result of extensive contestation) to 'the personal is political' realm, as modern feminists have convincingly argued–indicates that the domain of politics is not 'naturally' defined, but is ideologically constructed. Consequently, its boundaries shift historically as the result–among other things–of the process of ideological contestation and struggle.

The Marxist legacy

The critical argument about the social role of ideology was, of course, first formulated in its most contested form by Marx and Engels. It is not simply that the most developed set of arguments and positions about ideology are to be found within the marxist perspective. The fact is that, whether you adopt a marxist position on the question of ideology or not, *any* theory of ideology must deal, sooner or later, with Marx's challenging theses about ideology and with how these conceptions have been debated and reshaped within the different marxist traditions. That is why, in the rest of this introduction, we have given space to following through one strand in this debate.

The most searching formulation Marx offered was about the *epistemological* status of ideology–its status as a mode of thought, inquiry or explanation; its 'truth' status. This arises from Marx's insistence, in line with his general materialist theory, that ideas arise from social relations, not the other way around. Ideas, he said, have no independent or autonomous status, but are, in the end, 'expressions of' the material relationships in society and are governed or determined, not by their own internal logic, but by material relationships themselves. This constituted a serious assault on the basically 'idealist' position, that ideas arise independently of society and, in constituting their 'truth', float free of material relationships. Its generally unmasking thrust is shared by many classical and modern theorists who are *not* marxist–for example, Hobbes and Nietzsche. This led to Marx's famous 'inversion' of Hegel ' . . . it is not consciousness which determines being but . . . being which determines consciousness'. The problem with this formulation is that it gives ideas a wholly *dependent* status – a second-order type of reality – in the scheme of things. Their 'truth' now lies, in a sense, outside them, in the content of the real relations which they merely 'reflect'. In its *hard* form, this proposition leads to the metaphors of the 'economic base' determining, more or less directly – given various loops, lags and short-circuits – the 'ideological superstructure', or what has subsequently been known as the 'base/superstructure' problem in the theory of ideology.

This metaphor of 'base and superstructure' has subsequently been much criticized by social analysts, including some marxist theorists, as being too reductionist in form, too mechanistic and too 'economistic'. Marx gave the economy the determining role in 'the base'; and so ideas came to be, in 'vulgar marxist' terms, nothing but the ideal expression of the *economic* relationships of society. There has been an extended and unfinished debate, which Engels himself set in motion shortly after Marx's death, as to whether anything so simple and uni-directional – base-to-superstructure – was what Marx 'really' intended.

More directly germane to the study of political ideologies is the other, equally contested, formulation by Marx:

> . . . the ideas of the ruling class are in every epoch the ruling ideas, i.e. the class which is the ruling *material* force of society, is at the time, its ruling *intellectual* force. The class which has the means of material production at its disposal, has control at the same time over the means of mental production, so that thereby, generally speaking, the ideas of those who lack the means of mental production are subject to it. The ruling ideas are nothing more than the ideal expression of the dominant material relationships grasped as ideas; hence of the relationships which make the one class the ruling one, therefore, the ideas of its dominance.
> (Marx and Engels, *The German Ideology*)

This passage extends directly into the political dimension the general point about the material basis of ideas. It identifies ideology with classes; above all, with the *dominance* of one class/set of ideas and the *subjection* of another class/set of ideas to it. (Dominance and subjection here are the basic polar points in any political or 'power' relationship.) This puts the point about the politics of ideas into very sharp focus. However, the passage is very condensed. Marx elaborates so little on the actual mechanisms and processes by which such an effect of direct correspondence between class and ideology could be achieved. Nevertheless, virtually the whole of the subsequent argument in social science about political ideology could be regarded as a set of elaborate and conflicting footnotes to this seminal passage.

Marx was writing here at a very 'high' level of generalized abstraction. The subsequent problems may have arisen because commentators attempted to interpret what is a very general statement, about the relationship between the dominance of a particular class and the dominance of 'the ideas of its dominance', as if it was intended to be applied literally to every concrete historical situation.

When Marx went on to analyse such a historical conjuncture – the events in France of 1851 (*The Eighteenth Brumaire of Louis Bonaparte*) – he presented a far more complicated, less reductionist, account. For example, he no longer treated classes as single, homogeneous entities, each with 'its' appropriate 'ideas'. Instead, he gave considerable attention to the complex interplay of different ideas, symbols and slogans and to the different class strata which became organized behind them during the subsequent course of events. He sketched a complex relationship between ideas and their 'class representatives'. For example, at one point he argued:

> . . . one must not take the narrow view that the petty bourgeoisie explicitly sets out to assert its egoistic class interests. It rather believes that the particular conditions of its liberation are the only general conditions within which modern society can be saved and a class struggle avoided.

In other words, ideology is not necessarily a deliberate, conspiratorial 'cover' for class interests. It provides the imaginary forms of consciousness in which a class authentically 'lives' in relation to its conditions of existence. He added the general point that

> . . . one must not imagine that the democratic representatives are all shopkeepers or their enthusiastic supporters . . . What makes them representatives of the petty bourgeoisie is the fact that their minds are restricted by the same barriers which the petty bourgeoisie fails to overcome in real life, and that they are driven in theory to the same problems and solutions to which material interest and social situation drive the latter in practice. This is the general relationship between the political and literary representatives of a class and the class which they represent.

This is a far less 'class reductionist' way of posing the relationship between ideology and class than is common in most marxist analyses. But, unfortunately, Marx left these formulations at the level of the concrete analysis of a historical conjecture and did not give them a more general theoretical formulation. As Colin Mercer shows in his article on fascist ideology, however, subsequent marxists have had to address this question of the relationship between ideology and class.

Gramsci took the argument considerably further in the direction of a non-reductionist reading of ideology in his scattered formulations (in *Selections From The Prison Notebooks*, 1971). He gave cultural and ideological factors their own 'relatively autonomous' weight. He emphasized the critical role which the organization of different conceptions of the world plays in the construction and maintenance of hegemony. But his major contribution lies in his conceptualization of the social role and function of ideologies. He pointed to their role in 'preserving the ideological unity of the entire social bloc which that ideology serves to cement and to unify', and the 'psychological validity' they must have if they are to 'organize human masses and create the terrain on which men move, acquire consciousness of their position, struggle, etc.'.

Althusser

One seminal contribution in more recent years to the development of a non-reductionist marxist approach to the relationship between class, politics and ideology is to be found in the work of the French philosopher, Louis Althusser. The important point about Althusser's contribution is that it attempted to combine, but in novel and challenging ways, the two key insights which Gramsci had advanced. But it did so within a theoretical framework heavily influenced by modern structuralist and semiotic approaches.

If indeed, ideologies have the 'internal' and psychological and organizational capacity which Gramsci argued, then we have to pose the question of *how* this operates and what are the mechanisms by which it is effected. One way of answering this question is to argue, as Althusser did, that ideology is 'a system (with its own logic and rigour) of representations (images, myths, ideas or concepts, depending on the case) endowed with an historical existence and role within a given society' (Althusser, 1969). This suggests that ideology is not a question of consciously-held and formulated sets of beliefs but is actually the social 'atmosphere' in which we live. Althusser also gave a more semiotic or discursive definition of ideology itself. He treated ideologies, essentially, as 'systems of representation'. More specifically, he argued that the representations which comprise ideologies work in a *structural* way. As he put it, '...it is above all as *structures* that they impose on the vast majority of men, not via their "consciousness". They are perceived-accepted-suffered cultural objects and they act functionally on men via a process that escapes them' (Althusser, ibid.). Ideology, in other words, works on us to a large extent *unconsciously*, in the structures of, for example, 'common sense' and in our acceptance that things are 'natural', 'obvious' and pre-given. Ideology provides us with the bedrock of *presuppositions* by and in which we make sense of our everyday lives and organize them into the categories of our experience. However, if we follow Althusser's line of reasoning, we come up against another question: How do this 'system of mass representations' or these 'structures' actually work on us internally? How, to put it bluntly, do they 'recruit' us into their perspectives of the world?

Althusser answered this question by deploying the philosophical and juridical category of the *subject*. The subject is not the same as the human person, it is not the 'biological person' which you or I are: it is, rather, the *social* category in which we exist as social beings – as a legal subject, as a family subject, as a sexual subject, as a grammatical subject, 'I' etc. The important thing to note about this particular category is that it is not a naturally occurring entity but a *symbolically constructed* one. This was Althusser's point: that the *subject* of ideology is a constructed category and that it is precisely this construction of the category of the subject which is the key mechanism in the functioning of ideology: 'The category of the subject is constitutive of all ideology insofar as all ideology has the function (which defines it) of "constituting" concrete individuals as subjects' (Althusser, 1971).

In the next stage of the argument, Althusser used another term – *interpellation* – in order to describe the more precise mechanisms of recruitment. This term has the double function of both *naming* you and *positioning* you as, for example, a 'subject of law'. Althusser called this mechanism a form of 'hailing', in which you immediately recognize that it is *you* that is being addressed; and in that process of recognition you also submit or subject yourself to the consequences of the positioning:

> Ideology 'acts' or 'functions' in such a way that it 'recruits' subjects among the individuals (it recruits them all), or 'transforms' the individuals (it transforms them all) by the very precise mechanism that I have called interpellation or 'hailing'. (Althusser, 1971)

The mechanism is therefore based on a process of what we might call spontaneous identification as, for example, when somebody speaks of the 'British people'. If we are British we automatically recognize our place within that discourse and we also recognize the sorts of characteristics which that discourse involves, and identify ourselves in that place as a potential 'author' of the statement. This is where we come to the crunch. It is clear that in an interpellation like 'the British people', we tend to recognize certain principles of unity, certain elements which are included and certain elements which are marginalized or excluded. All ideologies perform this work of exclusion and inclusion. Such an interpellation thus works both to identify and to circumscribe a set of limits. The British people may or may not include, for example, people who are black, or people of a different set of religious or political beliefs, or who subscribe to a different way of life. The criteria for that circumscription, for those processes of inclusion and exclusion, are not *given* in the words 'British people'. They vary according to its discursive and ideological location. To take a contemporary example, it is clear that when Enoch Powell used the notion of 'British people', his criteria for demarcation were quite different from those included in Tony Benn's use of the same expression.

Laclau

In *Politics and Ideology in Marxist Theory* (1977), Ernesto Laclau developed further this concept of interpellation and its discursive and ideological function. He argued, for example, that it played a significant role in the operation of fascist ideology (an example discussed in this volume). Instead of following the more orthodox marxist argument, which states that fascist ideology is a more or less straightforward expression of the most retrograde sections of the bourgeois class and monopoly capital, Laclau engages more fully with the problem, central to our own analysis, of the *popularity* of fascism across different classes. He is aware that different classes share the same ideological and linguistic universe. Different ideologies intersect within the same space and sometimes are structured around the same concepts, though giving them a different meaning or connotation. Thus fascism, by virtue of its active 'anti-nature', anti-liberal, anti-democratic, anti-pacifist, anti-communist, anti-compromise, but above all *anti-power bloc*, character was able to articulate to its own discourses an ensemble of radical, jacobin and popular positions and mobilize them against the 'power-bloc' of an exhausted and over-compromised liberal regime. Therefore, Laclau advances the argument that 'far from being the typical ideological expression of the most conservative and reactionary sectors of the dominant classes . . . ' fascism was, rather, *'one of the possible ways* of articulating the popular-democratic interpellations into political discourse.' (Laclau, 1977). He is not arguing here that fascism was therefore democratic or that, in a blanket way, it was popular. But he is arguing that the concepts of *democracy* and the *people* were articulated within fascist discourse in such a way as to provide, for sections of different classes, some principles of ideological unity. These particular substantive elements therefore have no 'necessary class-belongingness'. Neither of the politically potent concepts of 'people' or 'democracy' actually belongs *irretrievably* to any one class or ideological discourse. Their position in different discursive formations cannot therefore be analysed or reduced to purely class terms. Rather than having a single, unequivocal class connotation, these ideological terms are *multidiscursive*. They are concepts which can mobilize support across class, region and gender. In fact, they became articulated into a bloc which then developed society in a particular economic and social direction and was underpinned by a particular alliance of class forces.

Laclau therefore argues that particular ideological elements do not have a pre-given class location. Taken in isolation, we cannot designate a particular element, whether it be patriotism, familial duty, sacrifice or opposition to the state, as *essentially and necessarily* the prerogative of one given class or social group. It is true that, historically, a given element may have been consistently associated with a given political position – say, patriotism with the political Right. But that is because of the historical success of right-wing politics in consistently articulating this particular conception, with its now dominant associations, to a particular political position or place in discourse. (Hugh Cunningham, also extracted in this volume, has effectively demonstrated, for example, that in eighteenth-century Britain, the concept of patriotism was more frequently associated with radical politics than conservative politics.) Laclau argues that such ideological elements have 'no necessary class connotation' and that their connotation, or association, where it is seen to exist (as in the case of patriotism), is, first, the result of the articulation of those elements into a concrete ideological discourse; and second, the effective articulation of that discourse to different class forces and political positions. The precondition for analysing this ensemble of discourses within the 'chameleon' of fascist ideology is not to pick out particular elements and to identify them as typically 'fascist' or typically 'petty-bourgeois' or typically reactionary but rather to examine the ways in which these elements were effectively *condensed* into particular unities, to understand the ways in which they came – and hung – together in a relative but precarious unity over a twenty year period; and how these discourses were linked to a particular configuration of social forces. This shifts the focus of analysis from the given class basis of ideology to the process of disarticulation and articulation or what is sometimes called the 'class struggle *in* ideology'.

These, then, are some of the ways in which recent theorists have tried to build on the critical conception of political ideology and the notions of ideological dominance and subjection which are at the heart of any serious theory of political ideology. They have tried to expand on the actual ways in which these ideological effects have been achieved, not by focusing on the ascription of a *necessary* link between classes and ideological elements. Instead, the aim has been to develop a conception of ideology as the articulation of a number of concepts within a particular discourse; and to expand on the social connection or function of ideology, not in terms of 'class belongingness', but in terms of the process of ideological struggle and contestation – the practices by which ideologies are articulated and disarticulated to different social, political and class positions in society. These advances certainly do not as yet constitute an adequate or satisfactory theorization of the problem of the social function of political ideology. But they do represent a series of interesting strategic theoretical advances which, between them, help to define the current 'state of play' in this field of inquiry.

References

ALTHUSSER, L. (1969) *For Marx,* Harmondsworth, Penguin.
ALTHUSSER, L. (1971) *Lenin and Philosophy, and other Essays,* London, New Left Books.
GRAMSCI, A. (1971) *Selections from the Prison Notebooks,* London, Lawrence and Wishart.
LACLAU, E. (1977) *Politics and Ideology in Marxist Theory,* London, New Left Books.

Acknowledgements

1.4 Reprinted from K. Marx & F. Engels, *The German Ideology* (Ed C.J. Arthur), Lawrence & Wishart, 1970, by permission of Lawrence & Wishart.

1.5 Reprinted from K. Marx, 'A Contribution to the critique of Political Economy' in *Karl Marx: Early Writings* (Pelican Marx Library 1975), pp 425-6, selection and notes   New Left Review, 1974, by permission of Penguin Books Ltd and Random House Inc.

1.6 Reprinted from M. Weber, 'Politics as a vocation' in Gerth & Wright Mills (Eds), *On Max Weber*, Routledge & Kegan Paul, 1948, by permission of Oxford University Press (New York).

1.7 Reprinted from A. Gramsci, 'The Study of Philosophy' in Hoare & Nowell-Smith (Eds), *Selections from the Prison Notebooks*, Lawrence & Wishart, 1971, by permission of Lawrence & Wishart.

1.8 Reprinted from F. Hayek, *Economic Freedom and Representative Government*, Institute of Economic Affairs, 1973, copyright   The Wincott Foundation 1973, by permission of the Wincott Foundation.

2 Reprinted from E. Laclau, *Politics and Ideology in Marxist Theory*, New Left Books, 1977, pp. 100-111, by permission of Verso.

3 Original article by Stuart Hall   The Open University 1985, by permission of the Open University.

4 Reprinted from J. Mitchell & A. Oakley (Eds), *The Rights and Wrongs of Women*, Pelican 1976, by permission of Deborah Rogers Ltd.

5 Reprinted from E.J. Hobsbawm, *Worlds of Labour*, Weidenfeld and Nicolson, 1984, copyright   E.J. Hobsbawm, by permission of Weidenfeld (Publishers) Ltd.

6 Reprinted from B. Anderson, *Imagined Communities: Reflections on the Origins and Spread of Nationalism*, New Left Books, 1983, pp. 14-40, copyright   B. Anderson 1983, by permission of Verso.

7 Reprinted from R. Scruton, *The Meaning of Conservatism*, Pelican 1980, copyright   Roger Scruton 1980, by permission of Penguin Books.

8 Reprinted from H. Seton-Watson, *Nations and States*, Methuen, 1977, pp. 28-42 copyright   Hugh Seton-Watson 1977, by permission of Associated Book Publishers (UK) Ltd.

9   Reprinted from T. Nairn, *The Break-up of Britain*, New Left Books, 1977, pp. 153–163, copyright   Tom Nairn, by permission of Verso.

10   Reprinted from D. Cannadine, 'Context, Performance and Meaning' in E. Hobsbawm & T. Roger (Eds) *The Invention of Tradition*, Cambridge University Press, 1983, pp. 101–164, copyright   David Cannadine, by permission of Cambridge University Press.

11   Reprinted from H. Cunningham, 'The Language of Patriotism, 1750–1914' in *History Workshop Journal*, Autumn 1981, by permission of Routledge & Kegan Paul plc.

12   Original article by Bill Schwarz   The Open University 1985, by permission of The Open University.

13   Reprinted from E. Said, *Orientalism*, Random House, 1978,   Edward W. Said 1978, by permission of Random House Inc and Routledge & Kegan Paul plc.

14   Reprinted from H. Bhabha, 'Of Mimicry and Man', *October*, Spring 1984,   Homi Bhabha 1984, by permission of Homi Bhabha and MIT Press.

15   Original article by Colin Mercer   The Open University 1985, by permission of The Open University.

16   Reprinted from V. de Grazia, *The Culture of Consent*, Cambridge University Press, 1981, pp. 187–224, by permission of Cambridge University Press.

PART I

Politics and ideology

1 Extracts

1.1 Two Treatises on Government (1690)

John Locke

From 'Of the State of Nature', Chapter II, The Second Treatise, *Two Treatises on Government* by John Locke.

To understand Political Power right, and derive it from its Original, we must consider what State all Men are naturally in, and that is, a *State of perfect Freedom* to order their Actions, and dispose of their Possessions, and Persons as they think fit, within the bounds of the Law of Nature, without asking leave, or depending upon the Will of any other Man.

A *State* also *of Equality*, wherein all the Power and Jurisdiction is reciprocal, no one having more than another: there being nothing more evident, than that Creatures of the same species and rank promiscuously born to all the same advantages of Nature, and the use of the same faculties, should also be equal one amongst another without Subordination or Subjection, unless the Lord and Master of them all, should by any manifest Declaration of his Will set one above another, and confer on him by an evident and clear appointment an undoubted Right to Dominion and Sovereignty [. . .]

But though this be a *State of Liberty,* yet it is *not a State of Licence*, though Man in that State have an uncontroleable Liberty, to dispose of his Person or Possessions, yet he has not Liberty to destroy himself, or so much as any Creature in his Possession, but where some nobler use, than its bare Preservation calls for it. The *State of Nature* has a Law of Nature to govern it, which obliges every one: and Reason, which is that Law, teaches all Mankind, who will but consult it, that being all equal and independent, no one ought to harm another in his Life, Health, Liberty, or Possessions. For Men being all the Workmanship of one Omnipotent, and infinitely wise Maker; All the Servants of one Sovereign Master, sent into the World by his order and about his business, they are his Property, whose Workmanship they are, made to last during his, not one anothers Pleasure. And being furnished with like Faculties, sharing all in one Community of Nature, there cannot be supposed any such *Subordination* among us, that may Authorize us to destroy one another, as if we were made for one anothers uses, as the inferior ranks of Creatures are for ours. Every one as he is *bound to preserve himself*, and not to quit his Station wilfully; so by the like reason when his own Preservation comes not in competition, ought he, as much as he can, *to preserve the rest of Mankind*, and may not unless it be to do Justice on an Offender, take away, or impair the life, or what tends to the Preservation of the Life, the Liberty, Health, Limb or Goods of another.

And that all Men may be restrained from invading others Rights, and from doing hurt to one another, and the Law of Nature be observed, which willeth the Peace and *Preservation of all Mankind*, the *Execution* of the Law of Nature is in that State, put into every Mans hands, whereby every one has a right to punish the transgressors of that Law to such a Degree, as may hinder its Violation. For the *Law of Nature* would, as all other Laws that concern Men in this World, be in vain, if there were no body that in the State of Nature, had a *Power to Execute* that Law, and thereby preserve the innocent and restrain offenders, and if any one in the State of Nature may punish another, for any evil he has done, every one may do so. For in that *State of perfect Equality*, where naturally there is no superiority or jurisdiction of one, over another, what any may do in Prosecution of that Law, every one must needs have a Right to do.

And thus in the State of Nature, *one Man comes by a Power over another;* but yet no Absolute or Arbitrary Power, to use a Criminal when he has got him in his hands, according to the passionate heats, or boundless extravagancy of his own Will, but only to retribute to him, so far as calm reason and conscience dictates, what is proportionate to his Transgression, which is so much as may serve for *Reparation* and *Restraint*. For these two are the only reasons, why one Man may lawfully do harm to another, which is what we call *punishment*. In transgressing the Law of Nature, the Offender declares himself to live by another Rule, than that of *reason* and common Equity, which is that measure God has set to the actions of Men, for their mutual security: and so he becomes dangerous to Mankind, the tye, which is to secure them from injury and violence, being slighted and broken by him. Which being a trespass against the whole Species, and the Peace and Safety of it, provided for by the Law of Nature, every man upon this score, by the Right he hath to preserve Mankind in general, may restrain, or where it is necessary, destroy things noxious to them, and so may bring such evil on any one, who hath transgressed that Law, as may make him repent the doing of it, and thereby deter him, and by his Example others, from doing the like mischief. And in this case, and upon this ground, every *Man hath a Right to punish the Offender, and be Executioner of the Law of Nature* [. . .]

1.2 Reflections on the Revolution in France (1790)

Edmund Burke

From *Reflections on the Revolution in France* by Edmund Burke

The Revolution [of 1688] was made to preserve our *antient* indisputable laws and liberties, and that *antient* constitution of government which is our only security for law and liberty. If you are desirous of knowing the spirit of our constitution, and the policy which predominated in that great period which has secured it to this hour, pray look for both in our histories, in our records, in our acts of parliament, and journals of parliament, and not in [. . .] the after-dinner toasts of the Revolution Society [. . .]. The very idea of the fabrication of a new government, is enough to fill us with disgust and horror. We wished at the period of the Revolution, and do now wish, to derive all we possess as *an inheritance from our forefathers*. Upon that body and stock of inheritance we have taken care not to inoculate any cyon alien to the nature of the original plant. All the reformations we have hitherto made, have proceeded upon the principle of reference to antiquity; and I hope, nay I am persuaded, that all those which possibly may be made hereafter, will be carefully formed upon analogical precedent, authority, and example.

Our oldest reformation is that of Magna Charta. You will see that Sir Edward Coke, that great oracle of our law, and indeed all the great men who follow him [. . .] are industrious to prove the pedigree of our liberties. They endeavour to prove, that the antient charter, the Magna Charter of King John, was connected with another positive charter from Henry I, and that both the one and the other were nothing more than a re-affirmation of the still more antient standing law of the kingdom. In the matter of fact, for the greater part, these authors appear to be in the right; perhaps not always: but if the lawyers mistake in some particulars, it proves my position still the more strongly; because it demonstrates the powerful pre-possession towards antiquity, with which the minds of all our lawyers and legislators, and of all the people whom they wish to influence, have been always filled; and the stationary policy of this kingdom in considering their most sacred rights and franchises as an *inheritance* [. . .]

The same policy pervades all the laws which have since been made for the

4

preservation of our liberties. In the 1st of William and Mary, in the famous statute, called the Declaration of Right, the two houses utter not a syllable of 'a right to frame a government for themselves'. You will see, that their whole care was to secure the religion, laws, and liberties, that had been long possessed, and had been lately endangered. 'Taking into their most serious consideration the *best* means for making such an establishment, that their religion, laws, and liberties, might not be in danger of being again subverted,' they auspicate all their proceedings, by stating as some of those *best means*, 'in the *first place*' to do '*as their ancestors in like cases have usually* done for vindicating their *antient* rights and liberties, to *declare*;'—and then they pray the king and queen, 'that it may be *declared* and enacted, that *all and singular* the rights and liberties *asserted and declared* are the true *antient* and indubitable rights and liberties of the people of this kingdom.'

You will observe, that from Magna Charta to the Declaration of Right, it has been the uniform policy of our constitution to claim and assert our liberties, as an *entailed inheritance* derived to us from our forefathers, and to be transmitted to our posterity; as an estate specially belonging to the people of this kingdom without any reference whatever to any other more general or prior right. By this means our constitution preserves an unity in so great a diversity of its parts. We have an inheritable crown; an inheritable peerage; and an house of commons and a people inheriting privileges, franchises, and liberties, from a long line of ancestors.

This policy appears to me to be the result of profound reflection; or rather the happy effect of following nature, which is wisdom without reflection, and above it. A spirit of innovation is generally the result of a selfish temper and confined views. People will not look forward to posterity, who never look backward to their ancestors. Besides, the people of England well know, that the idea of inheritance furnishes a sure principle of conservation, and a sure principle of transmission; without at all excluding a principle of improvement. It leaves acquisition free; but it secures what it acquires. Whatever advantages are obtained by a state proceeding on these maxims, are locked fast in a sort of family settlement; grasped as in a kind of mortmain for ever. By a constitutional policy, working after the pattern of nature, we receive, we hold, we transmit our government and our privileges, in the same manner in which we enjoy and transmit our property and our lives. The institutions of policy, the goods of fortune, the gifts of Providence, are handed down, to us and from us, in the same course and order. Our political system is placed in a just correspondence and symmetry with the order of the world, and with the mode of existence decreed to a permanent body composed of transitory parts; wherein, by the disposition of a stupendous wisdom, moulding together the great mysterious incorporation of the human race, the whole, at one time, is never old, or middle-aged, or young, but in a condition of unchangeable constancy, moves on through the varied tenour of perpetual decay, fall, renovation, and progression. Thus, by preserving the method of nature in the conduct of the state, in what we improve we are never wholly new; in what we retain we are never wholly obsolete. By adhering in this manner and on those principles to our forefathers, we are guided not by the superstition of antiquarians, but by the spirit of philosophic analogy. In this choice of inheritance we have given to our frame of polity the image of a relation in blood; binding up the constitution of our country with our dearest domestic ties; adopting our fundamental laws into the bosom of our family affections; keeping inseparable, and cherishing with the warmth of all their combined and mutually reflected charities, our state, our hearths, our sepulchres, and our altars.

Through the same plan of a conformity to nature in our artificial institutions, and by calling in the aid of her unerring and powerful instincts, to fortify the fallible and feeble contrivances of our reason, we have derived several other, and those no small benefits, from considering our liberties in the light of an inheritance. Always acting as if in the presence of canonized forefathers, the spirit of freedom, leading in itself to misrule and excess, is tempered with an awful gravity. This idea of a liberal descent inspires us with a sense of habitual native dignity, which prevents that upstart insolence almost inevitably adhering to and disgracing those who are the first acquirers of any distinction. By this means our liberty becomes a noble freedom. It carries an imposing and majestic aspect. It has a pedigree and illustrating ancestors. It has its bearings and its ensigns armorial. It has its gallery of portraits; its monumental inscriptions; its records, evidences, and titles. We procure reverence to our civil institutions on the principle upon which nature teaches us to revere individual men; on account of their age; and on account of those from whom they are descended. All your sophisters cannot produce any thing better adapted to preserve a rational and manly freedom than the course that we have pursued, who have chosen our nature rather than our speculations, our breasts rather than our inventions, for the great conservatories and magazines of our rights and privileges.

You [the French] might, if you pleased, have profited of our example, and have given to your recovered freedom a correspondent dignity. Your privileges, though discontinued, were not lost to memory. Your constitution, it is true, whilst you were out of possession, suffered waste and dilapidation; but you possessed in some parts the walls, and in all the foundations of a noble and venerable castle [. . .]. You had all that combination, and all that opposition of interests, you had that action and counteraction which, in the natural and in the political world, from the reciprocal struggle of discordant powers, draws out the harmony of the universe. These opposed and conflicting interests, which you considered as so great a blemish in your old and in our present constitution, interpose a salutary check to all precipitate resolutions; They render deliberation a matter not of choice, but of necessity; they make all change a subject of *compromise*, which naturally begets moderation; they produce *temperaments*, preventing the sore evil of harsh, crude, unqualified reformations; and rendering all the headlong exertions of arbitrary power, in the few or in the many, for ever impracticable. Through that diversity of members and interests, general liberty had as many securities as there were separate views in the several orders; whilst by pressing down the whole by the weight of a real monarchy, the separate parts would have been prevented from warping and starting from their allotted places.

1.3 Considerations on Representative Government (1861)

John Stuart Mill

From *Considerations on Representative Government* by J. S. Mill.

There is no difficulty in showing that the ideally best form of government is that in which the sovereignty, or supreme controlling power in the last resort, is vested in the entire aggregate of the community; every citizen not only having a voice in the exercise of that ultimate sovereignty, but being, at least occasionally, called on to take an actual part in the government, by the personal discharge of some public function, local or general [. . .].

The ideally best form of government, it is scarcely necessary to say, does not mean one which is practicable or eligible in all states of civilization, but the one which, in the circumstances in which it is practicable and eligible, is attended with the greatest amount of beneficial consequences, immediate and prospective. A completely popular government is the only polity which can make out any claim to this character. It is pre-eminent in both the departments between which the excellence of a political constitution is divided. It is both more favourable to present good government, and promotes a better and higher form of national character, than any other polity whatsoever.

Its superiority in reference to present well-being rests upon two principles, of as universal truth and applicability as any general propositions which can be laid down respecting human affairs. The first is, that the rights and interests of every or any person are only secure from being disregarded, when the person interested is himself able, and habitually disposed, to stand up for them. The second is, that the general prosperity attains a greater height, and is more widely diffused, in proportion to the amount and variety of the personal energies enlisted in promoting it.

Putting these two propositions into a shape more special to their present application; human beings are only secure from evil at the hands of others, in proportion as they have the power of being; and are, self-*protecting*; and they only achieve a high degree of success in their struggle with Nature, in proportion as they are self-*dependent*, relying on what they themselves can do, either separately or in concert, rather than on what others do for them.

7

The former proposition—that each is the only safe guardian of his own rights and interests—is one of those elementary maxims of prudence, which every person, capable of conducting his own affairs, implicitly acts upon, wherever he himself is interested. Many, indeed, have a great dislike to it as a political doctrine, and are fond of holding it up to obloquy, as a doctrine of universal selfishness. To which we may answer, that whenever it ceases to be true that mankind, as a rule, prefer themselves to others, and those nearest to them to those more remote, from that moment Communism is not only practicable, but the only defensible form of society; and will, when that time arrives, be assuredly carried into effect. For my own part, not believing in universal selfishness, I have no difficulty in admitting that Communism would even now be practicable among the *élite* of mankind, and may become so among the rest. But as this opinion is anything but popular with those defenders of existing institutions who find fault with the doctrine of the general predominance of self-interest, I am inclined to think they do in reality believe, that most men consider themselves before other people. It is not, however, necessary to affirm even thus much, in order to support the claim of all to participate in the sovereign power. We need not suppose that when power resides in an exclusive class, that class will knowingly and deliberately sacrifice the other classes to themselves: it suffices that, in the absence of its natural defenders, the interest of the excluded is always in danger of being overlooked; and, when looked at, is seen with very different eyes from those of the persons whom it directly concerns. In this country, for example, what are called the working classes may be considered as excluded from all direct participation in the government. I do not believe that the classes who do participate in it, have in general any intention of sacrificing the working classes to themselves. They once had that intention; witness the persevering attempts so long made to keep down wages by law. But in the present day, their ordinary disposition is the very opposite: they willingly make considerable sacrifices, especially of their pecuniary interest, for the benefit of the working classes, and err rather by too lavish and indiscriminating beneficence; nor do I believe that any rulers in history have been actuated by a more sincere desire to do their duty towards the poorer portion of their countrymen. Yet does Parliament, or almost any of the members composing it, ever for an instant look at any question with the eyes of a working man? When a subject arises in which the labourers as such have an interest, is it regarded from any point of view but that of the employers of labour? I do not say that the working men's view of these questions is in general nearer to the truth than the other; but it is sometimes quite as near; and in any case it ought to be respectfully listened to, instead of being, as it is, not merely turned away from, but ignored. On the question of strikes, for instance, it is doubtful if there is so much as one among the leading members of either House, who is not firmly convinced that the reason of the matter is unqualifiedly on the side of the masters, and that the men's view of it is simply absurd. Those who have studied the question, know well how far this is from being the case; and in how different, and how infinitely less superficial a manner the point would have to be argued, if the classes who strike were able to make themselves heard in Parliament.

It is an inherent condition of human affairs, that no intention, however sincere, of protecting the interests of others, can make it safe or salutary to tie up their own hands. Still more obviously true is it, that by their own hands only can any positive and durable improvement of their circumstances in life be worked out. Throughout the joint influence of these two principles, all free communities have both been more exempt from social injustice and crime, and have attained more brilliant prosperity, than any others, or than they themselves after they lost their freedom. [. . .]

Of the Extension of the Suffrage

Such a representative democracy as has now been sketched, representative of all, and not solely of the majority—in which the interests, the opinions, the grades of intellect which are outnumbered would nevertheless be heard, and would have a chance of obtaining by weight of character and strength of argument, an influence which would not belong to their numerical force—this democracy, which is alone equal, alone impartial, alone the government of all by all, the only true type of democracy—would be free from the greatest evils of the falsely-called democracies which now prevail, and from which the current idea of democracy is exclusively derived. But even in this democracy, absolute power, if they chose to exercise it, would rest with the numerical majority; and these would be composed exclusively of a single class, alike in biases, prepossessions, and general modes of thinking, and a class, to say no more, not the most highly cultivated. The constitution would therefore still be liable to the characteristic evils of class government: in a far less degree, assuredly, than that exclusive government by a class, which now usurps the name of democracy; but still, under no effective restraint, except what might be found in the good sense, moderation, and forbearance, of the class itself. If checks of this description are sufficient, the philosophy of constitutional government is but solemn trifling. All trust in constitutions is grounded on the assurance they may afford, not that the depositaries of power will not, but that they cannot, misemploy it. Democracy is not the ideally best form of government unless this weak side of it can be strengthened; unless it can be so organized that no class, not even the most numerous, shall be able to reduce all but itself to political insignificance, and direct the course of legislation and administration by its exclusive class interest. The problem is, to find the means of preventing this abuse, without sacrificing the characteristic advantages of popular government.

These twofold requisites are not fulfilled by the expedient of a limitation of the suffrage, involving the compulsory exclusion of any portion of the citizens from a voice in the representation. Among the foremost benefits of free government is that education of the intelligence and of the sentiments, which is carried down to the very lowest ranks of the people when they are called to take a part in acts which directly affect the great interests of their country [. . .].

It is by political discussion that the manual labourer, whose employment is a routine, and whose way of life brings him in contact with no variety of impressions, circumstances, or ideas, is taught that remote causes, and events which take place far off, have a most sensible effect even on his personal interests; and it is from political discussion, and collective political action, that one whose daily occupations concentrate his interests in a small circle round himself, learns to feel for and with his fellow-citizens, and becomes consciously a member of a great community. But political discussions fly over the heads of those who have no votes, and are not endeavouring to acquire them. Their position, in comparison with the electors, is that of the audience in a court of justice, compared with the twelve men in the jury-box. It is not *their* suffrages that are asked, it is not their opinion that is sought to be influenced; the appeals are made, the arguments addressed, to others than them; nothing depends on the decision they may arrive at, and there is no necessity and very little inducement to them to come to any. Whoever, in an otherwise popular government, has no vote, and no prospect of obtaining it, will either be a permanent malcontent, or will feel as one whom the general affairs of society do not concern; for whom they are to be managed by others; who 'has no business with the laws except to obey them,' nor with public interests and concerns except as a looker-on. What he will know or care about them from this position, may partly be measured by what an average woman of the middle class knows and cares about politics, compared with her husband or brothers.

Independently of all these confrontations, it is a personal injustice to withhold from any one, unless for the prevention of greater evils, the ordinary privilege of having his voice reckoned in the disposal of affairs in which he has the same interest as other people. If he is compelled to pay, if he may be compelled to fight, if he is required implicitly to obey, he should be legally entitled to be told what for; to have his consent asked, and his opinion counted at its worth, though not at more than its worth. There ought to be no pariahs in a full-grown and civilized nation; no persons disqualified, except through their own default. Every one is degraded, whether aware of it or not, when other people, without consulting him, take upon themselves unlimited power to regulate his destiny [. . .].

There are, however, certain exclusions, required by positive reasons, which do not conflict with this principle, and which, though an evil in themselves, are only to be got rid of by the cessation of the state of things which requires them. I regard it as wholly inadmissible that any person should participate in the suffrage, without being able to read, write and, I will add, perform the common operations of arithmetic. Justice demands, even when the suffrage does not depend on it, that the means of attaining these elementary acquirements should be within the reach of every person, either gratuitously, or at an expense not exceeding what the poorest, who earn their own living, can afford. If this were really the case, people would no more think of giving the suffrage to a man who could not read, than of giving it to a child who could not speak; and it would not be society that would exclude him, but his own laziness. When society has not performed its duty, by rendering this amount of instruction accessible to all, there is some hardship in the case, but it is a hardship that ought to be borne. If society has neglected to discharge two solemn obligations, the more important and more fundamental of the two must be fulfilled first: universal teaching must precede universal enfranchisement. No one but those in whom an *a priori* theory has silenced common sense, will maintain, that power over others, over the whole community, should be imparted to people who have not acquired the commonest and most essential requisites for taking care of themselves; for pursuing intelligently their own interests, and those of the persons most nearly allied to them [. . .].

It is also important, that the assembly which votes the taxes, either general or local, should be elected exclusively by those who pay something towards the taxes imposed. Those who pay no taxes, disposing by their votes of other people's money, have every motive to be lavish, and none to economize. As far as money matters are concerned, any power of voting possessed by them is a violation of the fundamental principle of free government; a severance of the power of control, from the interest in its beneficial exercise. It amounts to allowing them to put their hands into other people's pockets, for any purpose which they think fit to call a public one [. . .].

I regard it as required by first principles, that the receipt of parish relief should be a peremptory disqualification for the franchise. He who cannot by his labour suffice for his own support, has no claim to the privilege of helping himself to the money of others. By becoming dependent on the remaining members of the community for actual subsistence, he abdicates his claim to equal rights with them in other respects. Those to whom he is indebted for the continuance of his very existence, may justly claim the exclusive management of those common concerns, to which he now brings nothing, or less than he takes away [. . .]

But though every one ought to have a voice—that every one should have an equal voice is a totally different proposition. When two persons who have a joint interest in any business, differ in opinion, does justice require that both opinions should be held of exactly equal value? If with equal virtue, one is superior to the other in knowledge and intelligence—or if with equal intelligence, one excels the other in virtue—the opinion, the judgement, of the higher moral or intellectual being, is worth more than that of the inferior: and if the institutions of the country virtually assert that they are of the same value, they assert a thing which is not. One of the two, as the wiser or better man, has a claim to superior weight: the difficulty is in ascertaining which of the two it is; a thing impossible as between individuals, but, taking men in bodies and in numbers, it can be done with a certain approach to accuracy. There would be no pretence for applying this doctrine to any case which could with reason be considered as one of individual and private right. In an affair which concerns only one of two persons, that one is entitled to follow his own opinion, however much wiser the other may be than himself. But we are speaking of things which equally concern them both; where, if the more ignorant does not yield his share of the matter to the guidance of the wiser man, the wiser man must resign his to that of the more ignorant, by acquiring any amount of instruction, to make sure of the corresponding rise in station, that this foundation of electoral privilege is always, and will continue to be, supremely odious. To connect plurality of votes with any pecuniary qualification would be not only objectionable in itself, but a sure mode of discrediting the principle, and making its permanent maintenance impracticable. The Democracy, at least of this country, are not at present jealous of personal superiority, but they are naturally and most justly so of that which is grounded on mere pecuniary circumstances. The only thing which can justify reckoning one person's opinion as equivalent to more than one, is individual mental superiority; and what is wanted is some approximate means of ascertaining that. If there existed such a thing as a really national education, or a trustworthy system of general examination, education might be tested directly. In the absence of these, the nature of a person's occupation is some test. An employer of labour is on the average more intelligent than a labourer; for he must labour with his head, and not solely with his hands. A foreman is generally more intelligent than an ordinary labourer, and a labourer in the skilled trades than in the unskilled. A banker, merchant, or manufacturer, is likely to be more intelligent than a tradesman, because he has larger and more complicated interests to manage. In all these cases it is not the having merely undertaken the superior function, but the successful performance of it, that tests the qualifications; for which reason, as well as to prevent persons from engaging nominally in an occupation for the sake of the vote, it would be proper to require that the occupation should have been persevered in for some length of time (say three years). Subject to some such condition, two or more votes might be allowed to every person who exercises any of these superior functions. The liberal professions, when really and not nominally practised, imply, of course, a still higher degree of instruction; and wherever a sufficient examination, or any serious conditions of education, are required before entering on a profession, its members could be admitted at once to a plurality of votes. The same rule might be applied to graduates of universities; and even to those who bring satisfactory certificates of having passed through the course of study required by any school at which the higher branches of knowledge are taught, under proper securities that the teaching is real, and not a mere pretence. The 'local' or 'middle class' examination for the degree of Associate, so laudably and public-spiritedly established by the Universities of Oxford and Cambridge, and any similar ones which may be instituted by other competent bodies (provided they are fairly open to all comers), afford a ground on which plurality of votes might with great advantage be accorded to those who have passed the test. All these suggestions are open to much discussion in the detail, and to objections which it is of no use to anticipate. The time is not come for giving to such plans a practical shape, nor should I wish to be bound by the particular proposals which I have made. But it is to me evident, that in this direction lies the true ideal of representative government; and that to work towards it, by the best practical contrivances which can be found, is the path of real political improvement.

1.4   The German Ideology (1845-6)

Karl Marx and Friedrich Engels

From *The German Ideology* (edited and introduced by C.J. Arthur), London, Lawrence and Wishart, 1970.

The ideas of the ruling class are in every epoch the ruling ideas, i.e. the class which is the ruling *material* force of society, is at the same time its ruling *intellectual* force. The class which has the means of material production at its disposal, has control at the same time over the means of mental production, so that thereby, generally speaking, the ideas of those who lack the means of mental production are subject to it. The ruling ideas are nothing more than the ideal expression of the dominant material relationships, the dominant material relationships grasped as ideas; hence of the relationships which make the one class the ruling one, therefore, the ideas of its dominance. The individuals composing the ruling class possess among other things consciousness, and therefore think. Insofar, therefore, as they rule as a class and determine the extent and compass of an epoch, it is self-evident that they do this in its whole range, hence among other things rule also as thinkers, as producers of ideas, and regulate the production and distribution of the ideas of their age: thus their ideas are the ruling ideas of the epoch. For instance, in an age and in a country where royal power, aristocracy, and bourgeoisie are contending for mastery and where, therefore, mastery is shared, the doctrine of the separation of powers proves to be the dominant idea and is expressed as an 'eternal law'.

The division of labour, which [has been] one of the chief forces of history up till now, manifests itself also in the ruling class as the division of mental and material labour, so that inside this class one part appears as the thinkers of the class (its active, conceptive ideologists, who make the perfecting of the illusion of the class about itself their chief source of livelihood), while the others' attitude to these ideas and illusions is more passive and receptive, because they are in reality the active members of this class and have less time to make up illusions and ideas about themselves. Within this class this cleavage can even develop into a certain opposition and hostility between the two parts, which, however, in the case of a practical collision, in which the class itself is endangered, automatically comes to nothing, in which case there also vanishes the semblance that the ruling ideas were not the ideas of the ruling class and had a power distinct from the power of this class. The existence of revolutionary ideas in a particular period presupposes the existence of a revolutionary class [. . .].

If now in considering the course of history we detach the ideas of the ruling class from the ruling class itself and attribute to them an independent existence, if we confine ourselves to saying that these or those ideas were dominant at a given time, without bothering ourselves about the conditions of production and the producers of these ideas, if we thus ignore the individuals and world conditions which are the source of the ideas, we can say, for instance, that during the time that the aristocracy was dominant, the concepts honour, loyalty, etc. were dominant, during the dominance of the bourgeoisie the concepts freedom, equality, etc. The ruling class itself on the whole imagines this to be so. This conception of history, which is common to all historians, particularly since the eighteenth century, will necessarily come up against the phenomenon that increasingly abstract ideas hold sway, i.e. ideas which increasingly take on the form of universality. For each new class which puts itself in the place of one ruling before it, is compelled, merely in order to carry through its aim, to represent its interest as the common interest of all the members of society, that is, expressed in ideal form: it has to give its ideas the form of universality, and represent them as the only rational, universally valid ones. The class making a revolution appears from the very start, if only because it is opposed to a *class*, not as a class but as the representative of the whole of society; it appears as the whole mass of society confronting the one ruling class.[1] It can do this because, to start with, its interest really is more connected with the common interest of all other non-ruling classes, because under the pressure of hitherto existing conditions its interest has not yet been able to develop as the particular interest of a particular class. Its victory, therefore, benefits also many individuals of the other classes which are not winning a dominant position to raise themselves into the ruling class. When the French bourgeoisie overthrew the power of the aristocracy, it thereby made it possible for many proletarians to raise themselves above the proletariat, but only insofar as they become bourgeois. Every new class, therefore, achieves its hegemony only on a broader basis than that of the class ruling previously, whereas the opposition of the non-ruling class against the new ruling class later develops all the more sharply and profoundly. Both these things determine the fact that the struggle to be waged against this new ruling class, in its turn, aims at a more decided and radical negation of the previous conditions of society than could all previous classes which sought to rule.

This whole semblance, that the rule of a certain class is only the rule of certain ideas, comes to a natural end, of course, as soon as class rule in general ceases to be the form in which society is organised, that is to say, as soon as it is no longer necessary to represent a particular interest as general or the 'general interest' as ruling.

Note

[1][Marginal note by Marx:] Universality corresponds to (1) the class versus the estate, (2) the competition, world-wide intercourse, etc., (3) the great numerical strength of the ruling class, (4) the illusion of the *common* interests (in the beginning this illusion is true), (5) the delusion of the ideologists and the division of labour.

1.5 A Contribution to the Critique of Political Economy (1859)

Karl Marx

From *Early Writings* (trans. R. Livingstone and G. Benton), Harmondsworth, Pelican, 1975.

My inquiry led me to the conclusion that neither legal relations nor political forms could be comprehended whether by themselves or on the basis of a so-called general development of the human mind, but that on the contrary they originate in the material conditions of life, the totality of which Hegel, following the example of English and French thinkers of the eighteenth century, embraces within the term 'civil society'; that the anatomy of this civil society, however, has to be sought in political economy. The study of this, which I began in Paris, I continued in Brussels, where I moved owing to an expulsion order issued by M. Guizot. The general conclusion at which I arrived and which, once reached, became the guiding principle of my studies can be summarized as follows. In the social production of their existence, men inevitably enter into definite relations, which are independent of their will, namely relations of production appropriate to a given stage in the development of their material forces of production. The totality of these relations of production constitutes the economic structure of society, the real foundation, on which arises a legal and political superstructure and to which correspond definite forms of social consciousness. The mode of production of material life conditions the general process of social, political and intellectual life. It is not the consciousness of men that determines their existence, but their social existence that determines their consciousness. At a certain stage of development, the material productive forces of society come into conflict with the existing relations of production or—this merely expresses the same thing in legal terms—with the property relations within the framework of which they have operated hitherto. From forms of development of the productive forces these relations turn into their fetters. Then begins an era of social revolution. The changes in the economic foundation lead sooner or later to the transformation of the whole immense superstructure. In studying such transformations it is always necessary to distinguish between the material transformation of the economic conditions of production, which can be determined with the precision of natural science, and the legal, political, religious, artistic or philosophic—in short, ideological forms in which men become conscious of this conflict and fight it out. Just as one does not judge an individual by what he thinks about himself, so one cannot judge such a period of transformation by its consciousness, but, on the contrary, this consciousness must be explained from the contradictions of material life, from the conflict existing between the social forces of production and the relations of production. No social order is ever destroyed before all the productive forces for which it is sufficient have been developed, and new superior relations of production never replace older ones before the material conditions for their existence have matured within the framework of the old society. Mankind thus inevitably sets itself only such tasks as it is able to solve, since closer examination will always show that the problem itself arises only when the material conditions for its solution are already present or at least in the course of formation. In broad outline, the Asiatic, ancient, feudal and modern bourgeois modes of production may be designated as epochs marking progress in the economic development of society. The bourgeois mode of production is the last antagonistic form of the social process of production—antagonistic not in the sense of individual antagonism but of an antagonism that emanates from the individuals' social conditions of existence—but the productive forces developing within bourgeois society create also the material conditions for a solution of this antagonism.

1.6 Politics as a Vocation (1919)

Max Weber

From 'Politics as a Vocation', in H. H. Gerth and C. Wright Mills (eds. and trans.) *From Max Weber*, London, Routledge and Kegan Paul, 1948.

'Every state is founded on force,' said Trotsky at Brest-Litovsk. That is indeed right. If no social institutions existed which knew the use of violence, then the concept of 'state' would be eliminated, and a condition would emerge that could be designated as 'anarchy', in the specific sense of this word. Of course, force is certainly not the normal or the only means of the state—nobody says that—but force is a means specific to the state. Today the relation between the state and violence is an especially intimate one. In the past, the most varied institutions—beginning with the sib—have known the use of physical force as quite normal. Today, however, we have to say that a state is a human community that (successfully) claims the *monopoly of the legitimate use of physical force* within a given territory. Note that 'territory' is one of the characteristics of the state. Specifically, at the present time, the right to use physical force is ascribed to other institutions or to individuals only to the extent to which the state permits it. The state is considered the sole source of the 'right' to use violence. Hence, 'politics' for us means striving to share power or striving to influence the distribution of power, either among states or among groups within a state [. . .].

Like the political institutions historically preceding it, the state is a relation of men dominating men, a relation supported by means of legitimate (i.e. considered to be legitimate) violence. If the state is to exist, the dominated must obey the authority claimed by the powers that be. When and why do men obey? Upon what inner justifications and upon what external means does this domination rest?

To begin with, in principle, there are three inner justifications, hence basic *legitimations* of domination.

First, the authority of the 'eternal yesterday,' i.e. of the mores sanctified through the unimaginably ancient recognition and habitual orientation to conform. This is 'traditional' domination exercised by the patriarch and the patrimonial prince of yore.

There is the authority of the extraordinary and personal *gift of grace* (charisma), the absolutely personal devotion and personal confidence in revelation, heroism,

17

or other qualities of individual leadership. This is 'charismatic' domination, as exercised by the prophet or—in the field of politics—by the elected war lord, the plebiscitarian ruler, the great demagogue, or the political party leader.

Finally, there is domination by virtue of 'legality', by virtue of the belief in the validity of legal statute and functional 'competence' based on rationally created *rules*. In this case, obedience is expected in discharging statutory obligations. This is domination as exercised by the modern 'servant of the state' and by all those bearers of power who in this respect resemble him.

It is understood that, in reality, obedience is determined by highly robust motives of fear and hope—fear of the vengeance of magical powers or of the power-holder, hope for reward in this world or in the beyond—and besides all this, by interests of the most varied sort [. . .]. However, in asking for the 'legitimations' of this obedience, one meets with these three 'pure' types: 'traditional', 'charismatic,' and 'legal.' [. . .]

1.7 Prison Notebooks (c. 1933)

Antonio Gramsci

From: 'The Study of Philosophy', in Q. Hoare and G. Nowell-Smith (eds. and trans.) *Selections from the Prison Notebooks*, London, Lawrence and Wishart, 1971.

Philosophy in general does not in fact exist. Various philosophies or conceptions of the world exist, and one always makes a choice between them. How is this choice made? Is it merely an intellectual event, or is it something more complex? And is it not frequently the case that there is a contradiction between one's intellectual choice and one's mode of conduct? [. . .]

This contrast between thought and action, i.e. the co-existence of two conceptions of the world, one affirmed in words and the other displayed in effective action, is not simply a product of self-deception [*malafede*]. Self-deception can be an adequate explanation for a few individuals taken separately, or even for groups of a certain size, but it is not adequate when the contrast occurs in the life of great masses. In these cases the contrast between thought and action cannot but be the expression of profounder contrasts of social historical order. It signifies that the social group in question may indeed have its own conception of the world, even if only embryonic; a conception which manifests itself in action, but occasionally and in flashes—when, that is, the group is acting as an organic totality. But this same group has, for reasons of submission and intellectual subordination, adopted a conception which is not its own but is borrowed from another group; and it affirms this conception verbally and believes itself to be following it, because this is the conception which it follows in 'normal times'—that is when its conduct is not independent and autonomous, but submissive and subordinate. Hence the reason why philosophy cannot be divorced from politics. And one can show furthermore that the choice and the criticism of a conception of the world is also a political matter.

What must next be explained is how it happens that in all periods there co-exist many systems and currents of philosophical thought, how these currents are born, how they are diffused, and why in the process of diffusion they fracture along certain lines and in certain directions. The fact of this process goes to show how necessary it is to order in a systematic, coherent and critical fashion one's own intuitions of life and the world, and to determine exactly what is to be understood by the word 'systematic', so that it is not taken in the pedantic and academic sense. But this elaboration must be, and can only be, performed in the context of the history of philosophy, for it is this history which shows how thought has been elaborated over the centuries and what a collective effort has gone into the creation of our present method of thought which has subsumed and absorbed all this past history, including all its follies and mistakes. Nor should these mistakes themselves be neglected, for, although made in the past and since corrected, one cannot be sure that they will not be reproduced in the present and once again require correcting.

What is the popular image of philosophy? It can be reconstructed by looking at expressions in common usage [. . .]

But at this point we reach the fundamental problem facing any conception of the world, any philosophy which has become a cultural movement, a 'religion', a 'faith', any that has produced a form of practical activity or will in which the philosophy is contained as an implicit theoretical 'premiss'. One might say 'ideology' here, but on condition that the word is used in its highest sense of a conception of the world that is implicitly manifest in art, in law, in economic activity and in all manifestations of individual and collective life. This problem is that of preserving the ideological unity of the entire social bloc which that ideology serves to cement and to unify. The strength of religions, and of the Catholic church in particular, has lain, and still lies, in the fact that they feel very strongly the need for the doctrinal unity of the whole mass of the faithful and strive to ensure that the higher intellectual stratum does not get separated from the lower. The Roman church has always been the most vigorous in the struggle to prevent the 'official' formation of two religions, one for the 'intellectuals' and the other for the 'simple' souls' [. . .]

The question posed here [is . . .] this: is a philosophical movement properly so called when it is devoted to creating a specialised culture among restricted intellectual groups, or rather when, and only when, in the process of elaborating a form of thought superior to 'common sense' and coherent on a scientific plane, it never forgets to remain in contact with the 'simple' and indeed finds in this contact the source of the problems it sets out to study and to resolve? Only by this contact does a philosophy become 'historical', purify itself of intellectualistic elements of an individual character and become 'life'.

A philosophy of praxis [i.e. Marxism] cannot but present itself at the outset in a polemical and critical guise, as superseding the existing mode of thinking and existing concrete thought (the existing cultural world). First of all, therefore, it must be a criticism of 'common sense', basing itself initially, however, on common sense in order to demonstrate that 'everyone' is a philosopher and that it is not a question of introducing from scratch a scientific form of thought into everyone's individual life, but of renovating and making 'critical' an already existing activity. It must then be a criticism of the philosophy of the intellectuals out of which the history of philosophy developed and which, in so far as it is a phenomenon of individuals (in fact it develops essentially in the activity of single particularly gifted individuals) can be considered as marking the 'high points' of the progress made by common sense, or at least the common sense of the more educated strata of society but through them also of the people. Thus an introduction to the study of philosophy must expound in synthetic form the problems that have grown up in the process of the development of culture as a whole and which are only partially reflected in the history of philosophy. [. . .]. The purpose of the synthesis must be to criticise the problems, to demonstrate their real value, if any, and the significance they have had as superseded links of an intellectual chain, and to determine what the new contemporary problems are and how the old problems should now be analysed.

The relation between common sense and the upper level of philosophy is assured by 'politics' [. . .]

The active man-in-the-mass has a practical activity, but has no clear theoretical consciousness of his practical activity, which nonetheless involves understanding the world in so far as it transforms it. His theoretical consciousness can indeed be historically in opposition to his activity. One might almost say that he has two theoretical consciousnesses (or one contradictory consciousness): one which is implicit in his activity and which in reality unites him with all his fellow-workers in the practical transformation of the real world; and one, superficially explicit or verbal, which he has inherited from the past and uncritically absorbed. But this verbal conception is not without consequences. It holds together a specific social group, it influences moral conduct and the direction of will, with varying efficacity but often powerfully enough to produce a situation in which the contradictory state of consciousness does not permit of any action, any decision or any choice, and produces a condition of moral and political passivity. Critical understanding of self takes place therefore through a struggle of political 'hegemonies' and of opposing directions, first in the ethical field and then in that of politics proper, in order to arrive at the working out at a higher level of one's own conception of reality. Consciousness of being part of a particular hegemonic force (that is to say, political consciousness) is the first stage towards a further progressive self-consciousness in which theory and practice will finally be one. [. . .]. That is why it must be stressed that the political development of the concept of hegemony represents a great philosophical advance as well as a politico-practical one. For it necessarily supposes an intellectual unity and an ethic in conformity with a conception of reality that has gone beyond common sense and has become, if only within narrow limits, a critical conception [. . .].

A human mass does not 'distinguish' itself, does not become independent in its own right without in the widest sense organising itself; and there is no organisation without intellectuals, that is without organisers and leaders, in other words, without the theoretical aspect of the theory-practice nexus being distinguished concretely by the existence of a group of people 'specialised' in conceptual and philosophical elaboration of ideas. But the process of creating intellectuals is long, difficult, full of contradictions, advances and retreats, dispersals and regroupings, in which the loyalty of the masses is often sorely tried [. . .].

The process of development is tied to a dialectic between the intellectuals and the masses. The intellectual stratum develops both quantitatively and qualitatively, but every leap forward towards a new breadth and complexity of the intellectual stratum is tied to an analogous movement on the part of the mass of the 'simple', who raise themselves to higher levels of culture and at the same time extend their circle of influence towards the stratum of specialised intellectuals, producing outstanding individuals and groups of greater or less importance. In the process, however, there continually recur moments in which a gap develops between the mass and the intellectuals (at any rate between some of them, or a group of them), a loss of contact, and thus the impression that theory is an 'accessory', a 'complement' and something subordinate [. . .]. One should stress the importance and significance which, in the modern world, political parties have in the elaboration and diffusion of conceptions of the world, because essentially what they do is to work out the ethics and the politics corresponding to these conceptions and act as it were as their historical 'laboratory'. The parties recruit individuals out of the working mass, and the selection is made on practical and theoretical criteria at the same time. The relation between theory and practice becomes even closer the more the conception is vitally and radically innovatory and opposed to old ways of thinking. For this reason one can say that the parties are the elaborators of new integral and totalitarian intelligentsias and the crucibles where the unification of theory and practice, understood as a real historical process, takes place.

1.8 Economic Freedom and Representative Government (1973)

F.A. Hayek

From *Economic Freedom and Representative Government*, London, Institute for Policy Studies, 1973.

The Danger of Unlimited Government

For some time I have been convinced that it is not only the deliberate attempts of the various kinds of collectivists to replace the market economy by a planned system, nor the consequences of the new monetary policies, which threaten to destroy the market economy; the political institutions prevailing in the Western world necessarily produce a drift in this direction which can be halted or prevented only by changing these institutions. I have belatedly come to agree with Joseph Schumpeter who 30 years ago argued that there was an irreconcilable conflict between democracy and capitalism (Schumpeter, 1943)—except that it is not democracy as such but the particular forms of democratic organisation, now regarded as the only possible forms of democracy, which will produce a progressive expansion of governmental control of economic life even if the majority of the people wish to preserve a market economy.

Majority rule and special interests
The reason is that it is now generally taken for granted that in a democracy the powers of the majority must be unlimited and that a government with unlimited powers will be forced, to secure the continued support of a majority, to use its unlimited powers in the service of special interests—such groups as particular traders, the inhabitants of particular regions, etc. We shall see this most clearly if we consider the situation in a community in which the mass of the people are in favour of a market order and against government direction, but, as will normally happen, most of the groups wish an exception to be made in their favour. In such conditions a political party hoping to achieve and maintain power will have little choice but to use its powers to buy the support of particular groups. They will do so not because the majority is interventionist, but because the ruling party would

not retain a majority if it did not buy the support of particular groups by the promise of special advantages. This means in practice that even a statesman wholly devoted to the common interest of all the citizens will be under the constant necessity of satisfying special interests, because only thus will he be able to retain the support of a majority which he needs to achieve what is really important to him.

The root of the evil is thus the unlimited power of the legislature in modern democracies, a power which the majority will be constantly forced to use in a manner that most of its members may not desire. What we call the will of the majority is thus really an artefact of the existing institutions, and particularly of the omnipotence of the sovereign legislature, which by the mechanics of the political process will be driven to do things that most of its members do not really want, simply because there are no formal limits to its powers.

It is widely believed that this omnipotence of the representative legislature is a necessary attribute of democracy because the will of the representative assembly could be limited only by placing another will above it. Legal positivism, the most influential current theory of jurisprudence, particularly represents this sovereignty of the legislature as logically necessary. This, however, was by no means the view of the classical theorists of representative government. John Locke made it very clear that in a free state even the power of the legislative body should be limited in a definite manner, namely to the passing of laws in the specific sense of general rules of just conduct equally applicable to all citizens. That all coercion would be legitimate only if it meant the application of general rules of law in this sense become the basic principle of liberalism. For Locke, and for the later theorists of Whiggism and the separation of powers, it was not so much the source from which the laws originated as their character of general rules of just conduct equally applicable to all which justified their coercive application.

What is law?

This older liberal conception of the necessary limitation of all power by requiring the legislature to commit itself to general rules has, in the course of the last century, been replaced gradually and almost imperceptibly by the altogether different though not incompatible conception that it was the approval of the majority which was the only and sufficient restraint on legislation. And the older conception was not only forgotten but no longer even understood. It was thought that any substantive limitation of the legislative power was unnecessary once this power was placed in the hands of the majority, because approval by it was regarded as an adequate test of justice. In practice this majority opinion usually represents no more than the result of bargaining rather than a genuine agreement on principles. Even the concept of the arbitrariness which democratic government was supposed to prevent changed its content: its opposite was no longer the general rules equally applicable to all but the approval of a command by the majority – as if a majority might not treat a minority arbitrarily.

The Fundamental Principle

Today it is rarely understood that the limitation of all coercion to the enforcement of general rules of just conduct was the fundamental principle of classical liberalism, or, I would almost say, its definition of liberty. This is largely a consequence of the fact that the substantive (or 'material') conception of law (as distinguished from a purely formal one) which underlies it, and which alone gives a clear meaning to such ideas as that of the separation of powers, of the rule of law or of a government under the law, had been rarely stated explicitly but merely tacitly pre-supposed by most of the classical writers. There are few passages in their seventeenth and eighteenth century writings in which they explicitly say what they mean by 'law'. Many uses of the term, however, make sense only if it is interpreted to mean exclusively general rules of just conduct and not every expression of the will of the duly authorised representative body.

Tyranny of majorities

Though the older conception of law survives in limited connections, it is certainly no longer generally understood, and in consequence has ceased to be an effective limit on legislation. While in the theoretical concept of the separation of powers the legislature derived its authority from the circumstance that it committed itself to general rules and was supposed to impose only general rules, there are now no limits on what a legislature may command and so claim to be 'law'. While its power was thus once supposed to be limited not by a superior will but by a generally recognised principle, there are now no limits whatever. There is therefore also no reason why the coalitions of organised interests on which the governing majorities rest should not discriminate against any widely-disliked group. Differences in wealth, education, tradition, religion, language or race may today become the cause of differential treatment on the pretext of a pretended principle of social justice or of public necessity. Once such discrimination is recognised as legitimate, all the safeguards of individual freedom of the liberal tradition are gone. If it is assumed that whatever the majority decides is just, even if what it lays down is not a general rule, but aims at affecting particular people, it would be expecting too much to believe that a sense of justice will restrain the caprice of the majority: in any group it is soon believed that what is desired by the group is just. And since the theoreticians of democracy have for over a hundred years taught the majorities that whatever they desire is just, we must not be surprised if the majorities no longer even ask whether what they decide is just. Legal positivism has powerfully contributed to this development by its contention that law is not dependent on justice but determines what is just.

Mirage of 'social justice'

Unfortunately, we have not only failed to impose upon legislatures the limitations inherent in the necessity of committing themselves to general rules. We have also charged them with tasks which they can perform only if they are not thus limited but are free to use coercion in the discriminatory manner that is required to assure

F.A. Hayek

benefits to particular people or groups. This they are constantly asked to do in the name of what is called social or distributive justice, a conception which has largely taken the place of the justice of individual action. It requires that not the individuals but 'society' be just in determining the share of individuals in the social product; and in order to realise any particular distribution of the social product regarded as just it is necessary that government directs individuals in what they must do.

Indeed, in a market economy in which no single person or group determines who gets what, and the shares of individuals always depend on many circumstances which nobody could have foreseen, the whole conception of social or distributive justice is empty and meaningless; and there will therefore never exist agreement on what is just in this sense. I am not sure that the concept has a definite meaning even in a centrally-directed economy, or that in such a system people would ever agree on what distribution is just. I am certain, however, that nothing has done so much to destroy the juridical safeguards of individual freedom as the striving after this mirage of social justice.

Reference

SCHUMPETER, J. (1943). *Capitalism, Socialism and Democracy,* Allen & Unwin (Unwin University Books, No. 28, 3rd edn., 1950).

2 Class Interpellations and Popular-Democratic Interpellations

Ernesto Laclau

From *Politics and Ideology in Marxist Theory* by Ernesto Laclau, 1977. Reproduced by permission of the publisher, NLB.

[We must try to answer two essential questions: What constitutes the unity of an ideological discourse? and, How are ideologies transformed?]

Louis Althusser's most important and specific contribution to the study of ideologies [has been] the conception that the basic function of all ideology is to interpellate/constitute individuals as subjects. According to Althusser – who in this instance is strongly influenced by the conception of Lacan in which the 'mirror-phase' plays a decisive role in the formation and moulding of the self, 'The category of the subject is constitutive of all ideology, but at the same time and immediately I add that the category of subject is only constitutive of all ideology insofar as all ideology has the function (which defines it) of "constituting" concrete individuals as subjects'. (Althusser, 1971, p.160) *Individuals*, who are simple bearers of structures, are transformed by ideology into *subjects*, that is to say, that they live the relation with their real conditions of existence as if they themselves were the *autonomous principle* of determination of that relation. The mechanism of this characteristic inversion is interpellation.

Althusser writes: 'Ideology "acts" or "functions" in such a way that it "recruits" subjects among the individuals (it recruits them all), or "transforms" the individuals into subjects (it transforms them all) by the very precise operation that I have called interpellation or hailing, and which can be imagined along the lines of the most common everyday police (or other) hailing "Hey, you there!" ...' (*ibid*, p.162) If, therefore, the basic function of all ideology is to constitute individuals as subjects, and if through interpellation individuals live their conditions of existence as if they were the autonomous principle of the latter – as if they, the determinate, constituted the determinant – it is clear that the unity of the distinct aspects of an ideological system is given by the specific interpellation which forms the axis and organizing principle of all ideology. Who is the interpellated subject? This is the key question in the analysis of ideologies. We can now answer our first question: *what constitutes the unifying principle of an*

27

ideological discourse is the 'subject' interpellated and thus constituted through this discourse. The isolated elements of a discourse have no meaning in themselves. In trying to analyze the ideological level of a determinate social formation, our first task must be to reconstruct the interpellative structures which constitute it [. . .].

There are different types of interpellations (political, religious, familial, etc.) which coexist whilst being articulated within an ideological discourse in a relative unity. In what way is one interpellation articulated with another, that is to say, what is it that enables them both to form part of a relatively unified ideological discourse? By unity we must not necessarily understand logical consistency – on the contrary, the ideological unity of a discourse is perfectly compatible with a wide margin of logical inconsistency – but the ability of each interpellative element to fulfill a role of condensation with respect to the others. When a familial interpellation, for example, *evokes* a political interpellation, a religious interpellation, or an aesthetic interpellation, and when each of these isolated interpellations operates as a *symbol* of the others, we have a relatively unified ideological discourse. Various efforts can be made to rationalize this unity in an explicit way, but they are always *a posteriori* attempts, which operate on the initial basis of an *implicit* unity of ideological discourse. In this regard we can point out a basic difference between two types of situations. In periods of stability, when the social formation tends to reproduce its relations following traditional channels and succeeds in neutralizing its contradictions by *displacements*,[1] this is when the dominant bloc in the formation is able to absorb most of the contradictions and its ideological discourse tends to rest more on the purely implicit mechanisms of its unity. This is when, generally, the correlation between the logical consistency of the elements of the discourse and its ideological unity reaches its lowest point. (Religious interpellations of an ascetic type can, for example, coexist with an increasing enjoyment of worldy goods without the social agents 'living' them as incompatible.)

In a period of generalized ideological crisis [. . .] the opposite tends to occur. The crisis of confidence in the 'natural' or 'automatic' reproduction of the system is translated into an exacerbation of all the ideological contradictions and into a dissolution of the unity of the dominant ideological discourse. As the function of all ideology is to constitute individuals as subjects, this ideological crisis is necessarily translated into an 'identity crisis' of the social agents. Each one of the sectors in struggle will try and reconstitute a new ideological unity using a 'system of narration' as a vehicle which disarticulates the ideological discourses of the opposing forces. What is important for the present problem is that one of the possible ways of resolving the crisis for the new hegemonic class or fraction is to deny all interpellations but one, develop all the logical implications of this one interpellation and transform it into a critique of the existing system, and at the same time, into a principle of reconstruction of the entire ideological domain. In our previous example, the incompatibility between religious asceticism and enjoyment of material wealth, formerly masked by the dominant ideological discourse, erupts in all its sharpness during a crisis period. There arises in these circumstances a religious reformer who blames all the evils on corruption and the abandonment of strict ascetic observance and who, through his interpellation, gives his followers a new subjectivity. The religious interpellation thus comes to be a chief re-organizer of all familial, political, economic, and other aspects. The coexistence of various relatively consistent interpellations in an ideological discourse has given way to an ideological structure in which *one* interpellation becomes the main organizer of all the others. In our example religious ideology fulfills this central role, but, in other historical contexts it could be political ideology. Whether the crisis is resolved in this way depends on many historical circumstances, but we can indicate at least two which would favour this type of solution: (1) the more separated is a social sector from the dominant relations of production, and the more diffuse are its 'objective interests' and consequently, less developed its 'class instinct'–the more the evolution and the resolution of the crisis will tend to take place on the ideological level; (2) the more central is the role of this type of sector in the social formation in question, the more central will be the role of the ideological level in the final resolution of the crisis on the part of the social formation as a whole [. . .]

We have omitted a central issue from our previous discussion: the relation between the ideologies and the class struggle. This is, however, a fundamental problem if we want to answer our second question: how are ideologies transformed? It must be pointed out in this respect that there has existed a basic ambiguity within the Marxist tradition about the use of the concept *class struggle*. In one sense, class struggle is posed at the level of the mode of production: the production relation which constitutes its two poles as classes is an antagonistic relation. Surplus-value, for example, constitutes *simultaneously* the relation between capitalists and workers and the antagonism between them; or rather, it constitutes that relation as an antagonistic one. Two conclusions follow from this: (1) that there are no classes except in a relation of struggle; (2) that the level of analysis which makes this antagonism intelligible is that of the mode of production. But the concept of class struggle has also tended to be applied to another kind of antagonism: to that where the struggle between classes only becomes intelligible if the overall political and ideological relations of domination characterizing a determinate social formation are brought to bear. Let us take, for example, the case of a social formation in which there is an articulation between a capitalist and a feudal mode of production and where a feudal landowning class is the hegemonic class in the dominant power bloc. It is not just the peasants who are exploited (those whom the hegemonic fraction exploits directly at the level of the mode of production), but the dominated sectors as a whole–petty-bourgeoisie, urban workers, perhaps part of the bourgeoisie, etc. Classes are, in this case, also in *struggle*, but can we speak strictly of a *class struggle*? This type of antagonism is distinct from the first in two basic senses: (1) unlike the first, it does not constitute classes as such (we cannot think of the concept of worker without thinking of the correlative concept of capitalist, but we can think of the concept of capitalist without thinking of the concept petty-bourgeois); (2) whilst the first antagonism is intelligible at the abstract level of the mode of production, the second antagonism is only intelligible at the level of a concrete social formation. The problem which then arises is: what is the relation between these two kinds of antagonism? Closely linked to the previous question is another: what is the relation between the ideologies in which both kinds of antagonism are expressed?

This presents no problem for a traditional Marxist conception: all ideological content has a clear class connotation and any contradiction can be reduced – through a more or less complicated system of mediations – to a class contradiction. The two kinds of antagonism are not articulated: in fact the second can be reduced to the first. In the paradigmatic case, the bourgeoisie exploits the working class at the level of the mode of production and constitutes the dominant class at the level of the social formation. Here the two kinds of struggle coincide and the only relevant distinction is the traditional one between *economic struggle* and *political* struggle. If, on the contrary, we have a situation as in our previous example where the power bloc is in opposition to the petty-bourgeoisie, the peasantry, the working class and certain sectors of the bourgeoisie, the picture becomes more complex but is not essentially modified: one would conclude that those sectors must establish a 'class alliance' to which each one must join within its own ideology, its own interests and, if possible, with its own party in the struggle against the common enemy. If this struggle created a series of ideological contents – values, symbols, etc., in short specific popular democratic interpellations which went beyond the ideologies of the different forces comprising the pact – this would be rejected as an element of rhetoric, propaganda, etc.; and anyone insisting on the automony of this aspect would be dismissed as 'idealist'. If, within this perspective, the priority of certain 'democratic' tasks is asserted, this is because there are some bourgeois tasks yet to be fulfilled: this is where 'combined and unequal development' is summoned to explain the more complex combinations and alliances, which never call into question the reduction of all contradictions to class contradictions.

To this reductionist approach we counterpose the following thesis: (1) Class struggle is only that which constitutes classes as such; (2) Consequently, not every contradiction is a class contradiction, but every contradiction is overdetermined by the class struggle. Let us start with the first thesis. Its obvious consequence is that the second type of antagonism cannot, strictly speaking, be regarded as a class struggle. Note that it is not possible to evade the problem by stating, in our previous example, that the petty-bourgeoisie is one class, the feudal landowners another and that therefore the conflict between them is a class struggle. This is the way in which the class struggle is typically presented in bourgeois literature of social history. But, in the first place, classes appear *already* constituted and the confrontation is relatively external to their nature; this has little to do with the Marxist conception of classes according to which they constitute themselves through the act of struggle itself. Secondly, even if there are two classes confronting each other, in the conflict mentioned, it is obvious that they are not in confrontation *as classes*, that their class nature – their insertion in the production process – is relatively external to the confrontation itself. We have *classes in struggle*, but not *class struggle*.

Consequently, if this antagonism is not a class antagonism, the ideologies which express it cannot be class ideologies. Through this kind of antagonism, the dominated sectors would not identify themselves as a class but as 'the other', 'the counterposed' to the dominant power bloc, as the *underdog*. If the first contradiction – at the level of mode of production – is expressed on the ideological level in the interpellation of the agents as a *class*, this second contradiction is expressed through the interpellation of the agents as *the people*. The first contradiction is the sphere of *class struggle*; the second, that of *popular-democratic struggle*.[2] The 'people' or 'popular sectors' are not, as some conceptions suppose, rhetorical abstractions or a liberal or idealist conception smuggled into Marxist political discourse. The 'people' form an objective determination of the system which is different from the class determination: the people are one of the poles of the dominant contradiction in a social formation, that is, a contradiction whose intelligibility depends on the ensemble of political and ideological relations of domination and not just the relations of production. If class contradiction is the dominant contradiction at the abstract level of the mode of production, the people/power bloc contradiction is dominant at the level of the social formation. We must ask ourselves, then, what is the relation between these two contradictions, and as part of the same problem, what is the relation between class interpellation (=ideology) and popular-democratic interpellation (=ideology).

This enables us to return to our second thesis: if not every contradiction can be reduced to a class contradiction, every contradiction is overdetermined by class struggle. According to basic Marxist theory, the level of production relations always maintains the role of determination in the last instance in any social formation. This in itself establishes the priority of the class struggle over the popular-democratic struggle, since the latter takes place only at the ideological and political level (the 'people' do not, obviously, exist at the level of production relations). This priority is revealed in the fact that popular-democratic ideologies never present themselves separated from, but articulated with, class ideological discourses. Class struggle at the ideological level consists, to a great extent, in the attempt to articulate popular-democratic interpellations in the ideological discourses of antagonistic classes. *The popular-democratic interpellation not only has no precise class content, but is the domain of ideological class struggle par excellence.* Every class struggles at the ideological level *simultaneously* as class and as the people, or rather, tries to give coherence to its ideological discourse by presenting its class objectives as the consummation of popular objectives.

The overdetermination of non-class interpellations by the class struggle consists, then, in the integration of those interpellations into a class ideological discourse. Since ideology is a practice producing subjects, this integration is the interpellation of a subject in whom partial interpellations are condensed. But as classes struggle to integrate the same interpellations into antagonistic ideological discourses, the process of condensation will never be complete: it will always have an ambiguity, a greater or lesser degree of openness according to the level of the class struggle, and various antagonistic attempts at fusion will always coexist. We are now in a position to answer our second question: how are ideologies transformed? The answer is: *through class struggle, which is carried out through the production of subjects and the articulation/dis-articulation of discourses* [. . .].

Not the least of the bourgeoisie's successes in asserting its ideological hegemony, is the consensus it has achieved – shared by many revolutionaries – that many of the constitutive elements of democratic and popular culture in a country are irrevocably linked to its class ideology. That this is not the case, that popular-democratic interpellations have no precise class connotation and can be incorporated into quite distinct political discourses, is something of which fascism provides eloquent proof. For the thesis we wish to present is the following: that fascism, far from being the typical ideological expression of the most conservative and reactionary sectors of the dominant classes was, on the contrary, one of the possible ways of articulating the popular-democratic interpellations into political discourse.

Notes

1 'In periods of stability the essential contradictions of the social formation are neutralized by displacement; in a revolutionary situation, however, they may condense or fuse into a revolutionary rupture.' (Ben Brewster, 'Glossary' to Louis Althusser, *For Marx*, Harmondsworth, Penguin, 1969).
2 Let us clarify two points to prevent any misunderstanding. Firstly, not every non-class interpellation is a popular democratic interpellation (otherwise the latter would be a purely residual category). To be able to speak of a popular-democratic interpellation, the subject addressed as 'the people' must be so in terms of an antagonistic relationship regarding the dominant bloc. Secondly, by democracy we do not mean anything which has a necessary relationship with Liberal parliamentary institutions [. . .]. By democracy we understand a set of symbols, values, etc.—in short, interpellations—through which the 'people' grows aware of its identity through its confrontation with the power bloc. These interpellations are necessarily united to institutions in which democracy is materialized, but both aspects are indissoluble. One cannot conceive an extension of democratic rights without the parallel production of the subjects capable of exercising them.

Reference

ALTHUSSER, L. (1971) *Lenin and Philosophy and Other Essays*, London, New Left
echoing one another or as Laclau puts it (see extract in this volume)

PART II

Politics in Liberal Democracy

3 Variants of Liberalism

Stuart Hall

Liberalism is the most intriguing of all the contemporary political ideologies. It is deeply embedded in English common sense and political culture, and represents a set of widely shared political values. Everyone wants to be known as a 'liberal' sort of person. Yet it is very diverse in its forms, and its outlines are difficult to pin down precisely. When Harold Macmillan, former Conservative Prime Minister, but by then a revered elder statesman, made his famous maiden speech as the Earl of Stockton in the House of Lords in 1985, he gently but firmly chided his successor in office, Mrs Thatcher, about the harsh excesses of her version of conservatism. It reminded him, he said, of what in his younger days used to be called 'Manchester School Liberalism'. Macmillan was referring to the extreme *laissez-faire* doctrines propounded by the nineteenth century Manchester school of political economists who were militant free-marketeers and believed the only sources of well-being to be individual self help. This exchange reminds us that the question of *liberalism* is still very much at stake in contemporary political debate; its concepts, however, are no longer confined to paid-up liberals or the Liberal Party, but are present within both social democracy and latter-day Conservatism. How did liberalism remain so significant for English political culture and yet become so widely diffused?

1 Definitions

The term 'liberal' usually denotes 'an attitude of mind rather than a political creed' (Eccleshall, 1984). Liberals are open-minded, tolerant, rational, freedom-loving people, sceptical of the claims of tradition and established authority, but strongly committed to the values of liberty, competition and individual freedom. 'Liberalism', as a proper noun, denotes the political creed, associated with the Liberal Party which dominated British politics in the nineteenth century. It stood for individualism in politics, civil and political rights, parliamentary government, moderate reform, limited state intervention, and a private enterprise economy. This political doctrine first emerged at the end of the eighteenth century, and was associated with the American Revolution, the French Revolutions, and in

England, the age of reform. Later it became a world current of political thought, linked with the struggles for national self-determination.

Relations between these two terms – liberal and Liberalism – have never been clear cut. The term 'liberal' has a longer history but many of its meanings have since been imported into the newer term, 'Liberalism'. Liberalism was also projected backwards to embrace ideas and events which had strictly preceded it in time but which were later held to belong to it. At the other end of the timescale, the 1980s have witnessed, within the Conservative Party, the revival of a conservative brand of what many describe as 'neo-liberalism'. Thus the meaning of the term has been continuously expanded, historically. Liberalism has acquired an extensive before- and after-life.

The subject of inquiry in this article is probably more accurately described as 'liberalism'. This includes what I have described as the characteristics of 'liberal' people as well as the ideas specific to nineteenth century Liberal political figures like Gladstone and philosophers like John Stuart Mill. The subject of the article is wider in at least two senses. First, I include within 'liberalism' the ideas of a range of thinkers and writers who, I believe, were central to the liberal tradition of thought, but who wrote long before the term 'Liberalism' had acquired either its nineteenth century name or its association with a specific political party. Second, and more important, I am concerned with mapping the contours of a much broader discourse about political, social and economic life – one which is widely diffused throughout English society and forms part of a shared language among people who would not normally think of themselves as Liberals in the strict party sense at all. I refer to this discourse as a *political ideology*. I mean by that that it has, for a very long time, historically, provided, and continues to provide a quite distinct framework for defining, explaining and calculating about political and social matters. It is organized around a number of basic propositions or 'core concepts'. These have been in the process of formation and development into a distinctive mode of thought in England since, at least, the seventeenth century. Though it has adapted to changing historical circumstances, this framework of thought still provides the basis of practical reasoning and thought for many ordinary people in English society today, even if they would not call themselves 'liberals'. It has become a central part of English 'common sense'. So much so that, to many of those who constantly think within its limits, it does not appear to be an ideology at all, but simply an obvious way of making sense of things – 'what everybody knows'. However, this 'obviousness' is itself a sign that the ideas *do* belong to a particular ideological configuration – they are 'obvious' only because their historical and philosophical roots and conditions have somehow been forgotten or suppressed. As a general current of thought, liberalism has a European, indeed a world-wide, history, though this article concentrates exclusively on its English dimension.

We can make three important points about defining liberalism as a political ideology in this way. First, the term ideology used to mean a clear-cut political doctrine or creed, whose concepts were logically linked to form a 'system' which had achieved internal consistency and been subject to rigorous philosophical elaboration. Nowadays, the term ideology includes the whole range of concepts, ideas and images which provide the frameworks of interpretation and meaning for social and political thought in society, whether they exist at the high, systematic, philosophical level or at the level of casual, everyday, contradictory, common-sense explanation.

Second, this way of defining ideology helps us to underline the point that *no* ideology is ever wholly logical or consistent. All the great organic ideologies bring together discordant elements and have to struggle to make contradictory ideas fit the scheme. There are always loose ends, breaks in the logic, gaps between theory and practice, and internal contradictions in *any* current of thought. Ideologies which attempt to remain consistent while explaining a changing historical reality, are subject to severe stretch and strain. Thus mid nineteenth century liberals were unswervingly committed to *laissez-faire* and free trade. The 'new liberals' of the 1880s and 1890s were the architects of the early welfare state. This does not mean that the latter were wholly inconsistent. But liberal principles did have to be reinterpreted so as to make sense in the new circumstances, and new concepts had to be produced–for example, a new definition of 'community'–to sustain and make plausible changes in the logic of the position.

The third point concerns the relationship between 'philosophical' and common-sense elaborations of an ideology. An ideology cannot be reduced to its philosophical essence. Of course it matters that ideas have been given a refined theoretical and philosophical development and in our account we will certainly draw on liberal political theorists and philosophers. But it also matters a great deal how these ideas appear within the taken-for-granted discourses of everyday life, and shape the 'practical consciousness' of the masses. The Italian marxist theorist, Antonio Gramsci (see the extract in this volume), argued that there are always two distinct arenas in ideology–philosophy and common sense. An ideology only becomes 'organic' to the broad contours of historical development when it is widely diffused through society and forms the basis, not only of philosophical reasoning but also of the 'naive' and spontaneous conceptions of the world held by ordinary people and thus becomes part of the common sense of the age.

Liberalism has indeed acquired something of this common-sense status in English social thought. This may owe something to the relative stability of English society, the evolutionary character of the changes in its social structure, the lack after the seventeenth century of the sharp ruptures and breaks more familiar to the history of continental European states, as well as to the lengthy dominance of empirical modes of thought. These have all helped liberalism over time to become almost as 'settled' and inescapable as the English weather. Liberal conceptions are now widely used in English political culture without people recognizing the stock from which they are drawing. 'An Englishman's home is his castle' (sic) has acquired the status of eternal proverbial English wisdom. It is, in fact, the product of an immensely complex and specific history. It was liberalism which first privileged private man in 'his' individual private space, made the domestic sphere, with its specific sexual divisions, into a symbol of 'his' sovereignty and constructed it as a form of private property. The whole liberal tradition of the 'free born

Englishman' and his rights and the whole history of the emergence of 'civil society' in the seventeenth and eighteenth centuries is already inscribed in that proverbial statement.

Antonio Gramsci argued that common sense is always 'disjointed and episodic'. It presents the appearance of 'eternal wisdom', but it is, in fact, historically quite specific. Many different philosophies and conceptions of the world have sedimented into it, in a rather chaotic and contradictory way. English common sense contains many such 'traces' of which liberalism is only one. Far from dismissing 'common sense' for this reason, Gramsci insists that *every* language or common linguistic usage is premised on 'the elements of a conception of the world'; and that *everyone* who thinks is, in this sense, a philosopher. Thus, philosophy is not 'watered down' or diluted by this engagement with practical, popular life and action. On the contrary, a philosophical current only becomes organic to society when it leaves behind a sedimentation in 'common sense' as the document of its historical effectiveness. This imprinting of different ideologies into common sense is the signal that certain 'ideas' have influenced practical thinking, are present in the 'effective action' of a group or class, inform the spontaneous intuitions of life and the world of the masses. Gramsci argues that it is only when a current of ideas has become, in this way, 'a cultural movement, a religion, a faith' that it is capable of performing its organic role – 'that of preserving the ideological unity of the entire social block which that ideology serves to cement and to unify'. New philosophies may then attempt to re-shape common sense – this is the basis of ideological struggle to win popular support for certain ideas but only on condition that these new ideas *engage* with common sense – with the structure of what everybody already takes for granted, the unwritten presuppositions of the social thought of an epoch. Gramsci consistently foregrounded this 'relation between common sense and the upper level of philosophy' which, he argues, is always 'assured by politics' (Gramsci, 1971, see the extract in this volume.)

Our argument follows Gramsci in this respect. It moves constantly between the 'philosophical' and 'common sense' aspects of liberalism. It is less concerned with the logical development of liberal concepts than with mapping the broad ways in which liberal ideas have entered into and shaped the practical consciousness of society. The article analyses how liberal conceptions of the world have informed the actions of specific historical classes, groups and individuals; their role in unifying different sections of society around certain ideas at different historical moments; the transformations which these ideas were obliged to undergo in order to remain relevant to new historical circumstances. It identifies where the major internal contradictions in this set of discourses arise and the 'limits' of this particular configuration of thought, which holds such a variety of bold and contentious ideas and thinkers within a defined discursive space. By looking at 'variants' I will try to show that liberalism is a diverse, not a unified, discourse and consequently identify its radical, conservative and 'social democratic' strands.

The specific questions addressed in the article are as follows. What are the distinguishing 'core concepts' of liberalism – how is its discursive field defined (Section 2)? How were liberal ideas shaped by the social and historical context in which they developed? This is a test, broadly, of what has come to be known as the materialistic theory about ideology (Section 3). What is the link between liberal ideas and specific social classes and class interests? This question explores the marxist thesis that ideologies 'belong' to specific classes (Sections 4 and 5). Finally, how has liberalism reworked and reconstituted itself in different historical epochs? – a look at the process of ideological transformation (Sections 6 and 7).

2 The core conceptions of liberalism

The first task is to identify the key propositions or core concepts of liberalism. These are the ideas which map out or define its distinctive discursive space as an ideology. Of course, liberal ideas are not static. Ideologies retain their relevance to changing historical circumstances only by constantly revising and 'up-dating' their basic concepts. Nevertheless, if an ideology is to exhibit a degree of internal coherence over time, it must have a distinctive core of concepts and propositions, an internal reference system of themes and questions. We may call this matrix of core concepts, propositions and questions the *problematic* of an ideology (Althusser, 1969). The 'core conceptions' summarized here really refer to *classic* liberalism – liberalism as it had cohered into a political ideology by the end of the eighteenth century. In philosophical terms, its twin pillars at this stage were the political theories of John Locke and the political economy of Adam Smith. In political terms, its main sources were the ideas of the English Civil War, the Glorious Settlement, which introduced parliamentary government to England, and the American and French Revolutions. I am focusing primarily on England throughout this discussion though that means leaving out the relevant history of liberalism in France, Germany, Italy and the US.

We cannot analyse these core conceptions in isolation. Ideas form a tradition. They 'hang together'. They mutually define and modify one another; they entail each other – they are inter-dependent. They tend to refer across, summoning up or echoing one another or as Laclau puts it (see extract in this volume) 'connoting and condensing each other' within a discursive chain of meaning. The concepts, working together, form a distinct discursive space of meanings, and sustain a particular 'logic' of thought. Thus, for example, we cannot give a *liberal* definition of 'liberty' without reference to the liberal conceptions of equality and the individual. Or, to take another example, references to 'the individual' in classic liberal discourse always assume that a man's interests are identical to the interests of 'his' wife and children. So in its early form, the liberal concept of the individual was implicitly *gendered*. Thus, when we analyse an ideology in terms of its 'key concepts' we are really mapping the whole web of meanings, the discursive space, which these core ideas, working together, constitute as that ideology's 'régime of truth' – to borrow Foucault's metaphor.

Liberalism 'designates those progressive ideas which accompanied the gradual breakdown of traditional social hierarchies. Understood in this way, liberalism is the ideology most intimately connected with the birth and evolution of the modern capitalist world' (Eccleshall 1984). It is absolutely essential to 'place' liberalism in this way, historically as a modernizing ideology. Much is clarified by remembering that, from its inception, liberalism was *opposed* to something – the old order of feudal or traditional society – and *aligned with* something else – the new, emerging social order of bourgeois society. The opposition made liberalism, in its inception, a progressive social ideology. The alignment made it subsequently supportive of a new social establishment. This historic tension between its progressive and conservative tendencies is still to be observed at the very core of liberalism today.

Some of its key concepts can be directly derived from this historical placing. Born in opposition to a world dominated by monarchy, the aristocracy and the church, liberalism has subsequently tended to *oppose* the arbitrary power of absolute monarchs and the privileges and prescriptive right to rule of the nobility, based on birth or ascribed position in the social hierarchy. It has remained suspicious of the claims to authority of Pope and established Church. It contested the whole traditional order of society characteristic of feudalism where individuals were permanently fixed in their appointed place in the 'Great Chain of Being'. It remains dubious of all traditional ideas claiming final authority. By contrast, liberalism has consistently *favoured* an 'open' meritocratic society, where the energetic individual can rise to respectability and success, whatever his humble origins. (Given what I said earlier about the gendered nature of liberal concepts, I have deliberately used the masculine forms of the pronoun, 'him' and 'his' when outlining liberal ideas). Liberalism maintains a contractual and competitive rather than an ascriptive idea of social order. It favours free-thinking, rationalist and sceptical modes of thought, regarding religion as a matter of private conscience, not a matter for the state to legislate. In place of the acceptance of static social hierarchies characteristic of conservative social philosophies, liberalism has always displayed optimism about the results of change, dynamism, growth, mobility, accumulation and competition.

At the centre of its conception of the world in the seventeenth century was a novel way of conceptualizing *individualism*. Now, people have always had some conception of what it is to be an individual. But individual*ism* – a whole conception of the world premised on the sovereign individual – was quite foreign to the social philosophies of feudal and Catholic Europe. It was the Reformation and Puritanism, which loosed the individual from the institutional supports of the Church and set 'him' in direct confrontation with God. This idea was then absorbed, in its more secular form, into the categories of the new social philosophy. This conception of the individual, stripped of status, position, relationship or place in the divine scheme of things was a highly atomistic and materialistic conception. Yet, it was also idealist and abstract – a category conceived as free of all constraints on action and endowed by Nature with certain inalienable rights. This stripped-down, atomistic version privileged Nature over society and destroyed the whole web of social and spiritual constraints in which, in the older philosophies, human beings were understood to be embedded.

This abstract individual was then ascribed with concrete characteristics and attributes said to be endowed by Nature and essential to its *human nature*. These explained what men naturally were, why they acted the way they did and what rights they had. Thus individuals were said to be 'naturally' driven by the search for security, power and self-interest. Man was competitive and aggrandizing 'by nature'. It was part of human nature to barter and truck, to compete, accumulate property unceasingly, to maximize one's advantages and struggle to rise in society. The state was essentially a set of external constraints on individual freedom, necessary for an ordered social existence, but arising outside of and artificially imposed on individuals.

The liberal concept of *society* is really the reverse side of this conception of the individual. The good society was that which guaranteed the liberty of the individual to maximize the self and its freedom of action. The purpose of the state was to create for individuals the conditions in which they could pursue their *private* affairs as equal members of society. Thomas Hobbes (1588-1679) had argued that competitive societies required a strong and sovereign power to impose constraints on individuals to prevent them from destroying one another in what he called the 'war of all against all'. On the other hand, classic liberals came to believe the state must interfere as little as possible with the individual's rights and freedom of movement. The only legitimate government was one to which individuals had freely ceded their inalienable rights and with which they had consented to make a contract-offering political loyalty, consent and obligation in return for good government, the protection of the individual's life, property and liberties. In short, classic liberalism had a strong but limited concept of the state and a contractual conception of the social bond.

The arena of individual interest and self-realization was called *civil society*-the domain of private voluntary association, beyond the reach and regulation of the state. Civil society became, in liberal doctrine, *the* privileged domain of action. Our common-sense view often is that individual liberty of this kind has existed since time immemorial, only gradually being encroached on by the state. The fact is that liberalism as a doctrine and the forces that created liberal society *carved* this space of private rights, interest and action out of a much more corporate type of society. Civil society contained three major zones; the private domestic world of the family; the arena of free and contractual economic activity-the market; and the domain of voluntary social and political association. The raising of civil society over the state-hitherto, the realm of public duties and responsibilities-and the 'privatizing' of the whole conception of society, represents a major *reversal* by liberalism of previous systems of social thought.

Natural rights, which now defined the individual's powers, were not thought of as arising from social intercourse, or from the struggles of groups to achieve certain collective powers, but 'belong to individuals as individuals in the state of nature and (are) therefore prior to entry into society'(Locke). Liberalism later abandoned this theory of 'natural rights': but this did not undermine the essentially individualist premises on which its theory was predicated. Thus only individuals could by their free consent abrogate their rights sufficiently to create society and government. Only this giving of consent made government legitimate.

This notion that individuals were already endowed with rights and liberties *outside* of society, led to a very distinctive way of conceptualizing the relationship *between* individuals and society. Many previous and later theories assume that individuals are at least in part formed by society. Liberalism maintains a strict logical separation between the individual and society, with what we might call 'external relations only' between them. Liberalism thus played a role in constructing our prevailing common sense or 'spontaneous' awareness of ourselves today as a separate, isolable and self-sufficient beings. This conception of individual rights is also the source of liberalism's particular claim to universality as a social doctrine. Its claims are 'not for this group or this nation in this time, but for all human beings at all times in all places' (Gamble, 1981).

The peculiarly liberal conception of *liberty* now falls into place. Liberty means freedom of the individual from constraint; freedom *for* the individual to exercise 'his' natural egoistic drives and instincts. Liberty is defined essentially in a *negative* way – freedom *from* constraint. Equality is a subordinate value to this and means primarily that all individuals are equal because they are born with *the same* rights. None therefore should have prior status as a consequence of birth or inherited position. Everyone must have an *equal* chance to enter the competitive struggle – there must be no barriers to entry. Everyone must be *free* to compete. Whatever their real differences in power and wealth, the law recognizes all individuals as equal 'legal subjects'. This is the 'liberal' conception of equality.

Note that it does *not* mean that people must have equality *of condition* so that they can compete equally; or that those who start from a poorer position should be 'positively advantaged' so that they can really, in fact, compete on equal terms; and certainly it does not mean that everyone should end up in roughly equal positions. Liberalism has always accepted that those who compete successfully must succeed. But since the fear of failure is the spur to competition, all cannot succeed. Hence, inevitably, many must lose in order for some to win. From its inception classic liberalism was identified with the 'free market' and opposed any intervention by the state to remedy the unequal consequences of market competition or to distribute goods, resources and opportunities more equitably between the competing classes. This is an inherently inegalitarian position if we conceive liberty in a more *positive* sense. The tension around this point constitutes a recurring contradiction within liberal discourse.

This underlines the argument that no ideology is wholly consistent. Great, organic ideologies like liberalism survive because of their capacity to 'bridge' the difficult transitions between contradictory ideas, their facility at 'squaring the circle'. Liberalism has subsequently shifted its position many times on this point but it has always come to rest firmly within the limits of what we might call an individualistic conception of equality. Liberty and equality are always articulated together in liberal discourse, but in ways which systematically privilege liberty *over* equality.

Liberalism's negative conception of liberty fits with its *legalistic* conception of equality. Liberalism has always placed considerable stress on equality before the law and the 'rule of law' itself. Rich and poor alike must be treated as equals by the law: 'The prince and the pauper are free in law to sleep beneath the bridges of Paris'. F.A. Hayek, a modern neo-liberal, argues that this is 'the fundamental principle of classic liberalism' – the limitation of government 'to the passing of laws', meaning 'general rules of just conduct applicable to all citizens' (Hayek, 1973). Of course, the law has nothing to say about the deeply unequal *condition* of those who appear before it. The prince, after all, is 'free' to go home to his palace; the beggar has nowhere else to go. But, for the purposes of legislation, all – rich and poor, who are manifestly *not* equal in fact – are treated as *formally* equal in the eyes of the law. This contrast between formal and substantive equality is another source of ambiguity in liberalism.

The law therefore appealed to liberals because it offered formal and systematic public criteria in place of the arbitrary power of earlier courts and judicial procedure. 'The law must no longer vary with the length of a Lord Chancellor's foot', as they said during the Civil War. The law thus maintained fairness between competing contenders without questioning or interfering with the basic dispositions of wealth and power in society. Also, the law secured the contracts which individuals 'freely' made with one another in civil society – and contract is a highly persuasive legalistic way of describing how sovereign individuals associate. The same liberal concern with submitting the state to the law also led liberals to be 'constitutionalists' – whether in the written form of the American or the unwritten form of the British Constitution. Finally, the law protected the individual's rights, liberties and property. 'The business of laws', John Locke once observed, 'is not to provide for the truth of opinions but for the safety and security of the commonwealth and of every particular man's goods and person.'

In terms of its *political* conceptions, then, liberals believed in good government: the state had to be strong but limited. Liberalism thus came to be associated with a range of mechanisms for weakening and dispersing the concentrated powers of government. For example, it affirmed the strict separation between the state and civil society; or later, between political and economic power – so that concentrations of wealth are held to be separable from political equality. The difference in wealth and power between the millionaire and the beggar does not undermine, in liberalism, their equality as voting persons – one-person-one-vote. Another favoured feature of liberal constitutionalism was the separation of powers between executive, legislature and judiciary: between Presidential executive and Congress in the US system, or between Crown, Lords and Commons in the English 'mixed' constitution.

In the feudal or traditional social order, political participation was limited exclusively to those estates at the apex of society. In liberalism only the consent of its citizens can confer legitimacy on government. Liberalism therefore favoured from the outset opening up the state to a wider political participation. One of liberalism's first historic tasks was to justify the entry into political society of those rising individuals hitherto excluded from the system of representation. However, as Dickinson (1977) has acutely observed, 'By the term "free man" the Whigs [who were the liberal heirs to the ideas of the Glorious Revolution] always meant a man of independent means'. Women, domestics, children and the labouring poor were not considered 'free-born Englishmen', in the same sense. Liberalism is therefore identified with the idea of representative government, but *not* with universal democracy. Liberalism provided the justification for a widening of the franchise. But it did not lead the struggle for universal suffrage. The liberal commitment to individualism has always been hard to reconcile with the idea of a mass democracy. The latter was only grafted on to liberalism at a relatively late date and Macpherson (1977) is right to suggest that one can still hear the grating sound which this grafting produced. This is yet another tension in liberalism – between its universalistic claims on behalf of all citizens and its alignment with the interests of particular sections of society; between its commitment to representative government and its doubts about universal democracy.

The liberal conception of political rights (free association and participation in the political process) and of civil and legal rights (freedom from arbitrary arrest, freedom of thought, religion and opinion, the freedom to be tried by a jury of one's peers) were matched by an equally vigorous *economic* liberalism, predicated on a notion of the possessive individual – or 'economic man'. The individual's rights included the 'right' to own and dispose of his own property, to buy and sell, to hire labour and make a profit. These were concretely rooted in the emerging economic relationships of commercial society which had begun to transform English society. This conception of the economy was materialist, because its operations no longer depended on moral ideas, fellow feelings, ethical idealism or good-will but on 'an immediate and earthly recompense for labour' (Laski 1936). It was utilitarian because it was grounded in the calculus of rationally pursued self-interest and the calculation of advantage. Its drives were held to be rooted in human nature – hence an economy built on these foundations was considered by most liberals to be a 'natural' economy. Competition was its governing principle. This produced a *dynamic* conception of economic life – perhaps the first systematically dynamic economic theory in modern history. Hostile to the fixed and static economic relationships of feudalism, liberalism was articulated around the idea of an infinitely expanding, developing economy, propelled by productive labour, individual risk-taking and reward. Property was central to the definition of, and enhanced, the individual. It was the material expression of 'his' powers. Its accumulation and disposal were the proper extention of 'his' rights and liberties into the economic domain.

The market was thus the perfect instrument of such a system because, in market society, 'central economic decisions...result from the impersonal movement of prices reflecting the push and pull of forces of demand and supply which arise from a multitude of individual decisions and wills' (Gamble, 1981). The market thus perfectly embodied the new economic individualism. Market relationships abolished the traditional restraints on the freedom to raise and invest capital, to fund loans and earn interest, sell property and realize a profit, hire and fire labour. They represented the 'setting free' of the individual in the economic sphere, creating the conditions for the private speculation in land, capital and labour which, by the end of the eighteenth century, had transformed English society into the most dynamic capitalist economy on earth.

3 Liberalism's historical conditions of existence

Having, for analytic purposes, treated liberalism's key ideas ahistorically, let us now situate them historically. Why these particular ideas *then* – at that particular historical moment? The claims of liberalism are universal. But what happens when these general conceptions are applied to specific societies, to particular historical circumstances and institutions? Does liberalism become imprinted with the interests of a particular class or group? Is it really the dominant ideology of a particular epoch or class?

You may recognize these as the kinds of question posed by the materialist theory of ideology, advanced by classical marxism. Their most seminal formulation appeared in *The German Ideology* (Marx, 1846), the only sustained theoretical treatment of the topic by Marx and Engels. Larrain (1983) reminds us that probably few of the original generation of marxists – Kautsky, Lenin, Gramsci, the young Lukacs – knew this text. They relied on the abbreviated version of the theory contained in a summary passage in Marx's 1859 Preface to *The Critique of Political Economy*, a notably compressed and ambiguous text.

The broad 'theses' Marx and Engels advanced can be summarized in the following propositions.

1 Ideas arise from actual social relations. It is men, as 'conditioned by the development of their productive forces and social intercourse' who produce conceptions, ideas, law, morality, religion, metaphysics etc. Consciousness is 'a social product', and is always 'interwoven with material reality'. Social being determines consciousness, not – as we imagine – vice versa. Therefore, we should 'explain the formation of ideas from material practice, consciousness from the contradictions of material life'. This is the *materialist* proposition about ideology. It is important to remember that, by 'reality' Marx did not mean a reality 'out there', which we could contemplate as fixed and already formed, but one constantly being produced and transformed by human practice. It was this social and material activity which produced ideas.

2 The second proposition concerns the social character or *class basis* of ideology. It is the proposition that ideologies arise from, express the interests of, and 'belong' to particular classes, and they reflect in thought the position of those classes in the economic structure. 'Ideas are the conscious expression – real or illusory – of the real relations and activities, of the production, of the intercourse, of the social and political conduct of particular classes'.

3 The third thesis contains a proposition about the *power and domination* of particular ideas. 'The ideas of the ruling class are in every epoch . . . the ruling ideas'. 'The class which is the ruling material force of society is at the same time its ruling intellectual force' (Marx, 1846). The class which monopolizes material power also monopolizes intellectual production and 'regulates' the production and distribution of the ideas of its age.

These theses contain many challenging and problematic formulations. They have been extensively criticized on three main grounds. First, on the grounds of *reductionism;* they tend to reduce ideas to their 'material basis' and therefore allow them little or no independent effectivity. Ideas become purely secondary factors – dependent variables – in history. Second, on grounds of *economism*; they are said to collapse ideas into the economy and make the latter the real content of ideas, which ideas merely mask or hide. Third, as *class essentialist*; they assume ideologies are only the expression of social classes and 'belong' exclusively to them. Ideas flow from and are ascribed to the position of a class in the productive system. Critics have also drawn attention to the unfortunate implication of the proposition that ideology is 'illusory'. It is said to disguise the true material interests of those who subscribe to it and thereby produces a 'false consciousness'. Others have criticized the notion that ideas are mere 'reflexes', 'echoes', 'sublimates' of material life, and therefore constitute a superstructure resting on, dependent on and determined by the economic 'base'. These criticisms have considerably weakened the specific form in which Marx and Engels first advanced their propositions and especially the 'vulgar' form in which these have been transmitted by some schools within the marxist tradition. The question is whether these criticisms have entirely disposed of the *broad* positions which the materialist theory advanced. In the following sections we will attempt to explore and test this question.

To do so we must turn again to the historical conditions of the emergence of classic liberalism. Liberalism is an ideology of the modern world. It appeared as the modern world emerged. For decades the idea of 'modernity' was 'thought' essentially, within its categories. A critical turning point in its evolution in England was the political, social and economic trends crystallized by the English Civil War of the 1640s. The founding arguments of liberalism were first rehearsed in these years and in direct relation to those epochal events. Hobbes' *Leviathan* (1651), a founding political text of liberalism which addressed the need of competitive society to have a strong and sovereign centre of power, was written in the wake of King Charles' execution of 1649. Thus its historical context was a period when Cromwell and Parliament were in command and debates about property, equality and the nature of political obligation and authority raged fiercely amongst the different Puritan sects who identified with the revolutionary cause. As Raphael observes about Hobbes, 'To be a great philosopher it is not enough to have a great talent. The talent must also be faced with an important real-life problem' (Raphael, 1977). Locke's *Two Treatises* (1690) were published around the time of the exclusion of James II from the throne and the Settlement of 1688 which consolidated a new political order based on a limited constitutional monarchy and representative government, religious toleration, a contractual theory of the state and a 'natural rights' conception of the sovereign individual. Almost a century later, in 1776, Tom Paine produced his book, *Common Sense*, the basis for that essential liberal document, the American Declaration of Independence, and Adam Smith published the classic analysis of capitalist market society, *The Wealth of Nations*. These dates help to establish classic liberalism's 'founding moment'.

Liberalism did not, however, suddenly appear. Many of its ideas have undergone a lengthy process of formulation, only gradually beginning to cohere into an organic conception of society. There are very few, if any, absolutely 'new starts' in the history of ideology. But, looking back, we can see older conceptions of society beginning to disintegrate, losing their coherence, their purchase on common sense and yielding gradually to new conceptions of the world.

We can only sketchily suggest the historical preconditons of liberalism. The Reformation had challenged papal jurisdiction and authority. It posited the individual as the sovereign judge of all conduct and a direct interlocutor with God. It was therefore pivotal in setting in motion that conception of the individual as 'captain of his destiny', without which liberalism could not have existed. The challenge to religious authority loosed upon the world the scandalous idea that men must follow the dictates of their own conscience guided by reason. It was the end of an absolutist notion of revealed truth.

Nature was no longer an order for men and women to contemplate but an external reality with which they must experiment, investigate, use the tools of science to explain, labour to transform and above all *master* (the masculine derivation was not fortuitous). Despite the religious impetus to these developments, their underlying thrust was inevitably secular. It committed men to free-thinking, rational, empirical and investigative modes of thought about the real and evident world. It liberated from the fetters of authority a new 'scientific' attitude to reality. From this point onwards, as Gamble (1981) remarks, 'Science appears as the essence of modernism' and becomes identified 'as the natural ally of liberalism and democracy and "open" societies'.

Laski (1936) has suggested that this ideological revolution had three main components: the evolution of a new political doctrine – the state as a self-sufficient, secular entity; a new theology – undermining the hold of faith on men and women's minds; and a new cosmology – a new scientific attitude to nature.

In economic life, this revolution was not only underpinned by a 'new spirit of enterprise', but appeared as a new 'feverish activity', a 'zest for innovation'. In contrast with the static structures of feudal society there emerged a dynamic economy, throwing over the old barriers to expansion, revolutionizing everything in its wake. Many of these 'barriers' had been the very forms of property and production in familial and feudal society. Some of the 'barriers' were also ideological: religious inhibitions on the pursuit of profit and on usury; the locking up of wealth and property in the fixed establishments of the Church; the dispersal of markets and legal authority under the fragmented feudal system of political, military, economic and ecclesiastical obligations. The Reformation not only sanctioned a new individualism, it transferred enormous wealth into secular hands. It unified the secular state. It freed men from the inhibition to trade, profit and expand which had been embodied in such notions as a 'just price' and a 'moral economy'. The pursuit of gain, Max Weber noted in *The Protestant Ethic*, is as old as recorded history. The systematic pursuit of profit through accumulation, however, was something new. When the individual seized this opportunity, the result was the whole material dynamic of commercial society. There was born the revolutionary idea of production without limit, of boundless accumulation. The unification of markets and territory under a single ruler created an entirely new economic and political framework – the secular sovereign state, whose boundaries are coterminous with a unified internal market under a single law and administrative regime. This is the point of origin of the nation-state and of modern ideas of sovereignty, which have dominated modern history from that time on. The promotion of free-thought, scepticism and religious toleration was followed by an expansion of the empire of reason. But this was matched by the material advances of the New Science – the microscope, the telescope, the advances in astronomy, mathematics, optics, hydro-mechanics, magnetism, electricity, medicine and botany. The period of exploration, navigation and discovery abroad paralleled the advances at home in agricultural production, engineering and mechanics. 'In their search for wealth they required new power over nature, new instruments to develop that power. Their needs defined new horizons . . . out of which emerged a new picture of the universe and a new control of nature' (Laski, 1936).

It seems, then, even from this brief sketch, that liberalism was undoubtedly 'of its time and place', profoundly shaped by its historical conditions of existence. Its forms of thought and consciousness were – as the first materalist proposition suggests – 'a social product . . . interwoven with material life'. We could not attempt to explain the formation of these ideas outside of material practice and changes in historical conditions. Of course the genealogy of the ideas of liberalism is lengthy and exceedingly complicated. The ideas cannot be treated as simple 'echoes' or 'sublimates' of other processes. They have their own relatively independent history. Furthermore, the early forms which liberalism assumed owe their character to a revolution in thought and cosmology as much as to a revolution in material or technological conditions. The birth of liberalism, in short, had both material and ideological conditions of existence. In its 'soft' form, then, the materialist proposition stands. But in its 'harder' form – explaining ideas directly *from* material practice – it is more difficult to substantiate. It is clear that historical developments give rise to and shape particular ideas. However, it is not clear how precisely the causal links can be drawn which prove that material factors fully determine ideological outcomes. What seems to be validated, however, is the general proposition concerning the social and historical basis of ideas.

4 Liberalism's 'class belongingness'

So far we have briefly considered the historical preconditions which made liberalism possible as a distinctive body of ideas. It was formed in the series of 'breaks' with the past which created modern society as we know it. However, the connections are too loose to serve as an adequate exploration of the materialist theory of ideology. Let us turn now to the period in the seventeenth and eighteenth centuries – liberalism's 'founding historical moment' – to explore the second materalist proposition: the 'class derivation or class belongingness' of liberal ideology.

Liberalism's historical emergence in England can be traced directly to the period of the English Revolution (1640-1688). The Civil War itself – as later historians have shown – had complex and diverse causes. It came from the long accumulation of frustrations which the gentry and other men of property experienced as a result of the attempts of the Stuart monarchy to impose absolute rule and ecclesiastical authority on the populace and to re-establish in English government – with its long parliamentary tradition – the claims of divine right. The English Revolution was carried along on the complex tides of religious argument set in motion by the Reformation and the rise of Puritanism. The actual Civil War (1640-1649) itself was triggered by a series of complicated, contingent events. The royalists and parliamentarians, both during and after the war failed to resolve themselves into two, broad, simple opposing factions. It is impossible to identify factions which were coherent within themselves, opposed at every point to each other, which represented the major classes involved: the landed nobility standing for the monarchy, the Church and the traditional order and the rising gentry – the new bourgeois classes, to put it crudely – standing for the new forces of capital, property, commerce and trade. If we try to explain the social and ideological character of the English Revolution in these neatly blocked out terms – with each 'class representative' carrying, so to speak, its appropriate ideology like a number plate on its back (Poulantzas, 1975) – we will be severely disappointed. Whole classes are rarely ever unified in this way or neatly aligned behind their appropriate banners. Within the Parliamentary forces, there were a variety of political and social groupings; ranging from the highly respectable and substantial men of property (led by Cromwell and Ireton) through Lilburn (who stood for the small men of the city against the big men of commerce) to the Levellers (with their radical programme of popular democracy for the poorer sections of society) and Winstanley (who spoke a kind of agrarian communism on behalf of the new landless labourers). Yet they all belonged to the Parliamentary cause. They were all opposed to the absolutism of the Stuart monarchy. But they also diverged widely in terms of their social class origins and their economic interests. And they substantially differed amongst themselves, and debated passionately, about a number of critical political positions such as the question of to whom the rights of political representation under the new franchise should be extended. There is thus no neat correspondence between the economic, political and ideological positions.

In fact, when the air finally cleared, it was manifest that there had been, effectively, not one but *two* revolutions. The revolution which won civil, political and economic rights for the new men of property, which enshrined their rights, liberties and property as the proper object of good government, which curbed the powers of the state, monarch, church and nobility over them and enlarged their sphere of action, succeeded. It is this which was later consolidated under the settlement of the so-called 'Glorious Revolution' of 1688. The second revolution, supported by the propertyless and designed to eliminate the poverty and social injustice experienced by the mass of the poorer classes – the 'poorest sort of us', as Lilburn put it – did not succeed.

Liberalism was, therefore, never in any simple sense '*the* ideology of *the* ruling class'. The Civil War was not fought out as a simple class vs class issue of this kind. It had more of the character of a political struggle *within* the ruling classes about which section should become the ruling or 'leading' class in society. Even so, it never became a straightforward duel between the landed nobility and the commercial bourgeoisie. The latter, if anything, were conspicuous by their relative absence in the actual ranks of the parliamentary leaders. The struggle assumed much more the character of a struggle between the declining and the emergent fractions of the propertied classes, to which the lower social ranks became, for a time, aligned. Liberalism was one discourse in which these different class fractions first fought out what they wanted, what their interests were, the justification for their actions. It was the framework of thought in which they came to consciousness. It was also an arena of struggle and contestation between different fractions *within* these emerging class formations.

Yet the Civil War did create the conditions in which capitalism developed and the bourgeois classes of society became the leading classes. And this historic outcome was inconceivable without the framework of classic liberal theory. Indeed, liberalism helped to *constitute* those ideas as a political tradition. It is here that we find invoked, as part of a concrete historical struggle, the liberal principle that a monarch who abuses the trust placed in him has broken a contract with society. It is here that we see advanced the claims to representation and political participation by the new classes rising to prominence in civil society. Here we find the case advanced that these rights arise not from society or the state but in nature itself. Here too is the argument that the only right to rule is that which flows from the consent of 'the people' and that therefore they have a right to rebel against an arbitrary tyranny. This is the basic liberal lexicon of representative government and individual civil rights. So liberal ideology was *articulated* to the emergence to dominance of a rising class, though it was not the exclusive product or property of that class.

This complex relation of ideology and class is demonstrated in the flood of radical and popular thought circulating by way of pamphlets and debates among Cromwell's army, the radical Puritan sects and the poor, where we find the seeds of a *second* strand or 'tradition' within liberalism. This represented a more radical line of thought, designed by and for the 'little people', the people without property and power, who articulated liberal principles into a more thorough-going egalitarian democratic programme. They called, within the general demand for liberty, for social justice and freedom from want. They argued that if *all* men were born equal then they must be 'free born Englishmen' too – a cry at once seized on and taken up, in an even more radical form, by the very first feminists among the Puritan sects, who used the natural rights argument to support their case (see Juliet Mitchell, in this volume).

It would therefore be wrong to attempt to give this emerging liberalism a finished, unified or coherent character attached exclusively by origin to a single class – *the* dominant ideology of the ruling class. Liberalism actually emerged as a contested space already divided into its more conservative and its more radical tendencies – a tension which has been repeated again and again throughout its history. Depending on which tendency was the dominant one, liberalism could be articulated to the demands of different social strata. It was not entirely 'class belonging' in its social basis. Both conservative and radical tendencies were premised on the fundamentally *liberal* concepts of individual liberties and rights and a conception of society as an association of free and rational persons bound by contract and consent. The quarrel between those who saw good government as the extension and preservation of *their* property and those who saw liberty as the end of 'one rule for the rich and one for the poor' was a quarrel between different classes initially *within liberalism*.

It was John Locke (1632–1704) who consolidated the former tradition as the dominant one in liberalism by elaborating it philosophically. He defined the principles of classic liberalism for two centuries in ways which identified it with the more conservative tendency. Locke powerfully stated the case for constitutional and representative government. He regarded the state as the result of a contract between the citizen and society. Men could only be bound in the first place into political obligation by giving up some of their rights with free consent. These rights were inalienable because they were natural rights – the first of which was the right of property. 'The reason why men enter society is the preservation of their property'. Each man was the 'sole proprietor' of his own person and capacities.

In the settlement of the Glorious Revolution, when Stuart claims to the throne were finally set aside and rule by constitutional monarchy and parliament installed, the Whig party (mainly representing the landed gentry who supported Parliament) set out to secure the gains which had been made by the Civil War, but at the same time to restore stability and continuity to the social order. The Glorious Revolution of 1688 was a 'historic compromise'. A limited monarchy, representative government and the consent of the people were moulded into 'the English form of government'. Research by Peter Laslett suggests that Locke's *Two Treatises on Government* were conceived and written before the year of the Glorious Revolution (Laslett 1967). Nevertheless, as Laslett himself acknowledges, the book 'did in actual fact justify the Revolution to posterity, as well as to contemporaries'. In Gough's judgement, Locke 'justified the constitutional principles of the Revolution Whigs . . . by making them appear to be in accordance with the conclusions of pure reason'. His discussion of the powers of government, however abstractly conceived, was 'in effect a description of the régime approved of in current Whig political thought, which his argument represented as the logical conclusion of ordinary common sense, but in fact [embodied] his observation of the traditional assumptions of the English constitution' (Gough 1968).

The subtle relationships between Locke's philosophy and Whig 'common sense' does not mean that Locke was simply a vulgar apologist for the Whig solution or deliberately dressed up his arguments to plead a special case. The thesis about the relationship between class and ideology does not require us to *reduce* political ideas conspiratorially to mere class propaganda. Locke and the Whigs in their different ways clearly *did* genuinely understand themselves and their society by means of these new categories and concepts. And they *were* in their time subversive even though not in the end as subversive as they believed. (Locke did not acknowledge he was the author of the *Treatises* because its defence of rebellion against tyranny was widely understood to be potentially seditious [Dunn, 1984]).

The thesis about the relationship between class and ideology does *not* require us to reduce all ideas to a mere expression of class interest.But it *does* require an explanation of why certain liberal assumptions came to be so widely and commonly held; why they gradually became the dominant taken-for-granted conception of politics; why this way of conceptualizing individuals, their rights, their relation to society and the state and their conceptions of property acquired, in this period, *both* the compulsory force of a natural attitude – obvious common sense – and the cogency of advanced philosophical Reason and sustained argument. It is the similarity or homology of structure between the new patterns which political thought assumed and the new patterns which political and economic relationships evolved, which establishes the basis of the connection.

The connection, provided it is not reductively treated, always enables us to provide a concrete reference for what is posed by ideology in an abstract or universal manner. Take for example the question of property. Locke gave, as we have seen, a central place to property in the 'natural rights' of the individual. However, he had to explain how men acquired a *private* right over God's common heritage. He reached the revolutionary conclusion that it was mixing *labour* with material objects which gave man 'his' right to the product of labour (Dunn 1984). He argued that since labour gave man 'an entitlement', property was something which men could also alienate or dispose of for money or a wage in the market. However, this argument did not make the labouring classes, in his view, a social interest like the propertied. Though in *abstract* terms, civil society was composed of a mass of free and equal individuals, in *concrete* terms it was implicitly acknowledged to be composed of the actual quite unequal classes of the propertied and the propertyless. This is not because Locke wished deliberately to 'do down' the poor or to disguise the class structure of his society. In this he merely reflected the common and widespread assumption that 'free born Englishmen' with rights of representation *were* inevitably *propertied men*. And yet, by way of this unstated presupposition, the whole class and gender structure of market society, the new relationships of property and capital, the emerging social order of bourgeois society and the structure of sexual divisions were *premised* at the heart of his doctrine as the silent but salient, absent/present assumption on which its logic was founded. In theorizing about it, he transferred these assumptions 'into a supposed state of nature' and generalized 'some attributes of seventeenth century society and man as attributes . . . of *man as such*' (Macpherson, 1962, our italics).

In fact, then, the link between ideology and class is forged, not because the former directly 'expresses' the latter, but by way of a more complex process in which a specific disposition of class power is unconsciously transferred or displaced into the unstated premise of an argument, which then structures the whole of the logic apparently beyond the conscious awareness of the so-called 'author' of the philosophy. Marx first drew attention to this mechanism in ideology in the *German Ideology* when he commented on the tendency of ideology to *universalize* the particular–giving what are in fact concrete, particular interests the form of a general and universal argument. Marx observed that 'increasingly abstract ideas hold sway, i.e. ideas which increasingly take on the form of universality'. He elaborated on the political *effect* this had on winning ascendancy for those ideas and winning support among *different* classes for those ideas. 'For each new class which puts itself in the place of one ruling before it is compelled, merely in order to carry through its aim, to represent its interests as the common interest of all the members of society, that is, expressed in ideal form: it has to give its ideas the form of universality and represent them as the only rational, universally valid one'. Marx also commented on the *naturalizing* or *eternalizing* effect of ideology: grounding what is historically specific in the apparently timeless and eternally changeless terrain of Nature. The problem is that these mechanisms or effects have usually been interpreted as deliberate and self-conscious conspiracy rather than as a result of the constitutive function of ideology. They are the mechanisms by which ideologies *construct* the world in definite ways, through certain distinct categories, which is the great positive role of an organic mode of thought.

5 Liberalism and the bourgeois revolution

Between the writing of Locke's *Two Treatises* in the 1680s and 1776, when Adam Smith published his *Wealth of Nations*, the whole system of economic and property relations, which were only opening premises in some of Locke's formulations, had become the dominant mode of economic organization through English society. The social classes which rose to social and political ascendancy with this transformation of traditional England into an agrarian and commercial capitalist society were those whose rise in social position depended on the clearing away of barriers to their advance–an idea articulated largely within liberal discourse. This is also the process by which what had begun as a 'revolutionary' doctrine, ultimately justifying turning the whole world 'upside down' (Hill, 1975) and cutting off the head of a king, was progressively assimilated into the legitimating ideology of a new social order. This recuperation of liberalism is also often explained in terms of the 'class-belonging' thesis about ideology–liberalism as the ideology of the bourgeois revolution. How well does that proposition stand up to inspection?

The landed Whigs had begun to deal in property as a commodity to be accumulated and worked on, entering trade and commerce and establishing from their estates, country seats and town residences a whole nexus of social connections, patronage and influence. They made sense of these new conditions of their existence within the categories of what can only be called 'common sense Lockeanism'. They regarded it as part of the natural order that their class should now become the leading class in society. They not only lived 'by the constitution';

they now projected it backwards into eternal time, asserting that the liberties of 'free born Englishmen' and their political institutions had *always* existed, were sanctified by ancient custom going back at least to Anglo Saxon times. It was the theory of divine right which was the real modern interloper. In this way they gave themselves roots in English history – in ways which later provided the basis for a close link between English liberalism and English nationalism. They sanctified their 'revolution' by *traditionalizing* it – another ideological mechanism. Of course, they believed with Locke that the only legitimate governments were based on the consent of 'free men' and that they were the class the state must now represent. Once the initial consent to government had been given, they actually expected people to submit to the authority of the state; and as the legal system came more and more to reflect their concept of property rights, they expected, and increasingly themselves enforced, widespread obedience to the new property regime and the market through the law (Thompson 1975). Liberalism thus came progressively to justify a new structure of power and interest, a new type of class society. Though Locke's viewpoint on this question is ambiguous he did not dissent from the idea of a legislature 'dominated by men of property or elected on a propertied franchise' (Dickinson, 1977).

If Locke first gave a formed and considered articulation to this social and political system, it was Adam Smith, a century later, and the political economists of the Scottish Enlightenment, who first 'codified' it as a functioning and dynamic economic system. From its inception, liberalism had assumed an intimate connection beween liberty, property and the market. Whatever variant of liberal thought we examine, we find it underpinned by new conceptions of profit, contract, risk and accumulation. Liberal 'man' was a rational, calculating, accumulating man – man conceived as naturally 'at home' only within the new bourgeois relations of agrarian and commercial capitalism. 'Now . . . man in general is . . . conceived in the image of bourgeois rational man' (Macpherson, 1962). It was Adam Smith who *explained* (rather than simply assuming) what the liberal economic revolution actually meant and how the new system actually worked. In this sense, *The Wealth of Nations* was 'ideological', because it took for granted the operations of a particular economic system as the eternal laws of the economy and premised its argument on that assumption. But, as Marx insisted, it was also 'scientific' because it deployed rich, carefully and consciously constructed categories, concepts and 'laws of relation', and produced a genuine, if not complete, knowledge of market society.

The 'bourgeois' character of Adam Smith's thought was evident in the fact that he first 'grasped the inherent dynamism of an economy organized around market exchange' (Gamble, 1981). He first observed how central to this dynamism was freeing the market and allowing the rapid advance of the social division of labour – the increasing specialization and coordination of economic functions. He first understood how much the nation's wealth depended on harnessing the productivity of labour. He gave the political concept of the social contract its corresponding position in economic life. He understood economic behaviour in competitive societies as rooted in men's natural egoism and governed by the national calculation of advantage. To the pessimistic Hobbesean image of competitive society only restrained from perpetual 'civil war' by a Leviathan state, Adam Smith brought the 'good news' that myriad individual wills and needs could be magically harmonized and regulated through the impersonal mechanisms, the 'hidden hand', of the market, yielding the *general* interest of society as a miraculous automatic result. Political economy finally broke the connection of liberalism with state-regulated or mercantilist conceptions of the economy, and applied the concept of liberty unremittingly to economic life. Left to itself, things would flow and exchange naturally and, like water, find their proper level. Required to consult only their own self-interest, rational calculating men would inadvertently maximize the wealth of the whole society. There were certain essential but limited tasks for governments to perform – among which he controversially included public education. Otherwise the sphere of economic liberty must be kept as open as possible. The burden of regulation must be lifted from the property owner, since the more single-mindedly he pursued profit, the greater the benefit he conferred on society. Essentially, Adam Smith believed that need itself and the spectacle of prosperity would provide the negative and positive spurs to everyone, including the propertyless poor, to engage in the competitive struggle. It was this systematic reorientation of economic thought around the conceptions of economic liberty and the identification of liberty with *laissez-faire* which enabled political economy to complete the edifice of classical liberalism.

The political revolution associated with the English Revolution and Locke and the economic revolution associated with market capitalism and Adam Smith transformed Britain, first of all the European nations, into a *bourgeois society* – a society in which 'bourgeois' social and economic relations became dominant and the classes linked with bourgeois types of development gradually became the leading social classes in society. Elsewhere this sort of development was delayed – in France until the 1790s, in Russia until the twentieth century. Nevertheless, in one society after another in Europe and North America, from the end of the eighteenth century, the ground was cleared of traditional social forms and ideas – the *ancien régime* – leaving the way free for this new type of bourgeois development. Its progress can be symbolized in the *three* revolutions. The industrial revolution transposed Adam Smith's new laws of political economy into the even more dynamic productive framework of industrial capitalism and set liberal ideas to work within the new industrial class structure. The American Revolution was modelled directly on Lockean principles. The American Declaration of Independence translated the theory of natural rights directly into a political programme which eventually opened the enormous potential wealth of the USA to capitalist development: 'We hold these truths to be self-evident, that all men are created equal, that they are endowed by their Creator with inalienable rights . . . that to secure these rights, Governments are instituted among men, deriving their just powers from the consent of the governed . . . '. The French Revolution not only marked the transition in France from the *ancien régime* to modern bourgeois society but set in motion, through the Napoleonic campaigns, a wave of constitutional, legal and administrative reforms throughout Europe and, in the *Rights of Man,* gave practical political articulation to one of the most radical versions of the liberal programme, condensed into the cry of 'Liberty, Equality and Fraternity'.

In what sense, then, was liberalism the ideology of the bourgeois revolution or, to put it more simply, a 'bourgeois' political ideology? This could mean that it was an ideology which arose from, or won its support from the new bourgeois classes, and reflected the objective interests which the bourgeois have, given their position in the class structure. A less 'economistic' or reductionist reading would require us to show how the ideas of liberalism helped to secure the long-term global position of the bourgeoisie and had as its main effect the organizing of the whole society around essentially bourgeois social relations and conceptions.

The former reading represents an interpretation of the 'class belongingness' of ideology, which is open to the danger of class reductionism. The latter adopts a more sophisticated and expanded notion of the class/ideology relationship, and is closer to Gramsci's conception of the part which ideology plays in securing hegemony in a social formation.

However, we have already noted the *fracturing* of liberalism into its conservative and radical tendencies and this affects how we understand liberalism's 'class belongingness'. As the new social order stabilized itself, what Eccleshall (1984) has called a sort of 'establishment liberalism' came to be identified with the Whig propertied classes, and was assimilated into the defence of the new dispositions of property, power and patronage. The alternative radical tendency, however, also vigorously survived. In the eighteenth century poor men and women, using the 'free born right' argument, laid claim to equality before the law. Feminists like Mary Wollstonecraft made use of the 'natural rights' argument to support their cause (see Juliet Mitchell in this volume). The argument around 'rights' was to surface in a more organized and sustained form in the 1790s and later, in sympathy with the French Revolution and Jacobinism, in the movements for parliamentary reform, in Chartist and Owenite politics, and generally as a central strand in nineteenth century artisan radicalism and the working class movement. Representation became a radical issue in the struggle for female suffrage. At the same time the more conservative tendency – 'establishment' liberalism – formed the basis of English middle class individualism, respectability, 'patriarchalism' and social paternalism; it fuelled the political moralism, the gospel of self-help, thrift, independence, philanthropy, enterprise, the commitment to free trade, retrenchment and evolutionary reform, which a popular political nineteenth century figure like Gladstone helped to canonize in the liberalism which dominated the Victorian period. Not only do the two strands persist: they persist in being articulated to cover the interests and political objectives of different class fractions or social strata. Thus we find, as liberalism becomes more organic and practical to lived social relations, its different elements were integrated into different political positions; and different social classes were articulated to these positions. From this point onwards, a progressive version of some liberal arguments appears as an important strand in radicalism, while the more establishment version becomes increasingly a strand within latter-day conservatism – to such a degree that 'it is not always easy to discern the dividing line between the two ideologies' (Eccleshall). This fracturing throws into question any *simple* view of liberalism as exclusively 'bourgeois' ideology.

Nowhere is this point more vividly evident than in the English reactions to the political revolutions of the eighteenth century. Tom Paine's *Rights of Man* (1791) acclaimed the French Revolution, his *Common Sense* (1776) called for an independent American republic: prophetic titles, both. Paine was a thorough-going radical, a champion of popular democracy, representative government, the abolition of slavery, the rights of women, free speech, freedom of opinion and religious toleration. His books became a sort of 'secular bible' in radical artisan and working class circles; 'foundation texts of the English working class movement' (Thompson, 1968). *The Rights of Man* was prosecuted as a seditious document.

Yet, what gave Paine his political cutting edge was a profound belief in the natural rights of *every* individual, however humble, to manage his or her affairs in every domain of life. His was a *radical* individualism. Moreover, Paine believed that the free market economy and the 'unceasing circulation of interest' were central to it. The guarantee of a person's independence, for Paine, was the ownership of property; though his *social image* of democracy was premised, not on the great estates of the Whig grandees, but on the independent small farmer or small property-owner. Paine, however, contested the traditional image of society as a human body. Instead, he said, it was 'like a body contained in a circle, having a common centre in which every radius meets; and that centre is formed by representation' (Eccleshall). The relationship between elements in Paine's thought is thus exceedingly complex. This enables us to understand how in the 1960s *both* the defence of American corporate capitalism and the radical critique of it were oriented in a liberal individualist philosophy – students and civil rights campaigners justifying their 'right to rebel' from the first article of the American Constitution.

This paradox is even more clearly brought out by contrasting Paine with his arch enemy, Edmund Burke, rightly seen today as one of the most profound of English conservative thinkers. Burke was driven into a deep conservative recoil by the French Revolution. He was one of the first political figures to articulate what we would now call an organic conservatism. Burke idealized custom and tradition, seeing in them the repository of true social authority. He urged the people to trust those hallowed institutions which had stood the test of time, to work from their *instincts* for order and authority, not from Reason. For him, 'Prescription and property (defined) the effective contours of the state' (Laski, 1936). He accepted a hierarchical society, and the duty of those placed lower to take guidance from those superior to them. The relations beween the different orders, he argued, *should* be like the parts of a body: necessarily subordinated to one another. This embedding of the established institutions of English society in a traditional conception of order fitted in with many aspects of the English ideological temperament and made Burke one of the great voices of English conservative common sense. His ideas have 'entered into the thoughts of Englishmen to a degree difficult to overestimate' (Laski, 1936).

Yet, the English Constitution which Burke revered was, of course, nothing more nor less than the very skilful constitutional compromise of 'checks and balances' at which the Glorious Settlement had arrived, which Locke looked forward to and which the Whigs, with profound relief, settled for. He was, in short, like Paine, a direct inheritor of Locke. Moreover, his traditionalism was also combined with a thorough-going commitment to *laissez-faire* economics. He regarded the laws of political economy as synonymous with the laws of nature and of God. It was wrong, he believed, for the state to intervene between a master and his servant, or to provide support for the poor. Wages must be strictly governed by the needs of subsistence. Labour 'is a commodity like every other and should rise or fall according to demand'. It must pay a due return to those who hire it. The poor must console themselves with 'patience, labour, sobriety, frugality and religion'. Burke's *conservatism*, in short, was paradoxically combined with a profound commitment to the doctrines of economic *liberalism*–a combination which has reappeared inside more recent forms of conservatism.

It is clear, then, that the elements of liberal ideology did *not* have any absolutely fixed class identity or connotation. They could be combined in different ways to constitute radically opposed ideological positions. The radical and subversive strand, represented by Paine's emphases, flowed into working class radicalism and later became a key element in the formation of English socialism. The traditionalist and *laissez-faire* emphases of Burke's ideas were absorbed into English conservatism. *Both* were premised on the liberal principles of political economy.

In the light of this, it is necessary to reconsider in what sense liberalism became the political ideology of bourgeois society. What we *cannot* mean by this is that it expressed exclusively the interests of a unified ruling class and justified the subordination of the lower orders. The 'ruling classes' were not unified by any single ideology. They took up and reworked different strands within liberalism–sometimes threading it with elements from other ideological traditions. Moreover, liberalism had no unitary structure of ideas. It was and remained fractured. The same basic set of concepts could, in combination with other elements, be used to generate *different* philosophical positions. Nevertheless, the result of the long historical transformations we have been describing *was* to 'make the economic, social and political position of the bourgeoisie predominant' in the English social formation. 'Wealth was enthroned, privilege cast down and a new, mobile, restless, aggressive, competitive and individualistic economic system began to emerge' (Gamble 1981). This transformation involved 'a comprehensive conflict and redefinition at every level as organic and magical views of society gave way before natural law and as the acquisitive ethic encroached upon an authoritarian moral economy' (Thompson, 1965). This acquisition of the leading or hegemonic position in society by bourgeois social, political and economic relations could not have been achieved without the moral and intellectual ascendency which liberal ideas gradually acquired within English political culture. To recognize this global outcome is to begin to conceive of the complex arch of bourgeois culture. Liberalism ·was undoubtedly one of its principal cornerstones.

6 The triumph and limits of liberalism

The nineteenth century marked the era of liberalism's triumph. From Waterloo until the outbreak of the First World War no other doctrine spoke with the same authority or exercised the same widespread influence. The great achievements of this period were all closely associated with liberal ideas. It served as the prophet of industrialism. It helped to transform Great Britain into the workshop of the world. It was the exponent of free trade which created the world market. It espoused the gospel of progress. It nourished and gave particular form to the currents of social reform. It was *laissez-faire* which cleared the last barriers to world trade and remodelled the Poor Law. It was liberalism which justified the extension of political power to the new entrepreneurial classes.

At the same time, as many have pointed out, liberalism was confronted by rival ideologies which began to challenge its hegemony. On the one side, a conservatism which set definite limits to the free play of the values of individual liberty with the contrary ideas of authority. On the other side, the critique of the liberal conception of equality and its identification with the propertied classes which, as the industrial working classes emerged as a historical force, deepened into the alternative positions of socialism. Industrial capitalism in itself represented a quite novel set of conditions and forces, and thus a challenge to classic liberalism which had been developed in quite different circumstances. How did liberalism survive these changed conditions? How did it remodel and refashion itself so as to be able to address and frame these new realities? What tensions or contradictions did this process of revision engender? The two key issues through which this question is focused are the questions of democracy and of equality.

The extension of the franchise and parliamentary reform were high on the agenda of two of the foremost liberal thinkers of the period, Jeremy Bentham and John Stuart Mill. Bentham is also noteworthy in a different context because, with him, one of the cornerstones of classical liberalism was finally swept away (the justification based on 'natural rights') and replaced by a new moral calculus which has underpinned the liberal argument ever since. This is *utilitarianism*, the idea that the moral criterion for measuring the social good lies in the rationalistic calculation of what provides 'the greatest happiness of the greatest number' of individuals. In Bentham's case, however, though the moral rationale for liberalism changed, the underlying premises did not. Bentham vigorously affirmed the pursuit of individual self-interest and the maximization of pleasure as the essential drives of human action. In his hatred of history and tradition he wished to 'rationalize' or modernize everything he could lay his hands on or set his mind to. In his calculative way, he was determined to find a way of *measuring* quantitatively which institutions were most urgently in need of reform in terms of their strict utility.

Bentham is therefore only one of the many figures in the period who helped to harness liberalism to the cause of steady and continuous legislative reform. For though Bentham believed that as much as possible of the state's functions should be 'privatized' and was firmly committed to the principle of *laissez-faire*, he also believed in the active intervention of legislation to clear away the old encumbrances to liberty and the need for efficient administration to instal by intervention from above, if necessary, the conditions of free and unrestrained action. Thus paradoxically, some of Bentham's followers – the philosophic radicals – were among the first organic state intellectuals in early nineteenth century society who, in the name of extending *laissez-faire* principles, were inadvertently instrumental in helping the state to play an increasingly interventionist role.

On the question of equality Bentham was just as contradictory. In his rationalistic way he himself made the formal case for equality. But, as had happened so many times in liberalism before, his concrete conception of how society actually functioned took for granted the existing distribution of wealth, the unequal consequences of market competition, the security of all property rights, the stimulus of starvation as the incentive for the propertyless to labour, the inevitability of 'near indigence' for the mass of the people. The commitment to political economy in Bentham clearly undermined his more egalitarian impulses.

On the question of democracy, Bentham was pushed by his own logic progressively towards reluctant support for the principle of universal suffrage. But like most liberals faced with the growing popular agitation for parliamentary reform, he was caught between his desires to erode the position of what he considered to be the idle and useless aristocracy and his fear of enfranchising an entirely new popular class. So, again, we find the ambiguities in liberal practice. Bentham was always willing to settle for a more limited franchise – sometimes proposing to exclude the poor and uneducated, sometimes those who were not householders or not taxpayers. Similarly, though *formally* he accepted the logic of female suffrage, *in practice* he recognized that public opinion would be against it.

John Stuart Mill, even more clearly, exemplified liberalism under the pressure of industrial class society, partly because he possessed what Bentham so conspicuously lacked – critical self-consciousness. Moreover, Mill confronted liberalism's need to renovate itself at a critical turning point – when the *social* question posed by the shattering impact of unregulated industrial capitalism and the rise of the working classes could no longer be either ignored or contained within an unreconstructed liberalism. The consequences of industrial capitalism and the pressures for democratization had profoundly unsettling effects on liberalism's certainties. Mill is important, not because he successfully resolved these issues, but because he exposed liberalism to searching self-questioning and self-doubt. It is Mill who first tried to negotiate liberalism through the working class challenge and who defined liberal democracy with all its compromises, hesitations and paradoxes.

At the risk of grossly oversimplifying Mill's thought, we can capture this image of liberalism at the turning point by considering how extensive his hesitations were at every critical juncture. He gradually came to acknowledge the one-dimensional character of Bentham's model of rational utilitarian man in which Mill had been at first rigorously educated. In its place he substituted a model of man and of human nature on which contemporary liberalism rests and which has passed into

English common sense. This is what Macpherson (1977) calls the *developmental model* – people as capable of infinitely developing their individual powers and capacities, in a society whose purpose must be to facilitate this life-long educative process. It is easy to see the affinity between a developmental model of human nature and the commitment to gradual evolutionary reform with which Mill in his lifetime, and liberalism ever since, has been identified. Mill's commitment to democracy was, then, linked with this developmental model. The test of democracy was what it could contribute to this process of self-realization and human development. Similarly, Mill pondered long and hard on whether the existing structure of class inequalities was reconcilable with the free development of individual choices and capacities. He came close to acknowledging the lack of 'fit' between political democracy and economic inequality and by the end of his life, his recognition that inequalities of wealth and power prevented the full development of most people in the working class had pushed him to the very frontiers of a theory of socialist redistribution. Yet in the last resort, he thought the incompatibility of democracy and inequality 'accidental and remediable': not an *inevitable* feature of the free-market capitalist system. As David Held has observed, Mill was 'fully committed to the moral development of all individuals but ... simultaneously justified substantial inequalities of power and reward' (Held, 1984).

Mill wrote the classic modern liberal statements, *On Liberty* (1859) and *Representative Government* (1869), and played an active part in the agitation for the extension of the franchise. He wrote a powerful and eloquent defence of the case for female suffrage – *The Subjection of Women*. Yet he worried most about the danger of despotic government, the overgrown state, the tyranny of the ignorant majority and the rule of mediocrity. The aim of government remained, for him, the protection of individual rights and civil liberties. Representative government and the freedom of speech and opinion were the best safeguards against excessive state intervention. But the degree of democracy must be limited. Mill therefore put the positive case for the educated classes to have two votes. He was a hesitant democrat as he had been a reluctant egalitarian.

Mill was haunted throughout by a sense of personal doubt. However, it would be wrong to see this intellectual unease as *personal* to Mill. He felt the weakness in the ruthlessly rationalist logic of Bentham without being quite able to abandon rationalism. He recognized Chartism as 'the revolt of nearly all the active talent, and a greater part of the physical force of the working classes against their whole relation to society', but he could not himself entertain such a root-and-branch, systemic response to industrial capitalism. He supported democracy. But his immediate concerns were for the rights of the minorities once the majorities were enfranchised. He opposed in a sound liberal manner all forms of state intervention; and yet his desire to see an educated democracy pushed him irrevocably towards secular state-sponsored education. Again and again he came up against the limits of liberal individualism when set to work in a fully developed class society. How could the free development of the individual be squared with the actual inequalities of the system? Could political democracy be insulated against the system of economic wealth and power in which it was embedded? Could the social question be resolved in individualist terms? These are some of the contradictions at the heart of liberal democracy itself which arise from the attempt to reconcile individual liberty and political democracy with class society.

Faced with these dilemmas, intrinsic to the very logic of thought he was deploying, Mill settled – as liberal democracy itself did – for a series of compromises and postponements. Liberal democracy has tried to temper democracy with meritocracy; leaven equality in one sphere with inequality in others; emancipate majorities *and* protect minorities; look with hope to personal self-development and the education of sensibility, while in its actual arrangements proposing to weight the talents of different classes differently; maintaining individualism at its centre while hoping to secure a more positive conception of the common good; maintaining intact an economic system based on competition and acquisitiveness while hoping somehow to constitute the conditions for the self-fulfilment and educative development of all. Mill's was a heroic defence of liberalism at a historical turning point. However, he also represented the moment when liberalism acquired one of its most enduring, least endearing, characteristics: the tendency to try to reconcile the irreconcilable, to have its cake and eat it too. As Eccleshall (1984) comments,

> Liberals . . . naturally gravitate towards the middle ground in politics from where they seek to mediate between the competing claims of capital and labour . . . (They) proclaim the merits of private enterprise yet renounce class privilege . . . seek to extend material security and cultural opportunities to the poor but refuse to identify themselves fully with any particular section of society.

It is in Mill that we can perhaps most clearly recognize this deeply ambiguous basis of liberal democracy.

Nowhere are the strengths and limits of the liberalism Mill advanced more clearly exemplified than in the example of feminism and female suffrage. When Mill was elected MP in 1867 female suffrage was a key point in his platform. His commitment to individual liberty and representative democracy pushed Mill into recognizing women's exclusion from equal rights and the consequences for women of their subordination to men. Indeed Mill understood the argument that, since in law, men 'covered' for their wives, this excluded them from being property holders so that a franchise qualification based on property would have excluded them. In *The Subjection of Women* Mill offered a passionate statement of the way women's subordination to men in marriage had created the most pervasive form of female subservience, which he understood as in no way 'natural' but 'an entirely artificial thing'. The text demonstrated the radical conclusion which can be reached by taking liberal principles seriously and applying them consistently. At the same time, because he could only conceptualize the feminist cause in terms of individual liberty and legal equality, not equality of both sexes as a social condition of freedom for all, he was led to advance what Juliet Mitchell (in this volume) rightly calls an 'abstract' rather than a social conception of emancipation. He could not conceive that women might genuinely choose a social role other than that of wife and mother, or that society itself had helped to construct this self-definition. 'It is not that all persons are equally qualified for everything' he argued, 'but that freedom of individual choice is known to be the only theory which procures the adoption of the best processes and throws each operation into the hands of those who are best qualified for it'. Mill's liberalism thus enabled him to adopt an advanced position on women's rights. But it also led him to *construct* the problem of women's subordination and its remedy in limited ways. This suggests how important are the ways in which political and social questions are ideologically constructed by different frameworks of thought.

By the closing decades of the great era of liberalism and reform, the conditions of existence of its ideas had altered so profoundly that liberalism could not survive as a coherent ideological discourse without massive reworking. In the face of the growing pressure on society from the industrial working classes and their organization, classic liberal individualism no longer sufficed to explain the great collective formations of English society or the persistent division of society into the classes of capital and labour, or the basic tendencies of industrial capitalism to create inequality. As the social and environmental problems arising in the wake of unbridled competitive industrial capitalism manifested themselves, it was clear that the 'hidden hand' of the market was no longer adequate to the task of defining and defending the general interest of society as a whole. As Britain's commercial hegemony came to be challenged by her industrializing rivals and British industry ceased to be able to transform itself to take advantage of the new methods and scale of capitalist production, so the liberal Victorian orthodoxies of *laissez-faire* collapsed. The night-watchman conception of the state which had provided the dominant frame for *all* governments, Liberal or Conservative, in the high Victorian period, was shown, against the experience in Germany and Japan, to be woefully inadequate to the task of raising the whole level of society to the new tasks of survival in the era of advanced capitalism and imperialist world rivalry. The trail of widespread poverty, destitution and unemployment which unregulated entrepreneurial capitalism had created in its wake now came back to haunt and threaten society. The pressure 'outside the gates' from the organized industrial classes and the residual poor alike for measures of sweeping reform, redistribution, state intervention and a shift of power became too much for the fragile compromises of liberalism to withstand. In the next section we will consider whether ideologies can profoundly refashion themselves and still retain their ideological coherence.

7   Liberalism in crisis and transition

Dangerfield (1935) has called the period from 1880 onwards, through the upheavals of the First World War into the post-war period, the 'Strange Death of Liberal England'. Not only because it witnessed the decline and virtual disappearance of the Liberal Party which had dominated political life in the decades of the mid-nineteenth century, but also because these years witnessed the disintegration of the imperatives and premises of a coherent liberalism. What had come to be taken for granted – respectability *and* reform; high mindedness *and* entrepreneurial energy; liberty *and* property stitched *together*; all in the great Victorian liberal synthesis, when liberal ideas became truly hegemonic and set the limits of thought and action for all the parties and classes which occupied the leading positions in society – were thrown into radical doubt and confusion.

Liberalism as a political discourse has never, since that period, been hegemonic. Liberal ideas, however, have remained as an essential component in the bedrock common-sense wisdom of English political culture. They have provided a basic political *repertoire* on which all the emergent political ideologies of the twentieth century have drawn. Liberalism disintegrated as a coherent tradition, but it survives as one of the first historic formations in English practical consciousness. It survived, principally by radically revising itself in the light of the new circumstances, or by emigrating under the cover or shadow of new discourses, with which it contracted intimate relations. This, in truncated form, is the story of how the 'Strange Death of Liberal England' yielded the 'new liberalism' as a constituent part of social democracy and 'neo-liberalism' as a major variant of conservatism.

This takes us back to questions concerning how ideologies develop and the social and material determinations of this process. If we reject the idea that whole ideologies are exclusively attached to or arise from whole, unified classes, then we cannot conceptualize ideological struggle as taking place between two self-supporting 'class ideologies', opposing one another. Therefore we cannot think of ideological change as consisting of the total replacement of one system of thought belonging to one class by another. We are pushed towards the Laclau position (spelled out elsewhere in this volume) that different ideological formations intersect in the same social space; and that different class fractions and other social forces can be articulated, under different historical circumstances, to different ideological positions, or mobilized beneath different ideological conceptions. The linkage between ideas and social forces depends more on the balance of forces in any specific conjuncture and how effectively the ideological struggle is waged. It is not finally determined by, say, the 'mode of production' or any such abstraction. Gramsci reminds us that the emergence of new forms of common sense in periods of social upheaval 'is not a question of introducing from scratch a scientific form of thought into everyone's life but of providing and making "critical" an already existing activity'. Ideologies are transformed by:

> a process of differentiation and change in the relative weight that the elements of the old ideologies used to possess. What was previously secondary and subordinate, or even incidental, is now taken to be primary – becomes the nucleus of a new ideological and theoretical complex. The old collective will dissolves into its contradictory elements since the subordinate ones develop socially, etc.
> (Gramsci, 1971)

This is exactly what happened to liberalism in the twentieth century.

The transformation of the 'old liberalism' into the 'new' was therefore partly the result of internal inconsistencies in the arguments which we have cited. Even more, it resulted from the fact that there was an increasing divergence between liberalism and the conditions in society to which it had classically referred and on which its existence depended. The open, competitive 'market capitalism' which made England the workshop of the world was giving way to the large combinations of industrial capital, operating in more corporate and quasi-monopolistic markets, in the context of the parcelling up of the world market into protected imperial spheres of influence. This more complex form of capitalist society depended increasingly on the whole institutional apparatus of social reproduction to keep it going – on a more educated workforce, and hence on state-provided systems of education (see James Donald's article in *Subjectivity and Social Relations*); on a healthy population, and hence on the whole state – supported structure of family and community welfare; on the network of infrastructural support for which only national and local governments could take the ultimate responsibility. All these tendencies eroded the *laissez-faire*/minimal state premises on which classic liberalism had been founded, and opened the floodgates to more 'collectivist' or interventionist state tendencies. Dicey, the liberal constitutionalist, saw the choices in the closing decades of the century clearly and starkly counter-posed 'liberal' tendencies against the threats to them from the 'collectivist' spirit – whether the collectivism of the 'right' (in such movements as National Efficiency and Social Imperialism) or the collectivism of the 'left' (in the form of more egalitarian socialist demands for state intervention to secure minimum conditions of life for the newly enfranchised majority and to bring about significant shifts in the distribution of wealth and power).

Liberalism was therefore increasingly pinned between these alternatives; and though no single coherent alternative emerged, liberalism was in effect massively and extensively reconstructed by a series of *ad hoc* 'revisions' spanning five decades. The political philosopher, T.H. Green, building on the breaches which Mill had already made in the edifice of classic liberal principle, went further in the direction of liberal collectivisim by arguing that it was a (new) duty of the state itself to *create* those conditions in which self-fulfilment of individuals could occur. Each person must have the *opportunity* for self-culture. In this lay the seed of an important revision, which extended the classic commitment to formal equality of the rights of all citizens into the broader idea of equality of opportunity. This was an important half-way stopping point on the way to a full social conception of equality as a condition, which liberals continued to regard as too root-and-branch (i.e. socialist) a conception for their tastes. Under this new argument, the state assumed extensive new duties and responsibilities. Another new liberal, Hobhouse, integrated into liberalism a version of sociology heavily influenced by biological thinking, which provided the basis for a more social, less competitive, conception of progress. His approach suggested a progress on the part of society towards higher stages of ethical value as it moved progressively from the competitive to a more cooperative ethic. This 'ethicalizing' of liberal doctrine and the erosion of its former dependence on competition as a core value was also significant. Hobson, another 'new liberal', went even further in his criticism of the accumulations of private wealth and its consequences for the poor. He argued for serious and extensive redistribution of wealth through progressive taxation in order to create minimally secure standards of life for the poorer classes of society. He made a searching critique of the inadequacy of 'market forces' to accomplish these conditions for the majority. This too became a common theme amongst all 'new liberals'. Both Hobhouse and Hobson virtually looked forward to a form of 'liberal socialism' (Hobhouse, 1911). They paved the way for the conversion of new liberals to the idea of a welfare state and the inevitable expansion of state intervention which this implies. In other fields, economists like Alfred Marshall began to transform economic theory from its basis in political economy to a new 'science' of human welfare; and Keynes pioneered new forms of state intervention which stopped short of socialist appropriation, but gave the state an enormously enhanced role in creating the economic conditions for welfare capitalism, which had the effect of 'salvaging the capitalist system in the most humane way' (Middlemas, 1979).

In these and other ways, liberalism gradually shed its militant *laissez-faire*, individualist and competitive skin and assumed a substantially new guise, more adapted to survival in the changed conditions of twentieth century corporate capitalism and mass democracy.

And yet this extensive renovation of the edifice of liberalism did not leave it entirely open to any wind of change or movement in any direction, rudderless or without a distinctive centre. Liberalism did not survive intact by holding fast to every concept and shibboleth of the past, for that would have guaranteed its irrelevance to the modern world. But new liberal ideas were generated, so to speak, *within* the limit or circumference of the liberal circle of thought.

Thus, liberalism embraced the need for social reform: not on the grounds of material need but by developing a deeper *ethical* basis. Reform became a moral imperative in politics. This provided liberalism with an alternative to the socialist emphasis of finding the roots of change in social interest and power. Liberalism distanced itself from individualism and *laissez-faire* - indeed, some modern critics would argue that *laissez-faire* was never as intrinsic to liberalism as has usually been thought. However, in its nineteenth century hey-day, there seemed to be a perfect 'fit' between the commitment to radical individualism and the passionate belief in *laissez-faire*. Now liberalism was refashioned so as to include much greater state intervention, especially in the fields of welfare and redistributive justice. But individual liberty remained an essential element in the liberal canon. Liberalism made considerable moves in the direction of welfare and the reform of the market mechanisms of the economy - 'capitalism with a human face', so to speak. Liberals, however, continued on the whole to value most local and voluntary efforts as checks against too much state intervention, and to be deeply suspicious of 'state socialist' solutions. Hobhouse, for example, addressed the question as to whether welfare would 'dry up the sources of energy and undermine the independence of the individual' and the will to work (Hobhouse, 1911). Though liberals now embraced a positive conception of the 'common good', this was deliberately articulated *against* notions of class (which, to liberals, remained too limited a vested interest) and oriented instead towards the much looser and vaguer idea of *community*, as the organizing concept. (Community can sometimes refer to real concrete historical formations – like 'mining communities'. But it can also acquire a vague reference to 'everybody with a common feeling of belonging', in ways which totally blur the real distinctions of wealth, power and position.) Liberalism acknowledged the wider influence of social factors; but social arguments were ultimately justified in terms of the fulfilment of individual potentialities.

In short, though in one sense liberalism in its new forms moved closer to socialism, especially of the more reformist variety, it was also at pains to articulate its difference from socialist and marxist types of theory. Its 'borrowings' from social reformist thinking helped to 'invest traditional liberal concepts with new meaning' (Freeden, 1978; Collini, 1979). 'We must take from Socialism what is good and reject what is bad or doubtful', one liberal apologist said. Instead of collapsing the difference between the two, the transformation of the old liberalism into the 'new liberalism' produced a novel hybrid ideological formation: neither 'pure' liberalism nor radical socialism but what we would recognize today as 'social democracy'. The paradox is that social democracy not only overlapped, in reality, into the territory of political thinking of the newly formed Labour Party but deeply influenced the whole reformist political philosophy and strategy of 'labourism'. Many of the early trade unions were formed within the traditions of radical or working-class liberalism, and adhered to 'lib-lab' politics up to and after the formation of the Labour Party. The effects of this long-standing connection are still to be seen in the utilitarianism of much labour and trade union thinking and in such factors as long-standing trade union commitment to 'free collective bargaining'. In effect, then, the transformation of liberalism helped to redraw fundamentally the disposition of the different major political ideologies across the spectrum in Britain. In this way liberalism, as a distinctive formation survived mainly by being partially absorbed or by 'taking cover'.

This indicates a shift in liberalism towards its more reformist side. But that is only to take one aspect of its remarkable fluidity. At the same time, many of the more individualist, competitive, free-market, political economy, *laissez-faire*, anti-statist elements of the liberal tradition, which were not absorbed into the 'new liberalism', social democracy or labourism, emigrated in the opposite direction. They became gradually absorbed as a sort of 'neo-liberal' sub-stratum within conservative ideas, bringing a passionate commitment to private capital, the laws of the market and free competition into a supporting role alongside the more organic conservative ideas of tradition, authority, patriotism, hierarchy and order. Thus the 'split' between the radical and conservative tendencies in liberalism reached its culmination in the twentieth century with the former moving in a more social reformist direction, and the latter drifting into the orbit of neo-liberal conservatism.

The apogee of this latter trend is to be found in the emergence of the 'radical right' in the Conservative Party in 1975 under Mrs Thatcher's leadership and in the country as a whole after the 1979 election. For 'Thatcherism' brilliantly *combines* within a single political ideology an organic conservative emphasis on the values of tradition, family, monarchy, patriarchy and nation with a 'neo-liberal' emphasis on the gospel of the free-market, the laws of supply and demand, the private economy, value for money and the private sphere of the citizen against the 'creeping socialist' threats to liberty from an overweening state and an overextended state welfare system. The first, 'organic' half of this ideological formation draws directly on the ancient repertoire of conservatism; the second neo-liberal half derives, directly, from the free market and libertarian traditions of classic liberalism and political economy. So the survival of one half of the liberal programme within social democracy, so to speak, is matched, today, by the resurgence of the neo-liberal side of the original liberal programme – only now under heavy conservative disguise!

Our conclusion to this compressed historical survey of the crises and transitions of modern liberalism takes us back, finally, to the basic propositions of the materalist theory of ideology which has provided our account with its theoretical scaffold. I think we can now see more clearly where the theses of the *German Ideology*, applied literally, are inadequate. It does not seem possible to 'read off' liberalism's ideological presuppositons directly from its material conditions of existence. We cannot, without doing excessive violence to its complex history, *reduce* liberalism to the ideology of a single class whose interests as a unified bloc it wholly and exclusively 'represents'. Liberalism did not belong exclusively to one set of class interests; nor did it mobilize classes into a single set of political positions. In its many forms, liberalism did contain distinct and recurring ideological premises – some of them logically contradictory. But it did not function as the blind 'false consciousness' of those subjects who were simply duped by it. Nor did its dominance arise from its conscious conspiratorial deception of the masses. All these deductions from the theory are too reductionist and simplistic in their thrust.

On the other hand, interpreted more broadly, conceived as a general approach rather than a set of specific theoretical 'laws', our study of liberalism suggests that the theoretical ideas first formulated in the materialist theory are absolutely essential. They provide us with critical starting points which no theory of ideology can afford to ignore. We could not hope to explain either liberalism's appearance or its subsequent transformations without reference to its historical and material 'conditions of existence'. Despite the philosophical complexities of the tradition, liberalism remained organized around certain key 'core concepts' which gave a particular ideological 'logic' or structure to its discourses. Whenever this logic is applied to the construction of a problem or to developing a political strategy, the results or effects bear the clear marks and inscription of the ideological character of the concepts and premises of liberalism which are deployed. Although liberalism did not 'represent' the class interests of a single whole class, there is little doubt that it did articulate, in different ways, the key conceptions of what has come to be recognized as 'bourgeois society'. Its fate, formation and fortune has been caught up at every point with the evolution and vicissitudes of the modern 'bourgeois' type of social formation. Moreover, within that, though its different strands have been articulated to different social class strata at different times – there is no automatic class belongingness – nevertheless, liberalism would be of little or no historical interest had it not been articulated to specific social interests and positions in this way. It clearly helped to shape and form English political 'common sense'. In that way it contributed to the complicated processes by which the hegemony of liberal conceptions was achieved. This 'taken for grantedness' of liberal ideas is one of its most systematic ideological effects. These starting points do not 'solve' the problems of the determinations of ideology, since they leave room for much more rounded and sophisticated formulations to be developed. But they do help to stake out certain absolutely critical and *necessary* starting points, even though they do not provide an adequate or complete theory of ideology.

References

ALTHUSSER, J. (1969) *For Marx*, Harmondsworth, Penguin Books.
BURKE, E. (1970) reprinted 1969 *Reflections on the Revolution in France*, Harmondsworth, Penguin Books.
COLLINI, S. (1979) *Liberalism and Sociology*, Cambridge, Cambridge University Press.
DANGERFIELD, G. (1935) *The Strange Death of Liberal England*, New York, Capricorn.
DICKINSON, H.T. (1977) *Liberty and Property*, London, Weidenfeld and Nicolson.
DONALD, J. (1985) 'Beacons of the future', in *Subjectivity and Social Relations* (eds) V. Beechey & J. Donald, Milton Keynes, Open University Press.
DUNN, J. (1984) *Locke*, Oxford, Oxford University Press.
ECCLESHALL, R. (1984) in *Political Ideologies* (ed) Eccleshall *et al.*, London, Hutchinson.
FREEDEN, M. (1978) *The New Liberalism*, Oxford, Clarendon Press.
GAMBLE, A. (1981) *An Introduction to Modern Social and Political Thought*, London, Macmillan.
GOUGH, J.W. (1968) *John Locke's Political Philosophy*, Oxford, Clarendon Press.
GRAMSCI, A. (1971) *Selections from the Prison Notebooks*, London, Lawrence and Wishart.
HAYEK, F. A. (1973) *Economic Freedom and Representative Government*, London, Institute of Economic Affairs.
HELD, D. (1984) 'Beyond liberalism and Marxism', in *The Idea of the Modern State* (eds) McLennan, Held and Hall, Milton Keynes, The Open University Press.
HILL, C. (1975) *The World Turned Upside Down*, Harmondsworth, Penguin Books.
HOBHOUSE, L. T. (1911) reprinted 1964 *Liberalism*, Oxford, Oxford University Press.
LARRAIN, J. (1983) *Marxism and Ideology*, London, Macmillan.
LASKI, H. (1936) *The Rise of Modern Liberalism*, London, Allen and Unwin.
LASLETT, P. (1967) Introduction to *Locke's Two Treatises of Government*, Cambridge, Cambridge University Press.
LOCKE, J. (1967) *Two Treatises of Government*, with an Introduction by P. Laslett, Cambridge, Cambridge University Press (originally published in 1690).
MACPHERSON, C.B. (1962) *The Political Theory of Possessive Individualism*, Oxford, Oxford University Press.
MACPHERSON, C.B. (1977) *The Life and Times of Liberal Democracy*, Oxford, Oxford University Press.
MARX, K. and ENGELS, F. (1846) reprinted 1965 *The German Ideology*, London, Lawrence and Wishart.

MIDDLEMAS, K. (1979) *The Politics of Industrial Society,* London, Deutsch.

MILL, J.S. (1910) *Utiliarianism, Liberty and Representative Government,* Dent, Everyman's Library Series.

PAINE, T. (1976) *Common Sense,* ed. I. Kramnick, Harmondsworth, Penguin (originally published in 1776).

PAINE, T. (1969) *The Rights of Man,* ed. H. Collins, Harmondsworth, Penguin (originally published in 1791).

POULANTZAS, N. (1975) *Political Power and Social Classes,* London, New Left Books.

RAPHAEL, D. D. (1977) *Hobbes,* London, Allen and Unwin.

RYAN, A. (1974) *J S Mill,* London, Routledge and Kegan Paul.

THOMPSON, E. P. (1965) 'Peculiarities of the English', *The Socialist Register,* London, Merlin.

THOMPSON, E. P. (1968) *The Making of the English Working Class,* Harmondsworth, Penguin Books.

THOMPSON, E. P. (1975) *Whigs and Hunters,* Harmondsworth, Allen Lane.

WEBER, M. (1930) *The Protestant Ethic,* London, Allen and Unwin.

4 Women and Equality

Juliet Mitchell

From *The Rights and Wrongs of Women* edited by J. Mitchell and A. Oakley, 1976.
Reproduced by permission of the publishers Penguin Books.

[. . .] Under capitalism 'equality' can only refer to equality under the law.
Because it cannot take into account the fundamental inequities of the class society
on which it is based, the law itself must treat men as a generalizable and abstract
category, it must ignore not only their individual differences, their different needs
and abilities, but the absolute differences in their social and economic positions.
Since the seventeenth century the law has expressed this, its precondition.

Bourgeois, capitalist law is a general law that ensures that everybody is equal
before it: it is abstract and applies to all cases and all persons. As the political
theorist Franz Neumann writes:

> [. . .] The formal structure of the law is, moreover, equally decisive in the
> operation of the social system of a competitive-contractual society. The need
> for calculability and reliability of the legal and administrative system was one
> of the reasons for the limitation of the power of the patrimonial monarchy and
> of feudalism. The limitation culminated in the establishment of the legislative
> power of parliaments by means of which the middle classes controlled the
> administrative and fiscal apparatus and exercised a condominium with the
> crown in changes of the legal system. A competitive society requires general
> laws as the highest form of purposive rationality, for such a society is
> composed of a large number of entrepreneurs of about equal power. Freedom
> of the commodity market, freedom of the labour market, free entrance into the
> entrepreneurial class, freedom of contract, and rationality of the judicial
> responses in disputed issues—these are the essential characteristics of an
> economic system which requires and desires the production for profit, and
> ever renewed profit in a continuous, rational capitalistic enterprise.
> (Neumann, 1964, pp. 167–8).

The law, then, enshrines the principles of freedom and equality – so long as you do
not look at the particular unequal conditions of the people who are subjected to it.
The concept 'equal under the law' does not apply to the economic inequities it is

there to mask. The law is general, therefore, as *men* – employer and employee – are equal, the law does not consider the inequality of their position. Equality always denies the inequality inherent in its own birth as a concept [. . .]

Those seem to me to be some of the limitations of the concept of equality – what of its strengths? When a rising bourgeoisie is struggling against an old feudal order, that is, before it has firmly constituted itself as the dominant class, in its aspirations it does in some sense represent all the social classes that were subordinate previously: its revolution initially is a revolution on behalf of all the oppressed against the then dominant class – the nobility. The ideological concepts that the bourgeoisie will forge in this struggle are universalistic ones – they are about *most* people and the society most people want. New formulations about 'human nature' will jostle with old ones and eventually set themselves as permanent truths. New values, such as a belief in the supremacy of reason, will be treated as though they have always been the pinnacle to which men try to ascend. These ideas will seem to be not only timeless but classless. Equality is one of them. Equality is the aspiration of the bourgeoisie at the moment when as the revolutionary class it momentarily represents all classes [. . .]

It is this universalistic aspect of the concept that has continued in the most ennobled liberal and social-democratic thought within capitalism; because it is instituted as a demand of the revolutionary moment it soars above the conditions that create it, but because this revolution is based on these conditions – the conditions of creating two new antagonistic 'unequal' classes – to these conditions it must eventually return, trapped by the hand that controls even its flight.

A history of the concept of equality would run in tracks very similar to a history of feminism. First introduced as one of the pinnacles of the new society's ideology in revolutionary England of the seventeenth century, the notion of equality next reached a further high in the era of enlightenment in the eighteenth century and then with the French Revolution. Feminism likewise has both the continuity and the fits and starts of this trajectory. Feminism as a conscious, that is self-conscious, protest movement, arose as part of a revolutionary bourgeois tradition that had equality of mankind as its highest goal. The first expressions of feminism were endowed with the strengths of the concept of equality and circumscribed by its limitations. Feminism arose in England in the seventeenth century as a conglomeration of precepts and a series of demands by women who saw themselves as a distinct sociological group and one that was completely excluded from the tenets and principles of the new society. The seventeenth-century feminists were mainly middle-class women who argued their case in explicit relation to the massive change in society that came about with the end of feudalism and the beginning of capitalism. As the new bourgeois man held the torch up against absolutist tyranny and argued for freedom and equality, the new bourgeois woman wondered why she was being left out.

Writing on marriage in 1700, Mary Astell asked:

> [. . .] If *all Men are born free*, how is it that all Women are born slaves? As they must be if their being subjected to the *inconstant, uncertain, unknown, arbitrary Will* of Men, be the perfect Condition of Slavery?

How could men proclaim social change and a new equality in the eyes of the Lord and consistently ignore one half of the population? It is to the values of the revolutionary society and against those of the old that the feminists appealed [. . .].

I want to select three aspects of the seventeenth-century feminists' arguments that make it clear this was the beginning of political feminism. First, in rejecting women as naturally different from men they are forced to define women as a distinct *social* group with its own socially defined characteristics. Second, as a result of this they see that men *as a social group* oppress women as a social group – they are not against men as such but against the social power of men; women's oppression as they put it is due to 'the Usurpation of Men, and the Tyranny of Custom'. Finally while they want to be let into men's privileged sphere they also want men to learn something from women; though they wouldn't have used exactly these terms, the feminization of men is as important as the masculinization of women – they do not undervalue female powers only their abuse[. . .]. There is a current Chinese slogan that says 'anything a man can do a woman can do too'; feminism in the seventeenth century, as today, would add: 'anything a woman can do a man can do too' – though the seventeenth-century terms for this sexual 'levelling' are slightly different[. . .].

As the Duchess of Newcastle somewhat fancifully wrote in 1662:

> . . . . men are so unconscionable and cruel against us, as they endeavour to Barr us all Sorts or kinds of Liberty, as not to suffer us Freely to associate amongst our own sex, but, would fain Bury us in their houses or Beds, as in a Grave; the truth is, we live like Bats or owls, Labour like Beasts, and Dye like worms.

The early feminists do not consciously congregate as a political movement but they do propose to establish female groups, usually for educational and self-educational purposes – they want to develop 'friendship' among women. (The urge for female friendship bears a resemblance to the desire for sisterhood as it is advocated in the Women's Movement today.) Clearly a larger rebellion crossed their minds:

> . . . women are not so well united as to form an Insurrection. They are for the most part Wise enough to Love their Chains, and to discern how very becomingly they sit. They think as humbly of themselves as their Masters can wish, with respect to the other Sex, but in regard to their own, they have a Spice of Masculine Ambition, every one would Lead, and none will Follow . . . therefore as to those Women who find themselves born for Slavery, and are so sensible of their own Meanness to conclude it impossible to attain to anything excellent, since they are, or ought to be, the best acquainted with their own Strength and Genius, She's a Fool who would attempt their Deliverance and Improvement. No, let them enjoy the great Honor and Felicity of their Tame, Submissive and Depending Temper! Let the Men applaud, and let them glory in, this wonderful Humility!
> (Mary Astell, 1700)

It was left to later generations of women to try and devise a way of solving the problem of the masculine ambition to lead and of overcoming the apathy of feminine contentment–both are struggles that still continue [. . .]. The seventeenth-century feminists are today frequently criticized for only wanting the liberation of the women of their own social class. Certainly whenever they explicitly thought of the labouring classes, it did not occur to them to consider that their own demands for access to education, the world of business and the professions were strikingly inappropriate for women (or men) of a lower class. When they talked of freeing 'half the world' they were oblivious of class differences. Yet I think to criticize them for being blinkered by their bourgeois vision is ahistorical and inaccurate. In so far as they came from the revolutionary class of that epoch and that they pointed out the oppressions that still existed, they did speak for all women [. . .]. Even the very precepts of a revolutionary change, in any era, cannot transcend the social conditions that give rise to them. In demanding entry into a male world, the end of men's social oppression of women and equality between the sexes, the women were truly revolutionary. They had explanations but they did not have a theory of how women came to be an oppressed social group, but still today we lack any such full theoretical analysis. They understood clearly enough that in their own time they were being made to live like bats and they saw the contradictions between this oppression and the ideology of liberty and equality; at that historical point to go beyond such insight and such forceful protest could only be millenianism–as they well knew [. . .].

When feminism next really reached a new crescendo, with Condorcet and Mary Wollstonecraft and the French Revolution, it was the hurtfulness not the uselessness of the oppression of women that was uppermost in the writers' minds. The principles were clear, Condorcet was emphatic in stating them. 'Either no member of the human race has real rights, or else all have the same; he who votes against the rights of another, whatever his religion, colour or sex, thereby abjures his own.' It is as bad to be tyrants as to be slaves, men and women are degraded by the oppression of women. But what is new to the argument, and best expressed in Mary Wollstonecraft's *A Vindication of the Rights of Women* (1792) is the constant analysis of the damage done to women and therefore to society by conditioning them into inferior social beings [. . .] Wollstonecraft inveighs against such false refinement:

> In short, women, in general . . . have acquired all the follies and vices of civilization, and missed the useful fruit . . . Their senses are inflamed, and their understandings neglected, consequently they become the prey of their senses, delicately termed sensibility, and are blown about by every momentary gust of feeling. Civilized women are therefore so weakened by false refinement, that, respecting morals, their condition is much below what it would be were they left in a state near to nature.

Between the end of the seventeenth and the end of the eighteenth century it would seem that among the middle classes the social definition of sexual differences had been more forcefully asserted; the behavioural characteristics of 'masculinity' and 'femininity' had drawn further apart. Behind Wollstonecraft's energetic analysis is a dilemma with which we are still familiar: if a woman strives not to fall for the lure of feminine subservience she is labelled 'masculine', in which case what happens to her legitimate femininity or 'femaleness'? How can one be a woman, indeed womanly, and avoid the social stereotypes? The answer is a concept of humanity which more urgently unifies the social characteristics of men and women:

> A wild wish has just flown from my heart to my head, and I will not stifle it, though it may excite a horse-laugh. I do earnestly wish to see the distinction of sex confounded in society, unless where love animates the behaviour.

In fact Wollstonecraft, while asserting equality as a human right, has to some degree moved away from what I have characterized as an essentially liberal position into one that we might describe as radical humanism. Though like the seventeenth century writers her highest good is reason and she demonstrates that women are inferior because they have been subjugated – not, as is usually argued, that they are subjugated because they are inferior – yet there is a new political dimension to her feminism. Where her English predecessors were demanding the practice consistent with the revolutionary values of their society, Wollstonecraft, living in the double context of by then reactionary Britain yet having the inspiration of the French Revolution, wanted not a change *within* society but a change *of* society:

> I do not believe that a private education can work the wonders which some sanguine writers have attributed to it. Men and women must be educated, in a great degree, by the opinions and manners of the society they live in . . . It may . . . fairly be inferred, that, till society be differently constituted, much cannot be expected from education.

The writer to whom I wish to refer finally in this sketch of the relationship between feminism and the concept of equality is John Stuart Mill. To offer a somewhat sweeping generalization, after Mill, in England the feminist struggle moves from being predominantly the utterances of individuals about a philosophical notion of equality to being an organized political movement for the attainment, among other things, of equal rights. Of course, the one does not exclude the other, it is a question of emphasis.

In a lucid and powerful manner Mill's essay, 'The Subjection of Women' (1869), written at the height of the Victorian repression of women, resumes with a new coherence the arguments with which we have become familiar. Thus he has a clear perspective on the argument that maddened the earlier writers, that women's characteristics and social status were 'nature': 'What is now called the nature of women is an eminently artificial thing – the result of forced repression in some directions, unnatural stimulation in others' and, 'So true is it that unnatural generally means only uncustomary, and that everything which is usual appears natural. The subjection of women to men being a universal custom, any departure from it quite naturally appears unnatural'. Mill also looks back with clarity on the history of democracry and of women's rights – or rather lack of them.

Where the seventeenth-century women looked to their own new society for change and Wollstonecraft, with the example of the first radical years of the French Revolution at hand, looked to change her society, Mill, writing from within an industrial capitalism that had hardened into fairly extreme conservatism had to stand aside and argue from the best of the past and the hope of the future. Most importantly, the justice and morality he wants have not yet been found in the world: 'Though the truth may not yet be felt or generally acknowledged for generations to come, the only school of genuine moral sentiment is society between equals' and – 'We have had the morality of submission, and the morality of chivalry and generosity; the time is now come for the morality of justice.'

But Mill's lucidity, unlike Wollstonecraft's exuberance, forces him to constrict his own vision. Although at one moment he speculates that the reason why women are denied equal rights in society at large is because men must confine them to the home and the family, he does not pursue the implications of this insight and instead programmatically demands these rights. When it comes down to it, his equality is, quite realistically, equality under the law:

> [. . .] the principle which regulates the existing social relations between the two sexes – the legal subordination of one sex to the other – is wrong in itself, and now one of the chief hindrances to human improvement.

I am not arguing against Mill's position but trying to indicate a lack that is implicit in this perspective. Mill's concept of human beings that are freed from the artificial constraints of a false masculinity or femininity is somehow more abstract than that of the earlier feminists. The seventeenth-century women thought if men and women were equal they could gain some quality from each other. Mary Wollstonecraft's vision combined in one being the best of a female world with the best of a male world. Mill correctly argues that we cannot know what men and women will be like when released from present stereotypes but out of this correctness comes an elusive feeling that Mill, seeing so accurately women's miserable subordination, failed to see their contribution. This turns on the question of the importance of the reproduction and care of human life – Mill does not see, as Wollstonecraft does, that there might be a gain in men really becoming fathers (instead of remote, authoritarian figureheads) as well as in women being freed to pursue the so-called 'masculine' virtues. That Mill's concept of humanity is abstract, that he did not seem to consider the contribution of 'femaleness' once freed of its crippling exclusiveness to oppressed women, may have been because he was a man; it may just as easily have been because of the different social circumstances from which he wrote. Because he was not living at the moment when the bourgeoisie was the revolutionary class, the universalistic aspect of such thought of which I spoke earlier must turn to abstraction, there is no other way in which it can refer to all people.

John Stuart Mill in a sense expresses the best and the last in the high liberal tradition. His ideals represent the best his society is capable of but they can no longer be felt to represent that society – as a consequence there is a sort of heroic isolation to his philosophy. Because of his isolation, because of his abstraction, in this field Mill's thought pinpoints and 'fixes' the essence of liberalism:

The old theory was, that the least possible should be left to the individual agent; that all he had to do should, as far as practicable, be laid down for him by superior powers. Left to himself he was sure to go wrong. The modern conviction, the fruit of a thousand years of experience, is that things in which the individual is the person directly interested, never go right but as they are left to his own discretion, and that any regulation of them by authority except to protect the rights of others, is sure to be mischievous. This conclusion, slowly arrived at, and not adopted until almost every possible application of the contrary theory has been made with disastrous result, now (in the industrial department) prevails universally in the most advanced countries, almost universally in all that have pretensions to any sort of advancement. It is not that all processes are supposed to be equally good, or all persons to be equally qualified for everything; but that freedom of individual choice is now known to be the only thing which procures the adoption of the best processes, and throws each operation into the hands of those who are best qualified for it.

Mill's philosophy is an overriding belief in the individual and in the right of the individual to fulfil his or her maximum potential. Mill's concept of equality is therefore an equality of opportunity. As a politician he fought for equal rights for women under the law.

Since Mill wrote there has, I think, been, in an uneven way, a decline in the tradition of liberal thought. Today, exactly three quarters of the way through the twentieth century, 'equality' would seem to have become a somewhat unfashionable concept. Equal rights are still strenuously fought for but equality as the principle of a just and free society rarely elicits the eloquent support it once received[. . .].

The fight for equal rights for women today takes place against this weakening of the liberal conception of equality. It is important both to remember that ideal and to realize its limitations. Too many revolutionary groups would skip the present and think that, given both a falseness in the conception and its ultimate unrealizability, 'equality' is not something to be fought for: too many not-so-revolutionary groups think that equal rights are attainable under class-antagonistic systems and are adequate. Equal rights will always be rights before the law but these have by no means been won yet nor their possible extent envisaged. A new society that is built on an old society that, within its limits, has reached a certain level of equality clearly is a better starting point than one that must build on a society predicated on privilege and unchallenged oppression.

Reference

NEUMANN, F. (1964) 'The concept of political freedom', in *The Democratic and the Authoritarian State*, New York, The Free Press of Glencoe.

5 Labour and Human Rights

E.J. Hobsbawm

From *Worlds of Labour* by E.J. Hobsbawm, 1984. Reproduced by permission of the publishers, Weidenfeld and Nicolson.

'Rights', whatever some philosophers say, are not abstract, universal and unchanging. They exist as parts of particular sets of beliefs in the minds of men and women about the nature of human society and the ordering of relations between human beings within it: a model of the social and political order, a model of morality and justice[. . .] To my knowledge, there is no society which does not recognize some rights, for at least some of its members, and rejects claims to others. It is doubtful whether any society could exist which fails to establish such distinctions.

Certainly the common labouring people of most of pre-industrial Europe believed they had or could claim some rights. What is more, even when these rights were not recognized as legally enforceable before the courts of the governing authorities, which they might or might not be, certain such entitlements were morally accepted even by governments and ruling classes [. . .]

This was part of that 'moral economy' which E.P.Thompson has discussed so well (Thompson, 1971). It was based on a general view of what constituted a just social order, and we know that it not only appeared to legitimize certain demands or expectations of poor labouring people, but also, insofar as this moral entitlement was infringed, their rebellions against it. Thus in the 1790s the noblemen and gentlemen landowners who monopolized the soil of England did their best to guarantee the rural poor a minimum income or social security by modifying the Poor Law, when the amount of rural pauperism seemed to increase beyond all precedent and reason [. . .] Conversely, when the British gentry established a class privilege which was believed contrary to the moral consensus, their constitutional right to do so was sharply distinguished from moral legitimacy. The Game Law of 1674 gave the monopoly of killing game [. . .] to people owning or renting land above a certain, for the time, quite enormous value or to the sons and heirs of noblemen and gentlemen. This was not only rejected by all countrymen on the grounds that God gave every man the right to take wild creatures if he could – hence poaching, widely indulged in, was not seen as a crime, though it was a legal offence. The same view in principle was taken by the great guru of the Common Law, whose views in the eighteenth century [. . .] carried vast authority, namely Blackstone (Munsche, 1981, pp. 117-119).

However, the system of 'rights' prevailing in most European pre-industrial societies differed from subsequent conceptions of rights in three ways. In the *first* place, it accepted inegalitarianism [. . .] ·That poor people had a right to earn a modest livelihood did not imply that they had the right to the same livelihood as lords. Rights depended on rank, hierarchical or personal status and situation, and could not necessarily be generalized. In the *second* place rights implied duties and the other way round. Protest and rebellion were legitimate insofar as those whose duty it was to guarantee that poor people could earn a living or buy bread at reasonable prices, failed in that duty. Conversely, [. . .] the right to a 'convenient proportion of wages' was inseparable from the duty to labour, i.e. to avoid 'idleness' [. . .] In the *third* place, these rights were rarely specified rigidly in law or at all, except in terms of precedent and consensus, which were of course much the same. In this sense, for instance, the modern conception of equality before the law is difficult to apply, even to people of essentially the same social status. At most, in legalistic societies, there was equality in the sense that all were subject to the same mandatory due process of law, so that any infringement of its formalities and rituals, however insubstantial, invalidated an accusation or verdict. Beyond this, we can say broadly that what was judged was the person and the circumstances in the light of the values of those who judged [. . .]

'Rights' in this sense formed a powerful component of the moral philosophy and – if the phrase is the right one – the political experience, of the men and women who emerged from their own past to form the novel phenomenon of labour movements. It is not possible to generalize further about them [. . .]

In the course of the later eighteenth century a *second* type of 'rights' was partly combined with these, partly superimposed on them. These were what may be called the 'Rights of Man', which still provide the basic model for programmatic Declarations of Human Rights. Such lists of basic rights [. . .] were not specifically formulated until the American and especially the French Revolution with its Declaration of the Rights of Man and Citizens. They are not to be confused with such documents of revolution as the seventeenth-century British Petition of Right of 1628 or the Bill of Rights in 1689, which were petitions against specific grievances rather than formulations of universally applicable human rights. I do not want to call this set of rights exclusively 'bourgeois' or embodying 'bourgeois revolution', though in fact they can be seen as one aspect of the system of beliefs about human nature and human society which finds another form of expression in the political economy of Adam Smith and his successors. I shall not treat them only as 'bourgeois' rights, both because they were plainly influential far beyond the range of supporters of bourgeois liberalism – Tom Paine's *Rights of Man* is a case in point – but also because many of the Rights formulated in the late eighteenth century context still correspond to what most people in modern societies want and need.

The new 'Rights of Man' type of human rights was novel and peculiar in three ways. *First*, such rights belong to individuals, conceived as such in the abstract, and not in the traditional manner as persons inseparable from their community or other social context. This was historically somewhat novel [. . .] 'Political associations' [. . .] are conceived of as bodies of persons who enter into association and can, as it were, be imagined outside them. The 'political associations' have the duty, or are set up to, protect the individual's rights against them (e.g. the state) as well as against other persons. Hence their power must be limited in scope and means, their agents must be held to account, and the rights of individuals must be guaranteed against them. We now take this approach for granted in constitutional societies, but it belongs to a specific historical view of human relations.

Second, [. . .] these rights are theoretically universal and equal since individuals conceived in isolation, can only have equal claims as such, even though as persons they are quite different. There can be no reason why, as abstract individuals, lords should have greater claims than peasants, rich men than poor men, Christians than Jews (or the other way round). They are regarded, as it were, like people who have bought a ticket at a standard price to a movie: never mind who they are, they have the same right to a seat. Hence Declarations of Rights have been, in theory, universally applicable. In fact their most powerful appeal has been that they provide *groups* who claim a better condition for themselves on *special* grounds – for instance as women or blacks or workers – with a *universal* justification for doing so, which makes it difficult for other people who accept the idea of such rights to resist the claim in principle [. . .]

Thirdly, and also in consequence of what has been said above, these rights were essentially political or *politico-legal*: since the whole point about proclaiming them was to provide institutional guarantees to human beings as citizens. The right to free speech in this sense must imply ways of protecting free speech, as Russian dissidents know well. Rights of the 'Rights of Man' type therefore implied political programmes and political action, insofar as these rights were not already effectively guaranteed by constitution and law. And of course in practice that was precisely the reason for drawing up Declarations of the Rights of Man.

But they did *not* imply a social and economic programme, because the freedoms guaranteed by such rights were negative: not to be interfered with. In Anatole France's famous phrase, 'the law in its majestic equality gives every man an equal right to sleep under a bridge or eat at the Ritz'. This was their *fourth* characteristic. Bourgeois-liberals welcomed this, since they argued that maximum economic welfare would be achieved by the untrammelled private enterprise of individuals. The bulk of modest farmers, small producers and traders did not want to be interfered with either by government or law, though they reserved the right to call on government to help them when times were bad: they were both for and against the unrestricted rights of property, which created intellectual problems that seldom troubled them but have troubled interpreters of Rousseau and Tom Paine. Yet, as Adam Smith knew well, for certain purposes a declaration of rights to negative freedom was not enough. And among those for whom it was quite evidently not enough, were the future constituency of labour movements, whose primary claim was to work at a decent wage, to social security which they certainly would need at some time in their lives, to benefits which poverty prevented their purchasing – such as health care and education – and to political rights not covered by the classical Declarations which would make it easier for them to fight for these, e.g. to form labour unions and strike.

How to combine the 'Rights of Man' rights with these [economic and social] demands? Later socialists and labour militants have been puzzled by such movements as Chartism in Britain, which was undoubtedly a working-class mobilization – probably the greatest in British history relative to the size of the population – but whose demands were exclusively for the democratization of elections [. . .] In fact there is little doubt that, in terms of their politics, radical and labour movements before the rise of socialist political parties were indistinguishable from non-socialist and non-working-class democrats. We may say – this is certainly the case in nineteenth-century Britain, but not only there – that until the rise of mass labour and socialist parties, or, ideologically, of Marxism, labour and socialist movements were not political as such, though their potential members as individuals often were. They operated outside politics by means of various collective initiatives such as unions, cooperative societies and communities or utopian colonies, though naturally they needed to acquire the legal/political rights to do so, which classical Declarations of Right did not include, and sometimes excluded [. . .] In politics pre-socialist labour militants were democrats [. . .] In general they did not look beyond the achievement of political democracy. Chartism may or may not have implied a social programme in the minds of its labouring supporters, but it certainly did not, as a movement, have such a programme. Now Socialist labour parties, especially the Marxist ones, obviously had such a programme and, apart from its intrinsic attractions, saw political democracy chiefly as a way of creating the conditions for achieving it. But, of course, since there were very few political democracies in Europe before the very late nineteenth century, the fight to establish or make effective democratic political rights remained primary [. . .]

Hence, insofar as they were politically active as movements, most nineteenth-century labour movements still operated in the framework of the American and French revolutions and their type of the Rights of Man. In other words, they fought for the rights of workers to be full citizens, even if they hoped to go on to fight for something more. They gave a special edge to the fight for these citizen rights, because they consisted largely of people who did not enjoy them, and because even those legal rights and civil liberties which were accepted in theory, were challenged in practice by the adversaries of labour. Nobody in Britain doubted the right to free speech, a free press and public demonstration, even though there was no clause in any legal document guaranteeing them. Yet, as we know, the effective right of free speech and assembly (e.g. on Trafalgar Square and in the royal parks of London) had to be fought for in a series of 'free speech fights' or mass demonstrations, and the effective right to a popular or radical free press had to be fought for similarly. The major nineteenth-century contribution of labour movements to human rights was to demonstrate that they required a lot of extension and that they had to be effective in practice as well as available on paper. This was, of course, a major and quite crucial contribution.

But it still left a number of potential human rights covered by neither of the two major families of rights which were the heritage of labour from the past [. . .]

The first group of such rights were the political and legal ones essential for the operation of any labour movement – for instance the right to strike and collective organization. I need hardly remind you that some of these were specifically excluded from the liberal-radical Declarations of the Rights of Man, or law-codes or constitutions, e.g. in France legally between 1791 and 1884. To this extent the era of classical bourgeois liberalism actually cut down the rights of corporate organization and action which pre-industrial societies had not only recognized in practice, but actually regarded as key institutions in the structuring of society. So these rights, and various consequential rights, had to be re-established and re-defined in terms of the nineteenth-century economy. The history of labour unions and struggles in all countries illustrates the chief field for the development of such human rights [. . .]

This is not true of the second group of neglected rights, of which the classical formulation is Roosevelt's 'freedom from want' [. . .] Now the dramatic, and indeed for most people the diabolical, innovation of bourgeois society and its capitalist economy was that it had no place for these positive rights and duties, and indeed tried to abolish them [. . .] The point was not that liberal economics did not mind if people died, let alone wanted them to. On the contrary, it argued with great force that the mechanisms of profit-making enterprise operating through the market would make most people better off than ever before. The point is that it could not, and did not want to, express this aspiration in the form of *rights*. There could be no place for, say, a right to employment or a right to earn a living wage in its system. Yet most people felt and still feel that they have such rights, or at least that they ought to have.

But for the great mass of the population who felt that way in the early nineteenth century [. . .] the appeal to the numerous old institutions designed to ensure these rights, was increasingly barred [. . .] Hence, while the infant labour movements were morally certain of these rights, and inspired by the memory that they had once actually been recognized, they could no longer directly appeal to them. And, of course, even if they could have done so, the old methods of ensuring them were no longer literally applicable in an industrializing society [. . .]

For obvious reasons no body of people was more acutely interested in this than the emerging working class and its movements. They were, after all, a historically new social and economic class, operating largely in novel, indeed sometimes unprecedented conditions, and above all they had, by definition, no significant independent access to all the means of production, but depended on the sale of their labour-power for wages [. . .] But hired men and women who had no resources except their wages, could encounter the denial of the right to survive at any moment, and might certainly come up against it at certain stages of their life-cycle – for instance as married couples with small children, and above all in old age. What is more, as we have seen, traditional provisions designed to protect it, broke down spectacularly in their case [. . .]

But just at this point we meet a paradox. There is absolutely no doubt that the poor, the working people and the potential or actual members of labour movements spoke the language of *rights* (and still do), if only because this is the natural language of anyone who sets up a model of morality and justice (of 'what is right' in the convenient vocabulary of Germanic languages) and makes claims in the light of this model.* It is also the natural language of politics, since it provides a built-in moral backing for any demand or action [. . .] When British labour movements demanded 'a living wage' or 'that wages should be the first charge on industry', they were patently speaking this language. [. . .]

On the other hand the theorists of labour movements did not universally talk the language of rights, at least after the early or middle decades of the century [. . .] There are two main reasons for this.

The first, and less significant, is that the most influential socialist theory by far, Marxism, specifically rejected the language of human rights for various reasons, which are not directly germane to the subject of this paper. Insofar as Marxism claimed to be an analysis of the operations of society, past, present and future, rather than a programme, that language was, of course, irrelevant to it, as indeed it was or is to Ricardo and Paul Samuelson. 'Rights' are not an analytical concept in science, any more than 'law' is, in the sense of something which *ought* to happen. A scientific 'law', if we choose to use the term, implies no claims or entitlements whatever. However, Marx was not merely indifferent to 'rights of man' but strongly opposed to them, since they are essentially individualistic, belonging to 'egoistic man . . . separated from other men and from the community'. In this sense Marx still speaks an ancient social language. This fundamental incompatibility of Marx' ideas with classical liberal theory has had far-reaching consequences for the position of individual citizens in states established on the Bolshevik model since 1917, though it is quite wrong to deduce from this incompatibility in theory a permanent incompatibility of Marxist regimes with legal and constitutional guarantees of citizen rights, either formally or in practice; any more than it is legitimate to suppose that no state based on the classical liberal rights of man can be a police state [. . .]

But the second, and much more significant reason is that rights in the sense of wide-ranging claims to a good or tolerable life, are not ends in themselves, but broad aspirations which can be realized only through complex and changing social strategies, on which they throw no specific light. It is possible, as Jefferson saw, to make 'the pursuit of happiness' into a 'natural right'.[. . .] But it is not possible to formulate a right to *be* happy in the same sense, since only advertising agencies would argue that there is a readily definable programme – e.g. drinking Coca Cola or smoking dope – which could guarantee happiness, which could thus be assured by a law to supply all citizens with the requisite quantities of the magic ingredient [. . .].

---

*In English and German the identification is linguistically clear. It is right to demand my rights, because they are themselves right. In German *Recht* may mean both law and entitlement and (as an adjective) the rightness of the claim.

To say that human beings have the right to freedom from want is merely another way of saying that public policy or private behaviour or both ought to be dedicated to this broad purpose. Such a declaration tells us nothing at all in itself about how this end is to be achieved in practice. There is no way it could do so. Some people might try to achieve it by a social revolution introducing a centrally planned socialist economy; others by a Reaganite trickle-down effect from unrestricted private enterprise in a market society; yet others by means of Scandinavian social-democratic strategies [. . .].

So the language of human rights was and is unsuited (except rhetorically and agitationally) to the struggle for the achievement of the economic and social changes to which labour movements were dedicated: whether reforms within existing society or gradual changes, or revolutionary transformations of the social and economic order. In short, it is possible to translate the Rights of Man of the classical Declarations, which are essentially concerned with individuals, into laws which specifically guarantee them even though the guarantees may be neither invariable nor unconditional, and even though experience shows that they do not guarantee them as simply and automatically as one might hope: as witness the right to equality irrespective of race and sex. But it is not possible to give the rights to a decent human life equal expression in law. They are not rights of individuals in the same sense, but programmes for society and social action. Everything depends on the strategies and mechanisms for achieving them, not to mention situations beyond legal control which may affect them.

So this is the paradox. More than any other force, the labour movement helped to unlock the politico-legal, individualist strait-jacket which confined human rights of the type of the French Declaration and the American Constitution. [. . .] At the same time labour movements demonstrated the limitations of a 'human rights' approach to politics [. . .] Such concepts as the right to live a decent life can become operational only in a society so constructed as to make them possible, and can be approached only indirectly through *policies* and ongoing institutional changes. This is clear even in the famous fifth chapter of the second part of Paine's *Rights of Man*. The crux of this chapter is not that men have economic and social rights, but in the *policies* of taxing the rich to create a fund for paying the poor, the unemployed and old as well as the cost of popular education. Without such policies, these human rights are entirely ineffective.

Now in pursuit of such policies, conflicts between the individual and the social rights inevitably develop. Almost any attempt to change society or to improve it in the interests of the poor in our century, has been shown to mean more public interference with the freedom of the individual than is provided for in the literal meaning of the American Bill of Rights: hence the exegetical contortions of the US Supreme Court in this century. The classical Rights (or rather freedoms from interference) have not only tended to be of little operational use to people trying to improve social arrangements. They have readily served the propaganda of their adversaries [. . .]. It is the paradox of liberty that it became the slogan of those who needed it least and wanted to deny it to those who needed it most: of the Liberty and Property Defence League which opposed socialism in Britian in the 1880s, of the Liberty League which fought the New Deal, or for that matter of General Pinochet, who used coercion and torture to persuade Chileans of the virtues of the free market economy, as understood by the disciples of Professor Milton Friedman, whom there is no reason to think of as other than sincerely devoted to libertarian ideals.

This observation is not to be understood as a criticism of liberty in the old-fashioned individualist sense of the French revolutionary Declarations of the Rights of Man. The theorist may regard this concept of freedom as inadequate, unsatisfactory and analytically feeble, but it is an empirically verifiable fact that for most human beings in the twentieth-century freedom from being told by outside (secular) authorities what to do and what not to do – beyond a varying minimum accepted as legitimate in the interests of society and its members – is a crucial component of what they consider liberty. No modern political order is likely to be considered satisfactory by its members which overlooks people's dislike of being coerced.

This needs to be said, for the other paradox of freedom is that those who want to change society in order to create the conditions for the free development of all individuals of which Marx dreamed, have tended to put the rights of the individual against state and society on the back burner, when they have been in a position to proceed to a reconstruction of society. In extreme cases, such as the Soviet Union under Stalin, they have taken them off the burner altogether. An entire polemical literature has therefore grown up, especially since 1945, which seeks but fails to demonstrate that this is the fundamental characteristic of revolutionary, socialist, or sometimes of all labour movements.

As against this it must be said that, historically, labour movements and the associated movements for social reform and social transformation have been movements for the Rights of Man in the individual as well as in the social sense; and their contribution to establishing and extending these rights has been capital. [. . .] They are children of the rationalist eighteenth-century Enlightenment, and unlike the traditionalist Right, Fascism or most ideologies of nationalism, they have never rejected or abandoned its hope and aspirations. This has been mostly due to the fact that [. . .] the constituency of these movements is one of people who are short of rights, who need them and demand them. Where labour and socialist movements have become powerful, they have naturally gathered in their neighbourhood protesters, defenders of civil liberties, champions of the rights of minorities and the rightless of all kinds – slaves, blacks, women, homosexuals or whoever – as well as libertarian believers in individual development and a new society, counter-culturists and new lifers of various sorts, who in turn demand their rights – from vegetarians to those who refuse compulsory vaccination.

Socialist movements of the late nineteenth and twentieth centuries – particularly in the early days – thus provided one of the few environments in which, say, emancipated women, Jews, and people with coloured skins could expect to be accepted on their merits as human beings and not suffer formal discrimination; perhaps the only such environments for those who had neither a great deal of money nor family connections. Perhaps they did not give the rights of such groups as exclusive a priority as their supporters might have wished, but they not only defended them, but actively campaigned for them, as part of the general championship of Liberty, Equality and Fraternity - slogans which early labour and socialist movements took over from the French Revolution - and of human emancipation. The struggle against social oppression implied the struggle for liberty.

References

MUNSCHE, P. B. (1981) *Gentlemen and Poachers: The English Game Laws 1671–1831,* Cambridge, Cambridge University Press.
THOMPSON, E. P. (1971) 'The moral economy of the English crowd in the eighteenth century', *Past and Present,* no. 50.

PART III

Politics and Nationalism

(a) National Identities

6 The Cultural Roots of Nationalism

Benedict Anderson

From *Imagined Communities: Reflections on the Origin and Spread of Nationalism* by Benedict Anderson, 1983. Reproduced by permission of the publishers, Verso.

Concepts and Definitions

Theorists of nationalism have often been perplexed, not to say irritated, by these three paradoxes: 1. The objective modernity of nations to the historian's eye vs. their subjective antiquity in the eyes of nationalists. 2. The formal universality of nationality as a socio-cultural concept – in the modern world everyone can, should, will 'have' a nationality, as he or she 'has' a gender – vs. the irremediable particularity of its concrete manifestations, such that, by definition, 'Greek' nationality is *sui generis*. 3. The 'political' power of nationalisms vs. their philosophical poverty and even incoherence. In other words, unlike most other isms, nationalism has never produced its own grand thinkers; no Hobbeses, Tocquevilles, Marxes, or Webers. This 'emptiness' easily gives rise, among cosmopolitan and polylingual intellectuals, to a certain condescension. Like Gertrude Stein in the face of Oakland, one can rather quickly conclude that there is 'no there there'. It is characteristic that even so sympathetic a student of nationalism as Tom Nairn can nonetheless write that: ' "Nationalism" is the pathology of modern developmental history, as inescapable as "neurosis" in the individual, with much the same essential ambiguity attaching to it, a similar built-in capacity for descent into dementia, rooted in the dilemmas of helplessness thrust upon most of the world (the equivalent of infantilism for societies) and largely incurable.' (Nairn, 1977, p.359).

Part of the difficulty is that one tends unconsciously to hypostasize the existence of Nationalism-with-a-big-N – rather as one might Age-with-a-capital-A – and then to classify 'it' as *an* ideology. (Note that if everyone has an age, Age is merely an analytical expression.) It would, I think, make things easier if one treated it as if it belonged with 'kinship' and 'religion', rather than with 'liberalism' or 'fascism'.

In an anthropological spirit, then, I propose the following definition of the nation: it is an imagined political community – and imagined as both inherently limited and sovereign.

It is *imagined* because the members of even the smallest nation will never know most of their fellow-members, meet them or even hear of them, yet in the minds of each lives the image of their communion. Renan referred to this imagining in his suavely back-handed way when he wrote that 'Or l'essence d'une nation est que tous les individus aient beaucoup de choses en commun, et aussi que tous aient oublié bien des choses.' (1947, p.892) With a certain ferocity Gellner makes a comparable point when he rules that 'Nationalism is not the awakening of nations to self-consciousness: it *invents* nations where they do not exist.' (1964, p. 169. Emphasis added). The drawback to this formulation, however, is that Gellner is so anxious to show that nationalism masquerades under false pretences that he assimilates 'invention' to 'fabrication' and 'falsity,' rather than to 'imagining' and 'creation'. In this way he implies that 'true' communities exist which can be advantageously juxtaposed to nations. In fact, all communities larger than primordial villages of face-to-face contact (and perhaps even these) are imagined. Communities are to be distinguished, not by their falsity/genuineness, but by the style in which they are imagined. Javanese villagers have always known that they are connected to people they have never seen, but these ties were once imagined particularistically – as indefinitely stretchable nets of kinship and clientship. Until quite recently, the Javanese language had no word meaning the abstraction 'society'. We may today think of the French aristocracy of the *ancien régime* as a class; but surely it was imagined this way only very late. To the question 'Who is the Comte de X?' the normal answer would have been, not 'a member of the aristocracy,' but 'the lord of X,' 'the uncle of the Baronne de Y,' or 'a client of Duc de Z'.

The nation is imagined as *limited* because even the largest of them, encompassing perhaps a billion living human beings, has finite, if elastic boundaries, beyond which lie other nations. No nation imagines itself coterminous with mankind. The most messianic nationalists do not dream of a day when all the members of the human race will join their nation in the way that it was possible, in certain epochs, for, say, Christians to dream of a wholly Christian planet.

It is imagined as *sovereign* because the concept was born in an age in which Enlightenment and Revolution were destroying the legitimacy of the divinely – ordained, hierarchical dynastic realm. Coming to maturity at a stage of human history when even the most devout adherents of any universal religion were inescapably confronted with the living *pluralism* of such religions, and the allomorphism between each faith's ontological claims and territorial stretch, nations dream of being free, and, if under God, directly so. The gage and emblem of this freedom is the sovereign state.

Finally, it is imagined as a *community*, because, regardless of the actual inequality and exploitation that may prevail in each, the nation is always conceived as a deep, horizontal comradeship. Ultimately it is this fraternity that makes it possible, over the past two centuries, for so many millions of people, not so much to kill, as willingly to die for such limited imaginings.

These deaths bring us abruptly face to face with the central problem posed by nationalism: what makes the shrunken imaginings of recent history (scarcely more than two centuries) generate such colossal sacrifices? I believe that the beginnings of an answer lie in the cultural roots of nationalism.

Cultural Roots

[...] In Western Europe the eighteenth century marks not only the dawn of the age of nationalism but the dusk of religious modes of thought. The century of the Enlightenment, of rationalist secularism, brought with it its own modern darkness. With the ebbing of religious belief, the suffering which belief in part composed did not disappear. Disintegration of paradise: nothing makes fatality more arbitrary. Absurdity of salvation: nothing makes another style of continuity more necessary. What then was required was a secular transformation of fatality into continuity, contingency into meaning [...]. Few things were (are) better suited to this end than an idea of nation. If nation-states are widely conceded to be 'new' and 'historical,' the nations to which they give political expression always loom out of an immemorial past, and, still more important, glide into a limitless future. It is the magic of nationalism to turn chance into destiny. With Debray we might say, 'Yes, it is quite accidental that I am born French; but after all, France is eternal.'

Needless to say, I am not claiming that the appearance of nationalism towards the end of the eighteenth century was 'produced' by the erosion of religious certainties, or that this erosion does not itself require a complex explanation. Nor am I suggesting that somehow nationalism historically 'supersedes' religion. What I am proposing is that nationalism has to be understood, by aligning it not with self-consciously held political ideologies, but with the large cultural systems that preceded it, out of which – as well as against which – it came into being.

For present purposes, the two relevant cultural systems are the *religious community* and the *dynastic realm*. For both of these, in their heydays, were taken-for-granted frames of reference, very much as nationality is today. It is therefore essential to consider what gave these cultural systems their self-evident plausibility, and at the same time to underline certain key elements in their decomposition.

The Religious Community

Few things are more impressive than the vast territorial stretch of the Ummah Islam from Morocco to the Sulu Archipelago, of Christendom from Paraguay to Japan, and of the Buddhist world from Sri Lanka to the Korean peninsula. The great sacral cultures (and for our purposes here it may be permissible to include 'Confucianism') incorporated conceptions of immense communities. But Christendom, the Ummah Islam, and even the Middle

Kingdom – which, though we think of it today as Chinese, imagined itself not as Chinese, but as central – were imaginable largely through the medium of sacred language and written script. Take only the example of Islam: if Maguindanao met Berbers in Mecca, knowing nothing of each other's languages, incapable of communicating orally, they nonetheless understood each other's ideographs, *because* the sacred texts they shared existed only in classical Arabic. In this sense, written Arabic functioned like Chinese characters to create a community out of signs, not sounds. (So today mathematical language continues an old tradition. Of what the Thai call + Rumanians have no idea, and vice versa, but both comprehend the symbol.) All the great classical communities conceived of themselves as cosmically central, through the medium of a sacred language linked to a superterrestrial order of power. Accordingly, the stretch of written Latin, Paoli, Arabic, or Chinese was, in theory, unlimited. (In fact, the deader the written language – the farther it was from speech – the better: in principle everyone has access to a pure world of signs.)

Yet such classical communities linked by sacred languages had a character distinct from the imagined communities of modern nations. One crucial difference was the old communities' confidence in the unique sacredness of their languages, and thus their ideas about admission to membership. Chinese mandarins looked with approval on barbarians who painfully learned to paint Middle Kingdom ideograms. These barbarians were already halfway to full absorption. Half-civilized was vastly better than barbarian. Such an attitude was certainly not peculiar to the Chinese, nor confined to antiquity. Consider, for example, the following 'policy on barbarians' formulated by the early-nineteenth-century Colombian liberal Pedro Fermin de Vargas:

> To expand our agriculture it would be necessary to hispanicize our Indians. Their idleness, stupidity, and indifference towards normal human endeavours causes one to think that they come from a degenerate race which deteriorates in proportion to the distance from its origin . . . *it would be very desirable that the Indians be extinguished, by miscegenation with the whites, declaring them free of tribute and other charges, and giving them private property in land.* (Emphasis added)

How striking it is that this liberal still proposes to 'extinguish' his Indians in part by 'declaring them free of tribute' and 'giving them private property in land', rather than exterminating them by gun and microbe as his heirs in Brazil, Argentina, and the United States began to do soon afterwards. Note also, alongside the condescending cruelty, a cosmic optimism: the Indian is ultimately redeemable – by impregnation with white, 'civilized' semen, and the acquisition of private property, *like everyone else*. (How different Fermin's attitude is from the later European imperialist's preference for 'genuine' Malays, Gurkhas, and Hausas over 'half-breeds', 'semi-educated natives', 'wogs', and the like.)

Yet if the sacred silent languages were the media through which the great global communities of the past were imagined, the reality of such apparitions depended on an idea largely foreign to the contemporary Western mind: the non-arbitrariness of the sign. The ideograms of Chinese, Latin, or Arabic were emanations of reality, not randomly fabricated representations of it. We are familiar with the long dispute over the appropriate language (Latin or vernacular) for the mass. In the Islamic tradition, until quite recently, the Qur'an was literally untranslatable (and therefore untranslated), because Allah's truth was accessible only through the unsubstitutable true signs of written Arabic. There is no idea here of a world so separated from language that all languages are equidistant (and thus inter-changeable) signs for it. In effect, ontological reality is apprenhensible only through a single, privileged system of re-presentation: the truth-language of Church Latin, Qur'anic Arabic, or Examination Chinese. And, as truth-languages, imbued with an impulse largely foreign to nationalism, the impulse towards conversion. By conversion, I mean not so much the acceptance of particular religious tenets, but alchemic absorption. The barbarian becomes 'Middle Kingdom', the Rif Muslim, the Ilongo Christian. The whole nature of man's being is sacrally malleable. (Contrast thus the prestige of these old world-languages, towering high over all vernaculars, with Esperanto or Volapük, which lie ignored between them.) It was, after all, this possibility of conversion through the sacred language that made it possible for an 'Englishman' to become Pope [1] and a 'Manchu' Son of Heaven.

But even though the sacred languages made such communities as Christendom imaginable, the actual scope and plausibility of these communities can not be explained by sacred script alone: their readers were, after all, tiny literate reefs on top of vast illiterate oceans. A fuller explanation requires a glance at the relationship between the literati and their societies. It would be a mistake to view the former as a kind of theological technocracy. The languages they sustained, if abstruse, had none of the self-arranged abstruseness of lawyers' or economists' jargons, on the margin of society's idea of reality. Rather, the literati were adepts, strategic strata in a cosmological hierarchy of which the apex was divine. The fundamental conceptions about 'social groups' were centripetal and hierarchical, rather than boundary-oriented and horizontal. The astonishing power of the papacy in its noonday is only comprehensible in terms of a trans-European Latin-writing clerisy, *and* a conception of the world, shared by virtually everyone, that the bilingual intelligentsia, by mediating between vernacular and Latin, mediated between earth and heaven. (The awesomeness of excommunication reflects this cosmology.)

Yet for all the grandeur and power of the great religiously-imagined communites, their *unselfconscious coherence* waned steadily after the late Middle Ages. Among the reasons for this decline, I wish here to emphasize only the two which are directly related to these communities' unique sacredness.

First was the effect of the explorations of the non-European world, which mainly, but by no means exclusively, in Europe 'abruptly widened the cultural and geographic horizon and hence also men's conception of possible forms of human life.' (Auerbach, 1957, p.282). The process is already apparent in the greatest of all European travel-books. Consider the following awed description of Kublai Khan by the good Venetian Christian Marco Polo at the end of the thirteenth century:

The grand khan, having obtained this signal victory, returned with great pomp and triumph to the capital city of Kanbalu. This took place in the month of November, and he continued to reside there during the months of February and March, in which latter was *our* festival of Easter. Being aware that this was one of *our* principal solemnities, he commanded all the Christians to attend him, and to bring with them *their* Book, which contains the four Gospels of the Evangelists. After causing it to be repeatedly perfumed with incense, in a ceremonious manner, he devoutly kissed it, and directed that the same should be done by all his nobles who were present. This was his usual practice upon each of the principal Christian festivals, such as Easter and Christmas; and he observed the same at the festivals of the Saracens, Jews, and idolaters. Upon being asked his motive for this conduct, he said: 'There are four great Prophets who are reverenced and worshipped by the different classes of mankind. The Christians regard Jesus Christ as their divinity; the Saracens, Mahomet; the Jews, Moses; and the idolaters, Sogomombar-kan, the most eminent among their idols. I do honour and show respect to all the four, and invoke to my aid *whichever amongst them is in truth supreme in heaven.*' But from the manner in which his majesty acted towards them, it is evident that he regarded the faith of the Christians as the truest and the best . . . (Emphasis added)

What is so remarkable about this passage is not so much the great Mongol dynast's calm religious relativism (it is still a *religious* relativism), as Marco Polo's attitude and language. It never occurs to him, even though he is writing for fellow-European Christians, to term Kublai a hypocrite or an idolater. (No doubt in part because 'in respect of number of subjects, extent of territory, and amount of revenue, he surpasses every sovereign that has heretofore been or that now is in the world.') And in the unselfconscious use of 'our' (which becomes 'their'), and the description of the faith of the Christians as 'truest', rather than 'true,' we can detect the seeds of a territorialization of faiths which foreshadows the language of many nationalists ('our' nation is 'the best' – in a competitive, *comparative field*).

What a revealing contrast is provided by the opening of the letter written by the Persian traveller 'Rica' to his friend 'Ibben' from Paris in '1712':[2]

The Pope is the chief of the Christians; he is an ancient idol, worshipped now from habit. Once he was formidable even to princes, for he would depose them as easily as our magnificent sultans depose the kings of Iremetia or Georgia. But nobody fears him any longer. He claims to be the successor of one of the earliest Christians, called Saint Peter, and it is certainly a rich succession, for his treasure is immense and he has a great country under his control.

The deliberate, sophisticated fabrications of the eighteenth century Catholic mirror the naive realism of this thirteenth-century predecessor, but by now the 'relativization' and 'territorialization' are utterly selfconscious, and political in intent. Is it unreasonable to see a paradoxical elaboration of this evolving tradition in the Ayatollah Rubollah Khomeini's identification of The Great Satan, not as a heresy, nor even as a demonic personage (dim little Carter scarcely fitted the bill), but as a *nation*?

Second was a gradual demotion of the sacred language itself. Writing of mediaeval Western Europe, Bloch noted that 'Latin was not only the language in which teaching was done, it was the *only language taught*' (1961, I, p.77. Emphasis added). (This second 'only' shows quite clearly the sacredness of Latin – no other language was thought worth the teaching.) But by the sixteenth century all this was changing fast [in large part as the result of the development of print-capitalism]. The reasons for the change need not detain us here [. . .] It is sufficient to remind ourselves of its scale and pace. Febvre and Martin (1976, p.248-9) estimate that 77 per cent of the books printed before 1500 were still in Latin (meaning nonetheless that 23 per cent were already in vernaculars). If of the 88 editions printed in Paris in 1501 all but 8 were in Latin, after 1575 a majority were always in French (ibid, p.321). Despite a temporary come-back during the Counter-Reformation, Latin's hegemony was doomed. Nor are we speaking simply of a general popularity. Somewhat later but at no less dizzying speed, Latin ceased to be the language of a pan-European high intelligentsia. In the seventeenth century Hobbes (1588-1678) was a figure of continental renown because he wrote in the truth-language. Shakespeare (1564-1616), on the other hand, composing in the vernacular, was virtually unknown across the Channel. And had English not become, two hundred years later, the pre-eminent world-imperial language, might he not largely have retained his original insular obscurity? Meanwhile, these men's cross-Channel near-contemporaries, Descartes (1596-1650) and Pascal (1623–1662), conducted most of their correspondence in Latin; but virtually all of Voltaire's (1694-1778) was in the vernacular (ibid, pp.330-32). 'After 1640, with fewer and fewer books coming out in Latin, and more and more in the vernacular languages, publishing was ceasing to be an international [sic] enterprise' (ibid, pp.232-33). In a word, the fall of Latin exemplified a larger process in which the sacred communities integrated by old sacred languages were gradually fragmented, pluralized, and territorialized.

The Dynastic Realm

These days it is perhaps difficult to put oneself empathetically into a world in which the dynastic realm appeared for most men as the only imaginable 'political' system. For in fundamental ways 'serious' monarchy lies transverse to all modern conceptions of political life. Kingship organizes everything around a high centre. Its legitimacy derives from divinity, not from populations, who, after all, are subjects, not citizens. In the modern conception, state sovereignty is fully, flatly, and evenly operative over each square centimetre of a legally demarcated territory. But in the older imagining, where states were defined by centres, borders were porous and indistinct, and sovereignties faded imperceptibly into one another. Hence, paradoxically enough, the ease with which pre-modern empires and kingdoms were able to sustain their rule over immensely heterogeneous, and often not even contiguous, populations for long periods of time.

One must also remember that these antique monarchical states expanded not only by warfare but by sexual politics – of a kind very different from that practised today. Through the general principle of verticality, dynastic marriages brought together diverse populations under new apices. Paradigmatic in this respect was the House of Habsburg. As the tag went, *Bella gerant alii tu felix Austria nube!* Here, in somewhat abbreviated form, is the later dynasts' titulature:

> Emperor of Austria; King of Hungary, of Bohemia, of Dalmatia, Croatia, Slavonia, Galicia, Lodomeria, and Illyria; King of Jerusalem, etc.; Archduke of Austria [sic]; Grand Duke of Tuscany and Cracow; Duke of Loth [a] ringia, of Salzburg, Styria, Carinthia, Carniola, and Bukovina; Grand Duke of Transylvania, Margrave of Moravia; Duke of Upper and Lower Silesia, of Modena, Parma, Piacenza, and Guastella, of Ausschwitz and Sator, of Teschen, Friaul, Ragusa, and Zara; Princely Count of Habsburg and Tyrol, of Kyburg, Görz, and Gradiska; Duke of Trient and Brizen; Margrave of Upper and Lower Lausitz and in Istria; Count of Hohenembs, Feldkirch, Bregenz, Sonnenberg, etc.; Lord of Trieste, of Cattaro, and above the Windisch Mark; Great Voyvod of the Voyvodina, Servia . . . etc.
> (Jászi, 1929, p. 34)

This, Jászi justly observes, was 'not without a certain comic aspect . . . the record of the innumerable marriages, hucksterings and captures of the Habsburgs.'

In realms where polygyny was religiously sanctioned, complex systems of tiered concubinage were essential to the integration of the realm. In fact, royal lineages often derived their prestige, aside from any aura of divinity, from, shall we say, miscegenation? For such mixtures were signs of a superordinate status. It is characteristic that there has not been an 'English' dynasty ruling in London since the eleventh century (if then); and what 'nationality' are we to assign to the Bourbons?[3]

During the seventeenth century, however – for reasons that need not detain us here – the automatic legitimacy of sacral monarchy began its slow decline in Western Europe. In 1649, Charles Stuart was beheaded in the first of the modern world's revolutions, and during the 1650s one of the more important European states was ruled by a plebeian Protector rather than a king. Yet even in the age of Pope and Addison, Anne Stuart was still healing the sick by the laying on of royal hands, cures committed also by the Bourbons, Louis XV and XVI, in Enlightened France till the end of the *ancien régime*. But after 1789 the principle of Legitimacy had to be loudly and self-consciously defended, and, in the process, 'monarchy' became a semi-standardized model. Tennō and Son of Heaven became 'Emperors'. In far-off Siam Rama V (Chulalongkorn) sent his sons and nephews to the courts of St. Petersburg, London, and Berlin to learn the intricacies of the world-model. In 1887, he instituted the requisite principle of succession-by-legal-primogeniture, thus bringing Siam into line with the 'civilized' monarchies of Europe. The new system brought to the throne in 1910 an erratic homosexual who would certainly have been passed over in an earlier age. However, inter-monarchic approval of his ascension as Rama VI was sealed by the attendance at his coronation of princelings from Britain, Russia, Greece, Sweden, Demark – and Japan!

As late as 1914, dynastic states made up the majority of the membership of the world political system, but [. . .] many dynasts had for some time been reaching for a 'national' cachet as the old principle of Legitimacy withered silently away. While the armies of Frederick the Great (r.1749–86) were heavily staffed by 'foreigners', those of his great-nephew Friedrich Wilhelm III (r.1797–1840) were, as a result of Scharnhorst's, Gneisenau's and Clausewitz's spectacular reforms, exclusively 'national-Prussian.'

Apprehensions of Time

It would be short-sighted, however, to think of the imagined communities of nations as simply growing out of and replacing religious communities and dynastic realms. Beneath the decline of sacred communities, languages and lineages, a fundamental change was taking place in modes of apprehending the world, which, more than anything else, made it possible to 'think' the nation.

To get a feeling for this change, one can profitably turn to the visual representations of the sacred communities, such as the reliefs and stained-glass windows of mediaeval churches, or the paintings of early Italian and Flemish masters. A characteristic feature of such representations is something misleadingly analogous to 'modern dress'. The shepherds who have followed the star to the manger where Christ is born bear the features of Burgundian peasants. The Virgin Mary is figured as a Tuscan merchant's daughter. In many paintings the commissioning patron, in full burgher or noble costume, appears kneeling in adoration alongside the shepherds. What seems incongruous today obviously appeared wholly natural to the eyes of mediaeval worshippers. We are faced with a world in which the figuring of imagined reality was overwhelmingly visual and aural. Christendom assumed its universal form through a myriad of specificities and particularities: this relief, that window, this sermon, that tale, this morality play, that relic. While the trans-European Latin-reading clerisy was one essential element in the structuring of the Christian imagination, the mediation of its conceptions to the illiterate masses, by visual and aural creations, always personal and particular, was no less vital. The humble parish priest, whose forebears and frailties everyone who heard his celebrations knew, was still the direct intermediary between his parishioners and the divine. This juxtaposition of the cosmic-universal and the mundane-particular meant that however vast Christendom might be, and was sensed to be, it manifested itself *variously* to particular Swabian or Andalusian communities as replications of themselves. Figuring the Virgin Mary with 'semitic' features or 'first-century' costumes in the restoring spirit of the modern museum was unimaginable because the mediaeval Christian mind had no conception of history as an end-less chain of cause and effect or of radical separations between past and present. Bloch observes that people thought they must be near the end of time, in the sense that Christ's second coming could occur at any moment: St. Paul had said that 'the day of the Lord cometh like a thief in the night.' It was thus natural for the great twelfth-century chronicler Bishop Otto of Freising to refer repeatedly to 'we who have been placed at the end of time.' Bloch concludes that as soon as mediaeval men 'gave themselves up to meditation, nothing was farther from their thoughts than the prospect of a long future for a young and vigorous human race' (Bloch, 1961, 1, pp.84-86).

Auerbach gives an unforgettable sketch of this form of consciousness:

> If an occurrence like the sacrifice of Isaac is interpreted as prefiguring the sacrifice of Christ, so that in the former the latter is as it were announced and promised and the latter 'fulfills' . . . the former, then a connection is established between two events which are linked neither temporally nor causally – a connection which it is impossible to establish by reason in the horizontal dimension . . . It can be established only if both occurrences are vertically linked to Divine Providence, which alone is able to devise such a plan of history and supply the key to its understanding . . . the here and now is no longer a mere link in an earthly chain of events, it is *simultaneously* something which has always been, and will be fulfilled in the future; and strictly, in the eyes of God, it is something eternal, something omnitemporal, something already consummated in the realm of fragmentary earthly event.
> (Auerbach, 1957, p. 64; emphasis added)

He rightly stresses that such an idea of *simultaneity* is wholly alien to our own. It views time as something close to what Benjamin (1973, p.265) calls Messianic time, a simultaneity of past and future in an instantaneous present. In such a view of things, the word 'meanwhile' cannot be of real significance.

Our own conception of simultaneity has been a long time in the making, and its emergence is certainly connected, in ways that have yet to be well studied, with the development of the secular sciences. But it is a conception of such fundamental importance that, without taking it fully into account, we will find it difficult to probe the obscure genesis of nationalism. What has come to take the place of the mediaeval conception of similtaneity-along-time is, to borrow again from Benjamin, an idea of 'homogeneous, empty time', in which simultaneity is, as it were, transverse, cross-time, marked not by prefiguring and fulfilment, but by temporal coincidence, and measured by clock and calendar (ibid, p.263).

Why this transformation should be so important for the birth of the imagined community of the nation can best be seen if we consider the basic structure of two forms of imagining which first flowered in Europe in the eighteenth century: the novel and the newspaper. For these forms provided the technical means for 're-presenting' the *kind* of imagined community that is the nation.

Consider first the structure of the old-fashioned novel, a structure typical not only of the masterpieces of Balzac but also of any contemporary dollar-dreadful. It is clearly a device for the presentation of simultaneity in 'homogeneous, empty time,' or a complex gloss upon the word 'meanwhile'. Take, for illustrative purposes, a segment of a simple novel-plot, in which a man (A) has a wife (B) and a mistress (C), who in turn has a lover (D). We might imagine a sort of time-chart for this segment as follows:

Time:	I	II	III
Events:	A quarrels with B	A telephones C	D gets drunk in a bar
	C and D make love	B shops	A dines at home with B
		D plays pool	C has an ominous dream

Notice that during this sequence A and D never meet, indeed may not even be aware of each other's existence if C has played her cards right. What then actually links A to D? Two complementary conceptions: First, that they are embedded in 'societies' (Wessex, Lübeck, Los Angeles). These societies are sociological entities of such firm and stable reality that their members (A and D) can even be described as passing each other on the street, without ever becoming acquainted, and still be connected. Second, that A and D are embedded in the minds of the omniscient readers. Only they see the links. Only they, like God, watch A telephoning C, B shopping, and D playing pool all *at once*. That all these acts are performed at the same clocked, calendrical time, but by actors who may be largely unaware of one another, shows the novelty of this imagined world conjured up by the author in his readers' minds.

The idea of a sociological organism moving calendrically through homogeneous, empty time is a precise analogue of the idea of the nation, which also is conceived as a solid community moving steadily down (or up) history. An American will never meet, or even know the names of more than a handful of his 240,000,000-odd fellow-Americans. He has no idea of what they are up to at any one time. But he has complete confidence in their steady, anonymous, simultaneous activity.

The perspective I am suggesting will perhaps seem less abstract if we turn to inspect briefly four fictions from different cultures and different epochs, all but one of which, nonetheless, are inextricably bound to nationalist movements. In 1887, the 'Father of Filipino Nationalism', José Rizal, wrote the novel *Noli Me Tangere*, which today is regarded as the greatest achievement of modern Filipino literature. It was also almost the first novel written by an 'Indio'.[4] Here is how it marvellously begins:

> Don Santiago de los Santos was giving a dinner party one evening towards the end of October in the 1880's. Although, contrary to his usual practice, he had let it be known only on the afternoon of the same day, it was soon the topic of conversation in Binondo, where he lived, in other districts of Manila, and even in the Spanish walled city of Intramuros. Don Santiago was better known as Capitan Tiago – the rank was not military but political, and indicated that he had once been the native mayor of a town. In those days he had a reputation for lavishness. It was well known that his house, like his country, never closed its doors – except, of course, to trade and any idea that was new or daring.
>
> So the news of his dinner party ran like an electric shock through the community of spongers, hangers-on and gate-crashers whom God, in His infinite wisdom, had created and so fondly multiplied in Manila. Some of these set out to hunt polish for their boots; others, collar-buttons and cravats; but one and all gave the gravest thought to the manner in which they might greet their host with the assumed intimacy of long-standing friendship, or, if

the occasion should arise, make a graceful apology for not having arrived earlier where presumably their presence was so eagerly awaited.

The dinner was being given in a house on Anloague Street which may still be recognized unless it has tumbled down in some earthquake. Certainly it will not have been pulled down by its owner; in the Philippines, that is usually left to God and Nature. In fact, one often thinks that they are under contract to the Government for just that purpose . . .

Extensive comment is surely unnecessary. It should suffice to note that right from the start the image (wholly new to Filipino writing) of a dinner-party being discussed by hundreds of unnamed people, who do not know each other, in quite different quarters of Manila, in a particular month of a particular decade, immediately conjures up the imagined community. And in the phrase 'a house on Anloague Street which may still be recognized . . . ' the recognizers are we-the-Filipino-readers. The casual progression of this house from the 'interior' time of the novel to the 'exterior' time of the (Manila) reader's everyday life gives a hypnotic confirmation of the solidity of a single community, embracing characters, author and readers, moving onward through calendrical time. Notice too the tone. While Rizal has not the faintest idea of his readers' individual identities, he writes to them with an ironical intimacy, as though their relationships with each other are not to the smallest degree problematic.

Nothing gives one a more Foucaultian sense of abrupt discontinuities of consciousness than to compare *Noli* with the most celebrated previous literary work by an 'Indio', Francisco Baltazar's *Pinagdaanang Buhay ni Florante at ni Laura sa Cahariang Albania* (The Story of Florante and Laura in the Kingdom of Albania), the first printed edition of which dates from 1861, though it may have been composed as early as 1838. For although Baltazar was still alive when Rizal was born, the world of his masterpiece is in every basic respect foreign to that of *Noli*. Its setting – a fabulous mediaeval Albania – is utterly removed in time and space from the Binondo of the 1880s. Its heroes – Florante, a Christian Albanian nobleman, and his bosom-friend Aladin, a Muslim ('Moro') Persian aristocrat – remind us of the Philippines only by the Christian-Moro linkage. Where Rizal deliberately sprinkles his Spanish prose with Tagalog words for 'realistic,' satirical, or nationalist effect, Baltazar unselfconsciously mixes Spanish phrases into his Tagalog quatrains simply to heighten the grandeur and sonority of his diction. *Noli* was meant to be read, while *Florante at Laura* was to be sung aloud. Most striking of all is Baltazar's handling of time. As Lumbera notes, 'the unravelling of the plot does not follow a chronological order. The story begins *in medias res*, so that the complete story comes to us through a series of speeches that serve as flashbacks.' Almost half of the 399 quatrains are accounts of Florante's childhood, student years in Athens, and subsequent military exploits, given by the hero in conversation with Aladin. The 'spoken flashback' was for Baltazar the only alternative to a straightforward single-file narrative. If we learn of Florante's and Aladin's 'simultaneous' pasts, they are connected by their conversing voices, not by the structure of the epic. How distant this technique is from that of the novel: 'In that same spring, while Florante was still studying in Athens, Aladin was expelled from his sovereign's court . . . ' In effect, it never occurs to Baltazar to 'situate' his protagonists in 'society,' or to discuss them with his audience. Nor, aside from the mellifluous flow of Tagalog polysyllables, is there much 'Filipino' about his text.

In 1816, seventy years before the writing of *Noli*, José Joaquin Fernandez de Lizardi wrote a novel called *El Periquillo Sarniento* (The Itching Parrot), evidently the first Latin American work in this genre. In the words of one critic, this text is 'a ferocious indictment of Spanish administration in Mexico: ignorance, superstition and corruption are seen to be its most notable characteristics.' (Franco, 1969, p.34). The essential form of this 'nationalist' novel is indicated by the following description of its content:

> From the first, [the hero, the Itching Parrot] is exposed to bad influences – ignorant maids inculcate superstitions, his mother indulges his whims, his teachers either have no vocation or no ability to discipline him. And though his father is an intelligent man who wants his son to practise a useful trade rather than swell the ranks of lawyers and parasites, it is Periquillo's over-fond mother who wins the day, sends her son to university and thus ensures that he will learn only superstitious nonsense . . . Periquillo remains incorrigibly ignorant despite many encounters with good and wise people. He is unwilling to work or take anything seriously and becomes successively a priest, a gambler, a thief, apprentice to an apothecary, a doctor, clerk in a provincial town . . . These episodes *permit the author to describe hospitals, prisons, remote villages, monasteries*, while at the same time driving home one major point – that Spanish government and the education system encourage parasitism and laziness . . . Periquillo's adventures several times take him among Indians and Negroes . . .
> (ibid, pp.35-36. Emphasis added)

Here again we see the 'national imagination' at work in the movement of a solitary hero through a sociological landscape of a fixity that fuses the world inside the novel with the world outside. This picaresque *tour d'horizon* – hospitals, prisons, remote villages, monasteries, Indians, Negroes – is nonetheless not a *tour du monde*. The horizon is clearly bounded: it is that of colonial Mexico. Nothing assures us of this sociological solidity more than the succession of plurals. For they conjure up a social space full of *comparable* prisons, none in itself of any unique importance, but all representative (in their simultaneous, separate existence) of the oppressiveness of *this* colony. (Contrast prisons in the Bible. They are never imagined as *typical* of this or that society. Each, like the one where Salome was bewitched by John the Baptist, is magically alone.)

Finally, to remove the possibility that, since Rizal and Lizardi both wrote in Spanish, the frameworks we have been studying are somehow 'European,' here is the opening of *Semarang Hitam* [Black Semarang], a tale by the ill-fated young Indonesian communist-nationalist Mas Marco Kartodikromo,[5] published serially in 1924:

> *It was 7 o'clock, Saturday evening;* young people in Semarang never stayed at

home on Saturday night. On this night however nobody was about. Because the heavy day-long rain had made the roads wet and very slippery, all had stayed at home.

For the workers in shops and offices Saturday morning was a time of anticipation – anticipating their leisure and the fun of walking around the city in the evening, but on this night they were to be disappointed – because of lethargy caused by the bad weather and the sticky roads in the kampungs. The main roads usually crammed with all sorts of traffic, the footpaths usually teeming with people, all were deserted. Now and then the crack of a horse-cab's whip could be heard spurring a horse on its way – or the clip-clop of horses' hooves pulling carriages along.

Semarang was deserted. The light from the rows of gas lamps shone straight down on the shining asphalt road. Occasionally the clear light from the gas lamps was dimmed as the wind blew from the east . . .

A young man was seated on a long rattan lounge reading a newspaper. He was totally engrossed. His occasional anger and at other times smiles were a sure sign of his deep interest in the story. He turned the pages of the newspaper, thinking that perhaps he could find something that would stop him feeling so miserable. All of a sudden he came upon an article entitled:

PROSPERITY

A destitute vagrant became ill and died on the side of road from exposure.

The young man was moved by this brief report. He could just imagine the suffering of the poor soul as he lay dying on the side of the road . . . One moment he felt an explosive anger well up inside. Another moment he felt pity. Yet another moment his anger was directed at the social system which gave rise to such poverty, while making a small group of people wealthy.[6]

Here, as in *El Periquillo Sarniento*, we are in a world of plurals: shops, offices, carriages, kampungs, and gas lamps. As in the case of *Noli*, we-the-Indonesian-readers are plunged immediately into calendrical time and a familiar landscape; some of us may well have walked those 'sticky' Semarang roads. Once again, a solitary hero is juxtaposed to a socioscape described in careful, *general* detail. But there is also something new: a hero who is never named, but who is consistently referred to as '*our* young man'. Precisely the clumsiness and literary naivety of the text confirms the unselfconscious 'sincerity' of this pronominal adjective. Neither Marco nor his readers have any doubts about the reference. If in the jocular-sophisticated fiction of eighteenth and nineteenth-century Europe the Trope 'our hero' merely underlines an authorial play with a(ny) reader; Marco's 'our young man,' not least in its novelty, *means* a young man who belongs to the collective body of readers of *Indonesian*, and thus, implicitly, an embryonic Indonesian 'imagined community.' Notice that Marco feels no need to specify this community by name: it is already there. (Even if polylingual Dutch colonial censors could join his readership, they are excluded from this 'ourness,' as can be seen from the fact that the young man's anger is directed at 'the', not 'our', social system.)

Finally, the imagined community is confirmed by the doubleness of our reading about our young man reading. He does not find the corpse of the destitute vagrant by the side of a sticky Semarang road, but imagines it from the print in a newspaper. Nor does he care the slightest who the dead vagrant individually was: he thinks of the representative body, not the personal life.

It is fitting that in *Semarang Hitam* a newspaper appears embedded in fiction, for, if we now turn to the newspaper as cultural product, we will be struck by its profound fictiveness. What is the essential literary convention of the newspaper? If we were to look at a sample front page of, say, *The New York Times*, we might find there stories about Soviet dissidents, famine in Mali, a gruesome murder, a coup in Iraq, the discovery of a rare fossil in Zimbabwe, and a speech by Mitterand. Why are these events so juxtaposed? What connects them to each other? Not sheer caprice. Yet obviously most of them happen independently, without the actors being aware of each other or of what the others are up to. The arbitrariness of their inclusion and juxtaposition (a later edition will substitute a baseball triumph for Mitterrand) shows that the linkage between them is imagined.

This imagined linkage derives from two obliquely related sources. The first is simply calendrical coincidence. The date at the top of the newspaper, the single most important emblem on it, provides the essential connection – the steady onward clocking of homogeneous, empty time. Within that time, 'the world' ambles sturdily ahead. The sign for this: if Mali disappears from the pages of *The New York Times* after two days of famine reportage, for months on end, readers do not for a moment imagine that Mali has disappeared or that famine has wiped out all its citizens. The novelistic format of the newspaper assures them that somewhere out there the 'character' Mali moves along quietly, awaiting its next reappearance in the plot.

The second source of imagined linkage lies in the relationship between the newspaper, as a form of book, and the market. It has been estimated that in the 40-odd years between the publication of the Gutenberg Bible and the close of the fifteenth century, more than 20,000,000 printed volumes were produced in Europe. Between 1500 and 1600, the number manufactured had reached between 150,000,000 and 200,000,000. 'From early on ... the printing shops looked more like modern workshops than the monastic workrooms of the Middle Ages. In 1455, Fust and Schoeffer were already running a business geared to standardised production, and twenty years later large printing concerns were operating everywhere in all (sic) Europe.' (Febvre and Martin, 1976, p.125). In a rather special sense, the book was the first modern-style mass-produced industrial commodity. The sense I have in mind can be shewn if we compare the book to other early industrial products, such as textiles, bricks, or sugar. For these commodities are *measured* in mathematical amounts (pounds or loads or pieces). A pound of sugar is simply a quantity, a convenient load, not an object in itself. The book, however – and here it prefigures the durables of our time – is a distinct, self-contained object, exactly reproduced on a large scale. One pound of sugar flows into the next; each book has its own eremitic self-sufficiency. (Small wonder that libraries, personal collections of mass-produced commodities, were already a familiar sight, in urban centres like Paris, by the sixteenth century.)

In this perspective, the newspaper is merely an 'extreme form' of the book, a book sold on a colossal scale, but of ephemeral popularity. Might we say: one-day best-sellers? The obsolescence of the newspaper on the morrow of its printing – curious that one of the earlier mass-produced commodities should so prefigure the inbuilt obsolescence of modern durables – nonetheless, for just this reason, creates this extraordinary mass ceremony: the almost precisely simultaneous consumption ('imagining') of the newspaper-as-fiction. We know that particular morning and evening editions will overwhelmingly be consumed between this hour and that, only on this day, not that. (Contrast sugar, the use of which proceeds in an unclocked, continuous flow; it may go bad, but it does not go out of date.) The significance of this mass ceremony – Hegel observed that newspapers serve modern man as a substitute for morning prayers – is paradoxical. It is performed in silent privacy, in the lair of the skull. Yet each communicant is well aware that the ceremony he performs is being replicated simultaneously by thousands (or millions) of others of whose existence he is confident, yet of whose identity he has not the slightest notion. Furthermore, this ceremony is incessantly repeated at daily or half-daily intervals throughout the calendar. What more vivid figure for the secular, historically-clocked, imagined community can be envisioned? At the same time, the newspaper reader, observing exact replicas of his own paper being consumed by his subway, barbershop, or residential neighbours, is continually reassured that the imagined world is visibly rooted in everyday life. As with *Noli Me Tangere*, fiction seeps quietly and continuously into reality, creating that remarkable confidence of community in anonymity which is the hallmark of modern nations.

Notes

1. Nicholas Breakspear held the office of pontiff between 1154 and 1159 under the name Adrian IV.
2. Henri de Montesquieu (1973) *Persian Letters*, Penguin, p. 81. The *Lettres Persanes* first appeared in 1721.
3. Gellner stresses the typical foreignness of dynasties, but interprets the phenomenon too narrowly: local aristocrats prefer an alien monarch because he will not take sides in their internal rivalries. *Thought and Change*, p. 136.
4. Rizal wrote this novel in the colonial language (Spanish), which was then the lingua franca of the ethnically diverse Eurasian and native elites. Alongside the novel appeared also for the first time a 'nationalist' press, not only in Spanish but in such 'ethnic' languages as Tagalog and Ilocano.
5. After a brief, meteoric career as a radical journalist, Marco was interned by the Dutch colonial authorities in Boven Digul, one of the world's earliest concentration camps, deep in the interior swamps of western New Guinea. There he died in 1932, after six years confinement.
6. As translated by Paul Tickell in his *Three Early Indonesian Short Stories by Mas Marco Kartodikromo (c. 1890–1932)*, p. 7. Emphasis added.

References

AUERBACH, E., (1957) *Mimesis: The Representation of Reality in Western Literature*, Garden City, NY, Doubleday Anchor

BENJAMIN, W., (1973) *Illuminations*, London, Fontana.

BLOCH, M., (1961) *Feudal Society* (2 vols), Chicago, University of Chicago Press.

FEBVRE, L., and MARTIN, H.-J. (1976) *The Coming of the Book*, London, New Left Books.

FRANCO, J., (1969) *An Introduction to Spanish-American Literature*, Cambridge, Cambridge University Press.

GELLNER, E., (1964) *Thought and Change*, London, Weidenfeld and Nicolson.

JASZI, O., (1929) *The Dissolution of the Habsburg Monarchy*, Chicago, University of Chicago Press.

NAIRN, T., (1977) *The Break-up of Britain*, London, New Left Books.

RENAN, E. (1947) 'Qu'est-ce qu'une nation?', in *Oeuvres Complètes*, vol. 1., Paris, Calmann Levy.

7 Authority and Allegiance

Roger Scruton

From *The Meaning of Conservatism* by Roger Scruton, 1980, Reproduced by permission of the publishers, Penguin Books.

[. . .] Conservatism originates in an attitude to civil society, and it is from a conception of civil society that its political doctrine is derived. But a political doctrine must contain a motive to action, and a source of appeal. The conservative, unable as he is to appeal to a utopian future, or to any future that is not, as it were, already contained in the present and past, must avail himself of conceptions which are both directly applicable to things as they are and at the same time indicative of a motivating force in men. And this force must be as great as the desire for the 'freedom' and 'social justice' offered by his rivals. There are three concepts which immediately present themselves, and whose contemporary application we must examine: the concepts of authority, allegiance and tradition.

Authority and Power

It is a remarkable fact that people recognize authority in their fellows, in social arrangements, in institutions, and in the state. It is equally remarkable that this authority can command their allegiance, to such an extent that they might as willingly die for its sake as for the sake of any ideal or any religious creed. In so far as people have shown this disposition to sacrifice their lives for something greater than themselves then, historically speaking, the nation and the social order must rival religion as the principal beneficiaries of the gesture.[. . .]

'Authority' can mean many things. In particular, it can mean either established or legitimate power. In either sense it can be granted, delegated, removed, respected, ignored, opposed. A person who has authority has it from a certain source – although it is well if he has authority in another sense, according to which it means not the legitimate or established principle of rule, but the natural gift to command allegiance.[. . .]

[An] analogy with the family is useful if we are to understand the role of authority in politics. It is clear from the start that a child must be acted upon by its parents' power: its very love for them will accord to them that power, and parents no more escape from its exercise by being permissive than does an officer cease to command his troops by leaving them constantly at ease. A child is what it is by virtue of its parents' will, and consequently the parent has an indefeasible obligation to form and influence the child's development. In this very process is power, and it is of necessity an established power since it resides already with the parent at the child's first coming into the world. Now there is a sense in which every child does not only need its parents to exercise that power, but will also demand that they do so, to the extent that it cherishes their protection. There can be no ministering to the love of a child, and no granting of love, that is not also, in the first instance, an exercise of established power. For how is the child to recognize, from all those beings that surround it, the object which is its parent, that is, its principle of protection and its source of love? Surely it must feel the influence of a will in its life, of a desire *for* its life, besides its own. It must feel the constraint of another's love for it. And it is only in recognizing the existence of an objective power over what it will do that the child is pulled out of its self-immersion into the recognition of its parent as an autonomous being, a being who not only gives love but gives it freely, and towards whom it owes love in return. The kind of personal love that we envisage as the end of family union requires, as its precondition, the sense of established power – the child's unformed recognition that, in respect of at least one other being, he is helpless – combined with the growing awareness that the power of that being is also an exercise of freedom. And it is a similar recognition of constraint, helplessness, and subjection to external will that heralds the citizen's realization of his membership of society; in this recognition love of one's country is born.

Consider the other side of family loyalties. We are apt to think of children as having a responsibility towards their parents, a responsibility that in no way reflects any merely contractual right, but which is simply *due* to the parents as a recognition of the filial tie. This sense of obligation is not founded in justice – which is the sphere of free actions between beings who *create* their moral ties – but rather in respect, honour, or (as the Romans called it) piety. To neglect my parents in old age is not an act of injustice but an act of impiety. Impiety is the refusal to recognize as legitimate a demand that does not arise from consent or choice. And we see that the behaviour of children towards their parents cannot be understood unless we admit this ability to recognize a bond that is 'transcendent', that exists, as it were 'objectively', outside the sphere of individual choice. It is this ability that it is transferred by the citizen from hearth and home to place, people and country. The bond of society – as the conservative sees it – is just such a 'transcendent' bond, and it is inevitable that the citizen will be disposed to recognize its legitimacy, will be disposed, in other words, to bestow authority upon the existing order. He will be deterred from doing so largely by acts of arbitrary power, or by a general 'unfriendliness' in the public order, of the kind experienced by the deprived and unfostered child.

Authority, in the sense that we have considered, is an enormous artifact. By which I mean, not that authority is intentionally constructed, but rather that it exists only in so far as men exercise, understand and submit to it. The condition of society presupposes this general connivance, and a conservative will seek to uphold all those practices and institutions – among which, of course, the family is pre-eminent – through which the habits of allegiance are acquired [. . .]. The conservative believes in the power of state as necessary to the state's authority, and will seek to establish and enforce that power in the face of every influence that opposes it. However, his desire is to see power standing not naked in the forum of politics, but clothed in constitution, operating always through an adequate system of law so that its movement seems never barbarous or oppressive, but always controlled and inevitable, an expression of the civilized vitality through which allegiance is inspired. The constitution, therefore, and the institutions which sustain it, will always lie at the heart of conservative thinking. The conservative places his faith in arrangements that are known and tried, and wishes to imbue them with all the authority necessary to constitute an accepted and objective public realm. It is from this that his respect for tradition and custom arises, and not from any end – such as freedom – towards which these practices are seen as a means.

Allegiance

Consider, then, the concept of allegiance. It is allegiance which defines the condition of society, and which constitutes society as something greater than the 'aggregate of individuals' that the liberal mind perceives. It is proper for a conservative to be sceptical of claims made on behalf of the value of the individual, if these claims should conflict with the allegiance necessary to society, even though he may wish the *state* (in the sense of the apparatus of government) to stand in a fairly loose relation to the activities of individual citizens. Individuality too is an artifact, an achievement which depends upon the social life of man. And indeed, as many historians have pointed out, it is a recent venture of the human spirit for men and women to define themselves as individuals, as creatures whose nature and value is summed up in their unique individual being. The condition of man requires that the individual, while he exists and acts as an autonomous being, does so only because he can first identify himself as something greater – as a member of society, group, class, state or nation, of some arrangement to which he may not attach a name, but which he recognizes instinctively as home. Politically speaking, this bond of allegiance – which, seen from the heights of intellectual speculation as 'my station and its duties', is experienced as a peculiar certainty in the activity of day to day – is of a value which transcends the value of individuality. For the majority of men, the bond of allegiance has immediate authority, while the call to individuality is unheard. It is therefore wrong to consider that a statesman has some kind of duty to minister to the second of these, and ignore the first [. . .].

A full understanding of the idea of allegiance will require in its turn an understanding of tradition, custom and ceremony – of the totality of practices through which the citizen is able to perceive his allegiance as an *end*. For the liberal, allegiance to society is a means: 'stick to this arrangement and on the whole you'll be left to yourself'. But the conservative cannot see it as a means to an end, since there is no description of the end in question that does not refer back to the values – and hence to the customs, institutions and allegiances – of those who pursue it. It follows that while the forms of patriotism will be many and varied, they will seek always to translate themselves into *symbolic* acts, acts which resist translation as 'means to an end'.

Consider the Englishman's allegiance to the Crown, as he envisages and enacts it. Monarchy is an institution, with a complex constitutional background, that elevates the person of the monarch above the realm of individual character and endows him or her with the dignity and, so to speak, the objectivity of office. It is not the personal qualities of the Queen that draw the Englishman to her nor is it any considered knowledge of the function and history of the Crown. It is rather a sense of the monarch as a symbol of nationhood, as an incarnation of the historical entity of which he is a part. His loyalty to the monarch requires ceremonial enactment, customary usage, an established code of deference: for this is the style of all symbolic gestures in which society and individual are merged.

Now a conservative is likely to value the institution of monarchy, and the kind of patriotism that it engenders. For the legitimacy of monarchical rule arises 'transcendentally', in the manner of the duties and obligations of family life. The monarch is not chosen for his personal attributes, nor does he have obligations and expectations which are the subject-matter of any 'social contract'. He is simply the representation of sovereignty, and its ceremonial presence. His will as monarch is not his individual will, but the will of state. The monarch forms part of that surface of concepts and symbols whereby the citizen can perceive his social identity, and perceive society not as a means to an end, but as an end in itself. Attachment to the monarch is therefore patriotism in a pure form, a form that could not be translated into attachment to a policy, or to a choice of means [. . .].

There is no general explanation of *how* men re-create and accept traditions. Nor is it easy to draw the line between genuine re-creation and the establishment of new and divergent social forms. But in all attempts to restore, re-create and assimilate tradition, the feature of continuity remains. When a man acts from tradition he sees what he *now* does as belonging to a pattern that transcends the focus of his present interest, binding it to what has previously been done, and done successfully. (This is obvious from the case of artistic creation.) Naturally there are rival traditions, and it would be vain to pretend that there is reason to belong to all of them. There are traditions of torture, crime and revolution. The traditions which the conservative fosters and upholds must therefore satisfy independent criteria. First, they must have the weight of a *successful* history – which is to say that they must be the palpable remainder of something that has flourished, and not the latest in a series of abortive starts. Secondly, they must engage the loyalty of their participants, in the deep sense of moulding their idea of what they are and should be. (Contrast the traditions of family life with those of torture.) Finally, they must point to something durable, something which survives and gives meaning to the acts that emerge from it.

But what does this tradition concretely amount to? It must include all those practices which serve to define the individual's 'being in society'. It constitutes his image of himself as a fragment of the greatest social organism, and at the same time as the whole of that organism implicit in this individual part. The institution of the family, as it has variously developed, provides a clear example [...]. But there are others, such as the customs which surround the momentous occasions of birth, coupling and death, the customs of hospitality, rivalry and class allegiance, of manners, dress and common courtesy. There are also the institutions of religion, in which man's desire for an identity greater than his nature provides reaches out of history altogether, to what is outside time and change. Only some of these institutions, it might be thought, are truly political. But to take such a view is to take too narrow a view of politics. Every tradition of any importance in the life of the citizen will tend to become part of the establishment of a state. This principle [...] is part of the natural history of politics, and shows the continuing necessity for political action to extend beyond the bounds of economic management. It is illustrated not only by the explicit establishment of the Church and, through the operation of law, of the family and private property, but by the implicit establishment of class rule in parliamentary institutions, by the more recent establishment of the traditions of organized labour in the trade-union movement, and by the extension of law (less automatic in America than in England, but manifest even there) to protect every aspect of social life, just so soon as it seems to be of more than individual concern [...].

Society exists through authority, and the recognition of this authority requires the allegiance to a bond that is not contractual but transcendent, in the manner of the family tie. Such allegiance requires tradition and custom through which to find enactment. But tradition is no static thing. It is the active achievement of continuity; it can be restored, rescued and amended as grace and opportunity allow.

8 National Consciousness in Britain

Hugh Seton-Watson

From *Nations and States: An Inquiry into the Origins of Nations and the Politics of Nationalism* by Hugh Seton-Watson, 1977. Reproduced by permission of the publishers, Methuen.

In the fourteenth and fifteenth centuries there slowly emerged a factor of decisive importance for English national consciousness: the formation of the English language.

At first two languages coexisted in England. The conquerors spoke a rather provincial form of French. Anglo-Saxons of the upper classes, and those who aspired to higher office or higher social status under the conquerors, learned this Norman French. The bulk of the population spoke various Anglo-Saxon dialects: the earlier supremacy of the Wessex dialect disappeared as there was now no significant Anglo-Saxon literature. For their part, many of the Normans learned an Anglo-Saxon speech in order to converse with their subjects. The accession of Henry II in 1154 brought an influx of Frenchmen from central France or Provence who were influenced by the literary renaissances of both Paris and Languedoc. From this time the cultural links of the upper class of England with France no longer went through Normandy. During the next two centuries, though higher French culture prevailed in court circles, the nobility of England came to speak increasingly the language of the country. However, this language itself rapidly changed. It was approximately from 1250 to 1400 that the language became flooded with French words: something like 10,000 can be traced to this period. In the fourteenth century the dialect of the area north-east of London, the most densely populated and commercially prosperous region, prevailed over other dialects, and from it emerged the language of the capital. The year 1362 is a date of symbolic importance: it was then that English replaced Norman French in the law courts, and that the opening of Parliament was conducted for the first time in English.

This process is usually known as the replacement of Old English (pre-Norman Anglo-Saxon) by Middle English. It is, of course, true that there is a continuity between Anglo-Saxon and English. The basic structure and syntax remained, and the basic words most used by simple people remained the original Anglo-Saxon

110

words, somewhat modified. One may therefore say that what had happened was that English had been enriched by the addition of French words. Yet this seems an inadequate description. The process was more than the acquisition of foreign loan-words – as Latin words passed through the church into German or Polish, or as Arabic words passed into Spanish. Rather, one should say that two languages, Anglo-Saxon and French, flowed together, and from them emerged a new language, neither Anglo-Saxon nor French but English. As English grew into a modern, rich, flexible language, evolving under the guidance of Wycliffe, Chaucer, Spenser and Shakespeare, innumerable concepts became expressible in synonyms of Anglo-Saxon or French origin [. . .].

One might therefore risk the generalisation that, though England was a land of human civilisation from the time of Julius Caesar, and even earlier, an English nation and an English language only came into existence in the fourteenth century. From this time only dates the history of England, as opposed to the history of the peoples of Britain. In Scotland, the diversity of peoples and languages remained greater until later: it is arguable that the formation of a Scottish nation was hardly completed before the sixteenth century.

English national consciousness, and the pride of educated Englishmen in their own language, were strengthened by the long wars with France and by the fluctuating discontent of churchmen with the claims made on their devotion by the foreign hierarchy of a church torn by schism. In the sixteenth century various forces came together to forge a strong sense of national identity. The Reformation was both a movement of ideas and a rejection of foreign domination. The English translations of the Bible, the religious polemical literature in English, enriched the language, and coincided with a great flowering of poetry. Tudor despotism appealed both to the greed of landowners and merchants for the wealth of the monasteries and to resentment against foreigners – both the Frenchmen who had been enemies of England for two hundred years and the Spaniards whose sea-borne wealth offered prizes to English raiders. In the reign of Elizabeth the upsurge of literature, the ferment of religious and political ideas, the rise of new social forces and the sense of mortal danger and crisis, all contributed to the emergence of an English nation. For hundreds of thousands, if not perhaps yet for all, subjects of the crown loyalty was now given not only to feudal superior, or church, or distant sovereign, but to the nation: the links which bound the population together were not only vertical but also horizontal.

The growing strength of the English proved to be a mixed blessing for the Welsh. In September 1400 a Welsh landowner, Owain Glyn Dwr (or Glendower), led a rebellion in the north. Its origin lay at least largely in Owain's personal grievances and land disputes, but it soon became a rising of the Welsh against the English, extending to a large part of the principality. The rebels were rather successful until 1406 when the English reconquest began to gain ground. By 1410 the revolt was almost over, and Owain had mysteriously disappeared. The accession of Henry VII, a Welshman, to the English throne aroused some hopes in Wales, but it was in fact the Tudor monarchs who effectively centralised government and insisted on the status of English as the sole official language, while

Welsh continued to be spoken by the humbler classes among themselves.

In Scotland, too, a language developed from the flowing together of Saxon and French, though with less of the latter, and with rather more from Celtic and Scandinavian sources, than in the south. This language was spoken not only in the east of Scotland but also in northern England. Scots, or 'northern English', was spoken at the Scottish court and by the social elite (who might or might not also speak Gaelic), as well as by the Lowland population as a whole. It was the language of the poets Robert Henryson and William Dunbar. It might have developed as a distinct literary language into modern times had not the union of the crowns in 1603 brought the predominance of southern English through its extension to the court, administration and upper class of Scotland [. . .].

The English and Scottish nations [. . .] both existed long before modern doctrines of nationalism were formulated. English nationalism never existed, since there was no need for either a doctrine or an independence struggle. English national consciousness certainly existed for five centuries or more; but it is arguable that during the nineteenth century it disappeared, merging into a British national consciousness, which the English tended to appropriate to themselves. Many Scots and Welsh also acquired this British national consciousness; but others continued to feel themselves members of Scottish and Welsh nations, while sharing loyalty to the British state and British empire, and being moved in turn by British patriotism, British imperialism and (after 1947) British inverted imperialism. However, among Scots and Welsh not only national consciousness but also nationalism existed, since varying but considerable numbers of those who constituted the Scottish and Welsh nations felt, as the English nation could not feel, the need to defend their national identities within the British state, or even to seek independence.

The Welsh were less disturbed by the Reformation than the English or Scots: they remained obedient to the old faith for longer, and passed over to the new with less commotion. It was in the eighteenth century that important religious differences appeared between Welsh and English, owing to the rapid spread of Methodism. The chapel became no less the symbol of Welsh nationality than the kirk of Scottish. The struggle to disestablish the official Church of Wales, which continued until the eve of the First World War, mobilised Welsh national feeling. Still more important was the revival of Welsh as a literary language, which dates, like Methodism, from the eighteenth century. The yearly *eisteddfod* festivals were instituted in 1789, their prime mover being Thomas Jones of Corwen. In the early nineteenth century Welsh was spoken by the great majority of the population of the still very rural principality. The threat to Welsh came from the industrial revolution, based on the rich southern coal fields. Industry brought to the Welsh, as to other peoples before and since, both wealth and misery, but it also brought floods of English immigrants into Wales as well as drawing Welshmen to jobs in England. At the beginning of the twentieth century less than half the population of the principality spoke Welsh, and by the mid-1970s only about a fifth. Massive unemployment in the 1930s brought mass support for socialism; but by the 1960s fear for the future of the language and resentment of the impact of uniform

English-controlled bureaucracy (which did not diminish when Labour came to power) was helping the nationalist party Plaid Cymru, which called in deliberately vague terms for Welsh self-government.

In Scotland difference of language was comparatively unimportant. Gaelic was still spoken by about 80,000 persons in the 1970s and there was a remarkable renaissance of Gaelic poetry. But though this gave hope that the language would be saved, it could not be seriously expected that it would become the chief language of Scotland. Attempts were also made to develop a literary non-Celtic language, Lallans, continuing the tradition of Henryson and Dunbar. This too produced some fine poems by Douglas Young and others; but the Scottish political revival in the twentieth century could not, to the same extent as the Welsh, be based on language. In Scotland industrial development had much the same effect as in Wales, a growth of both wealth and poverty and considerable immigration; but the latter consisted less of English than of Irishmen, coming usually from material conditions worse than those of the Scots. Scottish industry, like Welsh, suffered from greater unemployment than English in the 1930s and from greater loss of export markets after 1945; and as in Wales the resultant discontent was largely expressed in socialism or communism. However, the belief that the Scots as a nation should have not only their own kirk, law, and schools but also their own political institutions never died out after 1707. It was stimulated by the Irish movement for Home Rule, and grew with the combination of economic hardship and cultural revival in the 1930s and afterwards. In the 1970s the Scottish National Party made good use of the hopes aroused by oil exploitation in the North Sea, most of which was in Scottish rather than English waters. But national unease among Scots was much more widespread than the electoral support, let alone the active membership, of the SNP. There was resentment at the attitude of so many Englishmen who while sincerely believing themselves not to be in any sense English imperialists, yet refused to recognise the distinct nationality of the Scots, talking as if the future of Scotland were simply a problem of decentralisation. There was also a growing feeling that not only had the British empire ceased to exist but that the actual and potential rulers of Britain (of whatever political persuasion) had lost all belief in themselves. These views might be mistaken, but the English politicians of the mid-1970s were doing very little to prove it [. . .]. In 1976 the United Kingdom was not united, and Great Britain was no longer great, due to the actions not of its enemies but of its own citizens.

The centuries-long process of union of Saxon-Danish, Anglo-Celtic and Celtic-Norse territories into one kingdom appeared in the first half of the twentieth century to have been rather successful. It also seemed to have been accepted by the Celtic Welsh; and the wounds left by the separation and partition of Ireland seemed to be healing.

A quarter century later none of this was true. Yet loyalty to a common British homeland, devotion to the British crown and pride in the British form of civilisation were not dead, and were not confined to the middle-aged or middle class. This is not less true because these sentiments were seldom expressed by politicians or media-merchants. The truth was that the four nations were bound together, whether they liked it or not, and that it would be better to live together peacefully in some sort of agreed confederation than to hate and tear each other to bits. It was for English and Irish politicians to show not only that they were able to be generous to each other and to the Scots and Welsh, but that they cared sufficiently for Britain and for Ireland to put the lives of the people who lived in both islands above their dogmas, vanities and fears.

9 Kailyard Culture

Tom Nairn

From: *The Break-up of Britain* by Tom Nairn, 1977. Reproduced by permission of the publishers, NLB.

During the age of nationalism, it has come to be taken for granted that the distinctively modern consciousness of nationality is 'natural': people are naturally, instinctively, national*ists* (and not merely aware of being different from other folk). But in reality nationalism was a historical construct, associated with certain social strata, at a certain characteristic period of their development. Amongst these, none was more important than the intelligentsia. The new commercial and industrial middle class was indisputably the dominant force in the process; yet the way this dominance was exerted – the form of their class hegemony – owed its character to new intellectuals. It was the latter who formulated the new ideologies that were needed, and manned the first new societies, parties and other organizations. It was they who, initially, enabled the bourgeoisie to 'enlarge its class sphere technically and ideologically', and so 'pose itself as an organism . . . capable of absorbing the entire society', etc. By accomplishing this task, the intellectuals also won for themselves a new and greater social significance: no longer the servants of a closed aristocratic élite, they became vital elements in the cohesion of society as a whole.

Nationalism was the most important and effective of such new ideologies. Normally it developed through a recognizable number of phases, over several generations, in all those territories where new middle classes felt that tolerable 'development' for their people was impossible without rapid mobilization of their own resources and rejection of 'alien rule'. Normally, too, this process was a revolutionary one – whether or not it ever resulted in a successful *coup d'état* – in the sense that it meant trying to get rid of a non-adaptable landlord *ancien régime*, its 'reactionary' intellectual caste, corrupt and non-populist 'traditions', and so on. One may say that during this long period, over most of Europe, the standard function of an intellectual class was in this task. This is of course not to maintain that all intellectuals were xenophobes or flag-wavers. But the centre of gravity of their rôle *as* a class, their collective definition within modern social conditions, lay in the way they educated one folk or another.

In Scotland, the intelligentsia was deprived of this typical 'nationalist' rôle. Its new intellectual strata were to be, in a sense, unemployed on their home terrain. There was no call for the usual services. Here, the old régime and its intellectuals had crumbled away without firing a shot: they were overwhelmed by the burgeoning growth of the Scottish Industrial Revolution and the new entrepreneurial bourgeoisie linked to it. No prolonged cultural subversion was required to pull down its bastions. William Ferguson notes 'The decline of the specifically Scottish intellectualism which throughout the eighteenth century had without conscious effort sustained the concept of a Scottish nation' (1968, p.319). This decline was now to be counterpointed by the rise of a new 'specifically Scottish' culture, less intellectualist and more romantic, advancing the new concept of nationality appropriate to the age.

Clearly, the country did not cease to produce individual intellectuals from its own separate and quite advanced educational system. The point is simply that they could not constitute any longer a coherent, national 'class', in a sense which it is quite hard to define but easy to recognize. The fact was emphasized, rather than disproved, by the well-known prominence of so many Victorian Scots in fields like medicine, engineering, and the natural sciences. As Ferguson comments again: 'The reputation won by Scotsmen in science . . . did little to enhance the culture of their country. This is far from being a singular case, for science stands independent of national contexts . . . For good or ill, therefore, science cannot nurture the irrational bonds that make nations'. Irrational bonds: this overstates the case, and concedes too much to German-romantic theories of nationalism. The bonds are non-rational and non-intellectual, rather than those of unreason. But the underlying point is valid: a 'national culture', in that sense which had become newly important, entailed an intellectual class able to express the particular realities of a country, in a romantic manner accessible to growing numbers of the reading public – a class operating actively in the zone of general and literary culture (rather than the specializations Scots became celebrated for).

The relationship between civil society and State in Scotland precluded a fully national culture in this sense. Instead, what it led to was a strange sort of sub-national culture. An anomalous historical situation could not engender a 'normal' culture: Scotland could not simply be adapted to the new, basically nationalist, rules of cultural evolution. But since the country could not help being affected by this evolution, it produced something like a stunted, caricatural version of it. The best title for this is perhaps 'cultural sub-nationalism'. It was cultural, because of course it could not be political; on the other hand this culture could not be straight-forwardly nationalist either – a direct substitute for political actions, like (e.g.) so much Polish literature of the nineteenth century. It could only be 'sub-nationalist', in the sense of venting its national content in various crooked ways – neurotically, so to speak, rather than directly.

Among the numerous strands in the neurosis, two are especially prominent: cultural emigration, and the Kailyard School. As we shall see, the two phenomena are in fact (and contrary to appearances) closely connected. And they are connected in a way which permits one to focus much more clearly upon the significant popular-cultural reality underlying both of them: vulgar tartanry.

Cultural emigration

In the most authoritative study of the Scottish nineteenth century cultural scene, David Craig remarks: 'The historian is left calling Victorian culture in Scotland "strangely rootless" . . . We have to recognize that there did not emerge along with modern Scotland a mature, "all-round" literature . . . ' (1961, pp.13–14). Later, he ascribes this surprising 'void' in culture to intellectual emigration: 'During the nineteenth century the country was emptied of the *majority* of its notable literary talents – men who, if they had stayed, might have thought to mediate their wisdom through the rendering of specifically Scottish experience. Of the leading British "sages" of the time an astonishingly high proportion were of Scottish extraction – the Mills, Macaulay, Carlyle, Ruskin, Gladstone' (ibid, p.273). Unemployable in their own country, these and many later emigrés quite naturally found themselves a function in the development of English culture. For England was a milieu *par excellence* of just that 'mature, all-round' and literary thought-world Craig refers to. It was an organic or 'rooted' national-romantic culture, in which literature – from Coleridge and Carlyle up to F. R. Leavis and E. P. Thompson – has consistently played a major role.

The rootless vacuum, the great 'absence', the 'cultural schizophrenia' William Ferguson mentions in a similar context: these are metaphors, which in turn invite decipherment. What was the actual presence they denote, in Scotland – the books they wrote and read, the thoughts they had, and so on? They did not ponder mightily and movingly upon the reality of nineteenth century Scotland – on the great Glasgow bourgeoisie of mid-century and onwards, the new class conflicts, the continuing tragedy of the Highlands. So what was there, instead of those missing Zolas and George Eliots, those absent Thomas Manns and Vergas? What there was increasingly from the 1820s onwards, until it became a vast tide washing into the present day, was the Scots 'Kailyard' tradition.

The Kailyard tradition

This was, in effect, the cabbage-patch, the home 'backyard' left behind by the emigration of so much high-culture talent. Craig traces its origins to the time of John Galt's *Annals of the Parish* (1813) and *Blackwood's Magazine*, but its major triumphs were later. The opposite of mature all-roundness is presumably infantile partiality, or fragmentariness. This label certainly fits the Kailyard industry. In his *Literary History of Scotland* (1903) J. H. Millar notes that in the 1880s two books by J. M. Barrie (*Auld Licht Idylls* and *A Window in Thrums*) ' . . . for some mysterious reason caught the fancy of the English public to which the greater part of the dialogue must have been wholly unintelligible . . . The vogue of Mr Barrie's weaver-bodies and elders of the Original Secession was not long in bringing into the field a host of rivals; and the "Kailyard" School of Literature as it has been called, presently burst into existence . . . ' [. . .]

Kailyardism was the definition of Scotland as consisting wholly of small towns full of small-town 'characters' given to bucolic intrigue and wise sayings. At first the central figures were usually Ministers of the Kirk (as were most of the authors) but later on schoolteachers and doctors got into the act. Their housekeepers always have a shrewd insight into human nature. Offspring who leave for the big city frequently come to grief, and are glad to get home again (peching and hoasting to hide their feelings). In their different ways, village cretins and ne'er-do-wells reinforce the essentially healthy *Weltanschauung* of the place.

There is surely no need to go on. Everyone in Scotland knows only too well what is being referred to. The Penguin *Companion to Literature* defines the school as 'exploiting the sentimental aspects of Lowland life during the period 1880-1914', mainly through minor writers who 'pursued Scottish country quaintness into whimsical middens'. In fact it arose before 1880 and it prospers at the present day. Naturally, it has been transferred to the TV screen [e.g. in *Dr Finlay's Casebook*] . . . In Dundee our own cabbage-patch publishing Mafia, the D. C. Thomson gang, still thrives as George Blake observed it doing forty years ago, through 'the careful cultivation of the Kailyard strain' (1951, p.85).

What is the significance of this remarkably powerful and persistent sub-culture? In one sense, it may seem just another example of a widespread European trend, whereby in the nineteenth century provincial manners and characters were often made into *Kitsch* images for the new, mass reading public of the cities. Yet the very appeal and longevity of the phenomenon, as well as its huge popularity in Scotland itself, suggest more than this.[. . .]

The overall structure of this modern culture in fact corresponds exactly to the dilemma of Scotland's social structure since the Industrial Revolution. Emigration and Kailyardery are not merely individual, subjective responses to the situation, and it is therefore unjust to view them as treachery or loss of nerve. The cultural sub-nationalism they conspired to foster was, in its way, as much of a historical 'necessity' as the major national cultures produced in England, Germany, and the rest.

This may become clearer when one reflects on the extent to which the two main factors in the neurosis are connected. 'Thrums', 'Drumtochty' and 'Tannochbrae' were all creations of émigrés. They and their unspeakable progeny were produced, also, very largely for a foreign reading public (i.e. to pander to hankerings not themselves especially Scottish in origin).[. . .]

Whether as the pawky simplicities of village life, or as swaggering through the heather claymore in hand, 'Scotland' in the sub-romantic sense was largely defined by émigrés. The Kailyard was – and still is – very much the reverse of the coin of emigration. Its lack of 'human and political dignity' does not express some collective fault in the Scots psyche, but the 'historical fact' of the relationship between the intelligentsia and the people. This relationship was determined by the fact that the Scottish bourgeoisie did not face the need to form *its own* 'national community', through the mediation of a more rooted intellectual class and a more complex and sophisticated national culture (i.e. more 'mature, all-round', and so on). This is why it is vain to censure the writers and other intellectuals retrospectively for their failure to come up to European norms. They could not deal with modern experience in Scotland because in the relevant sense there *was no* 'modern experience': such experience was the product of culture, not its pre-existing social basis. And this culture arose in certain characteristic social and historical conditions which were, inevitably, lacking here.

Rendered jobless in these circumstances – without a middle class sufficiently exercised over the usual national problems, without a national capital-city of the kind which had become indispensable – what could the intelligentsia do? Its natural posture became to seek work outside, but at the same time (aware of its distinct origins and history) to look constantly backwards and inwards, in a typical vein of deforming nostalgia – constantly confirming a false, 'infantile' image of the country quite divorced from its 'real problems'. The real problem, of course, did not lie in the fact of factories, new cities, bourgeois family dramas, class conflicts, etc. – it lay, for the intellectuals (and therefore for the national culture) in the fact that these phenomena *did not pose* a cultural problem that had to be solved in specifically Scottish terms. [Thus a figurative 'schizophrenia' seems to have been] imposed upon an intellectual stratum which, although strongly national, was in its material conditions of existence quite unable to be national*ist* – unable to secrete a complete national-popular culture like its English or French peers.[. . .]

Popular tartanry

The dilemma is not 'merely' an intellectuals' one. Just as the two horns of it are in fact intimately connected, so the whole thing is related to the much larger field of popular culture. For Kailyard is popular in Scotland. It is recognizably intertwined with that prodigious array of *Kitsch* symbols, slogans, ornaments, banners, war-cries, knick-knacks, music-hall heroes, icons, conventional sayings and sentiments (not a few of them 'pithy') which have for so long resolutely defended the name of 'Scotland' to the world. Annie S. Swan and Cronin provided no more than the relatively decent outer garb for this vast tartan monster. In their work the thing trots along doucely enough, on a lead. But it is something else to be with it (e.g.) in a London pub on International night, or in the crowd at the annual Military Tattoo in front of Edinburgh Castle. How intolerably vulgar! What unbearable, crass, mindless philistinism! One knows that *Kitsch* is a large constituent of mass popular culture in every land: but this is ridiculous!

Ridiculous or not, it is obviously extremely strong. In this sense, as the main body of cultural sub-nationalism, it appears to represent a national-popular tradition which has persisted more or less in the way one would expect. Precisely because it has been unconnected with a 'higher' or normal, nationalist-style culture during the formative era of modern society, it has evolved blindly. The popular consciousness of separate identity, uncultivated by 'national' experience or culture in the usual sense, has become curiously fixed or fossilized on the level of the *image d'Epinal* and Auld Lang Syne, of the Scott Monument, Andy Stewart and the *Sunday Post* – to the point of forming a huge, virtually self-contained universe of *Kitsch*. [. . .]

References

BLAKE, G. (1951) *Barrie and the Kailyard School.*
CRAIG, D. (1961) *Scottish Literature and the Scottish People, 1680–1830.*
FERGUSON, W. (1968) *Scotland: 1689 to the Present* (vol. IV of the *Edinburgh History of Scotland*)

10 The Context, Performance and Meaning of Ritual: The British Monarchy and the Invention of Tradition

David Cannadine

From *The Invention of Tradition* edited by Eric Hobsbawm and Terence Ranger, 1983. Reproduced by permission of the publishers, Cambridge University Press.

[I]

In 1820, *The Black Book*, a radical critique of the corruption and power of the English Establishment, made this comment on royal ritual:

> Pageantry and show, the parade of crowns and coronets, of gold keys, sticks, white wands and black rods; of ermine and lawn, maces and wigs, are ridiculous when men become enlightened, when they have learned that the real object of government is to confer the greatest happiness on the people at the least expense.

Forty years later, Lord Robert Cecil, the future third marquess of Salisbury, having watched Queen Victoria open parliament, wrote with scarcely more approval:

> Some nations have a gift for ceremonial. No poverty of means or absence of splendour inhibits them from making any pageant in which they take part both real and impressive. Everybody falls naturally into his proper place, throws himself without effort into the spirit of the little drama he is enacting, and instinctively represses all appearance of constraint or distracted attention.

But he went on to explain:

This aptitude is generally confined to the people of a southern climate and of non-Teutonic parentage. In England the case is exactly the reverse. We can afford to be more splendid than most nations; but some malignant spell broods over all our most solemn ceremonials, and inserts into them some feature which makes them all ridiculous . . . Something always breaks down, somebody contrives to escape doing his part, or some bye-motive is suffered to interfere and ruin it all.

Taken together, these quotations exemplify contemporary attitudes towards the ceremonial of the British monarchy during the first three-quarters of the nineteenth century. The first argued that as the population was becoming better educated, royal ritual would soon be exposed as nothing more than primitive magic, a hollow sham. And the second suggested, on the basis of impeccable inside knowledge, that in any case the pageantry centred on the monarchy was conspicuous for its ineptitude rather than for its grandeur.

Today in England the situation is the exact reverse. With the possible exception of the papacy, no head of state is surrounded by more popular ritual than Queen Elizabeth II. The mass of the population may indeed have become better educated, as the authors of *The Black Book* had hoped; but they have not, as a result, lost their liking for the secular magic of monarchy. On the contrary, as Ian Gilmour has noted, 'Modern societies still need myth and ritual. A monarch and his family supply it.' (1969, p. 313). And, in additional contrast to this earlier period, the ceremonial is now splendidly performed, so much so that observers have assumed that this has always been the case. 'All the pageantry and grandeur of a thousand-year-old tradition'; 'a pageantry that has gone on for hundreds of years'; 'all the precision that comes from centuries of precedent'; 'the English are particularly good at ceremonial': these are the phrases of contemporary commentators and journalists as they describe the great royal ceremonials. However accurate may have been the accounts of *The Black Book* and of Cecil in their time, they have ceased to be valid today. The purpose of this [article] is to describe and explain the subsequent changes in the context and nature of English royal ceremonial which have rendered their comments irrelevant and confounded their predictions. [. . .]

Four distinct phases in the development of the ceremonial image of the British monarchy [can be discerned.] The first period, extending from the 1820s, and before, to the 1870s, is a period of ineptly managed ritual, performed in what was still preponderantly a localized, provincial, pre-industrial society. The second, beginning in 1877, when Victoria was made empress of India, and extending until the outbreak of the First World War was, in Britain as in much of Europe, the heyday of 'invented tradition', a time when old ceremonials were staged with an expertise and appeal which had been lacking before, and when new rituals were self-consciously invented to accentuate this development. Then, from 1918 until Queen Elizabeth's coronation in 1953 came the period in which the British persuaded themselves that they were good at ceremonial because they always had been – a belief in large part made possible because Britain's former rivals in royal ritual – Germany, Austria and Russia – had dispensed with their monarchies, leaving Britain alone in the field. Finally, since 1953, the decline of Britain as a great power, combined with the massive impact of television, suggests that the 'meaning' of royal ceremonial has once again changed profoundly, although as yet the outlines of this new period of change can only be dimly discerned. [. . .]

[II]

From the 1870s onwards, in England as in other western countries, the position of the head of state was ceremonially enhanced. A venerated monarch, conveyed in a splendid state coach along triumphal thoroughfares was no longer, as his predecessors had been, just the head of society, but was now seen to be the head of the nation as well. In England, as elsewhere in Europe, the unprecedented developments in industry and in social relationships, and the massive expansion of the yellow press, made it both necessary and possible to present the monarch, in all the splendour of his ritual, in this essentially new way, as a symbol of consensus and continuity to which all might defer. And, as international relations became increasingly tense, this added a further inducement to the 'invention of tradition', as national rivalry was both expressed and sublimated in ceremonial competition. Only in one major regard did the English experience differ from that of other western nations: in Russia, Germany, Italy, America and Austria, this efflorescence of ceremonial was centred on a head of state who still exercised real power. But in England, while the ceremonial shadow of power was cast over the monarch, the substance increasingly lay elsewhere.

In retrospect, these developments in context and circumstance seem a helpful way of explaining the changes in the performance and 'meaning' of ritual. But at the time, it was not, perhaps, as deliberate as this might imply. For it was only slowly, as one ceremony followed another, that this coherent syntax and language of symbols and meanings emerged. In 1887, after fifty years on the throne, the Widow at Windsor was persuaded – although only with the greatest reluctance – to participate in a grand state pageant in London. It was, indeed, a risk, for her recent unpopularity made it impossible to predict what sort of reception she would receive. And Victoria's emphatic refusal to wear the crown and robes of state only seemed to give substance to such forebodings. Even Princess Alexandra, whose powers of persuasion over the queen were unrivalled, failed in her attempts to get Victoria to change her mind. Nevertheless, the resulting Golden Jubilee, with its procession and service of thanksgiving in the Abbey, was a great success: 'Pageantry such as this generation never saw . . . The grandest state ceremony of this generation' (*Illustrated London News*, 25 June 1887). The Diamond Jubilee, planned with more confidence and certainty ten years later, was even more splendid. As the queen herself noted, with delighted surprise:

> No one, ever, I believe, has met with such an ovation as was given to me passing through these six miles of streets . . . The crowds were quite indescribable, and their enthusiasm truly marvellous and deeply touching.

Thereafter came Victoria's funeral, the coronation and funeral of Edward VII, the coronation and durbar of George V, and the investiture of his son as Prince of Wales at Carnarvon Castle. Indeed, by this time, departments of state and of the royal household, which had been woefully ignorant of precedent and ceremonial in 1887, had become expert. Hitches might still occur, as when the horses bolted at Victoria's funeral. But such mishaps were rare and, in this particular instance, were themselves immediately incorporated in 'tradition'. Meticulous planning, popular enthusiasm, widespread reporting and unprecedented splendour were successfully allied. Significantly, while the funerals of Nelson and Wellington were both more grand and more popular then those accorded to the early-nineteenth-century monarchs, the last rites of Victoria and Edward far outshone the state funeral accorded to Gladstone.

Insofar as the success of these pageants depended on improved performance, three people in particular were of major significance. The first was Reginald Brett, Viscount Esher, the *éminence grise* in British governing circles at the turn of the century, friend of Victoria, Edward VII and George V, secretary of the Office of Works from 1895 to 1902, and deputy constable and lieutenant governor of Windsor Castle from 1901-28. He was responsible, not only for the redecoration of the royal palaces and the sorting of the royal archives after Victoria's death, but also for the overall planning of every great state pageant from the Diamond Jubilee of Victoria to the funeral of Edward VII. In theory, responsibility for such occasions lay with the duke of Norfolk as hereditary earl marshal, the master of the horse, the lord steward and the lord chamberlain. But Esher's charm, tact, historical sense, flair for organization and love of ceremonial ensured that the lion's share of the work was done by him. And there was much to do. For it was so long since there had last been a major royal event that no one could remember what to do. 'The ignorance of historical precedent', Esher once noted in exasperation, 'in men whose business it is to know, is wonderful'. But despite such obstacles, his carefully rehearsed and meticulously researched pageants were triumphantly successful, bringing him 'scores of congratulatory letters' from the royal family and politicians alike. Although Victoria did feel, true to her lifelong antipathy to the Grand Old Man, that Esher's careful and tactful arrangements for Gladstone's state funeral in Westminster Abbey smacked of 'misdirected enthusiasm'.

Esher's interest in royal ritual was matched by that of Edward VII himself. For while his mother had been a reluctant participant in public ceremonial, who loathed splendid costume and public appearances, Edward was eager to 'show himself to his subjects, clothed in his attributes of sovereignty' (Bodley, 1903, p.205). He had been a constant critic of his mother's mournful gloom, and had also bitterly resented the way in which his nephew, the Kaiser, had outshone him in splendour. So, as king, there was a double incentive for him to enhance the grandeur of monarchy. And, with the assistance of Esher, he succeeded spectacularly. Indeed, it was Esher himself who paid tribute to his master's 'curious power of visualising a pageant', his 'promptness, imagination and *invention*', which were, he noted, significantly, 'the primary gifts without which *improvisation* is hopeless' (my italics). Sensing more acutely the competitive element in the new ceremonial, another courtier noted, with evident approval: 'Our King makes a better show than William. He has more graciousness and dignity. William is ungracious, nervous and plain'.

So it was entirely characteristic that one of Edward's earliest acts as king was to revive the state opening of parliament as a full-dress ceremonial occasion, with a procession in the state coach through the streets of London, and with the king, clad in his full regalia, personally reading the speech from the throne – something which Victoria had not done in forty years. And, ironically, it was Edward's funeral, in which the ubiquitous Esher once more had a hand, which was 'the grandest state pageant in which he was to take part'. Of special significance was the lying-in-state at Westminster Hall – 'an innovation which proved extremely popular'. One quarter of a million people filed past the coffin: never before had so many ordinary people, personally, individually, paid their last respects to a British monarch. And it was this novel precedent, combined with the long procession through the streets of London, with the coffin placed on a gun carriage pulled by naval ratings, followed by the more private interment at Windsor, which was emulated at the funerals of both George V and VI.

If Esher provided the expertise and organizing flair, and Edward himself supplied the enthusiasm and support, it was Elgar whose compositions raised ceremonial music from mere trivial ephemera to works of art in their own right. His 'Imperial March' of 1897 was the smash hit of the Diamond Jubilee, and successfully established him as the nation's unofficial musical laureate. Five years later, he composed the 'Coronation Ode' to commemorate the accession of Edward VII, which included, at the king's request, the choral setting of the broad and soaring melody of 'Pomp and Circumstance Number One' which has since gone round the world as 'Land of Hope and Glory'. Then, for the accession of George V, came the 'Coronation March', and the masque, 'The Crown of India' for the Delhi durbar. Such works, which reflected Elgar's genuine love of colour, pageantry, precision and splendour, provided the ideal martial, musical background to the great royal ceremonies. At the same time, they should not be seen as the embodiment of Edwardian bombast, pride, smugness and self-assurance. For his great melodies are more often than not funereal, melancholy, wistful, ruminative and introspective. Even the great motto theme of his first symphony, gloriously ennobled and triumphant as it appears towards the end of the last movement, never fully banishes the forces of doubt and darkness, diffidence and despair, which stalk through that work. But, even though the real tenderness of his music was often forgotten in the expansive brashness of the words fitted to his tunes, his marches and melodies nevertheless established themselves as the indispensable accompaniment of all great royal occasions – and have since so remained.

Assisted by the strong personal contribution of these three men, the public image of the British monarchy was fundamentally transformed in the years before the First World War, as the old ceremonial was successfully adapted in response to the changed domestic and international situation, and new ceremonial was invented and added. And such changes are well reflected in the unprecedented manner in which these royal occasions were commercially exploited. For, although no precise figures are available, it is clear that the massive outpouring of royal commemorative pottery dates from this time, as manufacturers cashed in on the appeal of royal ceremonial to a mass market which had never existed before. Likewise, new, consumer-oriented firms such as Rowntree, Cadbury and Oxo exploited royal events to help their advertising campaigns, and local authorities began to distribute beakers, mugs and other gifts in commemoration. In the same way, there were more private commemorative medals produced for sale for Victoria's Golden Jubilee than for the previous four great events combined, and the coronation of Edward VII was another medal-maker's paradise. In addition, in 1887, commemorative medals in the manner of campaign medals, to be worn on the left breast, were first issued, another novelty which was emulated at all subsequent coronations and jubilees in this period. So, in mugs and medals, as in music and magnificence, the last quarter of the nineteenth century and the first decade of the twentieth was a golden age of 'invented traditions', as the appeal of the monarchy to the mass of the people in an industrialized society was broadened in a manner unattainable only half a century before.

Nor was this greater stress on ritual limited to the royal family. In many other spheres of activity, too, venerable and decayed ceremonials were revived, and new institutions were clothed with all the anachronistic allure of archaic but invented spectacle. In London the Lord Mayor's Show was revised as a grand pageant, and in provincial cities, the new baroque town halls and the enhanced concept of civic dignity were further evidence of an efflorescence in civic ritual. In the same way, the new generation of redbrick universities, with their deliberately anachronistic styles of architecture, their aristocratic chancellors, their antique gowns and lavish degree ceremonies, were part of a similar trend. In the Dominions, the grand vice-regal régime introduced by Lord Dufferin to Ottawa when he was governor general of Canada (1872-8) set a precedent which was later emulated in Australia, New Zealand and South Africa. And in India, the three Delhi durbars of 1877, 1902 and 1911 marked a high point in the public face – although not the private power – of the Raj. At the same time, the honours system was greatly enlarged, with the creation of the Indian Orders, the Royal Victorian Order, the Orders of Merit and of Companions of Honour, and grand ceremonies of installation were revived for Knights of the Garter and of the Bath. In short, the enhanced and ritualized public face of the British monarchy was but one example of a more general proliferation of new or revived ceremonial during this period, which characterized English, European and American public life, not only at the level of the head of state, but in a more widespread manner as well.

[III]

During the third period, from 1914 to 1953, the context once again shifts profoundly, so that the ritual of the British monarchy ceased to be merely one aspect of widespread competitive inventiveness and became instead a unique expression of continuity in a period of unprecedented change. To begin with, the late-Victorian and Edwardian formula of a monarchy ceremonially grand but politically impartial was repeated in an even more strictly constitutional manner. For the limited power which Edward VII wielded was further eroded during the reigns of his three successors. Although, for example, George V was obliged to play some part in the constitutional crisis which he inherited on his accession, in the choice of a Conservative prime minister in 1923, and in the formation of the National Government in 1931, and although his private preferences were for the Conservatives, he maintained in his public, constitutional duties scrupulous rectitude and impartiality. He was a figurehead in politics, aptly reflecting his position as a figurehead in ceremonial, realizing the prediction of one radical in 1913 who observed: 'In England the king does what the people want. He will be a Socialist king'. The abdication of Edward VIII was further emphatic proof that it was parliament which made and unmade kings, and George VI was his father's son, not only in terms of his private preference for the Conservatives, but also in terms of his public impartiality. Even his rights to be consulted, to warn and to encourage were relatively attenuated. In 1940, he would have preferred Halifax as prime minister, and in 1945 was sorry to see Churchill depart. But on neither occasion did he have any power to influence events. The evolution of constitutional monarchy was complete.

From impotence to aloofness to veneration to grandeur the line ran unbroken, reinforced by the high reputation of the monarchs as individuals. In particular, George V, by allying the private probity of his grandmother with the public grandeur of his father, created a synthesis which both his long-serving successors have emulated. On the one hand, like his father, he was assiduous in attention to public ritual and ceremonial, and obsessed with matters such as the correct dress and manner of wearing decorations; but at the same time, his private life combined the unpretentiousness of the country gentleman with the respectability of the middle class. Perhaps accidentally, but certainly with great success, George V contrived to be both grand and domestic, a father-figure to the whole empire, yet also in his own right the head of a family with which all could identify. (Significantly, Edward VIII overrode both elements of the Georgian synthesis, caring not at all for ceremony, and living an eventful and indiscreet private life.) George VI, by contrast, deliberately took that name to emphasize the return to the style of his father. Indeed, on his accession, Baldwin noted that 'what will endear him to the people is that more than any of his brothers he resembles in character and mind his father'. Once again, the monarch assiduously carried out public, ceremonial duties, while at the same time enjoying a domestic life which was the very antithesis of his elder brother's. Like his father, his qualities were those of 'courage, endurance, kindliness, devotion': the man who conquered his stammer and resolutely refused to leave London during the Second World War (Ziegler, 1978, pp.76-77). If his father was 'George the Well-beloved', he in turn was 'George the Faithful'.

Under these circumstances, the monarchy appeared, particularly on grand, ceremonial occasions, as the embodiment of consensus, stability and community.

Indeed, the great royal rituals, the Armistice Day ceremonial, and the ever-expanding cult of Christmas (in both of which latter events the royal family figured strongly) were the three greatest celebrations of consensus, in which the royal family, individual families and the national family were all conflated. During the years 1914-53, Britain experienced a series of internal changes which far surpassed those of the preceding period in magnitude. Between 1910 and 1928, Britain moved from being a nation with one of the narrowest electoral franchises in Europe to full adult suffrage, with what was feared as 'a war-worn and hungry proletariat endowed with a huge preponderance of voting power' (Wheeler-Bennett, 1965, p.160). The Liberal Party was eclipsed by Labour as the second party in the state and, especially after the Second World War, the demise of the great aristocratic families left the crown increasingly isolated in London society. The General Strike and the Great Depression brought with them animosity and distress on an unprecedented scale, as did the two world wars. Accordingly, a politically neutral and personally admirable monarchy was presented, with great success, as 'the rallying-point of stability in a distracted age', the most effective aspect of which was its restrained, anachronistic, ceremonial grandeur (Longford, 1976, p.91).

In part, this was greatly facilitated by the continuing obsequiousness of the media, which continued to report the great ceremonies of state in an awed and hushed manner. Indeed, how else was it possible to treat an institution which combined political neutrality with personal integrity: there was nothing to criticize or caricature after the manner of Rowlandson or Gillray. From Partridge to Shepherd and Illingworth, royal cartoons were restricted to tableaux, congratulating members of the royal family on successful imperial tours, hailing the House of Windsor, or mourning the death of a sovereign. Significantly, when Low tried to publish a cartoon in 1936 which was critical of the monarchy at the time of the abdication, no newspapers in London would accept it. For editors and reporters, like cartoonists, remained deferential, as the gentleman's agreement among the press lords at the time of the abdication eloquently illustrated. In the same way, newspaper photographs, like newsreel films, were carefully edited [. . .].

But the most important development during this period was the advent of the B.B.C., which was of profound significance in conveying the dual image of the monarchy so successfully built up by George V. On the one hand, the Christmas broadcasts, instituted in 1932 and immediately adopted as 'traditional', enhanced the image of the monarch as the father-figure of his people, speaking to his subjects in the comfort and privacy of their homes. So successful a broadcaster was George V that his second son, although handicapped with a stammer, was obliged to continue the 'tradition'. At the same time, the B.B.C.'s first director general, Sir John Reith, himself a romantic devotee of pageantry and the monarchy, rapidly recognized the power of the new medium to convey a sense of participation in ceremonial which had never been possible before. So, from the time of the duke of York's wedding in 1923, 'audible pageants' became a permanent feature of the B.B.C.'s programmes, as each great state occasion was broadcast live on the radio, with special microphones positioned so that the listener could hear the sound of bells, horses, carriages and cheering. In a very special sense, it was this technical development which made possible the successful presentation of state pageants as national, family events, in which everyone could take part. And if the evidence of Mass Observation is any guide, they did: record audiences were a constant feature of the outside broadcasts of great royal occasions.

The combination of the novelty of the media and the anachronism of the ceremonial rendered royal ritual both comforting and popular in an age of change [. . .] In 1937, one commentator on the forthcoming coronation noted that 'an English Coronation is a thing apart from all other ceremonies: there is in fact no other spectacle of any kind so impressive, so awe-inspiring, to be witnessed anywhere else in the world' (Passingham, 1937, p.vii). By then, such words were, indeed, true. But only twenty-five years before, with similar ceremonial to be found in Moscow, Berlin, Vienna and Rome, they would have been demonstrably false. Of itself, survival had rendered venerable in an age of change that which had recently been novel in an era of competition. Percy Schramm, in his *History of the Coronation*, made the same point, with greater rhetorical luxuriance:

> Everything at Westminster remains as of yore, while Aachen and Rheims are desolate. There is no longer an *Imperator Romanorum*. Even the Habsburgs and Hohenzollerns have had to lay aside their imperial titles, and the Crown, sceptre and robes of the old imperial treasury are gazed at as exhibits in a museum. In France, not even this memory of the past survives . . . If we look more wisely about us, we shall see on every side old state traditions flung on the rubbish heap. There is hardly a country that has succeeded in so continually adapting her medieval institutions as to avoid their complete overthrow or their entire re-construction. Indeed, it is one of the symptoms of our age that countries, in the enjoyment of newly-awakened powers, create an entirely new form of state, and consciously throw the past aside.
> (Schramm, 1937)

[. . .] In Italy, as in Russia, the new political order brought with it strident, emotional, technologically sophisticated forms of ritual, the very antithesis of those prevalent in England. In Germany, in particular, the use of tanks, planes and searchlights implied a commitment to technology and an impatience with anachronism at odds with state coaches and ceremonial swords. Instead of lining the streets, cheering but orderly, as was the case with Londoners, one quarter of a million Germans participated annually in the Nuremberg rallies, where they listened with 'delirious rapture' to the 'unbridled emotionalism' of Hitler's oratory. The semi-liturgical chanting and intercession between speaker and audience; the manner in which the words seemed to erupt through the body of the Führer; the state of almost sexual exhaustion in which he was left after his speeches: all this contrasted strongly with the 'unassailable dignity' of George V and his queen.

However backward-looking and derivative much Fascist ritual (and building) has subsequently been discovered to be, to contemporaries in England, it was its strident, hysterical novelty that was noted, and compared with the more obvious traditionalism of the monarchy. As Bronislaw Malinowski explained (1938, p.112), at the time of the coronation of George VI, the dictators

> create in a hurry, from all kinds of ill-assorted odds and ends, their own symbolism and ritual, their own mythologies, and their directly religious and even magical creeds. One of them becomes the Aryan godhead incarnate; the other, blatantly, places the bays of the ancient Roman emperors on his own head . . . Pomp and ritual, legend and magical ceremonies, are enacted round them with an *éclat* which outshines the time-honoured, historically-founded institutions of traditional monarchy.

Of course, insofar as the traditions of British monarchy related to ritual, they were 'time-honoured' and 'historically-founded' in a relative sense; it was only when compared with recent rival rituals that they could plausibly be described in this way. But, in the inter-war years, this is exactly the viewpoint which was taken. In 1936, for example, the *New Statesman* compared the 'kind and fatherly common sense of the king's Christmas broadcast' with the Nazi official who 'ended by asking his audience all to join with him in offering the Nazi Christmas greeting to the leader – "Heil Hitler"'. Or, as Kingsley Martin put it even more pithily in the same year, 'if we drop the trappings of monarchy in the gutter .., Germany has taught us some guttersnipe will pick them up'.

In these diverse and disorienting national and international circumstances, the appeal of Empire, and the ceremonial association of the crown with it only increased – partly as a distraction from internal problems, and partly as an expression of the comforting belief that, in a newly competitive world of great power politics, Britain and her empire remained at the forefront. The Irish treaty, the independence of Egypt, the end of the Raj in India and the departure of Ireland and Burma may have implied that it was already on the wane. But the outstandingly successful tours of the Prince of Wales and the Duke of York to the Dominions and India only cemented the bonds between crown and empire the more closely, so that each royal ritual remained an imperial, as well as a domestic occasion. Here, for example, is Professor Malinowski's interpretation of the 'meaning' of the coronation of George VI:

> The Coronation was, among other things, a large-scale ceremonial display of the greatness, power and wealth of Britain. It was also an occasion on which the unity of the Empire, the strength of its bonds, was publicly enacted . . . Psychologically, I think there was no doubt that the Coronation generated an increased feeling of security, of stability, and the permanence of the British Empire.
> (Malinowski, 1938, pp.114-15)

Or, as George VI himself put it more succinctly in his own coronation broadcast: 'I felt this morning that the whole Empire was in very truth gathered within the walls of Westminster Abbey'. And the coronation of his daughter was seen in the same broad, ample perspective. As Philip Ziegler has explained:

The Empire was already crumbling, but the Commonwealth still seemed a powerful reality. Bound together by its common monarchy, it would grow in strength and cohesion. Britain, still clinging valiantly to the trappings of a great power, would regain her proper place in the world.
(Ziegler, 1978,p.97)

Indeed, it is in this context that Elizabeth's own words must be set: 'I am sure that this, my Coronation, is not a symbol of a power and a splendour that are gone, but a declaration of our hopes in the future'.

[IV]

Under these circumstances, the 'meaning' of royal ritual was further developed and extended. Assuredly, the political power and personal appeal of the monarch, the attitude of the media, the condition of London and the state of technology, all of which had changed profoundly during the previous period, remained unaltered. As before, the monarch was the father of his people, and the patriarch of Empire, and the royal ceremonial was as splendid and successful as in the days of Esher. Yet, paradoxically, it is such very real elements of *continuity* which both disguise and explain *changes* in 'meaning'. For it was the very fact of continuity, at a time of internal unrest and international revolution, which imparted to royal ritual in England those attributes of uniqueness, tradition and permanence which, in the previous period, they had so conspicuously lacked. It was not so much despite, as because of, the continuity in style and circumstance, that the 'meaning' of royal ritual altered once more.

Moreover, the impression of continuity and stability was further enhanced by innovation, as new ceremonials were invented.[. . .] The novelty of Abbey weddings for royal children and state funerals for dowager queens was far surpassed by the Silver Jubilee of George V, for which, again, there was no exact precedent, the twenty-fifth anniversary of Victoria's accession having fallen at exactly the time of Albert's death and her seclusion. Once more, the innovation was a great success, arousing widespread feelings of enthusiasm and support. In Lord Salisbury's opinion, the occasion represented 'an astonishing testimony to the deeply founded stability and solidarity of this country and empire under Your Majesty's authority'. And Ramsay Macdonald, who described the service on jubilee day as 'glowing with emotion', was even more moved by a reception for the Dominion prime ministers: 'Here the Empire was a great family, the gathering of a family reunion, the King a paternal head. We all went away feeling that we had taken part in something very much like a Holy Communion'.[. . .]

The remainder of the pageants of this period were of the type already established in the preceding phase of development. George V's funeral was an act of thanksgiving for the king who had survived the war and weathered the peace. George VI's coronation was an extravagant, imperial re-affirmation of the stability of monarchy after the interruption of the abdication. And, again, his funeral was a further expression of national appreciation for a man who had not wished to be king, but had triumphed over war and a stammer by a strong sense of duty. The

records of Mass Observation record widespread grief, shock and sympathy, so
much so, indeed, that it seems likely that Richard Dimbleby's famous radio
commentary describing the lying-in-state at Westminster Hall did in fact embody
the feelings of the majority of his audience:

> The oak of Sandringham, hidden beneath the rich, golden folds of the
> Standard. The slow flicker of the candles touches gently the gems of the
> Imperial Crown, even that ruby that Henry wore at Agincourt. It touches the
> deep, velvet purple of the cushion, and the cool, white flowers of the only
> wreath that lies upon the flag. How moving can such simplicity be. How real
> the tears of those who pass by and see it, and come out again, as they do at this
> moment in unbroken stream, to the cold, dark night and a little privacy for
> their thoughts . . . Never safer, better guarded, lay a sleeping king than this,
> with a golden candlelight to warm his resting place, and the muffled footsteps
> of his devoted subjects to keep him company . . . How true tonight of George
> the Faithful is that single sentence spoken by an unknown man of his beloved
> father: 'The sunset of his death tinged the whole world's sky.'

The contrast between this proud, loyal, reverential, popular broadcast, and the
savage *Times* editorial on the occasion of the death of George IV, well illustrates
the extent to which popular attitude towards royal ceremony and royal occasions
had altered.

The last great ceremony in this sequence, successfully conflating monarchy and
empire, stressing stability in an age of change, and celebrating the continuity of
Britain as a great power, was the coronation of Elizabeth II in 1953. For it was still
avowedly an *imperial* occasion, with the queen's dress containing embroidered
emblems of the dominions, with regiments of Commonwealth and colonial troops
marching in procession, with the prime ministers of the Dominions and India
present in the Abbey, and an assortment of heads of state from various exotic
colonial protectorates. At the time, it seemed as though the threats and challenges
of the war and austerity period had been surmounted: the empire was still largely
intact; the problem of Indian independence and republican status within the
Commonwealth had been triumphantly resolved; Churchill was back at 10
Downing Street; Britain had once more asserted her place as a great power; there
was a new Elizabethan age around the corner. All this was not only implicit, but
was self-consciously articulated at the time of the coronation. According to the
Delhi Express,

> the second Elizabethan era begins on a note of spiritual buoyancy which
> Britain has never experienced before. At no time in British history has she
> enjoyed the moral prestige which the Commonwealth, including Britain, now
> commands.

In this excessively euphoric context, it is not entirely surprising that the
archbishop of Canterbury should feel that Britain was close to the Kingdom of
Heaven on Coronation Day, or that Elizabeth herself should make her ringing
declaration of faith in the future.

The appeal of this sequence of ceremonies is well gauged by the high level of commercial exploitation and commemoration. Once more, at jubilees and coronations, commemorative pottery proliferated. Indeed, so anxious were domestic manufacturers to profit from the coronation in 1937 that a 100 per cent import duty was imposed on all foreign, imported souvenirs. In 1953, Birmingham Corporation offered local children a choice between a Bible, *Elizabeth Our Queen* by Richard Dimbleby, a spoon and fork, two commemorative mugs, a tin of chocolate, propelling pencils, a pen knife or a dish with a portrait of the queen. Commemorative medals in the manner of campaign badges were once more awarded, and collectors' medals were again privately produced. But these were in smaller numbers than before, largely because two new modes of commemoration were appearing. The first was the planting, throughout the empire, of trees, an innovation particularly noteworthy at the coronations of George VI and Elizabeth II. The second, dating from the time of George V's Silver Jubilee, was the issuing by the Post Office of specially designed commemorative stamps. Previously, the issuing of royal commemoratives had been limited to the empire, and in England only such secular festivals as the Empire Exhibition at Wembley had received notice. But from 1935, every royal jubilee, coronation, major wedding and wedding anniversary (but not, significantly, births or funerals) has been the subject of a special issue. Once more, it was an innovation; but well within 'traditional' moulds.

[V]

By definition, the period since the coronation in 1953 is too recent for detailed or satisfactory historical analysis. While it seems clear that the 'meaning' of royal ritual has entered a new phase, in which many of the presuppositions of the previous period have ceased to be valid, it is not as yet entirely clear how, positively, it might be described. But, in the interest of completeness, here are some observations consistent with the analysis employed thus far. To begin with, the political power of the monarch remains limited, or at least is exercised so discreetly that it seems not to matter. In a recent poll, 86 per cent of those asked felt that the queen 'was a figurehead, signing laws and doing what the government directs her to do'(Rose and Kavanagh, 1976, p.551). At the same time, the queen has carried on those traditions of 'extreme consciousness and dutifulness' which have characterized the British monarchy since the reign of her grandfather, and remained loyal to the Georgian synthesis of private probity and public grandeur. Above all, in a period when large parts of London have been rebuilt, men have been put on the moon, and Concorde has brought New York within commuting distance,the romantic glamour of anachronistic ceremony has become all the more appealing.[. . .]

Of greater significance has been the way in which royal ceremony has been an antidote to, or legitimation of, social change domestically, in a manner closely reminiscent of the previous period.[. . .] As a recent opinion poll put it:

Its existence means safety, stability and continued national prestige: it
promises religious sanction and moral leadership; it is 'above party' focus for
group identification; it means gaiety, excitement and the satisfaction of
ceremonial pageantry; it is an important, and perhaps an increasingly
important, symbol of national prestige.
(Harris, 1966, p. 137)

As those concluding words suggest, the role of royal ritual has also acquired a
new meaning in an international context, as Britain's world position has declined
profoundly. The fond, euphoric hopes of the coronation – that there was a new
Elizabethan age ahead – have proved vain. Indeed, to perceptive observers at that
ceremony, the writing was already on the wall. One American commentator, not
taken in by the buoyancy of the occasion, suggested that 'this show' was in part
'put on by the British for a psychological boost to their somewhat shaky empire'.
And, significantly, Elizabeth's title was much less grandly imperial than that of her
three predecessors. For she was neither empress of India, nor ruler of 'the British
Dominions beyond the Sea', but merely 'Head of the Commonwealth'. Since
then, the slide into impotence has only accelerated, with the break up of the
colonial empire, the disappearance of the last generation of imperial statesmen like
Smuts and Menzies, the fiasco of Suez, the problems of Biafra and Northern
Ireland, recurrent economic crises and the entry of Britain into the Common
Market. Indeed, the state funeral of Sir Winston Churchill in 1965, poised exactly
half way between Elizabeth's coronation and Silver Jubilee, was not only the last
rites of the great man himself, but was also self-consciously recognized at the time
as being the requiem for Britain as a great power.

So, 'as the power of Britain waned . . . pride grew in the Royal family as
something which was uniquely ours and which no country could match' (Ziegler,
1978, p.84). Just as, in previous periods of international change, the ritual of
monarchy was of importance in legitimating the novelty of formal empire and in
giving an impression of stability at a time of international bewilderment, so in the
post-war world it has provided a comfortable palliative to the loss of world-power
status. When watching a great royal occasion, impeccably planned, faultlessly
executed, and with a commentary stressing (however mistakenly) the historic
continuity with those former days of Britain's greatness, it is almost possible to
believe that they have not entirely vanished. As Richard Dimbleby noted
condescendingly at the time of the coronation, the Americans might be 'a race of
such vitality', but they were so 'lacking in tradition' that 'they must wait a
thousand years before they can show the world anything so significant or so
lovely'. And, since 1953, this attitude has become more widespread, as evidence of
decline has proved inescapable. In the words of D.C.Cooper (1970, p.260) 'while
people can see the gloved hand waving from the golden coach, they feel assured
that all is well with the nation, whatever its true state'. The 'tendency to elevate
royalty as national prestige declines', to stress as never before the grandeur and
uniqueness of its ceremonial in particular, has been especially marked in post-war
Britain (Harris, 1966, pp.18, 52).

As such, it has been greatly facilitated by the impact of television, which has made the royal pageants accessible in a vivid and immediate manner which neither the radio nor newsreels could achieve. Here, as in other ways, the coronation of Elizabeth was a bridge between an older era and a new phase of development. For while the tone of Richard Dimbleby's commentary placed it in a world which had more in common with 1935 (or even 1897) than 1977, the fact that it was a television commentary, and that more people *watched* the ceremony on television than *listened* to it on radio, made it clear that a new way of reporting the great occasions of state had been perfected. Largely as a result of television, Elizabeth was indeed the 'first British sovereign truly to be crowned, as the rubric requires, "in the sight of the people"' (Lacey, 1977, p.208). Hence the comment of Shils and Young, who regarded the whole occasion as an 'act of national communion' (1953, p.80). For never before had it been possible for the population as a whole to see the ceremonial as it happened, thereby obtaining an unprecedented sense of active participation.

But, as with the press or radio, the medium of television also contained a message. And, significantly, while television has cut politicians down to size, so that the grand manner in parliament or Whitehall is now no longer effective, it has continued to adopt the same reverential attitude towards the monarchy which radio pioneered in the days of Reith. On the one hand, such programmes as the film *Royal Family* have successfully perpetuated the picture of the queen and her family as quintessentially middle-class. On the other, the coverage of the great state ceremonials has enhanced the picture of grandeur and fairytale splendour which Reith and B.B.C. Radio did so much to promote. Of special significance in this regard were the commentaries of Richard Dimbleby, who covered every major royal occasion for the B.B.C. between the coronation and his death in 1965. For his eloquent, emotional commentaries, lit up by profound devotion to the monarchy and a romantic feeling for history and tradition, described royal ritual in the most fulsome, obsequious terms. By explaining the ceremonial and expressing a sense of history in the manner he did, Dimbleby's commentaries were of the greatest significance in presenting the ritual of monarchy as a festival of freedom and celebration of continuity in a worried and distracted age.[. . .].

So, despite the initial misgivings about the live broadcast of the coronation, it proved to be so successful that all subsequent royal ceremonial occasions have been primarily television spectaculars. Indeed, this element has brooked so large that it has even influenced the nature of the rituals themselves. At the Prince of Wales's investiture at Carnarvon, for instance, the canopy above the dais was deliberately made transparent so that the television cameras might see through it. As for the ceremonies themselves, they have again had more in common with the monarchies of George V and VI than with Victoria or Edward: they have been the rites of passage of a relatively young family, rather than the jubilees, funerals and coronations of venerable monarchs. The weddings of Princess Margaret (1960), the duke of Kent (1961), Princess Alexandra (1963) and Princess Anne (1973), the investiture of the Prince of Wales (1969) and the Queen's Silver Jubilee (1977), as well as the state opening of parliament since 1958 have all been essays in television ritual.

It is in this 'traditional' but changed context that the Silver Jubilee of 1977 may most usefully be set. At one level, that of public reaction, that occasion may be seen as part of a tradition harking back to the Silver Jubilee of George V and the more venerable celebrations of Victoria: a popular piece of well-planned pageantry which the public enjoyed. At another level, however, the grand, unrivalled pomp and circumstance of the occasion was seen as a perfect tonic to Britain's declining self-esteem:

> We were all sharing a rich piece of history . . . Somebody said that Britain may
> have lost out on a number of things, but we can still show the world a clean pair
> of heels when it comes to ceremonial. Yesterday's pageantry was a superb
> example . . . It proves there is something to be said for doing things the old-
> fashioned way.
> (*Daily Mirror*, 8 June 1977)

But, at the same time, the experts also recognized that the diminished scale of the ceremonial placed the event emphatically in a new, post-imperial age:

> Only a few members of the Royal Family would accompany the queen on her
> drive to St. Paul's; there would only be a handful of troops from overseas to
> supplement the anyway modest British contingent; no foreign potentates . . .
> would lend exotic glamour to the proceedings.
> (Ziegler, 1978, p.176)

In different ways, then, the jubilee ceremonial was an expression of national and imperial decline, an attempt to persuade, by pomp and circumstance, that no such decline had really taken place, or to argue that, even if it had, it really did not matter.

[VI]

The account of the evolution of royal ritual which has been sketched in here would certainly surprise both those nineteenth- and twentieth-century authorities quoted at the beginning of this article. Ceremonial which was badly performed has now become so well stage-managed that the British have been able to persuade themselves (despite overwhelming historical evidence to the contrary) that they are good at ritual because they always have been. And, however much literacy and education have increased, the liking which the British public has for royal pageant and display has grown rather than lessened. Old ceremonies have been adapted and new rituals invented, the combined effect of which has been, paradoxically, to give an impression of stability in periods of domestic change, and of continuity and comfort in times of international tension and decline. While there may be a sense in which the British monarchy legitimates the status quo, the fact remains that during the last two hundred years or so, the status quo has itself changed profoundly, and the public, ceremonial image of the monarchy has changed along with it. If, as seems possible, the next coronation takes place without a house of lords, a Commonwealth or an Established Church, the role of the ceremonial in creating the comforting picture of stability, tradition and continuity will only be further enhanced. The dynamic dialogue between ritual and society, between text and context, will continue.

At the same time, the picture of evolution, development and change which has been presented here may surprise those commentators and journalists who, on every great royal ceremonial occasion, talk glibly of a 'thousand-year-old tradition'. Of course it is true that the monarchy and some of its ceremonies are, genuinely, thus antique. Nor can it be denied that in England, as in much of Europe, there was a previous period in the sixteenth and seventeenth centuries when lavish and splendid royal ceremony abounded. But, as Professor Hobsbawm has argued (1983, pp.1, 11), the continuity which the invented traditions of the late nineteenth century seek to establish with this earlier phase is largely illusory. For while the materials out of which they were forged may have been on occasions genuinely venerable, their 'meaning' was specifically related to the social, political, economic and cultural circumstances of the time.[. . .]

References

BODLEY, J. E. C., (1903) *The Coronation of King Edward the Seventh*, London
COOPER, D. C., (1970) 'Looking Back in Anger' in V. Bogdanor and R. Skidelsky (eds.) *The Age of Affluence*, 1951–64, London
GILMOUR, I., (1969) *The Body Politic*, London
HARRIS, L., (1966) *Long to Reign Over Us?*, London
HOBSBAWM, E., (1983) 'Inventing Traditions', in E. Hobsbawm and T. Ranger, (eds.) *The Invention of Tradition*, Cambridge.
LACEY, R., (1977) *Majesty: Elizabeth II and the House of Windsor*, London.
LONGFORD, E., (1976) *The Royal House of Windsor*, London
MALINOWSKI, B., (1938) 'A nationwide intelligence service', in Madge, C., and Harrison, T., (eds.) *First Year's Work*, London
PASSINGHAM, W. J., (1937) *A History of the Coronation*, London.
ROSE, R., and D. KAVANAGH (1976), 'The monarchy in contemporary British culture', *Comparative Politics*, vii.
SCHRAMM, P.E., (1937) *A History of the English Coronation*, Oxford.
SHILS, E., and M. YOUNG, (1953), 'The meaning of the coronation', *Sociological Review*, new series, i
WHEELER-BENNETT, Sir J., (1965) *King George VI*, London
ZIEGLER, P.C., (1978) *Crown and People*, London

11   The Language of Patriotism, 1750-1914

Hugh Cunningham

From *History Workshop* No. 12, Autumn 1981. Reproduced by permission of the publishers, History Workshop Journal.

[English patriotism] cannot be ignored. Not only is it wheeled onto the historical stage as the natural resolution to crises in the nation's history (the Armada, the Napoleonic Wars, World War I, Dunkirk), but its strength or weakness, and its social location are also at the heart of debates about the non-revolutionary character of the working class, and about the sources and degree of loyalty to the modern state. However much they may otherwise disagree, admirers and opponents of patriotism have this in common, that they see it as a counterweight to class consciousness.

This unholy unanimity of opinion conceals important shifts in the meaning and significance of patriotism. In the later nineteenth and early twentieth centuries patriotism was extensively propagated by those in authority, and its political location was on the right. Its focus was sometimes the Empire or the United Kingdom rather than England, but even then it often resorted to the language and symbols of patriotism as they had developed in the eighteenth century. Yet in that century patriotism was the creed of opposition, and towards the end of it the vocabulary and rhetoric of patriotism was becoming the distinctive mark of extra-parliamentary radicalism. What happens to patriotism, we may ask, between the publication of *The Rights of Man* and the beginning of the French Wars on the one hand, and, on the other, Disraeli's famous speeches of 1872 when he claimed with resounding impact that the working class was both patriotic and Conservative? [. . .]. When, how and why did patriotism lose its links with radicalism and become identified with the political right? How, that is, did a particular word, patriotism, together with its associations which we must elaborate, shift towards the right of the political spectrum? And what light is shed by this linguistic shift on the patriotism of the age leading up to the First World War, and, more broadly, on the relationship between the state and the working class in the age of imperialism?

Patriotism in the Eighteenth Century

In the eighteenth century patriotism was the legitimation of opposition. If a 'formed opposition' was thought to be unconstitutional, an assertion that such opposition was motivated by patriotism might endow it with some legitimacy. That patriotism, first explicitly formulated by Bolingbroke in the 1720s, had three main sources.

First, and by a long way the most important for Bolingbroke, was a set of beliefs derived from Greek political thought and coming to England by way of Italian humanism and in particular Machiavelli. This tradition emphasised the virtues of balance and the dangers of corruption and had become familiar in English political thinking by the end of the seventeenth century. The balance between monarchy, aristocracy and democracy was translated in England to mean a balance between King, Lords and Commons. Corruption arose if any one of these three was under the undue influence of another. In the late seventeenth century it was the undue influence of the king, both through a standing army and through placing his men in the House of Commons, which caused alarm. It was Bolingbroke's coup, as Quentin Skinner has expressed it, to steal this ideological armour and reinforce it with the cloak of patriotism (Skinner, 1974, pp.112-13). Thenceforward every opposition to government in the eighteenth century, whether that of Chatham, or of Wilkes, or of radicalism in the 1790s, described itself as patriotic and accused the government of corruption.

But Machiavelli was not the only source of English patriotism. There was, secondly, an interpretation of English history which could lead to the same conclusion, that Government was corrupt and opposition patriotic. This interpretation stemmed from that belief in the Ancient Constitution which had nourished much seventeenth-century opposition to the King and the Court, and which posited an age, normally located in Saxon times before the Norman Yoke was imposed, when the constitution achieved perfection in securing liberty to the people. This was an argument for reform disguised as one for a return to the past, and it necessitated a constant battle over the interpretation of history.

Closely related to this historical root of English patriotism was the third source, the belief that the English were an Elect Nation, that 'God is English'. The extent to which English Protestant thinking had been infected by these ideas has probably been exaggerated, and by the eighteenth century may have been of relatively minor importance. On the other hand there was a powerful secular version of it, wherein in modern times England was seen to be the birthplace of liberty. 'Britain', as Milton put it, 'which was formerly styled the hot-bed of tyranny, will hereafter deserve to be celebrated for endless ages as a soil most genial to the growth of liberty'.

These three sources of patriotism, although they were each commandeered by the opposition, were none of them exclusive to it [...]. This rhetoric of patriotism was one to which appeal was as likely to be made by the Government and its supporters as by the opposition. More accurately there occurred in the eighteenth century, and as I shall argue for much of the nineteenth century, a dispute as to whether it was the Government or its opponents which could most rightly claim the label 'patriot'. While the Government never entirely surrendered the ground it increasingly conceded that a patriot was someone in opposition. This was largely because there was a patriot political programme, to which opposition politicians were almost invariably drawn, a programme which focused on the corruption of the constitution visible in the number of placemen in Parliament and in the strength of the standing army. If Bolingbroke had borrowed his ideological clothes from the Whigs, it was quite possible for Whigs to reclaim them, only to find that they had lost them again to radicals. Patriotism became more radical as the century progressed. We can trace the shift in Samuel Johnson's usage of the word. In the 1755 edition of his Dictionary he described a patriot quite straightforwardly as 'One whose ruling passion is the love of his country'. To this in 1773 he added 'ironically for a factious disturber of the government'. In 1774 he was trying to reclaim the title of patriot for his friends in his Southwark election pamphlet, *The Patriot*, but in the following year he gave up the struggle and produced the most famous definition in the English language: patriotism was 'the last refuge of a scoundrel'. By the 1770s, in fact, most government supporters had concluded that patriotism had been soiled and besmirched by Wilkes and the radicals to such an extent that it was better to taunt the latter with the name of a patriot than to try and reclaim the title for themselves. No man in his senses, claimed Dean Tucker in the mid-1770s, will pretend to say that the laws of Parliament are not binding 'till they have received the sanction of some patriotic club, or popular assembly convened for that purpose . . .'

In their senses or not, it was precisely at this time that radicals were beginning to make this kind of argument, proclaiming all the while their patriotism [. . .]. Wilkes, Cartwright and the radicals were taking the argument about patriotism out of the arena of parliamentary politics, and claiming that only a radical reform of parliament itself, only a restoration of lost rights, could root out corruption, remove the threat of tyranny, and preserve liberty. [. . .]

This radical patriotism was no mere rhetorical flourish. It derived from a sense that Englishmen had rights, rooted both in nature and in history, which were being violated. To think of themselves as patriotic, to invoke the 'martyred patriots' of the past, was both to legitimate and to reinforce the sense of the rightness of those activities which led some of them to transportation and death. It was a language of private correspondence as well as of public platform, a language which had been internalised and would not easily be shaken. For the radicals of the 1790s patriotism was not a cloak of deceit but an armour of righteousness.

Radicalism and Patriotism 1793–1850

War posed the first and major threat to that radicalisation of patriotism which was occurring in the later eighteenth century. Already in the American War, it is claimed, radicalism had been put on the defensive by the 'patriotic backlash'. All the more obvious does it seem that radical patriotism must have been stifled in the wars against France which began in 1793 and lasted, but for the brief intermission of the Peace of Amiens, until 1815 [. . .]. To an extent, of course, that stifling did happen, but [. . .] we may note two points about the patriotism generated by the invasion scares.

The first is a simple one, and would not be denied by the most ardently patriotic historian. Patriotism was not consistently evident throughout the war years; in fact for long years it was markedly absent, and if the public had an opinion it was for peace. It would be hard to claim that patriotism gave strength to Government in more than one-quarter of these twenty-two years of war. There were, in the language usually adopted, 'bursts' or 'waves' of patriotism preceded and followed by apathy or hostility (see Emsley, 1979).

The second point is that the language of propaganda, from which much of the evidence of patriotic fervour is taken, reveals both a concern to win over the doubtful and a sensitivity to the concerns of radical patriots. The outpourings from the presses are not so much a celebration of national unity as an exercise in persuasion. [. . .] The connections between 'Liberty' and 'Patriotism' remain strong and Government supporters both ceaselessly play on the connection, and at the same time reclaim from radicalism, for loyalism, the vocabulary of patriotism which had fast been slipping away from them between the 1770s and 1790s. The word 'patriot' occurs again and again in loyalist propaganda without any suggestion that a patriot could be anything other than a stout defender of his country and a firm believer in the 'blessings of our glorious constitution' [. . .].

The patriotism of the war years was not a unanimous declaration of national unity. On the contrary while the war made it possible for patriotism to be reclaimed in part from the radicals, at the same time it made it necessary for everyone to declare his or her patriotism–but not necessarily the same patriotism. The patriotism of loyalists was set against that of radicals, the patriotism of Evangelicals against that of prizefighters. While Methodists proclaimed their patriotism, others 'earnestly entreated' John Bull 'to avoid the *methodist conventicle, a place which is found woefully to debase all the nobler passions of the mind*'. Patriotism was a political prize much fought over in the war years, and while in the circumstances of war, or at least of invasion threat, it became more associated with loyalty to government, it never lost its accompanying rhetoric of liberty, nor did radicals and others cease to invoke it in pursuit of their own ends.

The second threat to radical patriotism in these years may be dealt with more briefly. It has to do with the impact of Tom Paine. E.P. Thompson has rightly noted that 'In coming forward as "Patriots" and constitutionalists, men like Major Cartwright and Baxter were attempting to take over the rhetoric of the age'. He goes on to suggest that this rhetoric had to be broken through because it implied respect for established institutions (Thompson, 1968, pp.88ff). Paine was the man who did the breaking, and certainly the liberalising impact of Paine's rationalism and irreverence is not to be denied. Yet those constitutional demands which were at the core of radical politics from Cartwright to the Chartists can hardly be dismissed as 'trivia'. More important the rhetoric of patriotism and the reference back to good King Alfred and the Norman Yoke could point to increasingly radical solutions to the present. Instead of abandoning the language, radicals changed the interpretation. As Iorwerth Prothero has put it '. . . the changes in radical ideology were often effected by a redefinition and reinterpretation of crucial and emotive words like "aristocracy", "people", "slavery", and "union" to meet a new analysis' (Prothero, 1974, p.143). To these words we might add 'patriotism', 'liberty', and 'tyranny' [. . .].

The Anglo-Saxon constitution was a potent myth for land reformers in the first half of the nineteenth century. But patriotism was used not only to justify a backward looking escape from industrialism, but also to combat head-on the threats to liberty which an industrialising civilisation increasingly posed. Constitutional issues such as the corruption of a ministry or the threat to liberty implicit in the new police continued to be argued about in terms of patriotism, but so also were issues which arose directly from urbanisation and industrialisation: the New Poor Law, work discipline and factory reform. And at the point where these issues coalesced, in Chartism, the language of patriotism was still being employed in defence of liberty against tyranny and slavery. While it had its continuity with the past, it derived its power from its ability to speak to the experience of working people in the first industrial revolution [. . .]. The Chartists were challenging the whole apparatus of the state, its economic foundations as well as its political and ideological buttresses. At the heart of this challenge was the claim that Parliament in no sense spoke for the people (hence the calling of a Convention), and that the Government had usurped rights which were both natural and had been enjoyed by the English in the past. These rights were not only the political ones of the six points of the Charter but rights to land, rights to enjoy themselves as they wanted to, rights to possess arms, rights to food and drink. These rights were demanded in the vocabulary of patriotism. 'We will have no Malthusian "Marcus" to poison the minds of the people with incitements to child-murder! We will have no Broughams and Martineaus to stigmatize marriage as a crime and charity as a folly! No; we are for the ancient laws of England . . . ' wrote the *Northern Liberator* in 1839, going on to recall 'constitutional' rights to poor relief, to annual parliaments and universal suffrage, to be armed, and not to have to 'submit to a *Bourbon Police*, whilst the old English name of constable is remembered'. The Chartists use the vocabulary of patriotism as a weapon of struggle, one which engaged with the enemy, and whose recollection of the past incorporated a vision of the future.

It was in the early days of Chartism that the vocabulary of radical patriotism reached its new peak. As the crisis of 1839-40 passed, and as the slump of 1842 bit deep, the Chartist analysis of the present and the future became more economic and social, more determined to dwell on the peculiarities of industrial capitalism rather than the peculiarities of the English. After the early 1840s the language of patriotism begins to pass out of the mainstream of English radical movements [. . .].

Patriotism: From Chartism to Jingoism

The vocabulary of patriotism came less instinctively to the lips of radicals in the third quarter of the century than it had done throughout the first half; and by the late 1870s the shift of patriotism to the political right had become established. The patriot was no longer, as Oastler had claimed, the person 'who can produce the greatest dissatisfaction', but rather a supporter of Disraeli's imperialist foreign policy [. . .]. Radical patriotism did not simply disappear; on the contrary it played a crucial role in easing the transition from the making of England's 'First Proletariat' in the first half of the nineteenth century to the making of a modern working class towards its close.

One of the hallmarks of radical patriotism was its deep-rooted suspicion of the state, and in the first half of the century, there were numerous issues, such as the New Poor Law or factory reform, in which the state could be seen as tyrant and the working class as patriots fighting for their rights and liberties. After mid-century, however, there was much less confrontation between the state and the working class. Ironically in this third quarter of the century it was sections of the middle class who perceived tyranny in the centralisation of the state or in the continuing dominance of the Church of England, and in their turn harked back to Anglo-Saxon freedoms. For the working class, however, one main plank of the radical patriot platform was being cut from under it by the liberalisation of the English state.

A second hallmark of radical patriotism was its internationalism. Patriots across the world saw themselves joined together in a struggle against reactionary governments. In September 1792 the London Corresponding Society told the National Convention how 'We, instead of natural enemies, at length discover in Frenchmen our fellow citizens of the world.' Many radical patriots were pacifists and opposed the French Revolutionary and Napoleonic Wars. Indeed they began to see the whole period since the Glorious Revolution as one of warfare, what Lovett in 1840 called '*the bleak record of the last hundred and fifty years of blood and human wretchedness*'. Against this despotism of rulers, 'patriots' of all nations should, as the *Black Dwarf* argued in 1823, 'melt down and amalgamate all national jealousies into harmony in the common cause . . . ' This fraternal internationalism was a powerful strain in radical thought from the 1790s through to the Chartist addresses to the beleaguered patriots of Europe, and reached its apogee with Harney and the Fraternal Democrats.

There coexisted with it, however, both the narrower English patriotism of Cobbett or O'Connor ('I will work only for home sweet home' wrote O'Connor in 1847), and more pervasively the sense that England, as the home of freedom, had a peculiar right and duty to spread its benefits to less fortunate nations. Palmerston shared these beliefs and in his skilful articulation of them weakened the instinctive hostility to the state and its doings which had been the mark of radical patriotism. In the era when England's world supremacy was at its height the language of patriotism provided a point of contact between rulers and people. Consider this song:

Shout, Britons, shout, till all the world throughout,
Your cheering voice shall hear O'er ev'ry land and sea;
Our duty is to fight,
For the cause of truth and right,
And to set the slave and tortur'd brother free;
Our cause is right and good,and we'll freely shed our blood,
Till the despot shall for ever hide his face,
Till dungeon, cell, and rack
Shall follow in his track,
And freedom dwell with all the human race.

The reference is to Italy, the date 1849. The song encapsulates the rhetoric of patriotism: slave, torture, despot, dungeon, freedom, they were words which stirred up generous and familiar emotions. In 1849 all except Catholics and extreme conservatives could agree with its sentiments. It was Palmerston's achievement to extract every ounce of political advantage from this rhetoric [. . .].

The path which Palmerston trod was a slippery one. Radicals remained suspicious, some of them deeply and incurably so. Conservatism at home alienated radical support as did bravado abroad and an increasing inability to match the rhetoric of patriotism with deeds. In the Crimean War he could draw on a tradition of Russophobia founded on Russian oppression of Poles and other subject nationalities. But in the 1860s Palmerston conspicuously failed to come to the aid of the Poles or to the inhabitants of Schleswig-Holstein. Working-class enthusiasm for the downtrodden people of Europe was becoming embarrassing, and the massive welcome which the London trades gave to Garibaldi in 1864 was in part a protest against the failure of government to support the great Italian patriot; the government was believed to have had some hand in his early departure.

Whatever hopes had been put in Palmerston had been dashed by the time of his death in 1865. But what Palmerston had done was to show that in foreign policy government and people were not poles apart, but rather shared common concerns. We can see one practical outcome of this in the working-class enthusiasm to enrol in the Volunteer Force, by intention exclusively middle-class, in the 1860s. To resist Louis Napoleon in the 1860s might be not only to defend Britain against an invasion threat, but also to link hands with radical Italian patriotism, and to offer a citizen's alternative to the aristocratic regular army. Such aspirations were short-lived within the Volunteer Force, and quickly quashed, and the outcome might be said to be the incorporation of the working class in the institutions of the nation as defined by government. The demarcation between the patriotism of radicals and the patriotism of government, so clearly defined in the 1790s or 1840s, was becoming blurred.

In the 1860s and 1870s radical patriotism was in some sort taken under the wing of both the Liberal and the Conservative parties. In the case of the Liberals there was a real point of juncture between working-class internationalism, as it had developed in the days of the Chartists, and liberal campaigns aginst tyranny and autocracy abroad. Working-class interest in the oppressed nationalities of Europe was one common ground, and much remarked upon. But the interest extended beyond Europe to America; and the Civil War, like the War of Independence, produced a broad-based radical alliance under Liberal leadership. Working-class support for the North came from the new generation of trade union leaders who in doing so effected solid links with reforming sections within the middle class. This pro-North alliance was soon to put strong pressure on Government for further constitutional reform in England, and to provide the popular base for the Gladstonian Liberal Party. The co-operation continued in the 1870s when, with the rise of Prussia, attention turned more to peace than to liberty. The Workmen's Peace Association, growing out of the Reform League and with many links with Chartism, was 'the largest political organization supported and led by working men in the 1870s.' Although distinct from the more middle-class Peace Society, the aims of the two organisations were broadly similar and there were many personal links between them. Both too looked to Gladstone to lead them into the promised land. As a crusader for liberty, as a supporter of Italian patriots, his credentials were good, while at the same time he was free of that hectoring quality which made radicals suspicious of Palmerston. The internationalist and pacifist strains within English radical patriotism had now become embodied within the Liberal Party.

From the other side of the political divide, the Conservatives were able to capture or co-opt some of the leading strains in radical patriotism, both in the period of the American Civil War, and later when Disraeli mobilised Russophobia in support of an imperialist foreign policy. Working-class support for the North in the American Civil war was by no means unanimous. Many supported the South, not because they favoured slavery, but out of a regard for self-interest, a recognition of the South as a nation struggling to be free, and a deep-rooted suspicion of any cause supported by Bright and the manufacturing interest. This was the policy which came naturally to anyone whose political teeth had been cut in the first half of the century. So also did fear of Russia. It was a feature of Russophobia in England that its adherents were either on the extreme right or on the extreme left: either fearful for the routes to the East and the future of the British Empire, or convinced that Russia instigated the suppression of democratic movements throughout Europe. It was thus not impossible for the greatest of all Russophobes, David Urquhart, who could describe himself as a 'Tory in the purest sense of the word – a Tory of the times of Anne', to have some impact on radical working men [. . .].

Russophobia was not alone in drawing part of the tradition of radical patriotism towards the Conservatives. There was also a popular John Bullish Toryism centred on Protestantism, which evoked the world of roast beef, plum pudding and good beer; it counterposed a frank and hearty enjoyment of life and sport to the more earnest world of Liberalism. In Lancashire, as Patrick Joyce (1980, pp. 251–2, 285–8) has shown, this cultural politics had a real attraction for many working people, and did so by drawing the radical teeth from the popular images of patriotism.

It was Disraeli who appreciated that through an appeal to patriotism it might be possible both to reassure the middle class that the Tories were truly Conservative and to win some of the new working-class voters. For Disraeli himself there was nothing very new in this. As he put it in Edinburgh in October 1867, ' . . . the national party is supported by the fervour of patriotism . . . I have always considered that the Tory party was the national party of England.' To convert his party to such beliefs, even more to use those beliefs to strengthen his exceedingly weak hold over the party, required much persuasion. In the 1867-8 Conservative government the Foreign Secretary, Lord Derby, gave much comfort to 'commercial Liberals' with his isolationist and non-intervention policy. Party propaganda noted that while the Conservatives had 'kept England aloof from entanglement with any contending party on the Continent, a quenchless thirst for interference, an insatiable appetite for meddling, has characterised the Liberal ascendancy.' In 1872 in his famous speeches at Manchester and the Crystal Palace Disraeli set out to educate his party, speaking to the working class, the great bulk of whom, he said 'are English to the core. They repudiate cosmopolitan principles. They adhere to national principles. They are for maintaining the greatness of the kingdom and the empire, and they are proud of being subjects of our Sovereign and members of such an Empire.' The stage was now set for the battle between the Liberal Party representing 'cosmopolitan principles' and a Conservative Party adhering to 'national principles'.

By the outset of the 1870s the radical patriotism of the Chartist era had been weakened and fragmented. The liberalisation of the English state had made the language of freedom and tyranny less obviously appropriate to domestic politics. At the same time the sense that it was England's duty and mission to spread freedom to the rest of the world came to be shared, though with differences of nuance, by working-class radicals and Palmerston. The consequences were twofold. First, as in the Crimean War, the working class became more likely to support the imperialist objectives of the state. And second, the cross-class absorption in foreign policy eased the way for the incorporation of the working class into one or other of the two main political parties. By the early 1870s the Liberals were the party identified with internationalism and peace, the Conservatives with nationalism and Russophobia. But it was only at the end of that decade that patriotism and Conservatism became firmly linked. In 1872 James Grant could write, 'The amount of man's patriotism has always been measured by the amount of his Liberalism . . . ' Within a few years that would cease to be the case.

The lead-up to this transference of the language of patriotism from the radicals to the right was long drawn out, stretching over quarter of a century. The decisive shift came suddenly in the space of a few months in late 1877 and early 1878. The occasion was the Eastern Question whose importance in English domestic politics it is now difficult to recall; on this matter at least we may heed the opinion of Lord Salisbury who in 1878 said that no question within the memory of man had 'so deeply excited the English people, moved their passions so thoroughly and produced such profound divisions and such rancorous animosity.' At heart the debate was one with which we are familiar: the claims of internationalism and peace set against that of national interest. The national interest was perceived by Disraeli to be the support of the Ottoman Empire so as to protect Britain's routes to the East against Russian encroachment. In 1876 news of Turkish massacres of Bulgarian Christians had thrown renewed doubt on this policy; there had been a massive agitation in support of the Bulgarian Christians whose outcome had been to bring Gladstone back into politics. In the spring of 1877 the Russians and Turks went to war, and while the Russians might claim this was a holy war in defence of Bulgarian Christians, Russophobes in Britain, both Conservative and left-wing, saw it in very different terms. Towards the end of 1877 the Russians were advancing on Constantinople, and the likelihood of British involvement against the Russians was becoming stronger. The outcome was a peace agitation of impressive proportions, stemming from that internationalist and pacifist opinion which had been so effectively propagated by the Workmen's Peace Association and the Peace Society. The first petition in favour of peace sent to the Foreign Office in December 1877 reads as follows: 'My Lord, As working Men we entreat you to use your utmost influence in Favour of Neutrality in the horriable War between Russia & Turkey, and alsow agains any increased expendeture on our armaments.' It comes from Mursley in Buckinghamshire, and was signed by fifty-three people, three of whom marked with the cross of the illiterate, and at least thirteen of whom were women. Some gave their occupations: there were fourteen labourers, two carpenters, two bricklayers, two farmers, a publican, a shoemaker, a builder, a farm bailiff, and an 'eadgecutter.' This petition was in no way untypical. The working-class contribution to the peace agitation was much stronger than it had been in the Bulgarian Atrocities agitation of 1876. And success seemed assured. On the eve of Parliament's meeting in January 1878 Stead could report exultantly that 'we have beaten the War party, hip and thigh, from Dan even to Beersheba'. Even the cautious Liberal Whip, Adam, spoke of 'the utter collapse of the war party in the country'.

They were words he would soon have to swallow. For it was the war party, and that new phenomenon, Jingoism, which were to be triumphant in public meetings in England in 1878. The left-wing Russophobes, including Marx and most particularly his contact Maltman Barry, had tried throughout 1877 to stir up an agitation, but though their press contacts were impressive they were weak on the ground. It was not left-wing Russophobia but Conservative Party organisation which roused the Jingo fervour. 'How marked the alliance of Toryism and rowdyism has been on this occasion!' wrote Goldwin Smith. It was 'the unpatriotic policy' of the Liberal Party and of 'the traitor Gladstone' which was attacked, and by contrast stress was laid on the patriotism of the Government supporters. Peace meetings were broken up, and Conservative demonstrations filled the public places of many of the big cities. The supporters of peace were cowed and could do nothing to prevent the association of patriotism and Conservatism. Probably they exaggerated the strength of Jingoism which was both socially and geographically less than a mass movement; but at the time the sense of defeat was nearly total, and the fear of Jingoism a lasting one.

The man who organised many of the Jingo meetings, Ellis Ashmead Bartlett, followed up his success by founding the Patriotic Association, and in 1880 the newspaper, *England*, the latter aimed particularly at 'the Working Class and the

Lower Middle Class'. Both Association and newspaper were nominally non-party but in fact financially supported by leading Conservatives. In his first editorial Bartlett referred to 'the chief political object we have in view and the field which we shall endeavour to fill. The field is Patriotism . . .' His efforts were suitably enough rewarded when Disraeli found him a pocket borough in the 1880 election.

Patriotism in the Age of Imperialism

Radical patriotism fragmented in the third quarter of the nineteenth century and was dealt a harsh blow in the Jingoism of the late 1870s. From that moment the initiative passed to the right. The ruling class sought in patriotism a means of diffusing the consciousness of the working class. The call for loyalty to the state rather than to any section of it was seen as a way both of reducing class conflict and of facilitating the imposition of greater demands on the citizen by the state. Patriotism, that is, became a key component of the ideological apparatus of the imperialist state.

Besides being Conservative this patriotism which was so ardently propagated was both royalist and racialist. For a brief moment in the early 1870s republicanism had both middle- and working-class support, but in the last quarter of the century royalist fervour was rising, reaching its peak in the Diamond Jubilee of 1897, an occasion which was both orchestrated and popular. If Royalty was to preserve and enhance its mystique it had to keep its distance from the people. Racialism, by contrast, derived its power from the felt presence of Jews, Irish or Germans in a context where social Darwinism was incessantly preached. In immigrant areas politicians ceaselessly played the racialist card. As the Jewish Conservative candidate for Romford put it in 1897, 'Now, gentlemen, I want to tell you that I am for "England for the English". I want England to come in first, second and third, and the foreigners to come a long way after.'

In the age of imperialism the English were constantly exhorted to be patriotic, and the measuring rod of patriotism was one erected by the Conservatives in the 1870s; the patriot was above class, loyal to the institutions of the country, and resolute in defence of its honour and interests. Liberals, radicals and socialists who protected their own patriotism were singularly unsuccessful in wresting the initiative from the right. Patriotism was firmly identified with Conservatism, militarism, royalism and racialism.

If the working class became patriotic in this period it was the outcome not only of the 'bribery' of the labour aristocrats, but, more importantly, of the bludgeoning of the whole of the working class by a weight of propaganda whose total impact it is difficult now to recapture. The process started with mothers whose role in breeding and rearing the race was increasingly insisted upon in the age of imperialism (Davin, 1978). They handed on the baton of socialisation into patriotism to the school which, through, for example, the history it taught and the drill it imposed, became the main agent of the state (see Chancellor, 1970; Hurt, 1977). At the same time popular reading material was infused with imperialist attitudes (James, 1973; Dunae, 1980). Once school days were over the youth organisations pioneered by the Victorians attempted to instil patriotism, along with other manly or womanly virtues (Springhall, 1977). In early manhood the Volunteer Force, largely working-class in composition, provided part-time and unpaid training in the patriotic task of defending the realm (Cunningham, 1975). The Regular Forces, too, once both in theory and practice the last resort of the outcast, had since the Crimean War been promoted as the embodiment of Christian heroism, and there had been much earnest talk about closing the gap between the armed forces and the nation.

Outside these relatively formal institutions the working class would be subject to patriotic propaganda in its leisure and in its politics. Music hall, it is argued, in London at any rate, became actively and self-consciously Tory in the last thirty years of the century, with consequences which, Laurence Senelick speculates, 'may help to explain the question that so fascinated Friedrich Engels: why the downtrodden British working class was so submissive and never rebelled' (Senelick, 1975, pp.155-6). And if the leisure hours were spent at chapel, particularly Wesleyan Methodist chapel, there too the congregation was more likely than in the early part of the century to hear patriotism being preached from the pulpit. And there was of course constant speculation about the relationship between patriotism and games playing, some of which may have percolated down to working-class players (see, e.g., Mason, 1980).

Historians have been in little doubt about the impact of all this. We are presented with a working class without political or cultural resources with which to resist patriotism, whether it spread by the flow of cash or by that entanglement of institutions through which the creed was preached; a class whose only mode of opposition to patriotism was half-hearted apathy: 'if the working class did not actively promote the jingoism', writes Gareth Stedman Jones, 'there can be no doubt that it passively acquiesced to it' (Stedman Jones, 1974, p.461). From the socialist perspective the outcome was at best what Victor Kiernan (1978, p.136) has called a merely 'half-accepted false consciousness'. It is a picture which needs to be qualified [. . .].

What is striking is the extent to which working-class people imposed their own interpretations on patriotic institutions and occasions [. . .]. There was a sense of the irrelevance of patriotism to most of working-class life, and this needs to be distinguished from apathy. And there was an ability to interpret patriotism in ways quite different to those intended by its propagators. Besides these responses, however, there was also outright opposition. It took two forms. The first inherited one strand of the radical patriotism of the early nineteenth century, its internationalism and pacifism, and continued the tradition of a working and middle-class alliance which had been forged in the 1860s and 1870s. It was most dramatically in evidence in the opposition to the Boer War, a moment of defeat certainly, but one testifying to a determination to resist Jingoism and militarism. It is a tradition which was by no means exhausted in the Boer War, and is clearly evident today.

The second form of opposition was distinctively socialist; to the claims of nation it counterposed those of class. In the radical patriotism of the 1830s and 1840s it can be seen in embryo, not often clearly articulated, but underlying much of the talk about the links between patriots of all countries in opposition to their rulers; its characteristic mode of thought, however, was political rather than social and economic. In the late nineteenth and early twentieth centuries, in the period of the Second International, socialists explicitly proclaimed the interest of the workers of all countries as indivisible. It is difficult to assess the depth of this thinking in England. It implied a total rejection of the language of patriotism. In a Red Sunday School in Glasgow in 1917 children were taught: 'Thou shalt not be a patriot for a patriot is an international blackleg'. Only rarely is the abandonment of the language of patriotism so explicit. More commonly socialists rejected the excesses of the patriotism that was thrust at them, arguing, as James Cunnington did in Bristol, that 'there were plenty of ways of inculcating patriotism of the highest type–the saving of life, instead of taking it–without influencing the passions of people against foreign nations'. The opposition to patriotism was more often seen in terms of fraternity than of class. But a sense of class was of course at the forefront of the domestic politics of the period, and the logic of the primacy of class placed socialists in inevitable opposition to those who preached the primacy of national unity.

It would, however, be illusory to suppose that this opposition to the patriotism of the age of imperialism was other than that of a small minority; nor can it be argued that the ability of working-class people to interpret patriotism in their own way immunized them in any thorough-going way from the virus of right-wing patriotism. Nor indeed can we forget that while some Socialists were firm in their loyalty to class above nation, others asserted a patriotism that was dangerously akin to the patriotism of the right. Hyndman and Blatchford in the very titles of their books (*England for All, Merrie England, Britain for the British*)harked back to the radical patriotism of the first half of the nineteenth century, but in the age of imperialism it was impossible to demarcate a patriotism of the left; the language had passed to the right and those who employed it did so too.

This history has happened, and however much we might wish it otherwise, it cannot be unwritten. Yet the legacy of radical patriotism remains with us, and is enjoying a resurgence. It can be seen in the socialist opposition to the EEC and to NATO, and in CND. Its hallmarks are an internationalist pacifism, a deep-rooted suspicion of the state and the invocation of a tradition of English freedom. Its relevance to the politics of today needs no stress [. . .].

References

CHANCELLOR, V. E., (1970) *History for their Masters*, Bath.
CUNNINGHAM, H., (1975) *The Volunteer Force*, London.
DAVIN, A., (1978) 'Imperialism and motherhood', *History Workshop*, No. 5, Spring.
DUNAE, P. A., (1980) 'Boys' literature and the idea of Empire, 1870-1914', *Victorian Studies*, Vol. xxiv.
EMSLEY, C., (1979) *British Society and the French Wars 1793-1815*, London.

HURT, J. S., (1977), 'Drill, discipline and the Elementary School ethos', in P. McCann, (ed.), *Popular Education and Socialization in the Nineteenth Century*, London.

JAMES, L., (1973) 'Tom Brown's imperialist sons', *Victorian Studies*, Vol. xviii.

JOYCE, P., (1980), *Work, Society and Politics: The Culture of the Factory in Later Victorian England*, Brighton.

KIERNAN, V., (1978), 'Working class and nation in nineteenth-century Britain', in M. Cornforth (ed.), *Rebels and their Causes*, London.

MASON, T., (1980), *Association Football and English Society 1865–1915*, Hassocks.

PROTHERO, I., (1974), 'William Benbow and the concept of the "general strike" ', *Past and Present*, no. 63, May.

SENELICK, L., (1975) 'Politics as entertainment: Victorian music-hall songs', *Victorian Studies*, Vol. xix, December.

SKINNER, Q., (1974), 'The principles and practice of opposition: the case of Bolingbroke versus Walpole', in M. McKendrick, (ed.), *Historical Perspectives*, London.

SPRINGHALL, J. O., (1977) *Youth, Empire and Society*, London.

STEDMAN JONES, G., (1974) 'Working-class culture and working-class politics in London, 1870–1900,' *Journal of Social History*, Vol. 7.

THOMPSON, E. P., (1968), *The Making of the English Working Class*, Harmondsworth, Penguin Books.

III   Politics and Nationalism

(b)   The Conservative Nation

12 Conservatism, Nationalism and Imperialism

Bill Schwarz

Since the late 1970s, it has been common for Conservative Party gatherings to feature the prominent display of Union Jacks, the singing of patriotic songs and other imperialist paraphernalia. Although it may not seem so, this is quite new. Until the 1950s, Conservative public meetings were generally accompanied by little more than some forlorn bunting and a single Union flag draped over a trestle table on the podium. Subsequently, imperial and national symbols began to look a little anachronistic as the conservative government of Harold Macmillan set in train the process of rapid decolonization and turned its attention to the EEC. In the 1960s, as the Union Jack took on connotations of Carnaby Street's joky chauvinism or the more menacing racism of the far right, the link between the Conservative Party and the imagery of Empire began to wane. But here we are in the 1980s with the Conservatives – or rather their corporate agents – eagerly recycling the symbols of Empire and nation in public displays carefully designed for television and radio.

How can we make sense of this new Conservative rhetoric? A clue is given by the historian Gareth Stedman Jones's observation that: 'Social alliances do not simply happen, they are brought into being and re-created by the construction and periodic reconstruction of a common political discourse' (1983, p.253). This suggests two lines of investigation: first, the discursive elements which are the building blocks of a political ideology like conservatism and, secondly, the historically variable articulations of such ideologies and the social alliances which they support. In studying attempts to create a popular English conservatism, we should look not just at the language of Conservative politicians and thinkers, but also at the imagery and symbols I have mentioned, at spectacular public rituals (especially those focused on the monarchy), and at representations of the nation and the people in a variety of media (such as the press or advertising) and forms of popular entertainment (music hall, cinema, television and so forth). Ideology involves *both* the production of such representations *and* their dissemination within popular culture as a means of organizing and managing social alliances. It follows that conservatism as a political ideology cannot be understood other than historically and empirically, through an account of its organizational strategies for

154

generating popular support.

At the same time, it is important to remember that the questions which this historical investigation seeks to answer are theoretical ones – essentially, they can be summarized in Ernesto Laclau's questions about what constitutes the unity of an ideological discourse and how ideologies are transformed (this volume, pp.27–32). In this article, therefore, I shall be examining a number of key moments in the formation of patriotic and conservative ideologies, roughly from the Civil War in the seventeenth century to the aftermath of the Second World War. I shall focus, first, on how elements like 'liberty', 'the individual', 'the nation', 'patriotism', 'Englishness' and 'the people' are worked into the relative coherence of a conservative ideology at these moments and, secondly, on how and why these articulations of conservatism change.

Before embarking on that historical account, a number of points should be noted. For a start, my account is based on the premise that there *is* an English nationalism and that assertion, in itself, is enough to upset some widely cherished myths. For many conservative writers on Englishness (regardless of their party allegiance), to interpret that deliberately vague notion as an ideology or a nationalism is to misconstrue the indefinable, felt, organic values which it entails. These,they suggest,can only be perceived and appreciated sensually, as they are embodied in England's language and literature, in its landscape and gardens, in its architecture and in the common sense of its people. These make up the threads that bind us invisibly to the past. Just as English nationalism is denied, so is the fact of its turbulent and contested history. What we get instead (especially in many of the older history books) is an emphasis on tradition and heritage, above all on *continuity*, so that our present political culture is seen as the flowering of a long, organic evolution.

But this idea of continuity is as much an imaginary construct as the idea of Englishness – and is equally central to the ideology of English conservatism. Indeed, these are among the categories which make up the 'system of narration' which defines what it means to be English in conservative terms (see Laclau, this volume, p.28). The logic of this system of narration is that patriotism is a natural human instinct, that there is an intrinsic relationship between their party and patriotism, and therefore that the Conservative Party is successful to the extent that it is able to express the nationalist sentiments of the people. This belief is only sustainable by ignoring the dramatic historical variations in both conservative and nationalist ideologies (and in the relationship between them) as well as the forms of British patriotism which have been far from conservative.

Nevertheless, the assumptions about the conservatism-nationalism link, or attempts to analyse it, do raise an important theoretical problem: the two sides of the equation are not really commensurable. Whereas it is possible to approach conservatism as a political ideology, in the sense that it comprises certain beliefs or values which are linked to the interests and social position of particular groups or classes, nationalism isn't an ideology in that strict sense. As Benedict Anderson comments,

> Part of the difficulty is that one tends unconsciously to hypostasize the
> existence of Nationalism-with-a-big-N . . . and then to classify 'it' as *an*
> ideology . . . It would, I think, make things easier if one treated it as if it
> belonged with 'kinship' and 'religion', rather than with 'liberalism' or
> 'fascism'.
> (Anderson, this volume, p.88)

The implication is that nationalism is a *cultural* rather than a purely political
phenomenon; hence its power to generate a sense of identity and allegiance.A neo-
conservative like Roger Scruton expresses the point like this:

> The condition of man requires that the individual, while he exists and acts as
> an autonomous being, does so only because he can first identify himself as
> something greater – as a member of a society, group, class, state or nation, of
> some arrangement to which he may not attach a name, but which he recognizes
> instinctively as home.
> (Scruton, this volume, p.107)

Pruned of its characteristic rhetoric about 'instinct' and 'the condition of man',
this is making much the same point as Benedict Anderson's argument (from a very
different perspective) about nationalism as membership of an 'imagined
community'.

Nationalism, like culture more generally, involves a sense of *belonging to* or *in* a
place, of being *at home in a place* (Said, 1984, p. 8). It might therefore be said, and
this is very much the emphasis given by Laclau, to form part of the 'political
unconscious' which political parties have to work on in their attempts to construct
social alliances. It is, in Gramsci's sense, 'historically organic'.

> One must therefore distinguish between historically organic ideologies, those,
> that is, which are necessary to a given structure, and those that are arbitrary,
> rationalistic, or 'willed'. To the extent that ideologies are historically necessary
> they have a validity which is 'psychological'; they 'organize' human masses,
> and create the terrain on which men move, acquire consciousness of their
> position, struggle etc. To the extent that they are arbitrary they only create
> individual 'movements', polemics and so on . . .
> (Gramsci, 1971, p.377)

The question is therefore how, or whether, conservatism as a political movement
has been able to organize and rework popular nationalist sentiment. This is what is
at stake in 'the attempt to articulate popular-democratic interpellations in the
ideological discourses of antagonistic classes' (Laclau, this volume, p.31).

So contemporary forms of nationalist conservatism, to return to my opening
example, do not represent the release of a single patriotism inherent in the British
people, let alone all the people in Britain. Rather, one particular conservative
version of patriotism – a popular-democratic interpellation articulating a specific
meaning of the British nation – has emerged as dominant, neutralizing or
marginalizing other voices on the way.

Note, however, that what is involved here is not ideological imposition but
ideological *struggle*. Although it is always difficult to judge popular responses to

nationalistic appeals, it is clear that such interpellations are always negotiated and often contested. George Orwell, for example, insisted that a subjective sense of Englishness cannot easily be escaped: 'Good or evil, it is yours, you belong to it, and this side of the grave you will never get away from the marks it has given you' (Orwell, 1970, p.76). Nevertheless, in another essay, he also suggested that formal and official exhortations to patriotism as such are popularly received with at least a degree of scepticism or indifference. He never read the proclamations of generals before going into battle or listened to national anthems, he wrote, 'without seeming to hear in the background a chorus of raspberries from all the millions of common men to whom these high sentiments make no appeal' (Orwell, 1970, p.193). Again, the point seems to be that nationalism can remain effective as a repertoire of images, values and responses feeding into subjectivity even when it is consciously ridiculed.

So far I have stressed some of the ways in which English nationalism is like other nationalisms. But it does, of course, have its own peculiarities, the legacies of the ideological struggles through which it has been formed. Most notable is the curious relationship between an unacknowledged but specifically *English* nationalism and the political compositon of the United Kingdom. Often, in England or outside the British Isles, the terms 'English' and 'British' are regarded as interchangeable. Not so in Ireland, Scotland or Wales, where separate identities forged in nationalist cultural strategies have been mobilized in opposition to the political and ideological hegemony of England. The reluctance of English nationalism to name itself as such is a paradoxical outcome of the long history of such struggles. Although it has been the most powerful component in the make-up of a British identity, Englishness has remained the most taken-for-granted and the least investigated of modern nationalisms. We must ask why.

In order to pin down the shifting relations between representations of England and Britain, it is necessary first to understand how, in various historical periods, England was placed in the configuration of Britain, and second to assess the expansion of English cultural and political rule not only throughout the British Isles but also throughout the Empire. Although never complete or uncontested, the absorption of subordinate national identities into a characteristically English identity became a powerful feature of British imperial rule at the end of the nineteenth century; its traces remain prominent in contemporary British culture. This, then, is the story of the expansion and contraction of England – an imaginary construct which presents itself as the outcome of tradition and continuity, but which achieves this appearance only by systematically concealing the conditions of its own formation and reproduction.

The legacy of revolution

The most dramatic instance in this history of national identity is the English Revolution of the 1640s and the cultural struggles which prefigured it. It was precisely in this break with the past that the idea of Englishness became fully formed – and formed, it must be stressed, as a *revolutionary* ideology.

The passage in this volume by Hugh Seton-Watson describes the earliest origins of English identity, rightly giving due attention to the importance of the development of the English language. By the middle ages the English state was in large part created, governing not only England and Wales but also portions of France. Its political rule, however, was concentrated in the south-eastern corner of the island, which happened to be the most highly cultivated and economically advanced region. The expansion of the market outwards from the south-east and the drive towards the integration of the economy as a whole were critical in creating the conditions in which a more fully formed idea of the English community could emerge. The construction of the Tudor state and the fierce imprint of protestantism together moulded for the first time an identifiable national consciousness. But it was only in the revolution of the mid-seventeenth century that the radicals were able to pose successfully the new political conception of the nation *as* the people.

The struggle for popular sovereignty, the defence of property and opposition to the established church became, during the revolution, the defining features of a new patriotism. This was a patriotism pitted against the existing state and self-consciously revolutionary. With a missionary zeal the puritans undertook what they believed to be the essential task of liberating from ignorance and superstition not just the English people but also those who inhabited 'the dark corners of the land'. From the Reformation to the civil war there had occurred a slow but steady expansion of the cultivated areas of England; puritanism spread along the inter-connecting trade routes. In 1650 this incipient process of cultural diffusion received official sanction and encouragement from the new state: an act of parliament was passed for the Propagation of the Gospel in Wales and in the four northern countries of Cumberland, Westmorland, Northumberland and Durham. 'Wales and the North were finally integrated during the interregnum into the civilization which was extending from London over the whole country' (Hill, 1974, p.34). With considerably more brute force the Scottish Highlands and Ireland were in the same decade first effectively conquered by English armies. In the baptism of fire of the revolution, drawing on the might of the new army and the cultural power of puritanism, the English state asserted its hegemony over the other nations of the British Isles. As Cromwell declared to parliament on 17 September 1656: 'We are English, that is one good fact' (Hill, 1970, p.i).

The combination of the revolution with the emergence of a popular patriotic ideology fused into one the ideas of liberty and Englishness (see Hall, this volume). The conception of English liberty and the frequent contrast made with the continental nations still subjected to the thrall of absolutism lay deep in the emerging plebian culture of the eighteenth century. In its very formation, English popular culture was steeped in a sense of its own particular, and special, national identity. Many did believe that it was providential to have been born English – or at least, an English man. The great patriotic songs – those heard today at Conservative displays – were the product of this time. They were, according to one author,

. . . struck up lustily when the opportunity offered. Choruses of 'God Save the King' greeted George III at the theatre – more out of patriotism than love specifically for the Hanoverians. William Hogarth, who signed himself 'Britophil', caught the mood with a flattering – though double-edged – series of national stereotypes. People loved his beer-guzzling, roast-beef-eating, four-square Englishmen, the 'dread and envy' of starveling, bare-foot, onion-nibbling French peasants, oppressed by lecherous Popish priests and mincing courtiers.
(Porter, 1982, p.22).

In fact these were strange sentiments with which to fuel a sense of national pride. Many English men and women were materially no better off than their counterparts in Europe, and travellers to England were genuinely nonplussed by the great draughts of beery chauvinism which greeted them.

This does suggest that for the English the boundaries of the nation were acknowledged by the majority of the population, even with some pride, from very early on in modern history. From the beginning of the eighteenth century, bar the Jacobite resistances in 1715 and 1745, and with the singular exception of Ireland, the British state existed within settled frontiers. The Union With Scotland Act was passed in 1707, Union With Ireland not until 1800. Outside Ireland, religious, regional and ethnic antagonisms were relatively few and muted. Thus the major conflicting forces, cohering primarily around class divisions, occurred within – and not against – the nation.

There is a central question which needs to be asked, however. If the idea of England signified so strongly the hopes of revolution and liberty, how and when did this assume a conservative idiom and eventually become a mainstay of conservative ideologies? There is no inherent or necessary relationship between the idea of England and the idea of liberty. Indeed, these two terms don't themselves tell us very much. They can mean almost anything to anyone. As Ernesto Laclau suggests, such terms only begin to make sense when systematically worked into a broader ideology or discourse. That is why the different linkages made between 'England' and 'liberty' need to be studied historically. The connection between them has less to do with logic than with their shared conditions of emergence in the revolutionary years of the seventeenth century. Thus, it cannot be assumed that the idea of Englishness ever denoted a single or straightforward idea of liberty. What matters – especially in tracing how these central elements have been appropriated for conservative ideologies – are the cultural and political struggles over their metaphorical connotations.

The transformation of the nation as a symbolic category in a conservative direction quickened during the course of the eighteenth century as the revolutionary period receded. This process can be traced in a wide range of ideologies – not just in political ideologies, but also in those discourses which came to be modelled on some concept of the constitution, in legal ideologies for example (Hay, 1977), or even in debates about the proper usage of the English language (Barrell, 1983). But the conditions for this shift into conservatism were given by the revolution itself. In the mid-seventeenth century the old absolutist order was destroyed and new liberties did become instituted in the new state. But at the same time many of the most revolutionary aspirations, particularly of the lower orders, were contained. The world was transformed by the revolution, but it was not turned upside down as some had hoped. Some advances in liberty had been achieved, but also many compromises. The Restoration and the constitutional settlement of 1688 represented the equlibrium of revolution and conservative compromise.

This political settlement, contradictory to its core, was represented in symbolic form in the idea of the English nation. By the end of the eighteenth century, the rhetoric of the tradition of English liberties was available, as a political language, to *both* radicals and conservatives. The visionary libertarianism of the revolutionary millenarial groups of the 1640s was rendered subordinate during the years of reaction, forced into a subterranean existence and kept alive only in fragmented form in small, often isolated dissenting groups in the eighteenth century. In the next period of radical advance, from the 1770s, this tradition appeared once more, in transmuted form, and contributed to the new voice of democracy which took hold of the popular culture. But at the same time, in direct response to this radical and democratic challenge, a philosophical revolution took place in which the symbol of the conservative nation was first delineated.

The conservative nation

Conservatism, and its invocation of national identity, first crystallized in clear form in the 1790s, in the age of English counter-revolution. The great democratic revolutions in North America (1776) and France (1789) reordered and extended the syntax of 'liberty'. British armies were sent against both revolutions in the hope of destroying them. In England the nation was riven in two between those who passionately supported the revolution in France, and those conservatives who feared that a Jacobinism was about to be ignited in England. One of the richest manifestations of this embattled engagement – which took as central the definition of the nation – was Edmund Burke's *Reflections on the Revolution in France* (1790). This became the founding text of the conservative nation.

Burke's text is supreme in its polemical artifice. It was written by an Irishman whose identity as an Englishman appeared to require no explanation; it was addressed as an epistle to a 'young gentleman' in Paris, thereby bestowing an illusory maturity and wisdom on its author; and although it purported to be a treatise on France, its primary object of alarmed concern was Britain.

The centrality of Burke's *Reflections* follows from a simple fact which belies these literary tricks. It was in this polemic that the thesis was first sustained, with a cogent flair and vigour, that the strength of the constitution in England derived pre-eminently from an organic relationship with the *past* and from its very conservatism. Liberty, in this view, would only be destroyed by the abstract and over-rationalistic philosophies of the Jacobins (see Hall, this volume pp.56–7). The only hope for liberty lay in the modest, pragmatic evolution of human history represented above all by English civil society. In this, the faith in England's revolutionary identity, as the nation most deeply wedded to liberty, was neatly but decisively overturned. In the *Reflections* England appeared as the mirror-image of this idea: still as unique and superior, still the foremost adherent of liberty, but now earning these attributes *because* of its conservatism, and the refusal of its people to indulge in the childish antics of the French.

During the seventeenth century a popular patriotism had been formed in the struggles against absolutism, conditions which allowed patriotic ideologies in the eighteenth century a continuing oppositional bite. In the last decade of the eighteenth century, however, on the impact of the *new* revolutions, Burke was a significant force in prising apart patriotism and radicalism. For Burke the *primary* meaning of England was of an ordered past and of a 'manly, moral, regulated liberty' (1969, p.89). English liberty was defined no longer in terms of the popular will but as the *attribute* of the dense institutional and discursive carapace of custom, tradition and the past. Henceforth, 'our liberty . . . has its bearings and its ensigns armorial. It has its gallery of portraits; its monumental inscriptions; its records, evidences and titles' (this volume, p.6). The weight of this institutionalized past is taken as the cultural and political insurance against disorder in the future. More than anything else, at this moment we can see emerging that unshakeable belief that English liberty, quintessentially, *is* tradition.

In the twenty or thirty years after 1790 there occurred a series of sustained social and political conflicts in which, so E.P.Thompson's argument goes, the English working class was first made (Thompson, 1968). Although tenaciously creating and extending their own particular culture, the working-class radicals of the time suffered serious political defeats. One dimension of these defeats was that alongside the older plebian conception of a democratic nation, the conservative variant inspired by Burke assumed a new dominance. This was the period when a *popular* idea of the nation first became assimilated into a systematically conservative image.

Even in the first quarter of the nineteenth century, however, this conservative dominance did not entirely eliminate an oppositional patriotism within the organized, radical working-class movement. Dormant for much of the 1790s and 1800s when the state made every effort to reclaim the language of patriotism during the Napoleonic wars, a radical conception of Englishness re-emerged which reached a new peak in the Chartist struggles of the 1840s. For these decades the idea of the nation was the object of bitter contention, and it was still possible for working-class radicals to claim themselves as the true patriots, against what they represented as the sham patriotic pretentions of the governing class. For radicals England, as a symbol, could still connote an uncompromising faith in liberty. In the 1870s a transformation occurred in the language of patriotism which was of the greatest significance. From this time patriotism comes to connote, almost exclusively, the ideas and ambitions of the conservative nation. More liberal and oppositional accents became increasingly fragmented, being displaced by a new popular voice, loudly proclaiming its chauvinism and bellowing its commitment to the hierarchies of the conservative nation. In 1878, this voice acquired a name – jingoism.

The determinations which gave rise to this phenomenon are not easy to explain in their totality, but certain features stand out. As Hugh Cunningham explains, the immediate context for the first great explosion of jingoism, in the crisis of 1877-78, was Disraeli's determination to send the navy to Constantinople to hold at bay the advances of the Russians – the fear of Russia giving a particular colouring to popular xenophobia long before the identity with Bolshevism was constructed.

Behind this, of course, the fortunes of the Conservative Party assume a prominent part of the explanation. In 1867 it had been under a Tory administration that parliamentary reform first gave the vote to working men. The new democratic imperatives ensured that if the Tory Party were to survive it would have to become, up to a point at least, a *popular* party. Until the 1860s there would have been no sense in which the Tories could have been perceived as laying any greater claim to be the party of the nation than any other party or grouping. This identity occurred, first, in response to the 'cosmopolitan' little-Englandism of the Liberals (a reworked sense of nation which was deeply rooted in the spirit of nonconformism), and, second, as the mechanism by which to create a new means of popular representation. The name most clearly associated with this shift was that of Disraeli.

In the year of the Second Reform Bill Disraeli had asserted: 'I have always considered that the Tory party was the national party of England' (quoted in Cunningham, in this volume, p.146). This may have appeared self-evident to Disraeli, with his idiosyncratic and rather naive radical Tory romanticism, but it sounded pretty startling to his political colleagues. Yet Disraeli was a sufficiently astute opportunist to understand the need for recreating the party in a new democratic, popular image. The greatest strength of the old Tory Party had been its defence of agriculture, and of the system of social relations – including those of paternalism – which sustained landed capital. 'The original core of the Conservative Party, the impregnable bastion from which it has never been shifted, is its domination of the English countryside – a domination completely consistent with the original Tory landowner base. Between 1847 and 1865 the Conservatives won between 62 and 75 per cent of the English country seats in every election' (Ross, 1983). This observation is important not only for emphasizing the dependence of Conservation upon agriculture, but also for suggesting that the striking emergence of ideologies of ruralism towards the end of the century was not contingent in so far as it touched the Conservative Party, but closely connected to the party's traditions. Furthermore, the continuing significance of the south-east needs to be stressed: 'Tory strength in the countryside is matched by its position in the South and South-East of England. If a line is taken across England from the Humber estuary in the North-West to the Bristol Channel, and then extended downwards to the South Coast, the Tories had a majority to the south of that line, excluding London, in every general election of the nineteenth century except for 1832 and 1885' (Ross 1983, pp.67-8). In breaking out, electorally, from this stronghold it was necessary to forge an appeal which would have meaning for the urban working class. It is a paradox that a primary means by which this was achieved was the construction of a ruralist ideology which looked *back* to the English society of the pre-industrial eighteenth century. It is from this period that English nationalism assumes its overwhelmingly rural connotations.

Alongside this, of course, the 1870s marked the opening of Britain's imperial high noon. In the 1870s Britain's 'informal' global hegemony came to an end, threatened by the territorial claims of powerful, industrialized metropolitan rivals. By 1900 England was at the hub of the largest empire the world had ever seen, administered at its pinnacle by a tiny group of men steeped in the mythologies of the classical world who devoutly believed in the eternity of the new civilization they were creating.

Disraeli's famous disparaging remark about colonies as 'millstones' makes sense in so far as the necessity actually to formalize, territorially, spheres of influence was indeed the source of much diplomatic and military inconvenience for the imperial rulers. Far better a system which required little policing and ran on the steam of Britain's economic might. Disraeli himself was far from modest in his imperial ambitions, recasting the idea of the conservative nation in an explicitly imperial mould. Before the 1870s the term 'imperialism' connoted within British political culture continental absolutism and authoritarianism on the model of a Bonaparte or Bismarck. Its accretion of new meanings and its insertion into the discourse of the free-born Englishman is a dazzling spectacle to behold.

A formative moment in this transformation took place in the incongruous setting of the Free Trade Hall, Manchester on 3 April 1872 when Disraeli (aided by two bottles of brandy) addressed the Conservative Association for a full three and a quarter hours. In response to the Radicals lodged inside the Liberal Party, Disraeli highlighted the commitment of his party to the established political institutions – the monarchy, the House of Lords and the Church, all of which had recently come under Radical attack. His emphasis was on the centrality of the throne to the well-being of the nation, as the *necessary* pivot on which constitutional issues turned:

> Since the settlement of [the] Constitution, now nearly two centuries ago, England has never experienced a revolution, though there is no country in which there has been so continuous and such considerable change. How is this? Because the wisdom of your forefathers placed the prize of supreme power without the sphere of human passions. Whatever the struggle of the parties, whatever the strife of factions, whatever the excitement and exaltation of the public mind, there has always been something in this country round which all classes and parties could rally, representing the majesty of the law, the adminstration of justice, and involving, at the same time, the security of every man's rights and fountain of honour.
> (Quoted in Buckle 1920, p.187)

The theme here, of liberty, justice and individual rights is neatly incorporated into a view of constitutionalism which has its theoretical inspiration in Burke, and which holds together – a recurring difficulty for conservative ideologues – *both* an appreciation of social change *and* the recourse to the essential 'continuity' of post-revolutionary English political development. In proportion to the demo-cratization of the political nation, Disraeli implied, so the stabilizing influences of the established institutions of the nation needed to be articulated. The speech closed, in terms quite uncharacteristic of the dominant political discourse of the day, with an invocation of political grandeur which carried an explicitly *popular* appeal:

> I express here my confident conviction that there never was a moment in our history when the power of England was so great and her resources so vast and inexhaustible. And yet, gentlemen, it is not merely our fleets and armies, our powerful artillery; our accumulated capital, and our unlimited credit on which I so much depend, as upon that unbroken spirit of her people, which I believe was never prouder of the Imperial country to which they belong.
> (Quoted in Buckle 1920, p.187)

The idea of an imperial conservatism fashioned to fit a democratic age was developed further in a speech at the Crystal Palace the following June. Disraeli insisted that the party had three great objectives: to maintain the institutions of the nation, to uphold the Empire and to elevate the condition of the people. Of these tasks, he expounded most fully the role of imperial England, rejecting Liberal arguments for granting self-government to the colonies and 'little-Englandist' objections to their cost. To take this attitude, however sincerely, meant for Disraeli:

> ... viewing everything in a financial aspect, and totally passing by those moral and political considerations which make nations great, and by the influence of which alone men are distinguished from animals.
> Well, what has been the result of this attempt during the reign of Liberalism for the disintegration of the Empire? It has entirely failed. But how has it failed? Through the sympathy of the Colonies for the Mother Country. They have decided that the Empire shall not be destroyed; and in my opinion no Minister in this country will do his duty who neglects any opportunity of reconstructing as much as possible our Colonial Empire, and of responding to those distant sympathies which may become the sources of incalculable strength and happiness to this land.
> (Quoted in Buckle 1920, pp.194-5)

This positive rendering of the concept of Empire, and the diligence with which Disraeli and the Tory leadership attempted to present their party as *the* party of Empire, launched a political project which, despite sometimes dramatic fluctuations, came to define the conservative nation until at least the end of the 1950s. And what was so remarkable in this achievement was that, in opposing liberalism and denouncing the ethics of a little Englandism, conservative nationalist ideologies appropriated and made their own the language of the free-born Englishman. As Hugh Cunningham rightly comments: 'in the age of imperialism it was impossible to demarcate a patriotism of the left; the language had passed to the right and those who employed it did so too.'

There is some contention about the degree to which Disraeli himself was responsible for this profound reorientation in Conservative ideology. Certainly, his ideas on Empire and the nation must have rather rapidly gained the acceptance of the majority of the party leaders and party managers. I have already implied that the agricultural basis to Toryism provided the discursive resources for the proliferation of ruralist ideologies which etched a very distinctive contribution to the idea of the conservative nation. In addition, the romantic and the radical in Disraeli's own temperament clearly cut across, at various points, older plebian traditions of community. But whatever the assessment of Disraeli's own contribution, there is no doubt that very soon after his death in 1881 a *concerted* job of ideological work was conducted inside Conservatism in order to enshrine his name as the founder of conservative nationalism. In the process, a shift of singular importance occurred in which traditions supposedly rooted in the immemorial past were 'invented' with breathtaking speed and audacity (Hobsbawm and Ranger, 1983).

We can take as an example the Primrose League; this was founded in 1883 by Randolph Churchill as a quasi-official organ of the Conservative Party, with the purpose of organizing the private rather than the more directly political terrain. Within seven years of its foundation it boasted a membership of one million – and even has a shadowy existence to this day. Its ideologies of romantic feudalism perpetuated the apparent naturalness of landed rule, its evocative themes proclaiming the defence of religion, the family, the estates of the realm and England's imperial ascendancy. It was decisive in that it also represented a major attempt by a dominant political party to incorporate women as – indirect – participants in public affairs, long before formal voting rights were won and women took their place as equal members of the political nation. Some of its 'habitations' were for women only, and they adopted an explicitly feminist platform. The Primrose League – which took its name, supposedly, from Disraeli's favourite flower – created a powerful set of ideologies which fused notions of democracy and participation with reverence for hierarchy and tradition, subsuming popular democratic connotations under the weight of the inherited, conservative past. But the popularity of the League was primarily due to its dedication to entertainment rather than formal political discussion. Meetings were the occasion for pierrots, jugglers, ventriloquists and, when possible, the ever-popular magic lantern – often relaying home images of the distant outposts of the empire. As Ostrogorski, one of the most astute conservative theorists of the time, observed, the League was 'a machinery which manufactures sentiments' and 'the greatest promoter of the "socialisation of politics" ' (Ostrogorski, 1902, pp. 551 and 440).

In this same spirit of popular conservatism a number of journals appeared within a year or two of each other, all dedicated – with different nuances – to commemorating the contribution of Disraeli. One such was *England*, edited by the founder of the Patriotic Association, Ellis Ashmead-Bartlett. In the first issue of another, *Merry England* in 1883, George Saintsbury looked back to the Young England movement and its contemporary relevance:

> Young England aimed at dissolving the rigid barriers between different classes
> of the population by the influence of natural good offices, by the humanizing
> effects of art and letters, by the common enjoyment of enjoyable religious
> functions, by popularising the idea of national tradition and historic
> continuity, and by restoring the merriment of life, by protesting against the
> exchange of money and receipt as sufficient summary of the relations of man to
> man.
> (Quoted in Lucas 1971,pp.178-9)

This desire to retrieve the imagined past in order to make a better future became
one of the most striking leitmotifs of conservative conceptions of Englishness from
this period until the First World War. The conservative image which emerged, as
if by some conjuring trick, from these ventures was, if nothing else, a coherent
picture. It was one which was critical in reproducing the sentiments and
allegiances to which Ostrogorski referred. How much it shaped Conservative
policies is a question of a different order, and not one directly relevant to this
article. There is good reason to think, however, that the direct impact was rather
slight.

More relevant, but even harder to assess, is the influence of these re-definitions
of the nation on popular culture. In the last decades of the nineteenth century, the
social and political institutions attempting to instil the imperial ethic into the
culture of the working class multiplied beyond belief. Not only institutions within
the orbit of the state – such as the military, elementary schools, prisons and
reformatories and so on – were suffused with the culture of Empire: so too were
those of a voluntary or private nature. There is now an abundant literature dealing
with many aspects of this process of ideological and cultural production.
Conclusions are tentative but it appears that despite the unprecedented weight of
this cultural domination, a working class built in the image of the middle-class
ideal of Empire failed to emerge.

Jingoism and a poisonous chauvinism undoubtedly existed, although not as a
generalized expression of working-class experience. Jingoism was as much a cross-
class response, drawing in elements from an expanding lower-middle class, as a
manifestation peculiar to the working class. To many workers patriotism appeared
primarily as an irrelevance, which, as Hugh Cunningham observes, needs to be
distinguished sharply from a notion of apathy. Nor did a formal commitment to
patriotism necessarily preclude forms of behaviour which, to the middle classes,
would have appeared as the most outrageous denial of the imperial ideal. Thus, to
take one example, an oral account suggests why Liberal cosmopolitanism was
received with hostility by some working people:

> Well the British people didn't like that because they had all been brought up
> on 'Rule Britannia'. I mean, even when they looted the West End in 1886,
> when the unemployed smashed up the jewellers' shops, trying to impress the
> people up west with their condition, they marched back to the East End
> singing 'Rule Britiannia'. Now what more patriotic, more conservative song
> can you have than that? But at that time every band played patriotic songs.
> (Quoted in Samuel 1981, p.263)

Popular patriotism, then, can lead to some unexpected places.

Not only did the concept of 'birthright' shift from a liberal to a conservative discourse at the end of the nineteenth century; it also assumed racist connotations. The 're-invention' of England in those years went hand-in-hand with the invention of the English *race*. One clear indication of this was the founding in 1894 of the Royal Society of St. George, which published a journal under the title *The English Race*. Its concerns were forcibly expressed in the first issue: 'there is some fear that the English stock is getting deficient in that healthy and legitimate egotism which is necessary to self-preservation . . . The Englishman must assert his indefensible birthright. . . . Above all other racial elements in the British system, the English needs to be distinguished and preserved' (quoted in Nairn, 1981, p. 258). Derivatives of ideas such as these could have alarming consequences.

Nowhere was this clearer than in the moves from the end of the nineteenth century to restrict 'alien' (mainly Jewish) immigration, a campaign based primarily in the East End of London. The first response, in the 1870s and 1880s, to Jews arriving in Britain to escape pogroms was one of general sympathy. The greatest anxieties were expressed by wealthy Anglo-Jews who were worried that destitute Jewish immigrants would give Jewry as a whole a poor reputation; so it was, in the first instance, Anglo-Jews who emphasized most strongly the importance of assimilation into the indigenous culture. By the mid-1880s, however, there were signs of an openly racist antagonism flaring in the East End. Local MPs and journalists quickly amplified these scares, addressing the 'respectable worker' whose job was threatened by immigrant labour. Arnold White, a notorious jingoist, offered himself as champion for the cause of free-born Englishmen dispossessed by aliens: 'the question is one which the inarticulate portion of the community feel with intensity and bitterness. If the House of Commons will order a real enquiry into the facts, I for one will undertake to prove the reality of the evil, the urgency of the situation, and the feasibility of effective prevention' (quoted in Fishman 1975, p.70). Such self-proclaimed spokesmen as these thrived by demonstrating their own alertness and their own sensitivity to popular fears, contrasting their own action to the feebleness of the government which, so the argument continued, preferred to adopt the line of least resistance and do nothing. Between 1887 and 1888 pressure mounted sufficiently for the government to agree to a Select Committee of Inquiry into the issue of immigration, although its final report made few recommendations. Occasional but regular racist outbursts still occurred in East London. Local trade unionists shared platforms with Conservative politicians, both decrying the Jewish 'threat'. In response, in 1892 as a piece of plain electoral opportunism, the Conservative Party agreed to the principle of an Aliens Bill. Lord Salisbury, frequently so averse to state intervention, introduced in July 1894 a private member's bill to restrict entry of destitute aliens and anarchists, the metaphors of contagion and crime adding force to his case. In the election the following year Joseph Chamberlain made the issue a prominent one in his speeches. From the turn of the century anti-immigrant organizations appeared in the East End, most notably the British Brothers' League, which held its first public meeting – packed to capacity – in

Stepney in May 1901. The intensity of the movement forced the government to appoint a Royal Commission in early 1903, and the eventual passing of the Aliens Bill in 1905, which empowered the Home Secretary to expel any aliens found to be criminal, vagrant, impoverished, or who lived 'under insanitary conditions due to overcrowding' (see Gainer, 1972).

It is difficult to assess with accuracy the extent to which the culture of the East End of London was influenced by racism, for it is evident from this account that there was a strong element of orchestration in play, with local Conservative activists repaying *their* perceptions of the situation to the government at the same time as lobbying on a racist platform. Nonetheless, it is one example of how thoroughly conservative opinion defined and made public on its own terms a key issue, and did so by deploying the language of the liberties of the English working man. In this context, the pursuit of liberty means not opposition to oppression imposed from above but the defence of one's own job or property from the 'invasion' of 'aliens'. From this point on, the interconnection between conservative ideologies and the anachronistic language of national liberty mesh to form a discourse which is peculiarly *closed* in its orientation, drawing from an array of common sense perceptions in which national characteristics – the freedom-loving, or inventive, or stoical Englishman – have a strategic position in organizing and producing new meanings and new political 'truths'.

The constitution

The period from the 1870s to the First World War marked the high-point of English imperial rule. This was also the period of the most intense remaking of English nationalism. For J.R.Seeley the two processes were one, linked by the concept of the 'expansion of England'. He looked forward to a time when 'Canada and Australia would be to us as Kent and Cornwall' (Seeley, 1883, p.63). It is significant that it was only to the 'white colonies' that his imagination could carry him.

This symptomatic absence raises most of all the problem of India. English people could not conceive of the Empire without India. It was the greatest proof of the civilizing mission of the nation, the 'jewel in the Crown of England' as Disraeli had called it. It held three-quarters of the population of the entire Empire and was the source of incomparable wealth and prestige. For two generations there can hardly have been a family in the Conservative oligarchy which did not at some point have intimate connections with the sub-continent. British Conservatism is unthinkable without India. But there existed one fundamental problem which did much to challenge the very basis of Conservative philosophy. The inhabitants of India did not have pink skins.

Before the First World War self-governing 'Dominion' status was conferred on the 'white colonies' (which due to its racial hierarchy could include South Africa) exactly as if their inhabitants hailed from Kent or Cornwall – and no doubt some did. But precisely because of the way in which the ruling race perceived and constructed the idea of 'Orientalism', as Edward Said explains, such a move proved impossible for India. No matter how anglicized the upper and professional classes of the sub-continent, no matter how perfect their accent and idiom, they could not cross the threshold and *become* English (see Homi Bhabha). Out of these impossible , desires there developed a new genre of 'English' literature, confirming the 'superiority' of Englishness and creating the comic figure of the aspirant anglicized Indian which was to root itself deeply in British culture.

From the last half of the nineteenth century the gradual realization by British Conservatives that 'something had to be done about India', that some concession to political freedom had to be made, proved traumatic. The idea of agreeing to equality of citizenship with the peoples of India was abhorrent to large numbers of Conservatives, for it brought into immediate crisis their own national and racial identity.

Moreover, from the time of the First World War, the Empire itself appeared in a very different light. Although the geographical size of the Empire increased dramatically as a result of the rich pickings made at the Versailles Peace Conference, Britain could no longer boast global hegemony. Economically, Britain had long ago ceased to be the most powerful nation and was embarking upon its protracted secular decline into economic crisis. The Easter Rebellion in Dublin in 1916 and the partition of Ireland in 1921 dislocated the metropolis at its very heart. In the wake of the Bolshevik Revolution in Russia and the upheavals in the aftermath of the world war there spread through the Empire movements seeking colonial liberation, most of all in India. And even at home, the political arrangement which had held together Conservatives and Liberals was in the very final moments of disintegration, with Labour appearing as a serious electoral contender.

The liberal response to these shifts inside the Conservative Party – as opposed to the incubation of a determined, diehard empire loyalism – can best be represented by Stanley Baldwin, the leader of the party from 1923 to 1937. With Baldwin the image of the conservative nation once more underwent a drastic transformation, defeating those who had adhered to the militaristic and jingoistic imperialism of the late nineteenth century. In its place there slowly emerged a version of conservatism in which the idea of English constitutionalism – of 1688 read through Burke and Lord Macaulay's *History of England* – became the organizing principle of what came to be understood as the very nature of politics.

What is significant in this context is less Baldwin's political career than the way in which he conceptualized his politics in terms of English culture. However, the paradox lies in the fact that at every turn he was determined to demonstrate that his idea of the nation was neither nationalistic (in the sense of 'other' nationalisms) nor political in that it was the shared *inheritance* of every English man and woman.

Baldwin's idea of the conservative nation enriched and extended the ideology of Englishness and drew it yet more deeply into the syntax of conservative discourse. It incorporated fully the rival motifs of liberalism (constitutionalism, liberty and individual justice) while denying that it had any political provenance. In this discourse Englishness came *to signify* liberal, parliamentary constitutionalism. But at the same time it was itself *signified by* a complex series of signs – the landscape and countryside, common sense and reasonableness, popular literature and language, pragmatism and modesty – which had no place in the formal, institutional political ideologies of the earlier period. Henceforth the central sign, England, carried an accumulation of meanings, 'civic' in inspiration rather than 'political', which could work by displacement and understatement. Indeed there occurred the transformation of the Baldwin persona itself in which the modest, popular, pipe-smoking figure, the carrier of a rural wisdom deriving from older traditions of folklore, came itself to signify the whole complex of the political philosophy merely by its appearance. This is in stark contrast to the late nineteenth century which witnessed an obsessional proliferation of explicitly nationalist and racial discourses. Although it directly works *from* this, carrying forward many of its interior meanings, in Baldwinism this explicit concern with a racial superiority diminished, for – when working at its best – it did not even have to be spoken.

Many of these themes are evident in a speech on 'England' which Baldwin delivered to the annual dinner of the Royal Society of St George's in 1924 (see Schwarz, 1984, pp.14-18). Here he implicitly repudiated politics in favour of a common national identity which stressed individual diversity while ignoring social antagonisms.

> Let us see to it that we never allow our individuality as Englishmen to be steam-rollered. The preservation of the individuality of the Englishman is essential to the preservation of the type of the race, and if our differences are smoothed out and we lose that great gift, we shall lose at the same time our power.

Significantly, Baldwin referred to the erosion of linguistic diversity in order to express this fear of uniformity:

> I regret that by a process which for want of a better name we have agreed among ourselves to call education, we are drifting away from the language of the people and losing some of the best English words and phrases which have lasted in the country through centuries, to make us all talk one uniform and inexpressive language.

The language is presented here as part of an essential historical *tradition*. Baldwin then eternalizes this ideology of Englishness by transposing it to the world of the landscape.

> To me, England is the country, and the country is England. And when I ask myself what I mean by England, when I think of England when I am abroad, England comes to me through my various senses – through the ear, through the eye, and through certain imperishable scents.

With almost mystical conviction, he invokes the temporal rhythms of the countryside:

> The sounds of England, the tinkle of the hammer on the anvil in the country smithy, the corncrake on a dewy morning, the sound of the scythe against the

whetstone, and the sight of a plough team coming over the brow of a hill, the sight that has been seen in England since England was a land, and may be seen in England long after the Empire has perished and every works in England has ceased to function, for centuries the one eternal sight of England. The wild anemones in the woods in April, the last load at night of hay being drawn down a lane as the twilight comes on, when you can scarcely distinguish the figures of the horses as they take it home to the farm, and above all, most subtle, most penetrating and most moving, the smell of wood smoke coming up in an autumn evening, or the smell of the scutch fires: that wood smoke that our ancestors, tens of thousands of years ago, must have caught on the air when they were coming home with the results of the day's forage, when they were still nomads, and when they were still roaming the forests and the plains of the continent of Europe. These things strike down into the very depths of our nature, and touch chords that go back to the beginning of time and the human race, but they are chords that with every year of our life sound a deeper note in our innermost being.

The recurring images of nature, home, harmony and (less explicitly) the continuity of human life through the family are then linked to the identity of the English people and their conception of Empire.

These are the things that make England, and I grieve for it that they are not the childish inheritance of the majority of the people to-day in our country. They ought to be the inheritance of every child born into this country, but nothing can be more touching than to see how the working man and woman after generations in the towns will have their tiny bit of garden if they can, will go to gardens if they can, to look at something they have never seen as children, but which their ancestors knew and loved. The love of these things is innate and inherent in our people. It makes for that love of home, one of the strongest features of our race, and it is that that makes our race seek its new home in the Dominions overseas, where they have room to see things like this that they can no more see at home. It is that power of making homes, almost peculiar to our people, and it is one of the sources of their greatness.

Although now it may be the extraordinary sentimentality of Baldwin's rhetoric that is most striking, that should not lead us to underestimate its political skill or impact. Here I want to stress just one aspect of the speech – its populism. Baldwin attempts to address 'the whole people' and – by activating subjective feelings of one's past and familial inheritances – to position 'the people' within his own reading of English history and the English character. This is not an *active* populist appeal in which the people are called upon to political action, but rather one which is more passive, which addresses the people in order to win their consent to this imaginary construct of England and to remind them of their place in the national order of things.

Why should the discourses of nationalism and Conservatism have been rearticulated in this populist mode at this time? For one thing, the pressure on Conservatives to extend the universalist or populist elements of their philosophy was increasing as a result of the extension of the franchise and the entry into the political nation of women and working-class men. This also accounts for the deep but hard-fought for *liberal* attachments of Conservatism in the 1920s. Conservatives did not (on the whole) wish to embrace an outwardly reactionary politics in which the advances of democracy were to be overturned, but rather to develop the institutions of democracy in such a way that the new electorate would learn a 'reasonable' political conduct and not threaten the fundamental political institutions. It may be for this reason that some of the elements of Disraelian Conservatism were reactivated in this period and assumed a new dominance, with the aim of instructing the electorate in the traditions of the established institutions of the realm.

Just as the French Revolution had a decisive impact on the idea of the conservative nation in Britain in the 1790s, especially through the writings of Burke, so in the 1920s the emergence of the Bolshevik state became the primary touchstone by which English constitutionalism could be judged. It can be argued that one effect of this long term political and cultural struggle was the effort to *constitutionalize* the conservative nation. Similarly, the Conservatives in the period after the First World War confronted not only a new political enemy at home, but also in the colonies. Baldwin hoped that it would be possible to constitutionalize the directive role of the 'mother country' toward her colonies and so save the Empire. In 1935, for example, the Government of India Act looked forward to a time of independence for India within the commonwealth of nations. In pursuing this strategy, Baldwin had to fight the diehards in his own party, not the least of whom was Winston Churchill, and this too forced Baldwin to emphasize the constitutionalist version of his concept of the conservative nation.

Baldwin's stress on the workings of civil society, and his repudiation of established political ideologies as a sufficient basis for Conservative philosophy, contributed to the dispersion of the Baldwinite conception far beyond the formal political institutions. The measure of his political success should perhaps be the influence of his thought on civic, 'voluntary' and 'private' ideologies whose adherents would in no way have declared formal allegiance to the Conservative Party. One area in which this process could be seen at work was the presentation of the monarchy.

Disraeli had identified the crown as the pre-eminent symbol of national unity, a constitutional bulwark against the corrosion of democracy. This *symbolic* power greatly increased as the crown progressively lost its real political influence (see Cannadine, this volume). Yet the nature of this power, as the fountainhead of the conservative nation, requires some concessions to democracy. The crown has to appear as a *popular* symbol, and its bearers (the royal family) as 'of' the ordinary people.

Whereas in the nineteenth century popular displays of the crown's majesty were rare, they have become common in a more democratic culture. By the 1920s and 1930s the means for representing the monarchy, with which we are familiar today, were already in place. Of great significance in the opening phase of this transition was the great Empire Exhibition of 1924 at Wembley – the first spectacle, running over a period of weeks – designed for *mass* domestic consumption. The new mass media played a particularly important role in organizing the opening. The *Daily Mail*, for example, relayed radio broadcasts up and down the country, renting the Albert Hall in London and local cinemas in all major towns. For the BBC it presented the first opportunity for a large-scale outside broadcast. Popular participation was massive – twenty-seven million people visited the exhibition – and the pageantry and spectacle unprecedented. The official programme proclaimed that 'the visitor will be able to inspect the Empire from end to end' (quoted in MacKenzie, 1984, p.108). To what extent this was the reason for the exhibition's popularity is hard to assess. But the excuse it provided for a good day out ensured that the idea of the exhibition certainly became lodged in the popular mind, giving rise to such forgotten popular songs as 'Wembling at Wembley with You' and 'In my Little Wigwam, Wembley Way'.

The new mass media *reconstituted* the monarch as a popular figure in this period, presenting the human individual as the living embodiment of sovereignty. This did not develop without contention. A ferocious struggle developed between the BBC, the Palace and the government over the ethics of the royal broadcast. The first Christmas address to the nation, made by George V in 1932, took five years to arrange. It was an immediate and great success. Sir John Reith, the head of the BBC, despaired of the caution of the politicians, simply unable to comprehend their short-sightedness. As late as 1937 he noted in his diary: 'Straight to Buckingham Palace. Hardinge said that Neville Chamberlain had felt that it was impossible for the King to broadcast every Christmas as they couldn't produce an interesting enough talk. How pathetic. Almost unbelievable. How typical of the attitude of politicians' (Stuart, 1975, p.197). Reith for one needed no persuading. Similarly, he had been campaigning since 1927 for the founding of a BBC Empire Service, which finally first broadcast in December 1932. On that occasion Reith proudly claimed that radio 'becomes a connecting and co-ordinating link between the scattered parts of the British Empire' (quoted in Mansell, 1982, p.2).

This imperial dimension to the monarch's presence was taken as crucial in the debates of the time. One commentator recalled: 'I heard in Canada King George V at the time of his Jubilee address to his people over the radio. Each individual heard his voice and had the feeling of being in his presence. He no longer seemed a symbol, something cold, abstract; he was a human being speaking to human beings' (quoted in Mansell, 1982, p.22).

In this sense the monarch personifies not only the links between all peoples of the Empire, but also the link to the *past*. And already, by the 1930s the royal family had become the representative of the *national* family – both unique and special on the one hand, but on the other living through the same woes and tribulations as the rest of us. Nowhere was this more forcefully presented than during the abdication crisis, a crisis which was resolved by Baldwin, his astute sense of political realities enabling him to see that the symbol of the crown was of greater political import than the fate of the person who wore it. The abdication was both a major constitutional crisis and an imperial crisis. As Baldwin emphasized, in terms reminiscent of Disraeli: 'The importance of the crown's integrity is, beyond all question, far greater than it has ever been, being as it is not only the last link of

Empire that is left, but the guarantee in this country, so long as it exists in that integrity, against many evils that have affected and afflicted other countries' (Baldwin, 1937, p.70). At the close of this crisis, Lucy Baldwin, the prime minister's wife, wrote to a friend proposing, with a touch of domestic common sense which Baldwin himself would have admired, 'Now what we have all got to do is to work to repolish the Throne' (quoted in Middlemas and Barnes, 1969, p.1017). The opportunity for this refurbishment came, of course, with the coronation the following May – a time for healing the spirit of the nation.

The royal radio broadcast, although designed for mass consumption, had no role for the people beyond listening quietly at their hearthside in their own homes. In contrast, spectacular 'live' occasions, such as coronations, *depend on* popular participation for their success. The people themselves are part of the show and, within limits, write their script as the drama unfolds. This provides great potential for confirming national identity and the place of the sovereign within the conservative nation. But, to prevent mishap, it also requires a high degree of direction, regulation and management. The boundaries of popular participation are carefully policed from the outset to position the *independent* voice of the people in the appropriate ordering of discourses. For this work – and are we not time and again reminded that no nation can match the English in such spectacular but tasteful displays of majesty – a consummate voice-over is needed to order and orchestrate the multiplicity of roles and to ensure that the correct hierarchy of *dramatis personnae* is adhered to.

Nearly eight thousand invitations were issued for the Coronation service in Westminster Abbey in 1937:

> The King has surprised and delighted four workpeople by personally inviting them to be present at the Coronation Service in Westminster Abbey on May 12. One is a Scotch woman weaver, another a South Wales steelworks foreman. Then there is a girl employed at the Birmingham Electricity Works and a young pit worker from Chesterfield.
> (Jennings and Madge, 1937, p.6).

Some of *us*, then, were permitted to witness the most symbolic moment of all. Others, especially from the colonies, were invited to take part in the processions, and themselves be a 'king or queen' for the day, representing their own peoples and communities.

> The most envied girl in Australia to-day is Miss Sheila Martin, of Wagga Wagga, New South Wales. She has been chosen to come to London as the best representative of Australian girlhood, and plans are being made to give her a Queen's reception in Britain.
> (Jennings and Madge, 1937, p.20).

Most of the audience, however, had to rely on the technology of the mass media. When the King and Queen came out of the Abbey 'instead of observers [i.e. commentators], four special "atmosphere" microphones will tell their own story by reproducing the sounds – the martial music, the cheers – as the procession passes.' To give the spectators the added sense of being there, and to highlight the humanity of the occasion, 'the largest telephoto lens in the world' was ordered by Paramount to film the key sequences (Jennings and Madge, 1937, p.16).

But the organizers clearly did not feel at ease giving the media specialists a free hand, although at the same time they recognized that without the mass media the event would be emptied of meaning. Due regard had to be paid to decorum and to the unique position of the monarch, and it was necessary to ensure that the right public images were relayed to the nation. Thus:

> After crowning King George VI at Westminster Abbey on May 12, Dr Lang, Archbishop of Canterbury, will go to a dark room in the West End to play a new role–film censor. His Grace, ever vigilant of public interest and good taste, will carefully scan the films of the Coronation made by the news reels. With him will be the Earl Marshall the Duke of Norfolk. The Primate and the Duke will have a free hand to cut from the film records anything which may be considered unsuitable for the public at large to see.
> (Jennings and Madge, 1937, pp.16–17).

What of those who participated 'on the day'? In fact, *everyone* had some role to play if they so wished. Most people could attend local parties. These were not the last word in decorum. For the day, everyone indulged in carnivalesque capers, symbolically turning the world upside down, indulging to excess (especially with liquor) and generally enjoying transient freedom denied by poverty or by the dull compulsion of daily labour. This, I believe, would have been the *predominant* popular experience of the coronation. (The Mass Observation reports also convey the sense of the weakening of sexual and gender taboos: many of the games in the local parties carried some element of bawdy transvestism.) There was no chance at these local celebrations to upset the *national* spectacle, only to ruffle the sense of occasion felt by respectable provincial dignitaries.

However, part of the drama of the day arose from the fact that at any moment anything could go wrong, and indeed, that the people might not stick to their allotted script. This very nearly happened. The transport strike, much to the horror of the transport workers' leader, Ernest Bevin, began on 1 May and very nearly continued up until the day of the coronation; a lightning strike by waiters on the eve of the 12 May was only resolved by the swiftest action on behalf of the employers.

But alcohol seems to have presented the greatest danger. The ushers in the Abbey, having seated everyone and with three hours to kill before the service commenced, managed to consume between them six cases of champagne. Many of the people who came to watch the procession were well drunk by the evening of 11 May, and spent much of the next day sleeping off their stupor in one of the parks. Rude and jocular songs–alongside frequent outbursts of *Land of Hope and Glory*–were frequent fare, especially as a response to the merest hint of some erotic or romantic display. 'Clapometers'–a nice indication of the importance of calibrating popular involvement–measured greatest applause, after the royal couple, for the boys who shovelled the horse manure from the streets.

On the whole popular exuberance was contained. But at one moment an outside microphone was commandeered by the crowd: 'someone managed to impersonate a BBC announcer and gave a commentary on the scene outside Buckingham Palace. The nervous strain of handing out the commentary to the 'unseen millions' seems to have told heavily on BBC officials, as there was a series of similar breakdowns and hoaxes' (Jennings and Madge, 1937, p.271). Thus it would seem that the conservative nation, despite the formal business of the day, did not get through unscathed. But the evidence also suggests that affection for the monarch and for the English institutions and customs – including here popular irreverence – was stronger at the end of the day than at the beginning, if only because the day was the occasion for good fun and high spirits. But the examples here also show the difficulties of directly incorporating the people as full participants of the nation. Such attempts at a *national* interpellation always have to negotiate the resistance embedded in existing forms of *popular* culture and subjectivity.

Another aspect to this popularizing of the monarchy involved the 'democratization' of the royal family. It was around this time that the monarch and his family began occasionally to engage in popular pastimes to prove their 'ordinariness'. This has become such a stereotyped media image that today it hardly merits attention, but before the 1930s it was thought far from proper for royal personages to indulge in activities which would bring such sustained publicity. And here particularly we can see developing, in the most patronizing of guises, the royal family participating (often with a look of calculated but pained pleasure) in specifically working-class pursuits. A random, but not untypical, example can illustrate this point.

It comes from the archetypal English populist entrepreneur Billy Butlin. In 1938 Butlin acquired sole rights to create an amusement park at the Empire Exhibition in Glasgow. With a sure combination of the popular and the deferential, Butlin persuaded the Duke and Duchess of Kent to visit his amusement park after they had opened the exhibition. Butlin recorded this, nearly forty years later, in loving, sycophantic detail. They went, he relates, 'on practically everything from the scenic railways – the Duke returned for a second trip on that – to the electric speedway. With that informality typical of the Royal Family, they happily went into the Crazy House, where visitors are assaulted by all manner of surprises' (Butlin, 1982, p.124). It is significant that this was an outer branch of the royal family: it was to be another twenty-five years before the monarch herself took the ultimate step and actually spent a day exploring the pleasures of a Billy Butlin holiday camp – an enticing reordering of the idea of the conservative nation.

The popularization of the conservative nation

The crystallization of what I have called, in shorthand, Baldwinism and the transformation of the symbolic power of the royal family suggest two of the crucial moments in the development of the idea of the conservative nation as a popular ideology, less emphatic than the jingoism of the late nineteenth century but perhaps all the more powerful for that very reason.

For a fuller picture of the various and diverse strands in this ideology it would be necesary to look at other strategic figures. Of key significance were those who had brought to bear on early and mid-twentieth century British politics an unprecedented 'English' rectitude and reverence for constitutionalism and its rituals. For example, it was George V who first made a common practice of visiting working-class communities and outlying areas of the Empire in an explicit attempt to extol the ideals of monarchy. As important, he dreamt of the nation as a kind of happy ship, ruled by an unbending but benevolent naval commander, a nostalgia deriving from his years as a young midshipman. This sort of idea, very different from earlier preconceptions of the monarchs, connected closely with Baldwinism.

Similarly, the career of Captain Clement Attlee, leader of the Labour Party from 1935 to 1955, could be placed within this same context. In this light we can see Attlee as representative of the officer class, devoted to a society in which the virtues of batmen, Indian manservants and boys' clubs could flourish. This paternalism touched the very core of his politics. Yet the role of the Labour Party in developing the new articulation of nationalist ideologies is of enormous significance, for it shows that the idea of the conservative nation was not the exclusive property of the Conservative Party. From the moment it appeared that there was a real possibility that Labour might become the party of government, the springs of respectability wound tight. At the 1923 Party Conference, a year before the Labour Party first took office, the question (not, it seems, a motion) was put: 'Is Republicanism the policy of the Labour Party?' The answer was clear. The vote against was 3,694,000; a mere 386,000 in the affirmative. This appeared to close the issue once and for all.

Through its subsequent history the Labour Party has been careful to abide by the rules of constitutionalism and its attendant rituals, even those which have little more than an apparently decorative function. There are countless anecdotes about the efforts of Labour politicians to conform to the etiquette of the day, especially in the earlier period when something akin to a class cultural apartheid existed. In January 1924, for example, the Labour Chief Whip had expressed the deepest concern that full court dress was beyond the means of all but one or two of the Labour leaders. The estimated cost was £73.2s.6d. These anxieties reached the ears of the king's secretary, Lord Stamfordham. Stamfordham went out of his way to be helpful. He wrote to the Chief Whip: 'I have ascertained from Messrs. Moss Bros., 20 King Street, W.C.2 (Telephone Gerard 3750), which is I believe a well known and dependable firm, that they have in stock a few suits of Household, Second Class, Levee Dress from £30 complete. This comprises trousers, coat, cock-hat, and sword and is the regulation dress' (Nicolson, 1952, p.392). Embarrassment was thus averted.

But the popularization of the conservative nation which occurred in the late 1920s and 1930s was not simply a matter of capitulation by the Labour Party. It touched working-class culture as a whole. Co-existing with the Baldwinite vision and working its same repertoire of elements, there appeared a specifically proletarian and urban rendering associated with such figures as Gracie Fields,

George Formby and Gracie Fields's occasional but pre-eminent script-writer, J.B. Priestley. All Baldwin's sentimentality was extended into this framework, but in an altogether more popular and sharper key. Gracie Fields in particular, born above the famed fish and chip shop in Rochdale, personifies this formation, becoming the prototype for the English, working-class star of the mass media. Anticipating the post-war history of stars, her symbolic function could at least obliquely converge with the acclaim more usually commanded by royalty. Thus 'during the 1930s, her tours across England were like royal processions' (Richards, 1984, p.169), earning her in 1938 that ambivalent recognition of CBE. The ideological formation represented by Gracie Fields, although distinctive in its popular claims, co-existed with the official culture of the dominant national institutions, but in a relationship which resolutely drove out any potentially antagonistic elements.

Through such channels, the idea of the domesticated Baldwinite nation extended out beyond the formal political institutions of the day. The break with jingoism entailed an attentuation of the 'masculine' symbolism of politics and the accentuation of a 'feminine' identity, in which, the figure of Gracie Fields is again central. In the 1930s and the 1940s the most powerful image of the English nation was projected through the ideas of the private sphere of the family and domesticity - the peculiar characteristics of 'our race', as Baldwin put it in his speech on 'England'. This, too, indicates another sharp break in the diffusion of a popular nationalism in modern British culture.

But a major paradox follows from this, which inexorably draws us back to the established political stage. Increasingly during the 1930s, the Conservative Party lost its authority to speak for nation and people. The miseries engendered by protracted economic deprivation and then, most startlingly, the Munich catastrophe of 1938 and the subsequent dismemberment of Czechoslovakia cut away the roots of popular Conservatism. For some, clearly, Munich represented the conservative nation triumphant. The elements exist in vivid form in popular memory. The quote from Disraeli; the courage and pluckiness of Chamberlain, the frail old man enduring the dangers and adventures of his first aeroplane trip for his country; the umbrella and bowler hat squaring up to the military regalia of the Germans and Italians; the relief and jubilation of the crowds at Heston and Downing Street. But in no sense was this response universal. Many were appalled at the Munich deal, regarding Chamberlain not as the naive negotiator outwitted by the double-dealing of unscrupulous foreigners, but as a treacherous participant, willing to sell Czechoslovakia down the river and extend to the limit appeasement of the aggressors so long as they left Britain alone. When in the spring of 1939 the policy of appeasement fell to pieces, once and for all, so too did the dominance of *Conservative* nationalism. This point has not received the attention it deserves. It opened the way, in the 1940s, for alternative variants of the nation, which had been prefigured in the popular culture of the 1930s. This was the greatest moment of humiliation for Conservatism which had haunted the party ever since, twice impelling it - in 1956 and 1982 - to engage in symbolic but murderous displays of imperial grandeur in order to atone for the treachery of the

1930s. Furthermore, Chamberlain was seen by his opponents as a representative of his class, a class grown soft and parasitic and no longer to be trusted to safeguard the interests of the nation. References to the French (whose upper classes were, as history showed, riddled with appeasers and quislings) became prominent, activating a popular chauvinism long present in English culture. The Foreign Office was presented as patrician through and through, as suspicions mounted that it was attempting to engineer an almighty sell-out. From this emerged the language of 'Guilty Men', of 'appeasers', of 'the old guard' and of the 'Colonel Blimps'. It was a language militantly populist, explicitly positioning those who used it against the state, the establishment and the power bloc. It was, above all, a language of the people and the nation. If the governing class could not be trusted, then it became the mission of the people to get on with the job. The popular rendering of the images of the conservative nation, and the icons which it had generated in the 1930s, proliferated in the moment of 1940.

This patriotic spirit came to a head in May and June 1940. Labour entered the coalition, Churchill replaced Chamberlain, Dunkirk was evacuated and France overrun, and the 'Battle of Britain' was fought in the summer skies. From these events there has been created a highly evocative nationalist mythology, almost complete in itself, which is still active in a range of political and nationalist discourses today. Read with hindsight, it is possible to distinguish an overarching figure in this drama, knitting all these episodes into one heroic moment, Churchill himself. Churchill was a Conservative, but one who had been out of step with his party for the previous decade, derided on the margins of political life. Indeed, he was a most incongruous character to appear as the saviour of democracy; but this he did, with an irrepressible faith in his own historic mission and his ability to lead his nation. On 13 May, three days after he assumed the premiership, he delivered the speech in the Commons in which he promised only 'Blood, toil, tears and sweat'. A little less than two weeks later, after the evacuation of Dunkirk, he made plain his determination never to surrender – a commitment which hitherto had not been spoken by the nation's governors:

> We shall go on to the end. We shall fight in France, we shall fight on the seas and oceans, we shall fight with growing confidence and growing strength in the air, we shall defend our Island, whatever the cost may be, we shall fight on the beaches, we shall fight on the landing grounds, we shall fight in the fields and in the streets; we shall never surrender. And even if, which I do not for a moment believe, this Island or a large part of it were subjugated and starving, then our Empire beyond the seas, armed and guarded by the British Fleet, would carry on the struggle, until, in God's good time, the New World, with all its power and might, steps forth to the rescue and the liberation of the Old. (Churchill, 1981, p.713)

A fortnight later, both to the House of Commons and as a radio broadcast, he delivered his verdict on the 'Battle of Britain':

> What General Weygand called the Battle of France is over. I expect that the Battle of Britain is about to begin. Upon this battle depends the survival of

Christian civilization. Upon it depends our own British life, and the long
continuity of our institutions and our Empire. The whole fury and might of the
enemy must very soon be turned on us. Hitler knows that he will have to break
us in this Island or lose the war. If we can stand up to him, all Europe may be
free and the life of the world may move forward into broad, sunlit uplands. But
if we fail, then the whole world, including the United States, including all that
we have known and cared for, will sink into the abyss of a new Dark Age made
more sinister, and perhaps more protracted, by the lights of perverted science.
Let us therefore brace ourselves to our duties, and so bear ourselves that, if the
British Empire and its Commonwealth last for a thousand years, men will still
say, 'This was their finest hour'.
(Churchill, 1981, p.729)

What is so striking about these speeches, read today (compared to listening to
them at the time) is their high and self-conscious rhetoric. The grand, almost
metaphysical, appeals to history, civilization and the Empire, counterbalanced by
the forebodings of a new Dark Age – clearly all this had an immense impact. What
is less obvious is exactly *how* these sentiments mobilized people and to what ends.
In assessing the events of 1940, the most difficult thing of all is to break through
the mythologies of 'Little England'. This is not to belittle the courage of those who
fought against Nazism nor to underestimate how desperately close won the fight
against the Axis powers was in the first year of the war. It is perfectly true that in a
critical period, Britain did stand alone against the might of the Third Reich. But it
is also the case that the public *representations* of these events were constructed in
the media – which at this date were heavily censored and managed – with an
astonishing alacrity. The myths were created in the moment the deeds themselves
occurred. In a sense, this was the mark of Churchill's greatness.

However it is also difficult, looking back with the advantage of hindsight, to
know how these Churchillian appeals accorded with the experiences of the people.
However much people may have respected him personally, his popularity as a
politician was by no means constant during the war, and in the 1945 election, as a
Conservative, he was thrown out, much to his own astonishment. The
discrepancies between a patriotism of greatness and Empire, and one drawn from a
common sense of the people pulling together in a time of crisis in order to create a
better world, could not have been more marked. Indeed, it is only in contrast to a
rather less mediated voice of the people – found in autobiographies, oral history
accounts, Mass Observation reports – that the Churchill voice begins to sound so
inflated, and so clearly divorced from popular experiences; from the blitz, or the
long hours in the munitions factories, or the daily routines of soldiers and sailors.

Churchill engineered the enduring myth of Churchill. For all his bluff attempts
to adopt a populist persona, he remained a Conservative of the old guard. Indeed,
there may be something here of the popular deference to leaders which was so
commonly seen by sociologists as an attribute of the Conservative hegemony of the
1950s. Churchill clearly knew about military matters (and may have had some gift
for military command as well), a knowledge which was the preserve of someone of
his class and background. In this respect, deference had a rational core.

Churchill is a complicated case. But the conservative nation, as it had been represented by the Conservative Party up until Munich, was clearly in crisis. Alternative conceptions of the nation, much more determinedly populist, provoked the inescapable challenge to the official political representations. Perhaps the foremost example, from the crisis of the summer of 1940, was in the famous radio *Postscripts* of J.B. Priestley. These were immensely popular, rivalling even Churchill's broadcasts. But the BBC mandarins suspected them of being vaguely subversive, and Priestley was eventually taken off the air.

His best known, and perhaps most characteristic, talk was probably the one broadcast on Wednesday 5 June, in the aftermath of Dunkirk. Priestley presented this in a self-conscious epic mode – it is 'as if we had turned a page in the history of Britain and seen a chapter headed "Dunkirk"'. This sense of continuity is linked to the idea of the national character in a way that recalls the epic form of Churchill's speeches:

> . . . let's do ourselves the justice of admitting too that this Dunkirk affair was also very English (and when I say 'English' I really mean British) in the way in which, when apparently all was lost, so much was gloriously retrieved. Bright honour was almost 'plucked from the moon'. What began as a miserable blunder, a catalogue of misfortunes and miscalculations, ended as an epic of gallantry.
>
> (Priestley, 1940, pp.1-2)

The striking contrast with Churchill lies in the populism of Priestley's style. Whereas Churchill invoked the heroism of 'our Island race', Priestley's image of the British people was closer to the comic imagery of seaside postcards –' the gents full of high spirits and bottled beer, the ladies eating pork pies, the children sticky with peppermint rock'. The common people here are *driven onto* the public stage by the vast and soulless machine of German might. It is the amateurishness and domesticity of Dunkirk that make it so English an epic. While Churchill thundered about the passing of empires, Priestley caught popular sentiment by condensing this history in the image of 'the little pleasure steamers' and their part in this 'difficult and dangerous embarkation'. This understatement is carried to its limits in the concluding reference to the good ship *Gracie Fields*, the 'pride of our ferry service to the Isle of Wight':

> . . . never again will we board her at Cowes and go down into her dining saloon for a fine breakfast of bacon and eggs. She has paddled and churned away – for ever. But now – look – this little steamer, like all her brave and battered sisters, is immortal. She'll go sailing proudly down the years in the epic of Dunkirk. And our great grand-children, when they learn how we began this War by snatching glory out of defeat, and then swept on to victory, may also learn how the little holiday steamers made an excursion to hell and came back glorious.
>
> (Priestley, 1940, pp.3-4)

The *Gracie Fields* becomes the sign of all that is decent and civil and heroic about the English people, and even the more conventionally political language of the final sentence is tempered by the homely connotations of 'excursion'.

Priestley's populism does not subvert the grandeur of Churchill's rhetoric; it complements it, is complicit with it. Priestley revives and broadens the idea of the conservative nation at a critical time. Although more closely, and perhaps more sympathetically, etched, the people in Priestley's account resemble closely the people in Baldwinism. They appear as passive bearers of 'Englishness', and no more.

Conclusion

We can bring the narrative to an end at this point. I have shown the early identification of English nationalism with a revolutionary constitutionalism, and how this was reversed during the counter-revolutionary period of the 1790s. Since the last quarter of the nineteenth century, English nationalism has most of all been articulated through Conservatism – first, in the language of high imperialism, and second, in what I have signalled here as Baldwinism. In highlighting the history of English nationalism in this way I have tried to give a sense of the discontinuity in its development, emphasizing the important turning points when the discursive formation was often quite radically refashioned. This stress on discontinuity and on the plurality of different versions of the English and conservative nation has been deliberate, an attempt to undermine the myths of continuity and singularity which are so often carried in the ideology of Englishness itself. However, in discussing each moment of transformation I have also insisted that there has existed a measure of continuity in that certain ideological elements have been carried forward into each new formation – thus, for example, Baldwinism in the 1920s contained within it recognizable features of the older, imperialist language, but in a new system and arrangement.

Much of this account depends on a reading of Laclau's analysis of ideology and of ideological transformation through a process of cultural struggle. To summarize briefly one or two of the central formulations, Laclau himself makes the distinction between the abstract elements within a particular ideology and the way in which these are combined in a historically specific, concrete ideology or discursive formation. He insists that the ideological elements themselves are relatively meaningless until they are combined with other signs or elements, and that what is crucial is precisely *how* they are combined. For example, we have seen here, and in the article on liberalism, the close proximity of two of the central signs or elements: England and liberty. These provide a potentially very rich raw material out of which political ideologies can be fashioned. But in themselves, outside a complete discursive framework, they mean little. Indeed, their meanings could be used in contrary ways. Thus for example in one discourse (Priestley or Churchill in 1940) the idea of the freeborn Englishman protecting hearth and home suggests a commitment against fascism, defending from Nazi terror those liberties which did exist in England. But on the other hand that very same idea could be mobilized in the 1970s or 1980s in order to protect 'hearth and home' from the perceived threat of Punjabis moving in next door – the same ideological elements, but inserted in a very different discursive framework, and leading to a quite contrary politics.

It is for this reason that Laclau places such emphasis on the sign as an object of cultural struggle. Political groupings or parties in a sense constitute themselves by attempting to elaborate a coherent discourse, unifying as far as possible a heterogeneous set of signs and symbols, contesting the meanings of certain fundamental concepts –liberty, democracy, morality and so on—with competing groups, and thereby aiming to formulate a full political and cultural programme. Thus by drawing on the accretion of meanings attached to the idea of England, reworking these meanings into a new unity, and appropriating newer ideological elements (in some instances from their political opponents) both Disraeli and Baldwin, for example, constructed a version of Conservatism with a new coherence and unity.

Now this in turn assumes that the construction of a unified discourse will, at least to some extent, address 'the people' and establish connections with the lived popular culture. If this objective fails, then the political party or grouping will remain merely sectarian, its programme academic, locked into an imaginary world of its own making. It is for this reason that Laclau introduces the concept of 'popular-democratic interpellations' in an attempt to theorize the relations between the popular and the political. As he sees it, the political project of a party (in its widest sense) is to win cultural and moral leadership by speaking to the people and expanding its objectives and constituency such that it achieves a real popular grounding. The party, then, comes to articulate its own programme as if it were universal, the programme of the people. And in so doing, the party exerts its own cultural authority by constructing the idea of 'the people' in its own image.

Something like this, I argued, occurred with the development of Baldwinism. There never appeared a full harmony between the sentiments of Stanley Baldwin, evoking the spell of rural Worcestershire, and the lived practices of the popular culture: the irreverence, bawdiness and drunkenness of the coronation of 1937 is sufficient to establish this difference. But the ways in which the Baldwinite vision of the conservative nation became popularized, especially after 1940, indicates the expansive potential of the Baldwinite ideology. Yet it is important to be clear on this. I am not suggesting that in the 1940s working people mouthed the language of Baldwin. Rather, it was a process in which working-class culture was an *active* agent in re-making the language of Baldwinism with its own pronounced inflection and accent. This is the significance of Priestley and such media stars as Gracie Fields. They spoke in a somewhat staged but nonetheless working-class idiom. It was a language which by virtue of its very separateness from the official culture proclaimed its difference from that culture, and indeed was composed of elements of a populist, anti-state and anti-power bloc strain: 'us' versus 'them'. This was the ground on which the range of radical ideologies of the 1940s flourished, against the Conservative 'old guard' and so on. But so far as the sentimental idea of England was reproduced in popular culture through such figures as Priestley, although identifiably different and separate from the upper classes, it was a discourse in which *antagonism* to the dominant culture was pared to a minimum. This antagonism was neutralized, difference preserved, and the conservative nation sustained, reproducing an ideology which was much more long-lived than the relatively circumscribed successes of Stanley Baldwin's Conservatism in political life.

Laclau's account is useful in making it possible to think of ideological transformations along these lines. It is perhaps a little more shaky on the question of determinations – on what social conditions make possible the emergence of one or other political force. Without going into the theoretical issues in detail here (see Hall, this volume, pp.44 ff.) it should be said, in the context of this article, that one of the central forces which gave shape to the play of discursive transformations was the expansion and contraction of the English state: the conquests of the seventeenth century, the establishment of the United Kingdom, the growth of empire, followed in our own time by imperial retreats and even pressures leading to what some have seen as 'the break up of Britain' (Nairn, 1981). The shifts in the imaginary and symbolic forms of England can only make sense in so far as they represent, in very complex ways, this protracted historical development.

The narrative in this article stops short of the next major transformation in the idea of England, which is also that which dominates today: the beginnings of decolonization and the end of Empire. In this modern period too it is clear that continuities exist within the discourses of Baldwinism, still reproduced in the dominant political institutions, if less frequently now in the broad range of cultural agencies. Some elements of the imperialist language of the late nineteenth century have also been reactivated, most especially around the issue of race and racial antagonism. It is still the case that the link between Conservatism and England is very strong, and effectively unchallenged: we still live in the conservative nation. Indeed, this has contributed a formidable current to the conservatism of the new right in the 1970s and 1980s.

But the situation in the 1980s is also one of ideological crisis – in which, so far as the themes of this article are concerned the process of decolonization has unhinged many of the unspoken assumptions of English nationalism. Conservatives now have to argue more stridently their claim to 'England', and in the process they create new points of antagonism. The expansive potentialities of the Baldwin idea of the nation have been severely diminished. At a higher level of abstraction Laclau writes about the nature of a generalized ideological crisis: 'The crisis of confidence in the "natural" or "automatic" reproduction of the system is translated into an exacerbation of all the ideological contradictions and into a dissolution of the unity of the dominant ideological discourse. As the function of all ideology is to constitute individuals as subjects, this ideological crisis is necessarily translated into an "identity crisis of the social agents" '. It could be argued, in the contemporary period, that the crisis of the English nation has produced exactly this crisis of *subjective* national identity.

Laclau has little to say about nationalism as such, and virtually nothing on England. In this sense I have drawn freely from his work. He does suggest that in moments of ideological crisis there is the possibility for the deployment of radically new discursive formations and the elaboration of new political philosophies. If one were to follow strictly the Laclau position, one might suppose that out of the contemporary crisis it might be possible to 'rediscover' the lost history of a radical English constitutionalism, and bring together an opposition with a patriotic voice, creating a viable political alternative to the conservative nation. Some attempts have been made at this. But what such ideas and strategies underestimate is the *weight* of tradition. The long duration of the idea of the conservative and English nation has a determinate history – the history of the Empire – which can't be dissolved in the flux of ideological crisis. The weight of this tradition has *itself* become an element in the contemporary ideological configuration. Hugh Cunningham's assessment of the imperial period holds good for the post-imperial epoch too: the language of the English nation is the language of conservatism.

References

BALDWIN, Earl (1937) *Service of Our Lives,* London, Hodder and Stoughton.
BARRELL, J. (1983) *English Literature in History, 1730–80,* London, Hutchinson.
BUCKLE, G. E. (1920) *The Life of Benjamin Disraeli, Earl of Beaconsfield,* Vol. V, London, John Murray.
BURKE, E. (1969) *Reflections on the Revolution in France,* Harmondsworth, Penguin.
BUTLIN, B. (1982) *The Billy Butlin Story,* London, Robson Books.
CHURCHILL, W. (1981) *Collected Speeches in Peace and War,* London, Windward.
FISHMAN, W. (1975) *East End Jewish Radicals, 1875–1914,* London, Duckworth.
GAINER, B. (1972) *The Alien Invasion. The Origins of the Aliens Act of 1905,* London, Heinemann.
GRAMSCI, A. (1971) *Selections from the Prison Notebooks,* London, Lawrence and Wishart.
HAY, D. (ed) (1977) *Albion's Fatal Tree,* Harmondsworth, Penguin.
HILL, C. (1970) *God's Englishman,* Harmondsworth, Penguin.
HILL, C. (1974) *Change and Continuity in the Seventeenth Century,* London, Weidenfeld and Nicolson.
HOBSBAWM, E.J. and RANGER, T. (eds) (1983) *The Invention of Tradition,* Cambridge, Cambridge University Press.
JENNINGS, H. and MADGE, C. (1937) *May 12th,* London, Faber and Faber.
LUCAS, J. (1971) *Literature and Politics in the Nineteenth Century,* London, Methuen.
MACKENZIE, J. (1984) *Propaganda and Empire. The manipulation of British public opinion, 1880–1960,* Manchester, Manchester University Press.
MANSELL, G. (1982) *Let the Truth be Told. Fifty years of BBC external broadcasting,* London, Weidenfeld and Nicolson.
MIDDLEMAS, K. and BARNES, J. (1969) *Baldwin. A biography,* London, Hutchinson.
NAIRN, T. (1981) *The Break-up of Britain,* London, Verso.
NICOLSON, H. (1952) *King George V,* London, Constable.
ORWELL, G. (1970) *Collected Essays, Journalism and Letters* Vol. II, Harmondsworth, Penguin.
OSTROGORSKI, M. (1902) *Democracy and the Organization of British Politics,* London, Macmillan.
PORTER, R. (1982) *English Society in the Eighteenth Century,* Harmondsworth, Penguin.
PRIESTLEY, J. B. (1940) *Postscripts,* London, Heinemann.
RICHARDS, J. (1984) *The Age of the Dream Palace: Cinema and Society in Britain 1930–1939,* London, Routledge and Kegan Paul.
ROSS, J. (1983) *Thatcher and Friends. The anatomy of the Tory Party,* London, Pluto.

SAID, E. (1984) *The World, the Text and the Critic*, London, Faber and Faber.

SAMUEL, R. (1981) *East End Underworld*, London, Routledge and Kegan Paul.

SCHWARZ, B. (1984) 'The language of constitutionalism. Baldwinite Conservatism' in *Formations of Nation and People*, London, Routledge and Kegan Paul.

SEELEY, J. R. (1883) *The Expansion of England*, London, Macmillan.

STEDMAN JONES, G. (1983) *Languages of Class*, Cambridge, Cambridge University Press.

STUART, C. (ed.) (1975) *The Reith Diaries*, London, Collins.

THOMPSON, E. P. (1968) *The Making of the English Working Class*, Harmondsworth, Penguin.

III   Politics and Nationalism

(c)   Colonial Discourse

13 Knowing the Oriental

Edward W. Said

From *Orientalism* by Edward W. Said, 1978. Reproduced by permission of the publishers Random House.

On June 13, 1910, Arthur James Balfour lectured the House of Commons on 'the problems with which we have to deal in Egypt.' These, he said, 'belong to a wholly different category' than those 'affecting the Isle of Wight or the West Riding of Yorkshire.' [. . .] Some members were questioning the necessity for 'England in Egypt,' the subject of Alfred Milner's enthusiastic book of 1892, but here designating a once-profitable occupation that had become a source of trouble now that Egyptian nationalism was on the rise and the continuing British presence in Egypt no longer so easy to defend. Balfour, then, to inform and explain.

Recalling the challenge of J. M. Robertson, the member for Tyneside, Balfour himself put Robertson's question again: 'What right have you to take up these airs of superiority with regard to people whom you choose to call Oriental?' The choice of 'Oriental' was canonical; it had been employed by Chaucer and Mandeville, by Shakespeare, Dryden, Pope, and Byron. It designated Asia or the East, geographically, morally, culturally. One could speak in Europe of an Oriental personality, an Oriental atmosphere, an Oriental tale, Oriental despotism, or an Oriental mode of production, and be understood. Marx had used the word, and now Balfour was using it; his choice was understandable and called for no comment whatever.

> I take up no attitude of superiority. But I ask [Robertson and anyone else] . . . who has even the most superficial knowledge of history, if they will look in the face the facts with which a British statesman has to deal when he is put in a position of supremacy over great races like the inhabitants of Egypt and countries in the East. We know the civilization of Egypt better than we know the civilization of any other country. We know it further back; we know it more intimately; we know more about it. It goes far beyond the petty span of the history of our race, which is lost in the prehistoric period at a time when the Egyptian civilisation had already passed its prime. Look at all the Oriental countries. Do not talk about superiority or inferiority.

Two great themes dominate his remarks here and in what will follow: knowledge and power, the Baconian themes. As Balfour justifies the necessity for British occupation of Egypt, supremacy in his mind is associated with 'our' knowledge of Egypt and not principally with military or economic power. Knowledge to Balfour means surveying a civilization from its origins to its prime to its decline – and of course, it means *being able to do that*. Knowledge means rising above immediacy, beyond self, into the foreign and distant. The object of such knowledge is inherently vulnerable to scrutiny; this object is a 'fact' which, if it develops, changes or otherwise transforms itself in the way that civilizations frequently do, nevertheless is fundamentally, even ontologically stable. To have such knowledge of such a thing is to dominate it, to have authority over it. And authority here means for 'us' to deny autonomy to 'it' – the Oriental country – since we know it and it exists, in a sense, *as* we know it. British knowledge of Egypt *is* Egypt for Balfour, and the burdens of knowledge make such questions as inferiority and superiority seem petty ones. Balfour nowhere denies British superiority and Egyptian inferiority; he takes them for granted as he describes the consequences of knowledge.

> First of all, look at the fact of the case. Western nations as soon as they emerge into history show the beginnings of those capacities for self-government . . . having merits of their own . . . You may look through the whole history of the Orientals in what is called, broadly speaking, the East, and you never find traces of self-government. All their great centuries – and they have been very great – have been passed under despotisms, under absolute govern-ment. All their great contributions to civilisation – and they have been great – have been made under that form of government. Conqueror has succeeded conqueror; one domination has followed another; but never in all the revolu-tions of fate and fortune have you seen one of those nations of its own motion establish what we, from a Western point of view, call self-government. That is the fact. It is not a question of superiority and inferiority. I suppose a true Eastern sage would say that the working government which we have taken upon ourselves in Egypt and elsewhere is not a work worthy of a philosopher – that it is the dirty work, the inferior work, of carrying on the necessary labour.

Since these facts are facts, Balfour must then go on to the next part of his argument.

> Is it a good thing for these great nations – I admit their greatness – that this absolute government should be exercised by us? I think it is a good thing. I think that experience shows that they have got under it far better government than in the whole history of the world they ever had before, and which not only is a benefit to them, but is undoubtedly a benefit to the whole of the civilised West . . . We are in Egypt not merely for the sake of the Egyptians, though we are there for their sake; we are there also for the sake of Europe at large.

Balfour produces no evidence that Egyptians and 'the races with whom we deal' appreciate or even understand the good that is being done then by colonial occupation. It does not occur to Balfour, however, to let the Egyptian speak for himself, since presumably any Egyptian who would speak out is more likely to be 'the agitator [who] wishes to raise difficulties' than the good native who overlooks the 'difficulties' of foreign domination. And so, having settled the ethical problems, Balfour turns at last to the practical ones. 'If it is our business to govern, with or without gratitude, with or without the real and genuine memory of all the loss of which we have relieved the population [Balfour by no means implies, as part of that loss, the loss or at least the indefinite postponement of Egyptian independence] and no vivid imagination of all the benefits which we have given to them; if that is our duty, how is it to be performed?' England exports 'our very best to these countries.' These selfless administrators do their work 'amidst tens of thousand of persons belonging to a different creed, a different race, a different discipline, different conditions of life.' What makes their work of governing possible is their sense of being supported at home by a government that endorses what they do. Yet

> directly the native populations have that instinctive feeling that those with whom they have got to deal have not behind them the might, the authority, the sympathy, the full and ungrudging support of the country which sent them there, those populations lose all that sense of order which is the very basis of their civilisation, just as our officers lose all that sense of power and authority, which is the very basis of everything they can do for the benefit of those among whom they have been sent.

Balfour's logic here is interesting, not least for being completely consistent with the premises of his entire speech. England knows Egypt; Egypt is what England knows; England knows that Egypt cannot have self-government; England confirms that by occupying Egypt; for the Egyptians, Egypt is what England has occupied and now governs; foreign occupation therefore becomes 'the very basis' of contemporary Egyptian civilization; Egypt requires, indeed insists upon, British occupation. But if the special intimacy between governor and governed in Egypt is disturbed by Parliament's doubts at home, then 'the authority of what . . . is the dominant race – has been undermined.' Not only does English prestige suffer; 'it is vain for a handful of British officials – endow them how you like, give them all the qualities of character and genius you can imagine – it is impossible for them to carry out the great task which in Egypt, not we only, but the civilised world have imposed upon them.'

As a rhetorical performance Balfour's speech is significant for the way in which he plays the part of, and represents, a variety of characters. There are of course 'the English,' for whom the pronoun 'we' is used with the full weight of a distinguished, powerful man who feels himself to be representative of all that is best in his nation's history. Balfour can also speak for the civilized world, the West, and the relatively small corps of colonial officials in Egypt. If he does not speak directly for the Orientals, it is because they after all speak another language; then he knows how they feel since he knows their history, their reliance upon such as he, and their expectations. Still, he does speak for them in the sense that what they might have to say, were they to be asked and might they be able to answer, would somewhat uselessly confirm what is already evident: that they are a subject race, dominated by a race that knows them and what is good for them better than they could possibly know themselves. Their great moments were in the past; they are useful in the modern world only because the powerful and up-to-date empires have effectively brought them out of the wretchedness of their decline and turned them into rehabilitated residents of productive colonies.

Egypt in particular was an excellent case in point, and Balfour was perfectly aware of how much right he had to speak as a member of his country's parliament on behalf of England, the West, Western civilization, about modern Egypt. For Egypt was not just another colony; it was the vindication of Western imperialism; it was, until its annexation by England, an almost academic example of Oriental backwardness; it was to become the triumph of English knowledge and power. Between 1882, the year in which England occupied Egypt and put an end to the nationalist rebellion of Colonel Arabi, and 1907, England's representative in Egypt, Egypt's master, was Evelyn Baring (also known as 'Over-baring'), Lord Cromer. On July 30, 1907, it was Balfour in the Commons who had supported the project to give Cromer a retirement prize of fifty thousand pounds as a reward for what he had done in Egypt. Cromer *made* Egypt, said Balfour:

> Everything he has touched he has succeeded in . . . Lord Cromer's services during the past quarter of a century have raised Egypt from the lowest pitch of social and economic degradation until it now stands among Oriental nations, I believe, absolutely alone in its prosperity, financial and moral.

How Egypt's moral prosperity was measured, Balfour did not venture to say. British exports to Egypt equalled those to the whole of Africa; that certainly indicated a sort of financial prosperity, for Egypt and England (somewhat unevenly) together. But what really mattered was the unbroken, all-embracing Western tutelage of an Oriental country, from the scholars, missionaries, businessmen, soldiers, and teachers who prepared and then implemented the occupation to the high functionaries like Cromer and Balfour who saw themselves as providing for, directing, and sometimes even forcing Egypt's rise from Oriental neglect to its present lonely eminence.

If British success in Egypt was as exceptional as Balfour said, it was by no means an inexplicable or irrational success. Egyptian affairs had been controlled according to a general theory expressed both by Balfour in his notions about Oriental civilization and by Cromer in his management of everyday business in Egypt. The most important thing about the theory during the first decade of the twentieth century was that it worked, and worked staggeringly well. The argument, when reduced to its simplest form, was clear, it was precise, it was easy to grasp. There are Westerners, and there are Orientals. The former dominate; the latter must be dominated, which usually means having their land occupied, their internal affairs rigidly controlled, their blood and treasure put at the disposal of one or another Western power. That Balfour and Cromer, as we shall soon see, could strip humanity down to such ruthless cultural and racial essences was not at all an indication of their particular viciousness. Rather it was an indication of how streamlined a general doctrine had become by the time they put it to use – how streamlined and effective.

Unlike Balfour, whose theses on Orientals pretended to objective universality, Cromer spoke about Orientals specifically as what he had ruled or had to deal with, first in India, then for the twenty-five years in Egypt during which he emerged as the paramount consul-general in England's empire. Balfour's 'Orientals' are Cromer's 'subject races,' which he made the topic of a long essay published in the *Edinburgh Review* in January 1908. Once again, knowledge of subject races or Orientals is what makes their management easy and profitable; knowledge gives power, more power requires more knowledge, and so on in an increasingly profitable dialectic of information and control. Cromer's notion is that England's empire will not dissolve if such things as militarism and commercial egotism at home and 'free institutions' in the colony (as opposed to British government 'according to the Code of Christian morality') are kept in check. For if, according to Cromer, logic is something 'the existence of which the Oriental is disposed altogether to ignore,' the proper method of ruling is not to impose ultrascientific measures upon him or to force him bodily to accept logic. It is rather to understand his limitations and 'endeavor to find, in the contentment of the subject race, a more worthy and, it may be hoped, a stronger bond of union between the rulers and the ruled.' Lurking everywhere behind the pacification of the subject race is imperial might, more effective for its refined understanding and infrequent use than for its soldiers, brutal tax gatherers, and incontinent force. In a word, the Empire must be wise; it must temper its cupidity with selflessness, and its impatience with flexible discipline.

> To be more explicit, what is meant when it is said that the commercial spirit should be under some control is this – that in dealing with Indians or Egyptians, or Shilluks, or Zulus, the first question is not to consider what these people, who are all, nationally speaking, more or less *in statu pupillari*, themselves think is best in their own interests, although this is a point which deserves serious consideration. But it is essential that each special issue should be decided mainly with reference to what, by the light of Western knowledge and experience tempered by local considerations, we conscientiously think is best for the subject race, without reference to any real or supposed advantage which may accrue to England as a nation, or – as is more frequently the case – to the special interests represented by some one or more influential classes of Englishmen. If the British nation as a whole persistently bears this principle in mind, and insists sternly on its application, though we can never create a patriotism akin to that based on affinity of race or community of language, we may perhaps foster some sort of cosmopolitan allegiance grounded on the respect always accorded to superior talents and unselfish conduct, and on the gratitude derived both from favours conferred and from those to come. There may then at all events be some hope that the Egyptian will hesitate before he throws in his lot with any future Arabi . . . Even the Central African savage may eventually learn to chant a hymn in honour in Astraea Redux, as represented by the British official who denies him gin but gives his justice. More than this, commerce will gain.

How much 'serious consideration' the ruler ought to give proposals from the subject race was illustrated in Cromer's total opposition to Egyptian nationalism. Free native institutions, the absence of foreign occupation, a self-sustaining national sovereignty: these unsurprising demands were consistently rejected by Cromer, who asserted unambiguously that 'the real future of Egypt . . . lies not in the direction of a narrow nationalism, which will only embrace native Egyptians . . . but rather in that of an enlarged cosmopolitanism.' Subject races did not have it in them to know what was good for them. Most of them were Orientals, of whose characteristics Cromer was very knowledgeable since he had had experience with them both in India and Egypt. One of the convenient things about Orientals for Cromer was that managing them, although circumstances might differ slightly here and there, was almost everywhere nearly the same. This was, of course, because Orientals were almost everywhere nearly the same.

Now at last we approach the long-developing core of essential knowledge, knowledge both academic and practical, which Cromer and Balfour inherited from a century of modern Western Orientalism: knowledge about and knowledge of Orientals, their race, character, culture, history, traditions, society, and possibilities. This knowledge was effective: Cromer believed he had put it to use in governing Egypt. Moreover, it was tested and unchanging knowledge, since 'Orientals' for all practical purposes were a Platonic essence, which any Orientalist (or ruler of Orientals) might examine, understand, and expose. Thus in the thirty-fourth chapter of his two-volume work *Modern Egypt*, the magisterial record of his experience and achievement, Cromer puts down a sort of personal canon of Orientalist wisdom:

> Sir Alfred Lyall once said to me: 'Accuracy is abhorrent to the Oriental mind. Every Anglo-Indian should always remember that maxim.' Want of accuracy, which easily degenerates into untruthfulness, is in fact the main characteristic of the Oriental mind.
>
> The European is a close reasoner; his statements of fact are devoid of any ambiguity; he is a natural logician, albeit he may not have studied logic; he is by nature sceptical and requires proof before he can accept the truth of any proposition; his trained intelligence works like a piece of mechanism. The mind of the Oriental, on the other hand, like his picturesque streets, is eminently wanting in symmetry. His reasoning is of the most slipshod description. Although the ancient Arabs acquired in a somewhat higher degree the science of dialectics, their descendants are singularly deficient in the logical faculty. They are often incapable of drawing the most obvious conclusions from any simple premises of which they may admit the truth. Endeavor to elicit a plain statement of facts from any ordinary Egyptian. His explanation will generally be lengthy, and wanting in lucidity. He will probably contradict himself half-a-dozen times before he has finished his story. He will often break down under the mildest process of cross-examination.

Orientals or Arabs are thereafter shown to be gullible, 'devoid of energy and initiative,' much given to 'fulsome flattery,' intrigue, cunning, and unkindness to animals; Orientals cannot walk on either road or a pavement (their disordered minds fail to understand what the clever European grasps immediately, that roads and pavements are made for walking); Orientals are inveterate liars, they are 'lethargic and suspicious,' and in everything oppose the clarity, directness, and nobility of the Anglo-Saxon race.

Cromer makes no effort to conceal that Orientals for him were always and only the human material he governed in British colonies. 'As I am only a diplomatist and an administrator, whose proper study is also man, but from the point of view of governing him,' Cromer says, ' . . . I content myself with noting the fact that somehow or other the Oriental generally acts, speaks, and thinks in a manner exactly opposite to the European.' Cromer's descriptions are of course based partly on direct observation, yet here and there he refers to orthodox Orientalist authorities (in particular Ernest Renan and Constantin de Volney) to support his views. To these authorities he also defers when it comes to explaining why Orientals are the way they are. He has no doubt that *any* knowledge of the Oriental will confirm his views, which, to judge from his description of the Egyptian breaking under cross-examination, find the Oriental to be guilty. The crime was that the Oriental was an Oriental, and it is an accurate sign of how commonly acceptable such a tautology was that it could be written without even an appeal to European logic or symmetry of mind. Thus any deviation from what were considered the norms of Oriental behavior was believed to be unnatural; Cromer's last annual report from Egypt consequently proclaimed Egyptian nationalism to be an 'entirely novel idea' and 'a plant of exotic rather than of indigenous growth.'

We would be wrong, I think, to underestimate the reservoir of accredited knowledge, the codes of Orientalist orthodoxy, to which Cromer and Balfour refer everywhere in their writing and in their public policy. To say simply that Orientalism was a rationalization of colonial rule is to ignore the extent to which colonial rule was justified in advance by Orientalism, rather than after the fact. Men have always divided the world up into regions having either real or imagined distinction from each other. The absolute demarcation between East and West, which Balfour and Cromer accept with such complacency, had been years, even centuries, in the making. There were of course innumerable voyages of discovery; there were contacts through trade and war. But more than this, since the middle of the eighteenth century there had been two principal elements in the relation between East and West. One was a growing systematic knowledge in Europe about the Orient, knowledge reinforced by the colonial encounter as well as by the widespread interest in the alien and unusual, exploited by the developing sciences of ethnology, comparative anatomy, philology, and history; furthermore, to this systematic knowledge was added a sizable body of literature produced by novelists, poets, translators and gifted travellers. The other feature of Oriental-European relations was that Europe was always in a position of strength, not to say domination. There is no way of putting this euphemistically. True, the relationship of strong to weak could be disguised or mitigated, as when Balfour acknowledged the 'greatness' of Oriental civilizations. But the essential relationship, on political, cultural, and even religious grounds, was seen – in the

West, which is what concerns us here–to be one between a strong and a weak partner.

Many terms were used to express the relation: Balfour and Cromer typically used several. The Oriental is irrational, depraved (fallen), childlike, 'different'; thus the European is rational, virtuous, mature, 'normal'. But the way of enlivening the relationship was everywhere to stress the fact that the Oriental lived in a different but thoroughly organized world of his own, a world with its own national, cultural, and epistemological boundaries and principles of internal coherence. Yet what gave the Oriental's world its intelligibility and identity was not the result of his own efforts but rather the whole complex series of knowledgeable manipulations by which the Orient was identified by the West. Thus the two features of cultural relationship I have been discussing come together. Knowledge of the Orient, because generated out of strength, in a sense *creates* the Orient, the Oriental, and his world. In Cromer's and Balfour's language the Oriental is depicted as something one judges (as in a court of law), something one studies and depicts (as in a curriculum), something one disciplines (as in a school or prison), something one illustrates (as in a zoological manual). The point is that in each of these cases the Oriental is *contained* and *represented* by dominating frameworks. Where do these come from?

Cultural strength is not something we can discuss very easily [. . .] it is better not to risk generalizations about so vague and yet so important a notion until a good deal of material has been analyzed first. But at the outset one can say that so far as the West was concerned during the nineteenth and twentieth centuries, an assumption had been made that the Orient and everything in it was, if not patently inferior to, then in need of corrective study by the West. The Orient was viewed as if framed by the classroom, the criminal court, the prison, the illustrated manual. Orientalism, then, is knowledge of the Orient that places things Oriental in class, court, prison, or manual for scrutiny, study, judgment, discipline, or governing.

During the early years of the twentieth century, men like Balfour and Cromer could say what they said, in the way they did, because a still earlier tradition of Orientalism than the nineteenth-century one provided them with a vocabulary, imagery, rhetoric, and figures with which to say it. Yet Orientalism reinforced, and was reinforced by, the certain knowledge that Europe or the West literally commanded the vastly greater part of the earth's surface. The period of immense advance in the institutions and content of Orientalism coincides exactly with the period of unparalleled European expansion; from 1815 to 1914 European direct colonial dominion expanded from about 35 per cent of the earth's surface to about 85 per cent of it. Every continent was affected, none more so than Africa and Asia. The two greatest empires were the British and the French; allies and partners in some things, in others they were hostile rivals. In the Orient, from the eastern shores of the Mediterranean to Indochina and Malaya, their colonial possessions and imperial spheres of influence were adjacent, frequently overlapped, often were fought over. But it was in the Near Orient, the lands of the Arab Near East, where Islam was supposed to define cultural and racial characteristics, that the

British and the French encountered each other and 'the Orient' with the greatest intensity, familiarity, and complexity. For much of the nineteenth century, as Lord Salisbury put it in 1881, their common view of the Orient was intricately problematic: 'When you have got a . . . faithful ally who is bent on meddling in a country in which you are deeply interested – you have three courses open to you. You may renounce – or monopolize – or share. Renouncing would have been to place the French across our road to India. Monopolizing would have been very near the risk of war. So we resolved to share.'

And share they did [. . .]. What they shared, however, was not only land or profit or rule; it was the kind of intellectual power I have been calling Orientalism. In a sense Orientalism was a library or archive of information commonly and, in some of its aspects, unanimously held. What bound the archive together was a family of ideas and a unifying set of values proven in various ways to be effective. These ideas explained the behaviour of Orientals; they supplied Orientals with a mentality, a genealogy, an atmosphere; most important, they allowed Europeans to deal with and even to see Orientals as a phenomenon possessing regular characteristics. But like any set of durable ideas, Orientalist notions influenced the people who were called orientals as well as those called Occidental, European, or Western; in short, Orientalism is better grasped as a set of constraints upon and limitations of thought than it is simply as a positive doctrine. If the essence of Orientalism is the ineradicable distinction between Western superiority and Oriental inferiority, then we must be prepared to note how in its development and subsequent history Orientalism deepened and even hardened the distinction. When it became common practice during the nineteenth century for Britain to retire its administrators from India and elsewhere once they had reached the age of fifty-five, then a further refinement in Orientalism had been achieved; no Oriental was ever allowed to see a Westerner as he aged and degenerated, just as no Westerner needed ever to see himself, mirrored in the eyes of the subject race, as anything but a vigorous, rational, ever-alert young Raj.

Orientalist ideas took a number of different forms during the nineteenth and twentieth centuries. First of all in Europe there was a vast literature about the Orient inherited from the European past. What is distinctive about the late eighteenth and early nineteenth centuries, which is where this study assumes modern Orientalism to have begun, is that an Oriental renaissance took place, as Edgar Quinet phrased it. Suddenly it seemed to a wide variety of thinkers, politicians, and artists that a new awareness of the Orient, which extended from China to the Mediterranean, had arisen. This awareness was partly the result of newly discovered and translated Oriental texts in languages like Sanskrit, Zend, and Arabic; it was also the result of a newly perceived relationship between the Orient and the West. For my purposes here, the keynote of the relationship was set for the Near East and Europe by the Napoleonic invasion of Egypt in 1798, an invasion which was in many ways the very model of a truly scientific appropriation of one culture by another, apparently stronger one. For with Napoleon's occupation of Egypt processes were set in motion between East and West that still dominate our contemporary cultural and political perspectives. And the

Napoleonic expedition, with its great collective monument of erudition, the *Description de l'Egypte*, provided a scene or setting for Orientalism, since Egypt and subsequently the other Islamic lands were viewed as the live province, the laboratory, theater of effective Western knowledge about the Orient. [. . .]

With such experiences as Napoleon's the Orient as a body of knowledge in the West was modernized, and this is a second form in which nineteenth-and twentieth-century Orientalism existed. From the outset [. . .] there was everywhere amongst Orientalists the ambition to formulate their discoveries, experiences, and insights suitably in modern terms, to put ideas about the Orient in very close touch with modern realities. Renan's linguistic investigations of Semitic in 1848, for example, were couched in a style that drew heavily for its authority upon contemporary comparative grammar, comparative anatomy, and racial theory; these lent his Orientalism prestige and-the other side of the coin-made Orientalism vulnerable, as it has been ever since, to modish as well as seriously influential currents of thought in the West. Orientalism has been subjected to imperialism, positivism, utopianism, historicism, Darwinism, racism, Freudianism, Marxism, Spenglerism. But Orientalism, like many of the natural and social sciences, has had 'paradigms' of research, its own learned societies, its own Establishment. During the nineteenth century the field increased enormously in prestige, as did also the reputation and influence of such institutions as the Société asiatique, the Royal Asiatic Society, the Deutsche Morgenländische Gesellschaft, and the American Oriental Society. With the growth of these societies went also an increase, all across Europe, in the number of professorships in Oriental studies; consequently there was an expansion in the available means for disseminating Orientalism. Orientalist periodicals, beginning with the *Fundgraben des Orients* (1809), multiplied the quantity of knowledge as well as the number of specialties.

Yet little of this activity and very few of these institutions existed and flourished freely, for in a third form in which it existed, Orientalism imposed limits upon thought about the Orient. Even the most imaginative writers of an age, men like Flaubert, Nerval, or Scott, were constrained in what they could either experience of or say about the Orient. For Orientalism was ultimately a political vision of reality whose structure promoted the difference between the familiar (Europe, the West, 'us') and the strange (the Orient, the East, 'them'). This vision in a sense created and then served the two worlds thus conceived. Orientals lived in their world, 'we' lived in ours. The vision and material reality propped each other up, kept each other going. A certain freedom of intercourse was always the Westerner's privilege; because his was the stronger culture, he could penetrate, he could wrestle with, he could give shape and meaning to the great Asiatic mystery, as Disraeli once called it. Yet what has, I think, been previously overlooked is the constricted vocabulary of such a privilege, and the comparative limitations of such a vision. My argument takes it that the Orientalist reality is both antihuman and persistent. Its scope, as much as its institutions and all-pervasive influence, lasts up to the present.

14   Of Mimicry and Man: The Ambivalence of Colonial Discourse

Homi Bhabha

From *October*, no.28, Spring 1984 pp.125-33. Reproduced by permission of the publishers, MIT Press.

Mimicry reveals something in so far as it is distinct from what might be called an itself that is behind. The effect of mimicry is camouflage . . . It is not a question of harmonizing with the background, but against a mottled background, of becoming mottled–exactly like the technique of camouflage practised in human warfare.
(Jacques Lacan, 'The Line and Light,' *Of the Gaze*.)

It is out of season to question at this time of day, the original policy of conferring on every colony of the British Empire a mimic representation of the British Constitution. But if the creature so endowed has sometimes forgotten its real insignificance and under the fancied importance of speakers and maces, and all the paraphernalia and ceremonies of the imperial legislature, has dared to defy the mother country, she has to thank herself for the folly of conferring such privileges on a condition of society that has no earthly claim to so exalted a position. A fundamental principle appears to have been forgotten or overlooked in our system of colonial policy – that of colonial dependence. To give to a colony the forms of independence is a mockery; she would not be a colony for a single hour if she could maintain an independent station.
(Sir Edward Cust, 'Reflections on West African Affairs . . . addressed to the Colonial Office,' Hatchard, London 1839).

The discourse of post-Enlightenment English colonialism often speaks in a tongue that is forked, not false. If colonialism takes power in the name of history, it repeatedly exercises its authority through the figures of farce. For the epic intention of the civilizing mission, 'human and not wholly human' in the famous words of Lord Rosebery, 'writ by the finger of the Divine' often produces a text rich in the traditions of *trompe l'oeil*, irony, mimicry, and repetition. In this comic turn from the high ideals of the colonial imagination to its low mimetic literary effects, mimicry emerges as one of the most elusive and effective strategies of colonial power and knowledge.

Within that conflictual economy of colonial discourse which Edward Said (1978, p.240) describes as the tension between the synchronic panoptical vision of domination – the demand for identity, stasis – and the counter-pressure of the diachrony of history – change, difference – mimicry represents an *ironic* compromise. If I may adapt Samuel Weber's formulation of the marginalizing vision of castration (1973, p.1112), then colonial mimicry is the desire for a reformed recognizable Other, as *a subject of a difference that is almost the same, but not quite.* Which is to say, that the discourse of mimicry is constructed around an *ambivalence*; in order to be effective, mimicry must continually produce its slippage, its excess, its difference. The authority of that mode of colonial discourse that I have called mimicry is therefore stricken by an indeterminacy: mimicry emerges as the representation of a difference that is itself a process of disavowal. Mimicry is, thus, the sign of a double articulation; a complex strategy of reform, regulation, and discipline, which 'appropriates' the Other as it visualizes power. Mimicry is also the sign of the inappropriate, however, a difference or recalcitrance which coheres the dominant strategic function of colonial power, intensifies surveillance, and poses an immanent threat to both 'normalized' knowledges and disciplinary powers.

The effect of mimicry on the authority of colonial discourse is profound and disturbing. For in 'normalizing' the colonial state or subject, the dream of post-Enlightenment civility alienates its own language of liberty and produces another knowledge of its norms. The ambivalence which thus informs this strategy is discernible, for example, in Locke's Second Treatise which *splits* to reveal the limitations of liberty in his double use of the word 'slave': first simply, descriptively as the locus of a legitimate form of ownership, then as the trope for an intolerable, illegitimate exercise of power. What is articulated in that distance between the two uses is the absolute, imagined difference between the 'Colonial' State of Carolina and the Original State of Nature.

It is from this area between mimicry and mockery, where the reforming, civilizing mission is threatened by the displacing gaze of its disciplinary double, that my instances of colonial imitation come. What they all share is a discursive process by which the excess or slippage produced by the *ambivalence* of mimicry (almost the same, *but not quite*) does not merely 'rupture' the discourse, but becomes transformed into an uncertainty which fixes the colonial subject as a 'partial' presence. By 'partial' I mean both 'incomplete' and 'virtual.' It is as if the very emergence of the 'colonial' is dependent for its representation upon some strategic limitation or prohibition *within* the authoritative discourse itself. The success of colonial appropriation depends on a proliferation of inappropriate objects that ensure its strategic failure, so that mimicry is at once resemblance and menace.

A classic text of such partiality is Charles Grant's *Observations on the State of Society among the Asiatic Subjects of Great Britain* (1792) which was only superseded by James Mill's *History of India* as the most influential early nineteenth-century account of Indian manners and morals. Grant's dream of an evangelical system of mission education conducted uncompromisingly in English was partly a belief in political reform along Christian lines and partly an awareness that the expansion of company rule in India required a system of 'interpellation' – a reform of manners, as Grant put it, that would provide the colonial with 'a sense of personal identity as we know it.' Caught between the desire for religious reform and the fear that the Indians might become turbulent for liberty, Grant implies that it is, in fact the 'partial' diffusion of Christianity, and the 'partial' influence of moral improvements which will construct a particularly appropriate form of colonial subjectivity. What is suggested is a process of reform through which Christian doctrines might collude with divisive caste practices to prevent dangerous political alliances. Inadvertently, Grant produces a knowledge of Christianity as a form of social control which conflicts with the enunciatory assumptions which authorize his discourse. In suggesting, finally, that 'partial reform' will produce an empty form of 'the *imitation* of English manners which will induce them [the colonial subjects] to remain under our protection,' Grant mocks his moral project and violates the Evidence of Christianity – a central missionary tenet – which forbade any tolerance of heathen faiths.

The absurd extravagance of Macaulay's *Infamous Minute* (1835) – deeply influenced by Charles Grant's *Observations* – makes a mockery of Oriental learning until faced with the challenge of conceiving of a 'reformed' colonial subject. Then the great tradition of European humanism seems capable only of ironizing itself. At the intersection of European learning and colonial power, Macaualay can conceive of nothing other than 'a class of interpreters between us and the millions whom we govern – a class of persons Indian in blood and colour, but English in tastes, in opinions, in morals and in intellect' – in other words a mimic man raised 'through our English School,' as a missionary educationist wrote in 1819, 'to form a corps of translators and be employed in different departments of Labour.' The line of descent of the mimic man can be traced through the works of Kipling, Forester, Orwell, Naipaul, and to his emergence, most recently, in Benedict Anderson's excellent essay on nationalism, as the anomalous Bipin Chandra Pal (Anderson, 1983, p.88). He is the effect of a flawed colonial mimesis, in which to be Anglicized, is *emphatically* not to be English.

The figure of mimicry is locatable within what Anderson describes as 'the inner incompatibility of empire and nation' (ibid, pp. 88–89). It problematizes the signs of racial and cultural priority, so that the 'national' is no longer naturalizable. What emerges between mimesis and mimicry is a *writing*, a mode of representation, that marginalizes the monumentality of history, quite simply mocks its power to be a model, that power which supposedly makes it imitable. Mimicry *repeats* rather than *re-presents* and in that diminishing perspective emerges [in Joseph Conrad's *Nostromo*] Decoud's displaced European vision of Sulaco as

> The endlessness of civil strife where folly seemed even harder to bear than its ignominy . . . the lawlessness of a populace of all colours and races, barbarism, irremediable tyranny . . . America is ungovernable.

Or Ralph Singh's apostasy in V.S. Naipaul's *The Mimic Men*:

We pretended to be real, to be learning, to be preparing ourselves for life, we mimic men of the New World, one unknown corner of it, with all its reminders of the corruption that came so quickly to the new.

Both Decoud and Singh, and in their different ways Grant and Macaulay, are the parodists of history. Despite their intentions and invocations they inscribe the colonial text erratically, eccentrically across a body politic that refuses to be representative, in a narrative that refuses to be representational. The desire to emerge as 'authentic' through mimicry – through a process of writing and repetition – is the final irony of partial representation.

What I have called mimicry is not the familiar exercise of *dependent* colonial reactions through narcissistic identification so that, as Fanon (1970, p.109) has observed, the black man stops being an actional person for only the white man can represent his self-esteem. Mimicry conceals no presence or identity behind its mask: it is not what Césaire (1972, p. 21) describes as 'colonization-thingification' behind which there stands the essence of the *présence Africaine*. The *menace* of mimicry is its *double* vision which in disclosing the ambivalence of colonial discourse also disrupts its authority. And it is a double-vision that is a result of what I've described as the partial representation/recognition of the colonial object. Grant's colonial as partial imitator, Macaulay's translator, Naipaul's colonial politician as play-actor, Decoud as the scene setter of the *opéra bouffe* of the New World, these are the appropriate objects of a colonialist chain of command, authorized versions of otherness. But they are also, as I have shown, the figures of a doubling, the part-objects of a metonymy of colonial desire which alienates the modality and normality of those dominant discourses in which they emerge as 'inappropriate' colonial subjects. A desire that, through the repetition of *partial presence*, which is the basis of mimicry, articulates those disturbances of cultural, racial, and historical difference that menace the narcissistic demand of colonial authority. It is a desire that reverses 'in part' the colonial appropriation by now producing a partial vision of the colonizer's presence. A gaze of otherness, that shares the acuity of the genealogical gaze which, as Foucault describes it, liberates marginal elements and shatters the unity of man's being through which he extends his sovereignty (Foucault, 1977, p.153).

I want to turn to this process by which the look of surveillance returns as the displacing gaze of the disciplined, where the observer becomes the observed and 'partial' representation rearticulates the whole notion of *identity* and alienates it from essence. But not before observing that even an exemplary history like Eric Stoke's *The English Utilitarians and India* acknowledges the anomalous gaze of otherness but finally disavows it in a contradictory utterance:

Certainly India played *no* central part in fashioning the distinctive qualities of English civilisation. In many ways it acted as a disturbing force, a magnetic power placed at the periphery tending to distort the natural development of Britain's character . . .
(Stokes, 1959, p.xi)

What is the nature of the hidden threat of the partial gaze? How does mimicry emerge as the subject of the scopic drive and the object of colonial surveillance? How is desire disciplined, authority displaced?

If we turn to a Freudian figure to address these isues of colonial textuality, that form of difference that is mimicry – *almost the same but not quite* – will become clear. Writing of the partial nature of fantasy, caught *inappropriately*, between the unconscious and the preconscious, making problematic, like mimicry, the very notion of 'origins,' Freud has this to say:

> Their mixed and split origin is what decides their fate. We may compare them with individuals of mixed race who taken all round resemble white men but who betray their coloured descent by some striking feature or other and on that account are excluded from society and enjoy none of the privileges.
> (Freud, 1915, pp.190-1)

Almost the same but not white: the visibility of mimicry is always produced at the site of interdiction. It is a form of colonial discourse that is uttered *inter dicta*: a discourse at the crossroads of what is known and permissible and that which though known must be kept concealed; a discourse uttered between the lines and as such both against the rules and within them. The question of the representation of difference is therefore always also a problem of authority. The 'desire' of mimicry, which is Freud's *striking feature* that reveals so little but makes such a big difference, is not merely that impossibility of the Other which repeatedly resists signification. The desire of colonial mimicry – an interdictory desire – may not have an object, but it has strategic objectives which I shall call the *metonymy of presence*.

Those inappropriate signifiers of colonial discourse – the difference between being English and being Anglicized; the identity between stereotypes which, through repetition, also become different; the discriminatory identities constructed across traditional cultural norms and classifications, the Simian Black, the Lying Asiatic – all these are metonymies of presence. They are strategies of desire in discourse that make the anomalous representation of the colonized something other than a process of 'the return of the repressed,' what Fanon unsatisfactorily characterized as collective catharsis (Fanon, 1970, p.103). These instances of metonymy are the nonrepressive productions of contradictory and multiple belief. They cross the boundaries of the culture of enunciation through a strategic confusion of the metaphoric and metonymic axes of the cultural production of meaning. For each of these instances of 'a difference that is almost the same but not quite' inadvertently creates a crisis for the cultural priority given to the *metaphoric* as the process of repression and substitution which negotiates the difference between paradigmatic systems and classifications. In mimicry, the representation of identity and meaning is rearticulated along the axis of metonymy. As Lacan reminds us, mimicry is like camouflage, not a harmonization or repression of difference, but a form of resemblance that differs/defends presence by displaying it in part, metonymically. Its threat, I would add, comes from the prodigious and strategic production of conflictual, fantastic, discriminatory 'identity effects' in the play of a power that is elusive because it hides no essence, no 'itself.' And that form of *resemblance* is the most terrifying thing to behold, as Edward Long testifies in his *History of Jamaica* (1774). At the end of a tortured, negrophobic passage, that shifts anxiously between piety, prevarication, and perversion, the text finally confronts its fear; nothing other than the repetition of its resemblance 'in part':

> (Negroes) are represented by all authors as the vilest of human kind, to which they have little more pretension of resemblance *than what arises from their exterior forms* (my italics).

From such a colonial encounter between the white presence and its black semblance, there emerges the question of the ambivalence of mimicry as a problematic of colonial subjection. For if Sade's scandalous theatricalization of language repeatedly reminds us that discourse can claim 'no priority,' then the works of Edward Said will not let us forget that the 'ethnocentric and erratic will to power from which texts can spring' is itself a theater of war (Said, 1979, p.184). Mimicry, as the metonymy of presence is, indeed, such an erratic, eccentric strategy of authority in colonial discourse. Mimicry does not merely destroy narcissistic authority through the repetitious slippage of difference and desire. It is the process of the *fixation* of the colonial as a form of cross-classificatory, discriminatory knowledge in the defiles of an interdictory discourse, and therefore necessarily raises the question of the *authorization* of colonial representations. A question of authority that goes beyond the subject's lack of priority (castration) to a historical crisis in the conceptuality of colonial man as an *object* of regulatory power, as the subject of racial, cultural, national representation.

'This culture . . . fixed in its colonial status,' Fanon suggests (1967, p.44), '(is) both present and mummified, it testified against its members. It defines them in fact without appeal.' The ambivalence of mimicry – almost but not quite – suggests that the fetishized colonial culture is potentially and strategically an insurgent counter-appeal. What I have called its 'identity-effects,' are always crucially *split*. Under cover of camouflage, mimicry, like the fetish, is a part-object that radically revalues the normative knowledges of the priority of race, writing, history. For the fetish mimes the forms of authority at the point at which it deauthorizes them. Similarly, mimicry rearticulates presence in terms of its 'otherness,' that which it disavows. There is a crucial difference between this *colonial* articulation of man and his doubles and that which Foucault (1970, pt.II, ch.9) describes as 'thinking the unthought' which, for nineteenth-century Europe, is the ending of man's alienation by reconciling him with his essence. The colonial discourse that articulates an *interdictory* 'otherness' is precisely the 'other scene' of this nineteenth-century European desire for an authentic historical consciousness.

The 'unthought' across which colonial man is articulated is that process of classificatory confusion that I have described as the metonymy of the substitutive chain of ethical and cultural discourse. This results in the *splitting* of colonial discourse so that two attitudes towards external reality persist; one takes reality into consideration while the other disavows it and replaces it by a product of desire that repeats, rearticulates 'reality' as mimicry.

So Edward Long can say with authority, quoting variously, Hume, Eastwick, and Bishop Warburton in his support, that:

> Ludicrous as the opinion may seem I do not think that an orangutang husband would be any dishonour to a Hottentot female.

Such contradictory articulations of reality and desire – seen in racist stereotypes, statements, jokes, myths – are not caught in the doubtful circle of the return of the repressed. They are the effects of a disavowal that denies the differences of the other but produces in its stead forms of authority and multiple belief that alienate the assumptions of 'civil' discourse. If, for a while, the ruse of desire is calculable for the uses of discipline soon the repetition of guilt, justification, pseudoscientific theories, superstition, spurious authorities, and classifications can be seen as the desperate effort to 'normalize' *formally* the disturbance of a discourse of splitting that violates the rational, enlightened claims of its enunciatory modality. The ambivalence of colonial authority repeatedly turns from *mimicry* – a difference that is almost nothing but not quite – to *menace* – a difference that is almost total but not quite. And in that other scene of colonial power, where history turns to farce and presence to 'a part,' can be seen the twin figures of narcissism and paranoia that repeat furiously, uncontrollably.

In the ambivalent world of the 'not quite/not white,' on the margins of metropolitan desire, the *founding objects* of the Western world become the erratic, eccentric, accidental *objets trouvés* of the colonial discourse – the part-objects of presence. It is then that the body and the book lose their representational authority. Black skin splits under the racist gaze, displaced into signs of bestiality, genitalia, grotesquerie, which reveal the phobic myth of the undifferentiated whole white body. And the holiest of books – the Bible – bearing both the standard of the cross and the standard of empire finds itself strangely dismembered. In May 1817 a missionary wrote from Bengal:

> Still everyone would gladly receive a Bible. And why? – that he may lay it up as a curiosity for a few pice; or use it for waste paper. Such it is well known has been the common fate of these copies of the Bible ... Some have been bartered in the markets, others have been thrown in snuff shops and used as wrapping paper.

References

ANDERSON, B., (1983) *Imagined Communities*, London, Verso.
CESAIRE, A., (1972) *Discourse on Colonialism*, New York, Monthly Review.
FANON, F., (1967) 'Racism and culture' in, *Toward the African Revolution*, London, Pelican.
FANON, F., (1970) *Black Skin, White Masks*, London, Paladin.
FOUCAULT, M., (1970) *The Order of Things*, New York, Pantheon.
FOUCAULT, M., (1977) 'Nitzsche, genealogy, history', in *Language, Counter-Memory, Practice* (trans. D. F. Bouchard and S. Simon), Ithaca, Cornell University Press.
FREUD, S., (1915) *'The Unconscious'*, SE, XIV, London, The Hogarth Press.

SAID, E., (1978) *Orientalism,* New York, Pantheon Books.
SAID, E., (1979) 'The text, the world, the critic', in Harari, J. V. (ed.), *Textual Strategies,* Ithaca, Cornell University Press.
STOKES, E. (1959) *The English Utilitarians and India,* Oxford, Oxford University Press.
WEBER, S., (1973) 'The sideshow, or: remarks on a canny moment', *Modern Language Notes,* Vol. 88, No. 6.

IV Italian Fascism

15   Fascist Ideology

Colin Mercer

The term 'fascist' – for good historical reasons – usually brings to mind images of an authoritarian and totalitarian society ruled by diktat and jackboot, of mass and disciplined rallies of the faithful, of the persecution and murder on a mass scale of ethnic minorities, or quasi-military police states, and so on. In short an image of *coercion*.

There are several problems with this popular image. First, it condenses a number of powerful historical memories into an undifferentiated whole: Hitler's National Socialism, Mussolini's Fascism, Franco's Phalangism and even Pinochet's authoritarian regime in contemporary Chile all become part of the same rubric. Though there may be many elements common to these regimes, it is equally important, in order to understand and analyse them, to mark out their economic, social and cultural differences.

Secondly, this generalized image of fascism takes for granted a binary view of politics in which all policies or strategies can be identified as belonging ultimately on the right, on the left or in the centre. But consider these policy initiatives:

(i)   The establishment of the eight-hour day.
(ii) A welfare and social assistance programme encompassing accident, employment, maternity and occupational disease insurance and benefits.
(iii) Suffrage rights for women.
(iv) Equality of employment for women in industry, the professions, arts and crafts.

Where would these fit into the left /right political spectrum? 'Common sense' might tell us to locate these within a progressive, perhaps socialist but at least liberal, political programme. In fact, these were all initiatives advocated by the Italian Fascist movement between 1921 and 1922. I stress that they were *initiatives* rather than actual concrete policies because they were only unevenly implemented or, in the case of women's employment rights, later revoked. Nonetheless, they

208

were at the forefront of Fascist social policy and visible to the public as such. Combine this with the fact that Mussolini himself was once a prominent figure in the revolutionary wing of the Italian Socialist Party (PSI) and editor of its paper *Avanti* and that anarcho-syndicalism played a major role in the formation of the syndicalist section of the Fascist Party (PNF), and what begins to emerge is a rather strange and indeterminate political beast. It is certainly one that does not quite fit into the received categories of left and right.

Another problem with the image of fascism as simply coercive is that it can dismiss such regimes merely as historical aberrations. It is therefore important to remember that, in Italy, fascism was dominant for the better part of twenty years. This duration, together with the political complexity of the phenomenon, poses a rather awkward question: How was Italian Fascism able to generate *consent* to its own existence? That means looking at the basis of this consent in a form of mass politics operating across a wide range of political, cultural and economic terrains. It also requires some understanding of the nature of this consent, particularly in relation to the organization of popular culture and leisure activities but also in terms of what might be called the 'semiotics' of Fascism. By this I mean the distinctive ways in which Fascism organized for itself a mass *public presence* not only in the spectacular public forms of mass ceremonies, demonstrations and the like, but also in its strategies for creating what Mussolini was to call the 'new man' by reshaping the family, the state, production and cultural life.

These then, are the aspects of Italian Fascism that I shall be focussing on: its *relative political indeterminacy*; its ability to generate *consent* to its existence and duration; and the *complexity* of its cultural make up. All of them involve the problematic relationship between politics and ideology.

The crisis of Italian liberal democracy

In order for us to understand the specific ideological forms which Fascism took in Italy between the two world wars, we need to know something of the background against which they emerged. What factors encouraged the emergence of these particular ideological forms and not others, for example?

Italy achieved national unity as a state as late as the 1860s. The movement which brought unity about was called the *Risorgimento* (literally, the revival or revolution) and was, in effect, Italy's bourgeois revolution, corresponding roughly with the English revolution of the seventeenth century and the French Revolution of 1789. In making this rather unsatisfactory comparison, we can note the relative historical 'lateness' of the event and the fact that it still held a significant place in popular memory for Italians living at the beginning of the twentieth century. This historical proximity of the *Risorgimento* was to play an important role in some of the initial popular appeal of fascist ideology, as we shall see. Another characteristic of the *Risorgimento* which was to play a strategic part in the political and ideological practices of Italian Fascism was the perceived *incompleteness* of the 'revolution'. This feeling that the revolution had not brought about all the desired changes lay, as commentators of all political persuasions were to argue, at the root of the fragility of Italian liberal democracy at the beginning of the twentieth century.

Victoria de Grazia notes the influence the *Risorgimento* had on Fascist ideology in its earliest stages: 'Coming to power with all the rhetoric of an unfulfilled *Risorgimento* tradition, fascist and nationalist ideologues continually paid homage to the idea of a unified and unifying national culture' (de Grazia, 1981, p.187). To pertinent political and philosophical ends, Giovanni Gentile, the foremost philosopher of fascism in its early stages and later the Minister for Education, was to trace in the *Risorgimento* a convenient conception of the state where there was a 'predominance of public interests over private interests particularly in those regional dictatorships of Garibaldi in Sicily and Ricasoli in Tuscany which were to lay the foundations of the process of unification' (Romano, 1982, p.227). Gentile then went on to argue that this conception of governmental and state priorities and balance had been fundamentally betrayed by liberalism since the first 'left' Government of 1876 and that the preference for the private sphere over the public sphere lay at the root of all of Italy's contemporary ills.

The constant appeal to the unifying *potential* of the *Risorgimento* was pitched against an imbalance between state and civil society. This was a relationship which was seen to be in a quasi-perpetual state of disphasure due, it was felt, to moral weakness on the part of politicians, spiritual incoherence in the population generally, disabling regionalisms and, above all, to the strategy which came to be known as *transformism*. This was the name given to the dominant tendency in post-unification Italian politics to govern by means of broad coalitions of parties within the constitutional framework. The expression derives from Agostino Depretis (1813-87) who, on becoming Prime Minister in 1876, called for a 'transformation of the parties' and the creation of a ruling parliamentary bloc which would, it was claimed, transcend the fundamental antagonisms of Left and of Right. The result of this doctrine of, as Antonio Gramsci (1971, p.59) put it, 'the gradual but continuous absorption . . . of the active elements produced by allied groups' was that the main parties which emerged from the *Risorgimento* broke down into a series of factions led by more or less charismatic leaders. The art of government thereby became the act of establishing a network of quasi-structural compromises and concessions between the competing factions.

The problem with this form of politics, as Gramsci was quick to point out and the fascists were to take up with differing intents, was that it was essentially a *passive* way of continuing the potential of the 'revolution' of the *Risorgimento*. Whereas, for example, in France, a radical Jacobin intelligentsia both during, and in the wake of, the 1789 Revolution, had been able to form strategic alliances with broad masses of people in order to overthrow the *ancien régime*, and thus form a link between the newly ascendant bourgeoisie and popular strata, no such cross-class, inter-regional alliance had been formed in Italy. Transformism thus came to be seen as a cynical 'power-play' at the 'top' with little or no popular involvement. Because of the failure of the *Risorgimento* to become, in Gramsci's words, a revolution which was 'profoundly popular, i.e. radically national' the necessary political and social cement which would bind together people and state, leaders and led, public and private, state and civil society, was fatally inadequate.

Fatally inadequate, because although the strategy of transformism was relatively effective for a period of forty years or so, when confronted with the major political, economic and social crises of the first part of the twentieth century, the doctrine, though skilfully manipulated by Giovanni Giolitti who dominated Italian politics between 1900-1914, had clearly reached its limits. This was, I should make clear, a *generally* perceived crisis and a general, not just fascist, disillusionment with the strategy of transformism which had by now become a symbol of compromise which deprived political parties of any idealist project and politico-moral rigour. But it was Fascism that was able to represent itself, in a variety of ways, as a solution to the catastrophic equilibrium of forces which had developed in Italy in the years before the March on Rome – the largely ceremonial display of Fascist power – which provoked the King to empower Mussolini to form a cabinet in October 1922. These years had been marked by a generalized crisis at all levels, punctuated dramatically by the First World War and the division of Italy's major political forces into interventionists and abstentionists. Politically they were to culminate in 1919-20 in the Biennio Rosso – the two red years – which, in the eyes of many, brought Italy to the very brink of a socialist revolution. Following the First World War, industrial expansion in Italy took place at breakneck speed and in a way which was to have serious consequences for the fragile and relatively 'immature' institutions of state and government. Steel production, a primary sector of the economy, rose from five per cent to ten per cent of gross national output; engineering from twenty-one per cent to thirty-one per cent; company capital increased by an average of fifty-six per cent and, in the case of engineering, by a massive 156 per cent. FIAT, founded in 1895, increased its workforce from 4,000 to 20,000 during the war years and increased its capital tenfold. Enormous 'combines' began to emerge in the primary sectors of the economy and were rapidly to spread their entrepreneurs and their influence throughout the entire economy including, characteristically, through the press and news media. A new form of politico-industrial organization – monopoly capitalism – had arrived in Italy with something of a bang whereas in other western countries its impact had been more gradual and dispersed. At the same time, however, the Italian economy was undergoing a severe fiscal crisis. The lira lost a massive eighty per cent of its value between 1914 and 1920; the budgetary deficit rose from 214 million lire in 1914-15 to 23,345 million lire in 1919-20. Aggravating already massive inequalities between the industrialized North and the agricultural South, wheat production fell dramatically and forty per cent of the balance of payments deficit was due to food imports. (Sources: Williams, 1975; Hoare, 1977). As Quintin Hoare comments:

> The political crisis of the older order was manifest: incapable of creating any coherent political party with a stable structure, mass base or clear programme, the shifting cliques of 'notables', with their personal followings, *clientele*, and hired vote-gathering enforcers, appeared impotent either to control the

worsening economic situation or to confront the inexorable growth of the socialist forces.
(Hoare, 1977, p.x)

This 'inexorable growth' was represented mainly by the PSI which, by the 1919 elections, had become the largest single political party with 156 seats out of a total of 508. The Socialist trade union federation, the CGL, witnessed a dramatic increase in membership from around 250,000 in 1918 to two million in 1920 including, significantly, 900,000 agricultural workers. Conflict between capital and labour reached its peak in 1919-20. With employers insisting on quasi-military discipline in the factories and pegging wage increases well below the rocketing levels of inflation the response from organized labour was first a series of localized strikes at the main industrial centres of the north, then a General Strike in April 1920 which effectively meant that the whole of the Piedmont region in the north was subject to a period of 'dual power'and an intense conflict between employers and the state on the one hand and labour organized into factory councils on the other. The Factory Council initiative quickly led to the occupation of the factories and the formation of temporary 'soviets' right across the key industrial sectors of the north – Turin, Milan, Genoa – accompanied by massive agitation and unrest in the countryside by the militant *braccianti*, the day-labourers.

Clearly this is the stuff of which socialist revolutions have been made. The fact that there was not a revolution was due to a number of factors. These included rifts within the socialist movement, strategic mistakes on the part of its leadership, an overemphasis on defensive economic initiatives and an underestimation of the nature of political power. But it was also due to the fact that the revolution had been promised from another directon by the likes of Mussolini and Gabriele D'Annunzio, the poet and essayist who led an expedition to recapture Fiume in Yugoslavia for Italy in September, 1919. Of this successful and exemplary Fascist adventure Mussolini was to say, 'The revolution exists already; started at Fiume, it can only be concluded in Rome' (cited in Macciocchi, 1976, p.25).

The formation of a 'revolutionary discourse' was a central component of the early ideological strategy of Italian Fascism in its transformation from a marginal to a mass phenomenon. In this appropriation of a vigorous and transformative political language, Mussolini, with his armed bands of *arditi*, was effectively able to pose as the perpetuator of the revolutionary tradition initiated by the key figures of the *Risorgimento* but then betrayed by transformist politicians. The Fascist leader was able to mobilize the 'spirit of Garibaldi', still potent within popular memory as the image of a para-military grouping fighting its way to national unity. Commenting on this point, Sergio Romano has noted that, as well as Garibaldi:

Mazzini, Pisacane and the Bandiera brothers had prepared Italian public opinion for the idea of a group of combatants who gradually become representatives of people, army and nation as they cross the country, of a people which is born along the route of the struggle in physically reconstructing the unity of the territory and eliminating en route the old secular frontiers.
(Romano, 1982, p.230)

Italy was distinctive in ths respect. Precisely because of the relative lateness of its bourgeois revolution, certain revolutionary traditions and possibilities were still ideologically acceptable in ways which would have been impossible or at best extremely difficult in the more secure liberal democracies of France or Great Britain. This was not, of course, some spontaneous element of Italian life; it emerged precisely as a *possible* political and ideological response to the crisis which Italy was facing in the second decade of the twentieth century.

The variable components of fascist ideology

> I warn you against the tendency to regard fascist ideology as something that is solidly formed, complete, homogeneous. Nothing more closely resembles a chameleon than fascist ideology. *Don't look at fascist ideology without considering the objectives which fascism proposes to reach at a given moment within a given ideology.*
> (Togliatti, 1976, p. 10)

These words of caution are important given my earlier statement about the relative political indeterminacy of fascism. Palmiro Togliatti, in a series of lectures given in Moscow in 1935, from which this passage is taken, was a leading figure in the Italian Communist Party (PCI), later to become its General Secretary. Having worked clandestinely in Italy after the banning of opposition parties in 1925 and having witnessed some of the complexity of fascism's social and cultural initiatives and its variable ideological positions, he was here expressing a view contrary to the orthodox marxist interpretation of fascism as a more or less unified expression of the most reactionary sectors of capital. He was attempting to explain some of the strong points of fascism in its appropriation of a 'revolutionist' rhetoric and its appeal to forms of radicalism active within Italian popular memory. Togliatti was arguing, in effect, that there is no such thing as fascist ideology *in general*. Fascist ideology is a pragmatic, rather than systematic or coherent set of responses to particular circumstances. This is not to deny any elaborated unity to fascist ideology: but there is no unity to it which we can assume *a priori*. This is a cardinal point in the argument which I shall be developing about the nature of Italian Fascist ideology: that in order to understand it we have to analyse it not on the basis of pre-judgements about which class or class-fraction, which sector of capital, which persons or agencies it best served the interests of, but rather how and by what means it was able to secure forms of consent and degrees of popular resonance in its long-term existence. This is not to say that fascism did not ultimately serve particular sets of interests better than others: simply that it was not a *necessary* outcome to a particular arrangement of class and political forces.

To support this argument I need first to say something about the conception of ideology with which I am working, then to consider some of the central components of fascist ideology and finally to consider how the different components of the ideology fused or condensed into more determinate unity.

A useful starting point here is the observation by Antonio Gramsci – formulated in some proximity to fascism in one of Mussolini's gaols – that ideologies 'have a validity which is "psychological"; they "organise" human masses, and create the terrain on which men move, acquire consciousness of their position, struggle, etc.' (Gramsci, 1971, p.377). If, indeed, ideologies have this 'internal' or psychological and organizational capacity, then we have to pose the question of *how* this process operates. The most useful methodological approach to these ideological mechanisms is via the concept of interpellation as initially formulated by Louis Althusser and developed, in an analysis of fascist and populist discourse, by Ernesto Laclau.

Ideologies, for Althusser, are not consciously held sets of beliefs but rather *structures* which 'act functionally on men via a process that escapes them' (Althusser, 1969, p.233). Ideology is therefore not a question of consciousness but rather of unconscious assumptions, presuppositions in the structures of, for example, 'common sense' and in our acceptance that things are 'natural', 'obvious' or 'spontaneous' in their occurrence. The question of how these structures work on us as individuals, 'internally', is answered by Althusser through the concept of interpellation which is, in effect, a sort of ideological recruitment mechanism which is designated as a form of 'hailing'. Thus, when somebody speaks of the 'British people' or the 'Italian people' we – if we are British or Italian – tend automatically to recognize our place within that discourse. And this is where we come to the crunch. It is clear that in an interpellation like the 'British people' we tend to recognize (accept as natural, spontaneous) certain principles of unity, thereby including some elements and excluding others. Interpellations of this sort work both to identify and to circumscribe a set of limits which may or may not include the idea of a different skin colouring, a different set of religious and political practices, or a different lifestyle. The criteria for that circumscription, for those processes of inclusion and exclusion, are not automatically or naturally given in the expression 'British people': they vary accordingly to its discursive and ideological location.

Ernesto Laclau develops this argument in a way which provides a clue to our concern with the popular resonance of fascist ideology. Refuting the more orthodox marxist argument which sees fascism as a more or less united ideological expression of the most reactionary sectors of the capitalist class, Laclau argues that this conception, in its over-emphasis on class, is theoretically misplaced. This, he argues, is because fascism operated not at the level of *class* struggle but rather in the area of *popular-democratic struggle*. Thus by virtue of its active 'anti-nature' – anti-liberal, anti-democratic, anti-pacifist, anti-communist, anti-compromise, but above all *anti power bloc* nature – fascism was able to articulate to its own discourses an ensemble of radical, jacobin and popular positions and mobilize them against the 'power bloc' of an exhausted and over-compromised liberal regime. Therefore, for Laclau, the argument is that 'far from being the typical ideological expression of the most conservative and reactionary sectors of the dominant classes . . . ', fascism was 'one of the possible ways of articulating the popular-democratic interpellations into political discourse' (Laclau, this volume, p.32). He is not arguing that fascism was thereby democratic or that in a blanket way it was popular, but he is arguing that the substantives of *democracy* and the *people* were articulated within fascist discourse in such a way as to provide some principles of ideological unity. Associated with these observations is another: that these particular substantive elements have no 'class-belonging' – that neither of the politically potent concepts of 'people' or 'democracy' actually belongs irretrievably to any one class and that they cannot therefore be analysed or reduced in or to purely class terms. As well as existing structurally as classes, individuals and groups they also exist as 'people', which is a *multidiscursive* term in so far as it is a concept which traverses class, region and gender. Following this logic, Laclau goes on to argue that no particular ideological element has a pre-given class location: that taken in isolation we cannot designate a particular element, whether it be patriotism, familial duty, sacrifice or opposition to the state as essentially the prerogative of one given class or social group. We may 'naturally' associate a given element with a given political position – say, patriotism on the right – but that is only because of the historical success of right wing politics in articulating this particular conception with its now dominant associations, to its particular discourse. Laclau argues that such ideological elements have 'no necessary class connotation' and that this connotation, or association, where it is seen to exist (as in the case of patriotism), is 'only the result of the articulation of those elements in a concrete ideological discourse . . .'. The precondition for analysing this ensemble of discourses within the 'chameleon' of fascist ideology is not to pick out particular elements and to identify them as typically 'fascist' or typically 'petty-bourgeois' or typically 'right-wing' and so on but rather to examine the ways in which these elements *condensed* into particular unities, to understand the ways in which they came – and hung – together in a relative but precarious unity over a twenty year period.

A frequent mistake in the analysis of fascism, commensurate with the tendency to identify it immediately as an extreme form of conservatism, is to isolate one or two features such as nationalism or statism or anti-semitism and to construe these as somehow typical features of its make up. In line with the argument developed above, I shall now consider some of the central components of Italian Fascist ideology – not to present them as essential features of fascist discourse but in order to analyse how they were articulated together into a relative unity.

The nation

It would be wrong to assume, for example, that fascism *equals* nationalism in an extreme form or that it is the ultimate outcome of the expression of national sentiments. Certainly there was a strong and identifiable current of nationalism within Italian Fascism but it is, at the lowest denominator, a *particular* way of articulating national sentiments which only assumes popular meaning and political power in relation to the other elements with which it is combined. In the following passage from an article called 'The Proletarian Nations and

Nationalism' by Enrico Corradini written in 1911, for example, images of national solidarity are combined with those of proletarian class solidarity:

> Nationalism asserts above all the need for Italy to acquire awareness of herself as a nation, an awareness which is a form of *esprit de corps* as well, a sense of solidarity among citizens, just as class-consciousness is a sense of solidarity amongst workers, which I have already praised.
> (Lyttelton, 1973, p.149)

This, perhaps now unfamiliar, inclusion of proletarian values within the discourse of nationalism is symptomatic of an important strand within the early development of Italian Fascism. It was to become a means of distinguishing Italy as a nation from the 'decadent plutocracies' which surrounded it and a way of including the working class within its general rubric. The latter were depicted not so much as workers with particular interests but as citizens of a vigorous and dynamic nationhood whose interests would transcend immediate economic concerns and become part of a 'living organism'. As one commentator later put it, this was an 'ethic, comprising all the criteria of behaviours which the common interest calls for. The duty both of the individual and of society is to find out what this ethic may be . . . only those can succeed who have a share in the "national consciousness" shaped over the course of the centuries' (Sternhell, 1976, p.333). This touches upon another characteritic of nationalism which fascism inflected in a particular way – the fact that, as Benedict Anderson has put it, 'If nation-states are widely conceded to be "new" and "historical", the nations to which they give political expression always loom out of an immemorial past . . . ' (Anderson, in this volume, p.90). For Italian Fascism, this 'immemorial past' was to be elaborated out of the achievements of the race and frequent references to the glory of Ancient Rome. The programme of the *Partito Nazionale Fascista* (PNF) construed the image of the nation as the 'supreme synthesis' of the spiritual and material values of the race (Bourderon, 1979, p.13). These values would be constantly affirmed in opposition to the recent past of 'a regime of tiny, timorous and inept governments' (Corradini, in Lyttelton, 1973, p.180), in opposition, in other words, to liberalism and especially to transformism.

The historical references are, in turn, articulated to organic metaphors in a liturgy which stresses the connection between the 'national subject' and the 'native soil'. According to Mussolini, for example, every individual is 'desperately linked' to his native land (Bourderon, 1979, p.13). The problem which fascism elaborated for itself was to 'alleviate' that despair and to restore the originality and authenticity of that link after the years of its deflection.

The state

Having elaborated a series of interpellations in order to encapsulate its own version of the nation, Fascism necessarily had recourse to means for fusing it with the idea of the state. Having presented the recent past as a period in which the nation – of the people, of culture, of Italian glories – has become increasingly alienated from the state, of 'timorous and inept governments', Fascism was able to represent the *new* state as the 'juridical incarnation' of the nation. More precisely, according to Mussolini's *Doctrine of Fascism*, the state 'realises the political, juridical and economic organisation of the nation' (cited in Bourderon, p.65). The *Duce* then goes on to establish a broader discursive range in arguing that, furthermore, the state is the 'guarantor of internal and external security, but also the guardian and transmitter of the spirit of the people which has been elaborated over the centuries in its language, its customs and its faith' (ibid., p.65). An absolute commonality of nation and state: an identity pitched in terms of an invocation, a series of connotations of other 'more spiritual' values. Constructed in the present, the identity of nation/state is consolidated by reference to the past as if this new fusion were the inevitable result of an inexorable historical and moral continuity. As the 'immanent consciousness of the nation' (Mussolini) and the incarnation of the 'will of the people', the state assumes all those characteristics – faith, spiritual guardian, moral guidance – which might, in other circumstances be left to the established church. Hence the famous slogan formulated (with assistance from Gentile) by Mussolini: 'everything in the state, nothing against the state, nothing outside the state' and, if further emphasis were needed, 'We are, in other words, a state which controls all forces acting in nature. We control political forces, we control economic forces . . .' (Sternhell, p.379). (Note the allocation of the first person plural pronoun to the state there.)

In the chain of metaphors, if the nation is likened to a living organism, then the state is its 'ethical will', which transforms the people even in their physical aspect. Clearly no problems here with the much lamented imbalance between public and private organisms: state and civil society become fused in an organic whole.

The fascist 'dynamo'

In order to understand the ways in which what Mussolini called 'our fierce totalitarian will' became, in varying degrees, ideologically acceptable, we have also to understand something of fascism's proclaimed vitality.

'Fascism is a dynamo' was the expression chosen by Mussolini to express its vital – and vitalist – *élan*. As a former leader of the 'maximalist' wing of the PSI Mussolini was no stranger to the language of struggle and contestation. Now, as leader of a new movement, Mussolini would pitch fascism 'against the easy life' in so far as that easy life would represent, in popular imagination, a range of attitudes – conspiratorial liberalism, plutocratic decadence, the luxury of democracy, the timorousness of transformist politics – of which fascism could now represent itself as the antithesis. Drawing on a range of sources, from the language of anarcho-syndicalism, the vitalist philosophy of Henri Bergson and Georges Sorel, the generalized 'revolt against positivism' and a range of popular prejudices and preconceptions, Mussolini was able to state that 'We stand for a new principle in the world, we stand for sheer categorical definitive antithesis to the world of democracy, plutocracy, free-masonry, to the world which still abides by the fundamental principles laid down in 1789' (Sternhell, p.356). To further elaborate the chain of connotations and establish both a philosophical and historical rationale for the concept of dynamism, Gabriele D'Annunzio would write, in his *Letter to the Dalmations* of 1919, that 'Civilisation is nothing but the glory of incessant struggle. When man is no longer a wolf for other men, a nation will, and must always be a lioness to other nations' (Lyttelton, 1973, p.185). In a country divided into 'abstentionists' and 'interventionists' prior to the entry of Italy into the First World War, appeals of this nature were to establish a popular, if not universal resonance. And in the aftermath of the war, the language of struggle, combat and dynamism was to be given a new inflection which was to serve Mussolini as a constant resource throughout the twenty years of his rule as he constantly returned to the theme of the 'glorious war dead' and 'war wounded' and, in a significant ideological recruitment of women, to the themes of the silent sacrifice (a gender specific form of struggle) of the 'war widows' and 'mothers of warriors': the image, lodged in the Catholic imagination, of the *mater dolorosa*.

Fascism and class

Ideology alone cannot explain the popular impact of fascism in Italy. Another reason was, as Nicos Poulantzas has noted, its spectacular ability to absorb unemployment in its first years of ascendancy:

> . . . its relative ability to supersede economic crises, directed by the imperatives of the change from competitive to monopoly capitalism by means of economic policies aimed at monopoly concentration . . . and also a forced and rapid policy of imperialist economic expansion and the growth of the armaments industry . . . this absorption played an important role in the popular impact of Fascism.
> (Poulantzas, 1976, pp.97-98)

But, in turn, these material achievements also have to be understood in relation to the ideological forms through which they operate. Of crucial significance here was the ability of fascism in Italy to articulate, in its early stages at least, a discourse of radical social change, heavily influenced by a *particular* image of the proletarian, in its favour.

The titles of some of Mussolini's early speeches signal the dimensions and associations of this range of interpellations: 'Workmen's Rights After the War' (1919); 'We are not against Labour, but against the Socialist Party. In as far as it remains anti-Italian' (1920); 'Fascism's Interests for the working class' (1921); and the tortuous 'My father was a blacksmith and I have worked with him. He bent iron, but I have the harder task of bending souls'! (1922). These early appeals were partly a response to the reality of the exploitation of the Italian working class by international (plutocratic) capitalism – hence Fascism's initial 'national' anti-capitalism – partly a response to the still powerful syndicalist wing within the

Fascist movement which was later to be eclipsed, and partly an attempt to disarticulate this set of discourses from the historical 'possession' of the Socialist movement. At this stage, however, it is clear that these attempts at the interpellation of the proletarian were far from successful. Massive and persistent unrest, spontaneous acts of sabotage, massive and deliberate absenteeism, systematic attempts to lower production-rates and a whole range of forms of resistance continued to cause serious problems for Fascist management of the economy.

In fact, the main class base for fascism was in the traditional and, increasingly, new petty bourgeoisie who formed the core of the membership of the PNF and provided its bedrock of explicit support in the new industries and the rapidly expanding administrative and service sectors. But if to identify a class base is a *necessary* condition for analysing a given ideological formation, it is by no means a *sufficient* condition. By mobilizing these particular strata of the population fascism was able to go beyond class limitations and to represent itself not as a class form but as a *popular* one in so far as, for these strata, 'the identity as *the people* plays a much more important role than the identity as *class* . . . popular-democratic interpellations are much more important than their specific class interpellations . . .' (Laclau, 1977, p.114). Thus, drawing on the various and flexible resources of nation, state, struggle, revolution and the 'people', fascism was able effectively to 'expand' the characteristic ideological aspirations of the petty-bourgeoisie beyond its class base by foregrounding its declared nature as representative of 'the people' against a decadent, liberal, democratic, corrupt and ineffective 'power bloc' in a significantly populist operation.

Old ideas, new ideas

'Old ideas which always go hand in hand must be separated' was the title of an article written by the futurist artist Marinetti in the fascist newspaper *L'Arditi* in March 1919. The aim of the piece may be discursively located at precisely that point of 'disarticulating' old ideas and ideological unities from their previous historical and political associations. Here is the opening section in full:

> Up till now, politics have always subsisted on platitudes, or rather on ideas that went along stupidly hand-in-hand, joined in a fictitious relationship that, in fact, doesn't exist.
>
> When someone says 'monarchy', we at once think of an army, war, fatherhood and patriotism. Nor is this unreasonable. But it's absurd, when we speak for example, of an enthusiastic army, to be forced to think of a reactionary monarchy.
>
> When you speak of nationalism, you immediately think of conservatism, a system of greedy imperialism, reactionary traditionalism, repressive police, militarism, a hereditary aristocracy, clericalism.
>
> Associations of ideas that must be forcibly broken.
>
> When you speak of democracy, you immediately think of the lack of any

warlike spirit, humanitarianism, pacifism, quietism, abnegation, anti-colonialism, humility, internationalism, lack of racial pride and rejection of any idea of race.

Associations of ideas that must be forcibly broken.

When you speak of a healthy outdoor upbringing, dash, guts, boldness, physical strength, a mania for setting up records, you immediately think of an imperialist or clerical monarchy.

Associations of ideas that must be forcibly broken.

When you talk of justice, equality, freedom, the rights of the proletariat, or the peasants and the under-privileged, the struggle against parasites, you immediately think of anti-patriotism, international pacifism, Marxism and collectivism.

Associations of ideas that must be forcibly broken.

(in Lyttelton, 1973, p.216)

This remarkable and symptomatic document, published in the same month as the *Fasci Italiano de Combattimento* (the fascist movement before it was organized into a political party) was formed, offers what might be called a 'poetics'of fascism – right down to the repeated assonance of the end-lines. (In the same article, incidentally, Marinetti was to utter the famous expression that political parties were doomed to become 'illustrious corpses' – just three years before the *Partito Nazionale Fascista* was formed.) The aim, clearly, is to disrupt those ideological unities on which the 'corruption' and lack of will of the 'old order' was based. The article attempts to intervene in the apparently smooth connotative flow which would tie the notion of, again, patriotism, to a particular conception of the monarchy. It wants to interrupt that ideological 'logic' which distributes and fixes certain positions in a relationship of inevitable association with other positions in order, in turn, to formulate a new grid of positionalities, a new set of interpellations. As Laclau puts it, the theoretical and political rationale for this procedure lies in the fact that 'each one of the sectors in struggle will try and reconstitute a new ideological unity using a "system of narration" as a vehicle which disarticulates the ideological discourses of the opposing forces'.

In a cogent movement of critique, Marinetti's article may be seen to sketch out the traces of that new 'system of narration'. It announces the first moment of antagonism; the questioning of the 'old associations' and the old connotative fluency in order to suggest, by negative association, by assumed opposites, or antonyms, the terms of the preferred reconstruction of a new discursive and ideological unity. If we take four of Martinetti's headings – politics, nationalism, democracy, justice/equality and the associations of discursive equivalences which go with them – it is clear that the 'unspoken' antonym of each of these terms is adding up to something. (See Table 1.) The implied oppositions, of course, are all *assumed*: they are not mentioned as such by Marinetti, but reading down the right-hand column, they do form a powerful substratum of presuppositions for the 'new associations' of ideas. Against a dominant discourse of *integration* which marked the transformism of Giolitti's Liberal government and a long political tradition, Marinetti is articulating by association a new *popular positionality* within his own

TABLE 1

Themes	Stated association	Implied opposition
1. Politics	Platitudes	Hard truth
	Fiction	Reality
2. Nationalism	Conservatism	Revolution
	Greedy imperialism	Moderate imperialism
	Reaction	Moving forward
		Progression
	Repressive police	Popular police
	Aristocracy	People
	Clericalism	Anti-clericalism
3. Democracy	Pacifism	Activism
	Quietism	Aggression
	Humility	Pride
	Internationalism	Nationalism
	Lack of racial pride	Racial pride/racism
4. Justice		
Equality	Marxism/collectivism	Fascism
	International pacifism	National activism
	Anti-patriotism	Patriotism

discourse pitched against the string of democratic associations which represent the old ideas to be 'forcibly broken'.

We could signal this particular text as a preliminary moment in the discursive strategy of Italian Fascism which, according to Laclau:

> ... was precisely to affirm in an antagonistic way an ensemble of popular positionalities – represented in the Italian ideological field at the beginning of the century by Mazzinian and Garibaldian ideological elements – and to construct a chain of equivalences in which elements like the defence of the family and the struggle against the trades unions came into play. This was how a radical popular space which permitted the reconstitution of a new system of domination within it was constructed. As part of this process democratic positionalities were disarticulated from the system of equivalences linking them to the popular field and so were isolated and deprived of any hegemonic capacity.
>
> (Laclau, 1980, p.93)

The old democratic positionalities, associated with the failure of liberalism and the liberal state, and the range of associations or, in Laclau's terms, equivalences which Marinetti constructs for them are, through a process of 'guilt by association', being ideologically 'edited out' and a new system of antagonistic popular equivalences are being instituted which will gather around the primary interpellation of fascist (and, for Marinetti, futurist). All of this does not, of course, happen just because Marinetti says so. To become a popular positionality it is not enough to generate some vague new *vox populi*: it has to assume concrete institutional forms.

The semiotics of power

Fascism never was and never has been a coherent philosophy or doctrine. In a sense it never had to be, precisely because of its earlier declared allegiance to 'irrationalism' and the centrality of a certain philosophical pragmatism in relation to its ideology. It was enough for Marinetti to say that 'Ideologies are created, dominated and formed by life' (Lyttelton, 1973, p.218) or for Mussolini to say that 'Our doctrine is fact' in order to establish its *raison d'être*. But noting its irrationalism and pragmatism as two distinct elements is not to say that, therefore, there is no systematic or analysable coherence to the phenomenon. A chameleon it may be but the beast does not disappear when you have identified each of its separate colours. If we were looking for the traces of logical inconsistency we would find plenty of them in fascism: it was 'anti-capitalist' yet effected a rapid consolidation of monopoly capitalism: it was 'anti-clerical' yet negotiated a solid and lasting agreement with the Catholic Church: it was 'anti-liberal' yet claimed that it was the most 'perfect form of liberalism' (Gentile). This is not surprising if we accept Laclau's argument that an ideological unity does not depend on logical consistency but rather on the ability of one interpellation to persuasively evoke or connote other interpellations.

The question of *style* was an important one for the ideological unity of fascist discourse. If it didn't achieve logical unity it did, in significant measure, achieve an important stylistic unity with the promise of a new 'way of life' and a 'new man'. According to Mussolini, democracy ' . . . has made the people's style of life disappear: that is to say, its sense of direction, its colour, its strength, the sense of the picturesque, of the unexpected, the mystical. In fact, all of that which comprises the soul of the masses' (cited in Bourderon, p.144). This is why it was so important for fascism to appropriate and reform the 'styles' of previous popular movements, be they religious, political or 'of the folk'. The Italian *fasci*, as an emblem, before symbolizing a political movement, symbolized, in popular consciousness, the glory of ancient Rome. In this juxtaposition also, fascism was able to bring together the apparently contradictory positions of romanticism and a more 'classical' respect for discipline:

> The desire for community rather than individualism was symbolically
> expressed in the love of uniforms. The discovery of shirts of different colours
> as a way of rejecting the individualized bourgeois business suit, at the same

time symbolized the rejection of the grey everyday life, the deviance from conventionality and the vicarious identification with the lower classes against the bourgeoisie.
(Linz, 1976, p.54)

This suggests why it is important to identify the criteria of co-ordination of the styles and images of fascism; the ways in which fascism took over old styles and combined them into a new political and ideological 'grammar' or semiotics:

> . . . Fascism never renounced its revolutionary vocation. Born to forge a 'new' Italian, it created a gigantic semiotics, the aim of which was to both evoke and represent the revolution. The process was theatrical. Instead of transforming Italy from within, Fascism revolutionalized the way of dressing, the style of human relations, the symbols of power, ceremonies and the calendar . . . Fascism attempts to correct Italian reality without altering its substance . . . it does not suppress the religious Sunday but flanks it with a Fascist Saturday; it does not suppress religious ceremonies but joins with them its lay masses and its acolytes to celebrate the new faith; it does not suppress the distinctive symbols of the pre-Fascist hierarchy but recuperates and renews them in a carnival of uniforms, standards and flags.
> (Romano, 1982, pp.237-8)

Fascism's discourse of revolution was pitched not at the level of a fundamental transformation of economic and social relations, but rather at the level of a pervasive *symbolism*. In its pragmatic responses to problematic political and economic forces it was indeed still guilty of a form of 'transformism' though no longer tied to the prerequisites of parliamentary democracy. Ideologically, this reality was handled in a particular way by insisting, as Romano puts it, that 'the present is almost always transformist; it is the past and the future which are revolutionary' (ibid). This is not to say that there were no structural changes in the Italian economy and society under Fascism but on the whole these were changes which were taking place in other industrial economies anyway. Among these, we would count the shift from competitive capitalism towards the concentration of monopoly capitalism, the modernization of industrial production methods, the 'taylorization' of work processes following American models of scientific management and industrial welfarism, the co-ordination of the modalities of state intervention not only in industry but also, with the rise of new forms of mass communication, throughout the fabric of civil society. Italy's version of the welfare state, or at least its basic or recognizable contours, first emerged under Fascism with a comprehensive policy relating to education, welfare benefits, the family, and income distribution.

It is clear from the experience of other industrial societies that none of these transformations provides an *automatic* possibility for the emergence of fascism. The specific nature of the phenomenon must be sought elsewhere: in the rapidity and concentration of this process in Italy, in the generally perceived crisis of the previous power bloc of liberal hegemony, in the strengths and weaknesses of other political parties and movements which might have provided more democratic alternatives and, for our purposes, in the ability of a fascist movement to wage and partially win what is sometimes called the 'struggle for hearts and minds' at all levels of society. This, as the phrase hints, is simultaneously a struggle to win over the 'subjective' dimension of ideology, the institutional forms in which that subjectivity might be realized, and the points of connection between those various institutional forms in order to establish a relative congruence between them. A struggle, in other words, at the *subjective, institutional* and *symbolic* levels. But how was this unity achieved? How did fascism elaborate this 'gigantic semiotic'?

Workers-citizens-producers

I have already noted the early identification of fascism with the working class and the various forces which compelled this form of identification. In the actual construction of the regime, however, it soon became clear to Mussolini, to the Fascist *gerarchi* (the leading members and officials of the PNF) and to industrial entrepreneurs that forms of class solidarity and identification had, in some way, to be transcended or marginalized and that the more *ouvrieriste* sections of the fascist syndicalists would have to be kept firmly in place. The need was to provide a form of identification-an interpellation-which would both stress the need for production and include those responsible for the production within a harmonized national and 'natural' community and an integrated industrial structure.

At the level of industrial organization it was the policy of *corporatism* which provided fascism with a means to integrate private industry and the state. In order to supersede the class divisions inherent in the industrial structure of society, the enterprise or, according to this new word, the 'corporation', was to become the site for a new national reconciliation, a new 'community of producers within which both interest groups and individuals would be held in a spirit of solidarity which would be non-antagonistic'. This new community would have as its aim the increase in production, individual enhancement, and a respect both for the 'natural hierarchy' in which everybody recognized their place and acknowledged the 'sacred' nature of the sanctity of labour. This in itself would not necessarily be sufficient, but for fascism it would provide an important link in the chain whereby 'social reconciliation within the enterprise becomes a crucial link for national reconciliation.'

Such links, or connotations, were not automatically given or naturally assumed: they had to be persuasively constructed through an immense ideological concentration on the notion of the worker *as producer*. It was this need to, as it were, 'interpellate out' the languages of class solidarity and conflict and 'interpellate in' a new associative chain of producer-citizen-nation-state which inspired the original plans for a national leisure-time organization-the *dopolavoro* which forms an important focus of this article. The idea itself was not intrinsically fascist: it was American in origin, based on various conceptions of scientific management which had developed in the heartland of monopoly capitalism. It was introduced in Italy by Mario Giani who was the manager of a subsidiary of the

Westinghouse Corporation at Vado Ligure. Giani was to argue that a national *dopolavoro* organization would promote a 'fusion of characters, of spirits, of regional tendencies into a new "national type", more fully representative of our ancient and glorious stock and more conscious of its duties to the nation' (in de Grazia, 1981, p.36).

Clearly we have here a significant expansion of discourse beyond the immediate physical and economic requirements of the workplace. The notion of the producer here is an ideological *condenser* of a whole range of images and associations which could be represented diagramatically as follows:

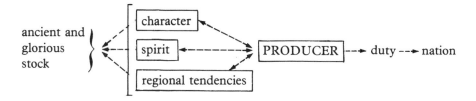

For fascism and for the initial development of the *dopolavoro*, this discursive field was to become crucial. The notion of producer fuses the heterogeneous elements of character, spirit and region in a historical line of continuity with a postulated 'ancient and glorious stock' and in a forward vector of duty and nation. Other possible elements which might impinge upon this unified discursive field are or were to be both ideologically marginalized or physically repressed or both: the classic interlopers would be class, ethnicity and gender. But in order for this discursive field to become in some way 'compelling' it was not enough just to utter it. It had to assume a mass institutional and popular form.

The culture of consent: the Opera Nazionale Dopolavoro (OND)

The OND or National Afterwork Agency was established by the Fascist government on May Day, 1925. It was a particular type of response to a 'problem' not specific to authoritarian regimes – the problem of after-work or leisure activities for working people. It was by no means a new problem and nor was it specific to Italy. Administrators and social reformers had been concerned with the issue in all advanced industrial countries. In Britain, for example, the organization of leisure had been the particular prerogative of a reforming bourgeoisie since the beginning of the Industrial Revolution in a response to the new requirements of industrial production for a relatively orderly and well-occupied workforce. Indeed, it was precisely these sorts of 'private initiatives' with a public character which had cemented, in Britain probably more successfully than any other industrial democracy, a 'sturdy civil society' in which the state would not – or would not be seen to – interfere. The encouragement of 'appropriate' leisure time activities by the likes of Hannah More, Samuel Smiles, Robert Owen and the Society for the Diffusion of Useful Knowledge in nineteenth century Britain and the resultant negotiated network of shared cultures and hierarchy of consensual values, formed the complex capillary vessels of civil society or what Gramsci was to call 'the "trenches" and the permanent fortifications of the front in the war of position . . . ' (Gramsci, 1971, p.243). A network, in other words, where, in spite of obvious and acknowledged class differences, a certain 'intellectual and moral leadership' or hegemony could be consolidated and reproduced.

In Italy the situation was radically different. Because of the historical and economic factors discussed above, there was no such mesh of negotiated ideological positions. The Italian working class and peasantry developed its own, largely autonomous cultural and political organizations and remained regionally and locally much more self-organised. It was therefore very resistant to anything which might smack of paternalism. Edward Tannenbaum argues that the Italians lacked 'what is called a civic culture. Unlike the French and Americans they had not acquired one by fighting together in a revolution' (Tannenbaum, 1973, p.13). There were strongly entrenched specific regional and political cultures: the working class and peasantry had for a long time enjoyed the benefits of an extensive network of clubs which were places to eat, drink, hold political meetings and discussions and to organize militant actions. These were the 'people's houses' or the *casi del popolo* which became some of the prime targets for Mussolini's armed bands of *squadristi*. The systematic vigour and brutality with which they were either destroyed or taken over gives us a clue that they were perhaps the site for a *potential* civic culture at a national level recognized by Mussolini who had had many years of experience in them. This first and preliminary destruction or 'war of manoeuvre' was, for fascism, necessary before setting out on a longer term 'war of position' to form its own version of a national civic culture.

Fundamental to this project, of course, is the recognition that leisure and popular cultural forms are ideologically and politically strategic: that, as de Grazia argues, a 'politics of culture' is integral to the stability of the capitalist system as such. The OND was located right at the heart of this strategic recognition in order, as de Grazia argues:

> To give a distinctively ideological cast to social experiences outside the workplace – to unite 'war veterans', 'tax payers', 'sports fans' or 'national citizens' . . . [which] . . . demanded the creation of a nationwide political culture that might persuade people that their shared goals transcended petty economic haggling, regional and ethnic disputes, or age-old social animosities. (de Grazia, 1981, p.2)

The OND was essentially a state-controlled agency, the aim of which was to *suture* the fatal political chasm between civil society and the state, between the 'private' and 'public' spheres, at first by encouraging employers to set up organized welfare and leisure schemes within the spirit of corporatism – a measure which met with some resistance from big business because they suspected that the OND was a syndicalist initiative – and later with the manifest success of the agency, by a complete takeover by the PNF with the realization of its full strategic potential. Its main ideological aim was 'the healthy and profitable occupation of workers' leisure hours by means of institutions for developing their physical, intellectual and moral capacities' with the aim of producing a 'totally reformed citizen-producer' (de Grazia, p.35).

But as the OND expanded and as the economic and political requirements of the fascist regime began to move in different directions, it was soon realized that this rather limiting *productivist* ethic, or what we might call this singular interpellation, needed to be expanded. As de Grazia puts it:

> Moving beyond the casual manipulations of worker community and home life typical of *laissez-faire* capitalism . . . the regime's own efficiency experts, moral reformers, government planners and political functionaries scrutinized for their susceptibility to organizing an entire range of social activities, from sports and entertainment to child rearing practices. From the mid-twenties on . . . the social and private domains were inexorably drawn into the public sphere. (ibid, pp.5-6)

There is probably no better testament to this perceived crisis of civil society and its impending state take-over than the mass of organizations which sprang up in this period to account for various 'social needs'. Amongst these the most important were the OND, and OMNI, the organization for mothers and infants, the *Balilla* for 'the civil education and physical preparedness of Italian youth' and the Fascist university groups (GUF). Alongside these organizations the government under Fascism attempted to 'reform custom'. A law of 1930 attempted to remove from the language the third person *Lei* as a form of polite address and also to replace the handshake with the Roman salute (see Tannenbaum, 1973, pp.281ff); an academy was established, based on the French model, for the standardization and diffusion of 'high culture'; and the Institute of the Italian Encyclopaedia was set up. From these events we can see something of the condensed, rapid and multi-faceted nature of cultural policy under Fascism.

But to return to the ideological dimension of these processes, the ways in which consent is organized, we have to consider not just the bare facts of the institutions but also the ways in which they can be seen to hold together symbolically. In Laclau's terms, we have to interrogate the nature of the *unity* of the various ideological discourses. This is a unity which depends upon the:

> ability of each interpellative element to fulfill a role of condensation with respect to the others. When a familial interpellation, for example, *evokes* a political interpellation, a religious interpellation, or an aesthetic interpellation, and when each of these isolated interpellations operates as a *symbol* of the others, we have a relatively unified ideological discourse. (Laclau, this volume, p. 28)

It is important to stress the words 'relatively unified' in that statement because we are not concerned here with questions of 'mind control' or a simple 'inculcation of the masses' or even an unproblematic moulding of public opinion. A given interpellation cannot simply be 'imposed': it has to be fought for at the level of 'the people' and of 'the popular'. This is a struggle which is far from being straightforward: it can engender contradictions and points of resistance by the very fact that it is a *popular* interpellation and therefore susceptible to other possible articulations. This was recognized, for example, by the Communist leader Togliatti when he insisted that the *dopolavoro* be treated not as a uniform and representative fascist organization but as a contradiction within fascism itself as effectively the first 'centralized class organization for satisfying the educational, cultural and sports needs of the masses' which had never before existed in Italy (Togliatti, 1976, p.74). Given this mass and centralized institutional character, Togliatti argued, it would be possible to engender within its forms, points of resistance to Mussolini's dictatorship.

Generating consent

The *dopolavoro* provided the Fascist regime with an opportunity to realize its image of a 'unified people' against the 'decadence' and 'disintegration' of the immediately preceding period characterised by Alfredo Rocco, one of fascism's most prominent ideologists and later the Minister of Justice, as 'a mass of particles, parties, associations, groups and syndicates' (quoted in de Grazia, p.7). More importantly, though, it would enable the regime to inflect this image in a particular direction, against, again according to Rocco, both the 'disruptive individualism' of liberalism and, on the same scale but more extreme, the 'unbridled individualism' of 'Bolshevism' (in Lyttelton, 1973, p.254). At the more elaborate and philosophical level it was Gentile who formulated the question of this new unity in terms of the strategic ideological importance of both subjectivity and the forms of language in which it is elaborated. He argues, in a formulation which shares something with marxism in its initial emphasis, that 'the human individual is not an atom. Immanent in the concept of individual is the concept of society . . . Man is, in an absolute sense, a political animal' (in Sternhell, 1976, p.364). More succinctly, though, Gentile goes on to emphasize that 'at the root of the "I" there is a "we" ' (ibid, p.365). The project of the OND, and indeed of fascist ideology in general, can be seen as a sometimes pragmatic, sometimes systematic series of transactions which would attempt to unite the subjective 'I' with the collective 'we'.

This fundamental problem of *identity* had to be established in two principal ways: 'at both a structural and an ideological level, on the one hand by the appropriation of popular associational forms and ideological motifs, and, on the other, by the imposition of dominant ideas and beliefs' (de Grazia, p.21). Inevitably contradictions would arise between the two processes, partly because of the historical association of previous popular forms with various aspects of the socialist movement (bowls, cycling excursions, popular theatre and so on) but nevertheless fascism achieved a considerable measure of success in establishing, with the OND and other politico-cultural organizations, a 'relative harmony' between force and consent.

By the 1930s, 20,000 *dopolavoro* circles had been formed in both workplace and residential branches along with adjacent fascist women's groups, 'rural housewife' sections, war veterans' organizations and cultural rallies or *littoriali*. Increased membership and participation in the various *dopolavoro* organizations in this period were not just due to its gradual acceptance on a mass scale, but also to a significant shift in policy in a more populist direction: 'a far more pronounced effort on the part of the state and the party to intervene systematically in the social life of the nation' (de Grazia, p.52). There was a significant shift away from the earlier productivist ethos, away from the more untenable aspects of activist fascist education and instruction towards, according to Achille Starace, National Secretary of the PNF and now Special Commissioner of the OND, a *dopolavoro* which would be both cheaper and 'more congenial to the habits and mentality of the working population' (ibid, p.52). There was also a move away from the emphasis on technical instruction which had been a keynote of its sections in clerical and service sectors of industry and the state sector, towards an emphasis on those sports and pastimes 'favoured by the masses'. This would be developed in such a way that it would become, in Starace's own words, an 'effective tool of assistance and propaganda among the masses'. Combined with this, and with the threat of fascist syndicalism now firmly under control, there would be a renewed effort to put pressure on employers to support *dopolavoro* initiatives both in the workplace and in the community.

If the initial appeal of the OND had been most successful within the petty bourgeoisie there was now an effort to expand its field of address most significantly to those areas where there had been, or which were traditionally associated with, labour unrest. In particular, a 'more rapid and active movement to penetrate the rural masses' (ibid, p.54).

In terms of membership figures and on a general level, the plan seems to have had some success. After 1932 membership of the OND increased rapidly from 1,744,000 to 2,376,000 in 1935, the year of the invasion of Ethiopia when the regime used the propaganda elements of the OND to its fullest extent, especially in the glossy magazine *Gente Nostra* (Our People) which reached its peak circulation figures at the same moment with its image of the grateful 'noble savages' of the invaded country. More significantly perhaps, the new membership was increasingly drawn from manual workers: by 1936 these, from both industrial and rural sections, constituted almost seventy per cent of the total OND membership. This meant, according to de Grazia, that 'in Italy as a whole, twenty per cent of the industrial labour force and seven per cent of the peasantry was enrolled in the OND, in addition to the "near totality" – eighty per cent – of state and private salaried employees . . . ' (ibid, p.55).

But, as Mussolini himself noted, 'Consent is as unstable as the sand formations on the edge of the sea'. To understand the ways in which the various forms of *dopolavoro* culture actively constructed and reconstructed the terms of these shifting and unstable formations, it is necessary to look more closely at the specific semiotics of its cultural work.

National treasures, myriad customs and the splendour of the past

One of the necessary ingredients for the formation of a popular-democratic positionality is the articulation of a sense of tradition or of heritage in which 'the people' can establish itself as part of a historical and cultural continuity. Giovanni Gentile, a former Minister of Education, in 1923 recognized the strategic importance of a 'dynamic new synthesis of the national heritage and fascist ideology . . . and . . . the utilization of the state as a positive education force to impart national values to a citizenry that hitherto had perceived state institutions as "mere names or external coercive forces"' (de Grazia, p.188). The corollary to that last expression would be that such values must therefore be transformed into 'internal and consensual forces' subjectively experienced and agreed upon. This formation of a new 'common sense' which Gramsci calls the 'sub-stratum' of ideology and which we might also call the 'unconscious structure' of Althusser's definition discussed above, was central to the range of preferred interpellations of fascist ideology.

Some of the more precise mechanisms of such 'work on subjectivity' can be observed in the OND's attempts to make popular customs and traditions a part of its ideological strategy. Some reference points in the discursive field of 'the popular' that was created in this way are identified by Victoria de Grazia in the article in this volume, especially in the section 'The return to traditions'. She shows how the 'heritage' of which Gentile speaks had to be exhumed and re-invented, how (after 1928) this revival shifted the reference of the term 'popular culture' from modern pastimes to a conception of 'the people' in terms of the *volk* of German Romaticism, and how civic festivals attempted to combine popular customs and religious or dynastic traditions with fascist rituals. But she also points out that, given the multi-discursive nature of the term, such *popular* occasions could potentially become moments of resistance, opposition and 'non-preferred' intervention. This was manifested in both structural forms in the contradictions which might emerge between an enthusiastic regional culture emphasizing communal soidarity and the 'essentially national orientation of the fascist regime' (p.247) and in the more explicit political possibility that such occasions, by dint of their mass nature, might well traverse the unstable line between orderliness and respect and riotous assembly (p.248).

This particular aspect of the *cultura dopolavoristica* provides a good deal of empirical material for the theoretical conception of ideology elaborated by Laclau. In a process of ideological and symbolic reorganization, selections, combinations and condensations of various 'available' or 'rediscovered' ideological elements are reworked into a grid of interpellations. The aim is to make structures which had been historically perceived as coercive and external 'internal and consensual'.

Let us now consider these processes in a little more detail in schematic form. If we take first the identifiable elements or motifs, we may list them as follows:

authenticity
harmony
continuity
national virtues
spirit
nature
fertility
virility
abundance
production
festivity

The nature of the ideological work applied to these elements – the nature, that is, of particular articulations, selections, condensations and combinations – can be summarized under three headings. These are:

(1) *Rediscovery – exhumation – equation*
folk *equals* authenticity
folk *equals* national virtues
folk *equals* people *equals* nation
(2) *Additions/assimilations*
folk *plus* civic virtue
folk *plus* instruction
folk *plus* state
(3) *Subtractions/exclusions*
folk *equals* people *minus* foreign influence
people *equals* folk *minus* modern corruption

The resultant ideological forms or interpellations may be summarized as the following dominant themes

national people/national folk
national fascist/producer as embodiment of national virtues
virile man/female woman

There are others, of course, but in this particular case these are probably the most pertinent. Through this schematic representation, my argument is that these elements are, not of themselves, intrinsically 'fascist'. Indeed, taken as isolated elements, each one of them could also be allocated to other political formations, from conservative to anarchist to socialist. It is, rather, in the specific and complex ways in which these elements are *condensed* into a particular framework of meanings, predominantly through the institutional form of OND, that they assume distinctively fascist interpellations which emerge as 'natural' and 'necessary' hierarchies of position.

The woman in black: Fascism's semiotics of gender

I have repeatedly stressed that the work of interpellation does not just consist of a process of 'naming' but also depends upon the material and institutional forms through which that naming and positioning may be transacted and negotiated. It was never enough, for example, for the *Duce* simply to *say* that a certain conception of virility, or masculinity, was appropriate to the idea of the fascist 'new man': this also had to take hold in a variety of directions in the context of a varying balance of political, economic and cultural forces. In this final section, I shall examine briefly both the preferred interpellations and the contradictions at work in the construction of the corresponding 'new woman' within that field of forces.

Mobilizing

According to Maria-Antonietta Macciocchi, on whose work this section is based, 'There has been no State demagogy as successful as Fascism in getting women into the streets as a mobilised political force' (Macciocchi, 1976, p.144). The author insists that a political revaluation of the role of women in the making of history must encounter this fact. It was women, for example, who played a very prominent role in the attacks on various socialist and communist organizations in the early days of fascism, organized into particular 'squadrons' which were both conscious of their gender identity and of their 'associated' roles as mothers and widows of the war-dead who, by ideological association, were now being reviled by the pacifists and anti-militarists of the opposition parties. This is not, of course, to argue, from an essentialist point of view, that this was some pregiven trait of women – women workers were also at the forefront of internal resistance to the fascist regime – but it is to stress something of the elaborated nature of the specific strategies which fascism addressed to women.

Fascism was not antifeminist *per se*, at least not in its early stages. As Gregor notes, many of the intellectuals and writers whose work was to become influential on the fascist movement had expressed early support for the demands of feminists. Roberto Michels had elaborated in his writings a position which was sympathetic to the major demands of sexual equality. Marinetti, discussed above in another context, also advocated 'radical equality' of the sexes in a swingeing attack on the 'bourgeois barbarism' of monogamy and marriage, speaking of 'the "cretinism" that made women the "slaves" of men in lifetime dependency' and, in a gesture which was probably more *against* the established Church than *for* women, argued for 'easy divorce and easy abortion to lift the burden of monogamy from both sexes' (Gregor, 1979, p.282).

In their programme of 1919 the Fascists advocated suffrage rights for women and, in the Statute of Carnaro, elaborated by Gabriele D'Annunzio while occupying Fiume, it was declared that 'all citizens, irrespective of sex, have complete rights in the pursuit of employment in industry, the professions, arts and crafts'. To be sure, formal equality is only a starting point and the direction in which Fascist policy was to move after these early years, when it did not revoke those formal rights entirely, certainly wanted to give them a particular ideological form where the image of woman, according to Mussolini, would stand as a *symbol* of the qualities of 'measure, equilibrium and wisdom' and where they would be seen to have, in particular ways, a ' "preponderant" influence in determining the destiny of society' (ibid, p.283).

This sort of emphasis is evident in the law of 1923 which accorded limited suffrage rights to women. Even if, in the early stages, it was *all* women who were addressed by fascist discourse, by now it was becoming clear that it was a certain version of woman which was to figure as the primary interpellation. The women allowed to vote by this law – only in municipal elections and disqualified from being elected themselves to council positions – were to be designated by seven categories: (i) women decorated with the military medal or the *croix de guerre*; (ii) women who had received an equivalent civil honour; (iii) mothers of soldiers who had been killed in the war; (iv) widows of soldiers who had not lost the rights to their pensions – in other words, only if they hadn't remarried or weren't 'living in sin'; (v) women who had assumed the role of legal guardian; (vi) women educated to secondary level; (vii) women who paid, in local taxes, an annual sum of not less that forty lire and who could read and write. These categories make it possible to assess of the particular *image* of women which was to be foregrounded in Fascist policy elsewhere. The effect of these seven categories was, in general, to underscore the petty-bourgeois nature of the core of fascism's support but the images of mother, widow and chastity were to have a broader political and popular resonance.

The 'hard core' of women's support for fascism was typified in the principal aims of the *fascii femminile* (the fascist women's organization): 'Assistance in the physical education of women with regard to the fundamental necessity to prevent the decline and decadence of the race by strengthening its roots in the reconstruction of the family, the resumption of woman's role in local and artisanal forms of work and in assistance programmes' (in Macciocchi, p.196). Again a particular inflection of the sort of work which women were supposed to do should be noted. Fascism never created an organization to represent specific women's interests in large-scale industrial production or the state sector: the emphasis was rather upon the accepted notions of women's work, particularly in the rural housewives sections which were created by the regime in order to offer 'the image of the joyful peasant women' who were to become so important in the forms of 'folk ceremonial' discussed above. If the countryside, according to fascism's rural myth, was the basis of fecundity and the health of the race, then the woman within this schema was to assume a very significant role particularly as, in the 1930s, Mussolini mounted a demographic campaign urging every wife to 'breed rapidly' and awarding the most prolific with special gifts and testimonials and a personal meeting at the presidential palace.

Protect and sacrifice: the Mater Dolorosa

The 'eternal widow' physically and spiritually embodying the glories of the war dead in order to maintain the hope of *future* generations was a powerful and frequently used theme of fascist discourse. It would be used to establish a theme of protection (of a memory, of a race) against the 'defilers of the tombs of the war dead' who might be, variously, socialists, communists, pacifists or, at its broadest, anybody who was not a fascist or who did not at least tacitly support the activities of the 'continuators of combat' in the *arditi* and *fascists*. In this ideological network, Mussolini was able, on the occasion of the parliamentary debate on women's suffrage in 1923, to say:

> From this tribune, ladies, I direct my thoughts towards the millions of mothers and wives who have supported in silence and in dignity the sacrifices and the suffering of the Great War: those who, although not represented here, have massively contributed, throughout this period, to the maintenance of the continuity of the course of national life.
> (Quoted in Macciocchi, 1978, p.158)

And as late as 1936–perhaps especially in 1936 after an imperial adventure in Ethiopia in which other forms of sacrifice had been called for–the leaders of the fascist women's groups were still responding in a mode which would directly echo Mussolini's discourse. As a response to the 'iniquity' of the sanctions imposed by the League of Nations after the invasion of Ethiopia, one prominent fascist woman was to echo that earlier symbolism by saying that 'The women of all Italy . . . will devote all their strengths in order that the fatherland (*patria*) should emerge triumphant from this iniquitous trial, and declare themselves ready for any necessary sacrifices' (Macciocchi, p.200). But between this ideological call and response, there is a degree of complexity which needs analysing.

The woman and the machine

The various interpellations concerning the role of women as mothers, widows, continuers of the race and guardians of its 'roots' and well-being are, again, not specific to fascism. They were also common themes in the discourses of politics, trades-unionism and social welfare in Britain in the 1920s (see for example, Rowan, 1984). And it is probably the case that *in general* they were about as successful in Britain as in Italy. In other words, beyond the perpetrators of the imagery, not very successful at all as a single mode of persuasion. But they assumed a particular urgency in Italy both in relation to the generalized ideological crisis and in relation to Fascism's specific problems concerning the employment of women in industry.

It was clear to the regime that women constituted not only a significant proportion of the public workforce but also that they constituted a potential political threat organized in this way. There is no better evidence of this than the mass resistance which Fascism encountered to its laws on women's suffrage precisely from this key sector. This factor, combined with the past history of women's involvement in socialist militancy (see Macciocchi, pp.152-55), meant that Fascist discourse had to resort to other ideological forms in order to convince this 'concrete individual' that she was indeed the subject *woman* and that this subject had particular attributes.

One of these attributes was that although she has a power of analysis, she had no power of *synthesis*. Thus, according to Mussolini, a woman could not be an architect since this form represents the 'synthesis of all the arts'. Furthermore, and again according to Mussolini, woman is incompatible with the machine for four reasons:

(1) in working the machine the woman becomes masculine;
(2) she causes masculine unemployment;
(3) she establishes an independence which is contrary to the natural laws of procreation and therefore prejudicial to the tendency to population increase;
(4) it causes men to lose their 'procreative powers' in distracting them from their essential activities.
(Macciocchi, 1978, pp. 184-5)

It wasn't long before this quasi-philosophical position became enshrined in various laws which would cut women's wage rates to fifty per cent of those for men in the same occupation (1927); ban women from teaching literature and philosophy in high schools (1927), from becoming directors of educational institutions (1928); and exclude them from the civil service (on discretion) in 1933 (followed by a ten per cent allocation in 1938). Clearly this was both a 'material force' due to rising unemployment and the generalized effects of the Depression and an 'ideological form' in its particular inflections and the sorts of imagery it involved. There is a consistency and complexity of imagery concerning the role of women which, in its density and intensity, is specific to fascism and probably to Mussolini who was, according to Macciocchi, the inventor of the relationship between women and fascism:

> . . . his first speeches addressed to women in order to gain their support as a fundamental element of the *consent* needed for the 'seizure of power' date from 1922-3; he poses the problem of votes for women (only in order later to rescind it); he invents the women's 'death squadrons' –widows, mothers in mounting or semi-mourning in an Italy which had come out of the War with 600,000 dead and 1,000,000 wounded; he invented a particular way of dressing for these women –the lugubrious black clothes and emblems of the *squadristi* in which, with the symbols of the death's head on their chests, they would attack the 'reds' with knives and hatpins; he structures a whole language, a feminine semiotic, around the initial invocation to 'widows, mothers of fallen soldiers, spouses' which later changed to 'sisters' and 'daughters'. It was Mussolini who was the first to engage with the demographic campaign and to announce the first commandment of the feminine decalogue: *Give Birth*: 'numbers are

powerful' . . . Fascism brought Italian women out onto the streets, into the
squares in a counter-explanation of politics . . . with a liturgy resembling that
of the church . . . accompanied with intense and fevered ritual.
(Macciocchi, 1978, p.71)

Gifts of gold: bonds of iron

A particular campaign which was to link an imperial necessity (funds for the
Ethiopia campaign) with a longer-term economic imperative (the population
campaign) and a preferred fascist symbolism was Mussolini's 'gift of gold'
strategy. Initiated in December, 1935, the scheme was to encourage the women of
the country to give up their wedding ring – in many cases their only valuable
possession – to the nation for the campaign being waged in Ethiopia. Macciocchi
describes this particular version of sacrifice whereby the women would
ceremonially offer up their possessions, as 'theatrical'. Women would file across a
stage decorated with various Fascist and Roman symbols – the emblems of
Fascism flanked by the burning Roman braziers of mythology – in order to proffer
their gifts of gold to Fascist dignitaries. But unlike similar campaigns in a more
earthy and utilitarian vein like 'digging for victory' in wartime Britain, Mussolini
multiplied the symbolism here. Instead of this just being a sacrifice, it was also to
become a 'day of alliance' between women and fascism as, in place of the gold
rings, the women were offered rings made of iron to establish a second contract of
union with fascism and with the *Duce* himself. In spite of what we might
retrospectively think of as an absurd episode we should note that, in Rome alone,
250,000 such 'alliances' were made and in Milan some 180,000. If the response was
not overwhelming then we at least have to concede that it was extremely
significant and some measure of the force of fascism's ideological symbolism (see
Macciocchi, 1976, p.198).

For fascism, women were relegated to the – not insignificant – role of an
ideological *chorus* befitting a system of images which had constant recourse to the
symbols of Ancient Rome. Woman as subject was discursively multiplied in fascist
philosophy into a 'mass and undifferentiated subjectivity' articulated with the
long-standing critique of liberalism and individualism. Gentile, for example,
wrote 'feminism is dead, with its false and rhetorical egalitarian visions of the man-
woman [which stem from the old enemy of] the libertarian egalitarianism of the
French Revolution and the Socialism of the last century'. Now, according to the
foremost philosopher of fascism, 'Woman no longer desires the rights for which
she fought . . . we have returned to the healthy conception of the woman who is a
woman and not a man, with her limits and, consequently, with her values'.
Ferdinando Loffredo, in his book *Politics of the Family*, was more pragmatically
explicit in stating that 'Fascism is against all individualist abstractions which have
a materialist basis' with the consequence that 'at the spiritual level' fascism is
'antifeminist'. The aim, of course, was to transform the biological nature of woman
into an *ideological* tie with the race and the nation. Woman is made the way she is

exclusively, according to this interpellation, in order to allow the child to flourish within her: 'If her functions were the same as men's, as in inferior species,then male and female organs would be undifferentiated, but on the contrary . . .' (Macciocchi, p.232-9). And, moving across the bestiary of fascist discourse, we return to Gentile for whom even the mention of the 'mind' of women is but a confirmation of their essentially corporeal nature: the mind 'does not liberate the woman from her (anatomico-physiological) sexuality, but bonds her to it . . . since the elevation of the mind cannot affect the body because it remains always the same body . . . with its dense and massive materiality which the woman will carry with her throughout her life as the mark of her destiny' (in Macciocchi, p.258).

Clearly again, though we may tend to identify these positions with certain conservative and reactionary versions of women's role which are still active today, there is nothing intrinsically *fascist* about them. That particular inflection only emerges as a result of the combination of these discourses with anti-liberalism, anti-democracy, anti-rationalism, anti-communism and anti-egalitarianism. The fact that they were able, with varying degrees of success, to attach themselves to dominant interpellations of the 'new man' and the corresponding but subordinate interpellation of the 'new/old woman' gives them a force and a popular resilience which they might, in isolation, not otherwise have achieved.

What we might call the *aestheticization* of politics and the *sexualization* of the social sphere were two key strategies of fascism in its articulation of popular-democratic discourses and the construction of a principle of unity around which such interpellations might relatively freely circulate. This is something of a testament to Gramsci's assertion that in regimes of this nature, the terrains of the *people* and of *culture* are of key strategic importance and are foregrounded in order to marginalize questions of politics of a broader nature, that 'in such parties cultural functions predominate . . . in other words, political questions are disguised as cultural ones' (Gramsci, 1971, p.149).

But such dense and connotative terms as *people* and *culture* are also dense and effective realities. The very nature of mass organization under fascism carried within it its own contradictions in so far as neither 'the people' nor the cultural forms which were constructed around them could be assumed to be irreducibly fascist by nature. As Macciocchi points out, in spite of the adherence of a significant proportion of women either to explicit fascist politics or to generalized forms of consent to fascism there were more women involved in the resistance to fascism and its final overthrow than in the resistance movements of the whole of Western Europe put together. The shifting sands of consent, consolidated temporarily in mass organizations such as the OND, the women's organizations, the mass rallies and the pervasive and active symbolism of fascism had engendered contradictions which, in the face of an Allied invasion, a declining regime, and a mass resistance movement organized around its own 'popular' objectives, could not be contained.

Conclusion

By way of conclusion it is perhaps worth both restating the central themes of my argument and also thereby marking a certain modesty of ambition. My aim here has not been to provide a history of Italian Fascism, nor to provide a comparative analysis which would establish points of connection with other forms of right-wing authoritarian political regime. This is due, in part, to self-imposed and necessary limitations of research. But it is also due to a resistance to viewing the particular forms of fascism as either generalizable across different contexts or, more crucially, to viewing fascism as a unified and monolithic phenomenon in which each of the parts can be recognized as a necessary component of the whole. As I stated at the beginning of the article, the awkward question of fascism's relative indeterminacy, its duration and the forms of consent which it generated in Italy would seem to provide ample empirical evidence for the argument that it is, in Togliatti's metaphor, something of a chameleon. But more than that, my argument has also been concerned with developing more appropriate theoretical conceptions in order to deal with the active and complex nature of ideological formations of this type. To elaborate these conceptions I have suggested that, in addition to the necessary historical criteria of locating fascism within a politico-economic context it is also important to focus on the equally real and material processes through which that context is lived. Thus, the subjective, institutional and symbolic levels of the ideological work of fascism have played a more significant role in my analysis than the average reader will be accustomed to. By way of justification and as an argument for taking ideology seriously, it is fair to say that, with the exception of certain authors important for my own analysis such as Laclau, de Grazia and Macciocchi, the great bulk of scholarly material on fascism has very little to say theoretically about how, to repeat Gramsci's terms, ideologies 'make men move, acquire consciousness of their position, struggle, etc'. Of all ideological formations it is fascism and related forms which pose that question most urgently.

References

ALTHUSSER, L., (1969) *For Marx*, Harmondsworth, Penguin.
ALTHUSSER, L., (1971) *Lenin and Philosophy, and other Essays*, London, New Left Books.
ANDERSON, B., (1983) *Imagined Communities. Reflections on the Origin and Spread of Nationalism*, London, Verso.
BOURDERON, R., (1979) *Le fascisme ideologie et pratiques*, Paris, Editions Sociales.
BUCI-GLUCKSMANN, C., (1975) *Gramsci et l'Etat*, Paris, Fayard.
DE FELICE, R., (1977) *Interpretations of Fascism*, Harvard, Harvard University Press.
DE GRAZIA, V., (1981) *The Culture of Consent: Mass Organisation of Leisure in Fascist Italy*, Cambridge, Cambridge University Press.
FAYE, J. P., (1973) *La critique du langage et son economie*, Paris, Editions Galilee.
FAYE, J. P., (1974) *Theorie du recit*, Paris, Hermann.

GRAMSCI, A., (1971) *Selections from the Prison Notebooks,* London, Lawrence and Wishart.

GRAMSCI, A., (1977) *Selections from Political Writings 1921-26,* London, Lawrence and Wishart.

GREGOR, A. J., (1979) *Italian Fascism and Developmental Dictatorship,* Princeton, New Jersey, Princeton University Press.

HOARE, Q., (1977) Introduction to Gramsci (*op. cit.*)

LACLAU, E., (1977) *Politics and Ideology in Marxist Theory,* London, New Left Books.

LACLAU, E., (1980) 'Populist rupture and discourse' in *Screen Education,* 34.

LAQUEUR, W., (1976) *Fascism: A Reader's Guide,* Harmondsworth, Penguin.

LINZ, J. J., (1976) 'Some notes towards a comparative study of Fascism in sociological and historical perspectives', in Lacqueur, *op. cit.*

LYTTELTON, A., (1973) (ed). *Italian Fascisms: From Pareto to Gentile,* London, Cape.

LYTTELTON, A., (1976) 'Italian Fascism' in Laqueur, *op. cit.*

MACCIOCCHI, M. A. (1976) (ed) *Elements pour une analyse du fascisme* (2 vols), Paris, UGE.

MACCIOCCHI, M. A. (1978) (ed) *Les Femmes et leurs Maitres,* Paris, Christian Bourgeois.

NOLTE, E., (1965) *Three Faces of Fascism,* New York, New English Library.

POULANTZAS, N., (1976) 'A propos de l'impact populaire de fascisme' in Macciocchi, (*op. cit.*)

ROMANO, S., (1982) 'Le fascisme' in *Dictatures et Legitimité,* (ed.) Duverger, Paris, PUF.

ROWAN, C., (1984) 'For the duration only: motherhood and nation in the First World War' in *Formations of Nation and People,* London, Routledge and Kegan Paul.

SAN SEVERINO, Q. di., (1923) *Mussolini as Revealed in His Political Speeches,* London, J. M. Dent.

STERNHELL, Z., (1976) 'Fascist ideology' in Laqueur, *op. cit.*

TANNENBAUM, E., (1973) *Fascism in Italy: Society and Culture 1922-45,* Harmondsworth, Allen Lane.

TOGLIATTI, P., (1976) *Lectures on Fascism,* London, Lawrence and Wishart.

WILLIAMS, G., (1975) *Proletarian Order,* London, Pluto Press.

16 The Formation of Fascist Low Culture

Victoria de Grazia

From *The Culture of Consent* by Victoria de Grazia, 1981. Reproduced by permission of the publishers Cambridge University Press.

The fascist regime had early recognized the instrumental value of *la cultura* in the consolidation of its rule. Coming to power with all the rhetoric of an unfulfilled Risorgimento tradition, fascist and nationalist ideologues continuously paid homage to the idea of a unified and unifying national culture. The formation of a single dominant culture would, it was understood, not only help to mask the patent inequalities of Italian society, but also serve to legitimate the regime according to a traditional bourgeois and even a popular cultural sensibility. But this said, there remained a wide spectrum of 'cultures' from which such a national culture might be forged, from the avant-garde to the popular; from technological utopias of the Futurists, whose pugilistic tactics had made them especially suitable companions for the *squadristi*, to the verities of elitist practitioners of the old high culture; and, in theory at least, the stock of folk traditions of precapitalist Italy. The regime demonstrated itself willing to espouse any one of these according to its need for support, and as a whole its cultural pretensions remained extremely eclectic in content. But in practice, and especially in the formation of the institutions for the dissemination of one or another kind of culture, fascism was inevitably drawn toward the reproduction of the already class-defined divisions between 'high' and 'low'. [. . .]

In the regime's definition, 'popular' culture simply involved the transmission of an already formulated body of precepts and information, whereas true culture was formed by the elite and purveyed to the masses. In keeping with this mechanistic division, 'artistic education' for the masses and 'popular culture' generally were treated as purely organizational questions. Cultural policy, to the extent that it existed, was relegated by default to a heterogeneous corps of intellectual collaborators: well-established cultural personalities at the national level; party functionaries, high-school professors, schoolteachers, and professional lecturers locally. By the thirties the resulting cultural *bricolage* had achieved an identity of its own, characterized by the institutions within which it was formed, as *cultura dopolavoristica*. In the end, distinguished less by its specific content than by its

240

style, it was easily digestible, crudely propagandistic, and as eclectic as the background of its organizers and the mixed social composition of their audience might indicate. [. . .]

Thus the culture that was brought to the working public with such virtuous images was no more than the world of high culture as perceived and vulgarized by the organizers of low culture; the servants of culture and not its creators, they propounded it with all the pompous condescension and mystification of acolytes opening up the world of the occult to the uninitiated. In one sense, the 'monumentalization of culture,' achieved by their efforts, was similar to that aspired to on another level by the regime itself as it reconstructed the Imperial *fora*, isolating them from the fabric of the medieval city and destroying the historical continuum that united modern Rome with its ancient past. The national tradition was thus reduced to a roster of illustrious but essentially static and isolated cultural 'monuments': Dante, Goldoni, Manzoni, Verdi, Puccini, D'Annunzio – an eclectic mixture, united solely by their similar packaging and consistent presentation to the public.

If embarrassing to the fascist cultural vanguard, as well as to academic culture, this distorted image of high culture at least allowed their world to remain intact. 'Low-brow' culture could be readily dismissed as *roba da dopolavoro* (trash) whereas respect for official culture and the traditional status of the intellectual was reinforced. Even as the regime was willing to tolerate and even foster a measure of avant-garde iconoclasm to perpetuate fascism's image as a dynamic, modern, aggressive force, so it found in traditional culture a mode of imparting fascism's conservative social ideals to a mass public. [. . .]

The return to traditions

Clearly rejecting a role in the development of a technological culture, the OND [*Opera Nazionale Dopolavoro* – National Afterwork Agency] turned its organizational energies and ideological strategems toward sustaining those very folk traditions that were gradually disappearing with the spread of literacy, urbanization, and improved communications. This so-called return to traditions was first announced by Beretta in 1929, when the regime, in its concern to reassure the crisis-stricken agricultural sector that its interests were being safeguarded, began to denounce the perils of urbanism and to defend sound rural virtues. By the early thirties the OND had become the leading celebrant of folk values, virtually ceasing its efforts to engender a more sophisticated identification with the fascist precepts. The term 'popular culture,' which was adopted by OND planners in the twenties to designate essentially modern cultural pastimes, came, at least until 1936, to be identified almost exclusively with folk traditions – whether genuine cultural survivals of the preindustrial community, long-extinct customs exhumed by diligent fascist ethnographers, or the many pseudo-popular festivities choreographed by the OND itself.

The apparent contradiction between the archaism and irrationality of folk custom and the commonly accepted notions of civil progress were reconciled by spokesmen in their explanations of the 'genuine educational functions' of popular traditions. Beretta staunchly defended the 'public utility' of popular customs against those 'students of social pedagogy' who persisted in believing that they 'constituted ancient and useless fossils that simply retarded the evolution of nations.' True education, now redefined to suit the reactionary social ideals of the regime, should not seek 'to level what was impossible to level' nor to destroy the 'perennial beauty of the race.' When traditional customs, beliefs, and usages were 'subject to the unifying action of modern civilization,' with its 'tendency to standardize men and manners as if they were machines or implements,' the national order inevitably deteriorated. A socially valuable education should have as its primary aim the retention of those traditions that lend cohesiveness to a nation and individuality to its people. Such national values had to be felt before being understood.

'To *educate* even before beginning to *instruct*'; such, in Beretta's words, was the OND's intention as it sought to 'revive the intimate character of traditions.' As the 'People' was inspired with a 'devotion to the past,' so folk traditions would be able to 'carry out their true and effective social functions' [. . .]

Having designated folk manifestations as the one cultural pastime where the people ostensibly gave spontaneous and free expression to its individuality, the OND tended naturally to obscure the degree to which it was actually involved in their revival. Sometimes it took full credit; more frequently, it emphasized that the 'reflowering' of popular traditions responded to a 'new spiritual need' and thus had not been 'provoked artificially': 'Judicious and vigilant propaganda' had sufficed to restore the 'splendor of the past.' The reappearance of historical processions and religious cortèges, celebrated with triumphal floats, ceremonial ships, funerary biers, litters, lilies, fronds, candelabra, and plastic images was 'in itself a manifestation of the innate religious devotion and patriotism of the people.'

In fact, however, folk ceremonial had in large part fallen into desuetude. Familiarity with urban habits through emigration, travel, the press, and military service had led – even in remote rural areas – to the replacement of customary dress by sober work garb. Relatively few of the resplendent municipal festivals, at their peak in the late eighteenth century when sponsored by the royal courts and organized by local guilds, had survived into the postwar period, especially in the northern industrial towns. Those that remained had lost their traditional luster, through lack of municipal funding or public interest. The revival of traditions therefore required considerable artifice.

'No means has been neglected,' acknowledged Beretta, to 'utilize popular traditions in a dignified way for purposes of national education.' Beginning in 1928, folklore sections were set up within each provincial board, their organization entrusted to persons with 'true competence,' 'profound knowledge' of local customs, and above all 'a passionate interest' in the community heritage. With the assistance of committees – made up of the traditional deputations responsible for managing municipal festivities, amateur historians, and ethnographers – the board sections sponsored meetings, competitions, and costume displays. The OND itself proved remarkably active, creating special choral groups (*camerate dei canterini*), organizing rustic bands playing traditional instruments, and promoting over 200 dramatic societies featuring plays in dialect, the most prominent among them being the Ruzzantini of Padua, which specialized in the works of the sixteenth-century popular dramatist Angelo Beolco, called il Ruzzante. The mass media were used extensively to popularize folk music and dances. The OND recorded popular songs for radio transmission, as well as cooperating with the Istituto Luce in producing a series of sound films of the Canterini groups of the Romagna and Sicily; a widely distributed film, *La sentinella della patria*, portrayed the essential *Italianità* of the long-disputed northeastern border regions. Although the OND made no pretense of engaging in 'scientific activity,' it nevertheless promoted the foundation of regional ethnographic museums, furnished them with local ethnographic lore and facsimiles of local costumes collected by its provincial boards.

In this one endeavor at least the OND obtained the full support of academic culture. Although the more qualified intellectuals were generally reluctant to involve themselves in strictly educational programs, they could easily endorse this 'return to traditions.' Folk culture represented a heritage free of the deforming influence of foreign ideologies. Even when unabashedly manipulated for propagandistic purposes, it could still be perceived as a serious cultural form. Re-enacted as living ceremonies by a robust populace, folk customs provided what for upper-class intellectuals was a comforting image–that of 'the people' as the repository and bearer of true national virtues.[. . .]

The event hailed by the OND as its 'first manifestation of national propaganda' was a giant costume rally held in Venice in August-September of 1928. The rally, initially conceived as a costume display for the Three Venices to demonstrate the distinctiveness of the region's people from the bordering populations of Teutons and Slovenes, was taken as an occasion to reaffirm the ethnic unity of the nation as a whole. Its overriding purpose, in the words of the presiding officials, was to familiarize Italians with the 'true Italy,' personified in the 11,000 costumed peasants who, on 18-19 August and again on 8-9 September, paraded through Piazza San Marco in elaborate dress. Beyond evoking the 'simple rural Italy, which cherished and preserved Italian traditions,' the festival had a practical aim in fostering the reconstruction and use of folk costumes in daily life.[. . .]

In a society where dress closely reflected the social status of the wearer, the widespread use of costume performed significant social and ideological functions. Dressing up was both a diversion from daily drudgery and a mode of affirming personal dignity, especially for those who could neither afford bourgeois fashion nor attain party uniform. The OND capitalized on this desire of ostentation, a desire further stimulated by the regime's own obsession with uniform. Decked out in the finery of an updated 'traditional' dress, no longer the sign of civic backwardness, peasants and artisans were endowed with social dignity as participants and protagonists in the numerous folk festivities. In the sense the folk costume served as the 'official dress,' so to speak, of *dopolavoristi*, who, alone among the organized fascist groups, had no special uniform of their own.

The pictorial iconography of fascism quickly absorbed the revived folk costumes as images of national virtues. The comely peasant women who adorned the covers of *Gente nostra*, together with the sturdy peasant men who were 'so mirthful, yet so indefatigable in their work and so sober and thrifty in their habits,' symbolized 'the People,' whose costumes, in Corso's words, expressed that 'passion and aesthetic sense' that 'beautifies their existence even amid the daily misery and drudgery of their lives.' An essentially desolate world – and an unfamilar one for most urban dwellers – was thus transformed into a rural haven; its undeniable but never-depicted hardships glossed over by an image of rejuvenating nature; its virtues, personified in solid patriarchs and 'rural housewives,' to be emulated by a promiscuous and frenzied urban world.

In 1930 the OND was instructed by the PNF [*Partito Nazionale Fascista* – National Fascist Party] to organize harvest and work festivals as a means of promoting artisan and agriculture-based industries. As OND propaganda stressed, any effective protection of jobs had to be accompanied by the preservation of the traditions associated with them. The festivals were organized to re-evoke the spirit of the rural community or the unity of the craft association in which professional activities and group social manifestaions were closely intertwined.[. . .] Much emphasis was put on the pagan-Christian, that is, the nonclerical origins of such festivities in bacchanalian or dionysian fertility rites.

The overwhelming majority of such festivities were celebrated in rural towns and villages. In the countryside surrounding Rome, the months of August through October were marked by numerous fairs sponsored by the city's Dopolavoro dell'Urbe: feting peaches at Castelgandolfo, grapes at Narino, strawberries at Nemi, apples at Nerviano, vines at Ostia.[. . .] Such modern notes as a lottery and the electrical illumination of the public square, designed to attract tourists and thereby involve a larger public within the community circle, marked the transformation of traditional rustic fete into modern consumer spectacle.

In urban centers celebrations appropriating the forms of the harvest, although they evoked the solidarity of rural community, were manifestly consumer orientated.[. . .] Even Milan, the nation's most modern city, had its version of Fruit Day, sponsored in 1934 by the Aeronautics Exposition. For the occasion the proper rural atmosphere was recreated within the city by importing contingents of costumed rustics from the surrounding provinces: The union of urban technology and rural fecundity was self-consciously celebrated in a central square by erecting an enormous iron scaffolding shaped in the futuristic form of the Littorial *fascio* and decorated with 1,000 kilograms of fresh fruit.

Arts and crafts shows performed not dissimilar functions in attempting to reassociate the craftsman and his product in a celebratory and often distinctly nationalistic atmosphere. Bolzano, as the northernmost outpost of *Italianità*, was the site selected in 1930 for the first National Exposition of Arts and Crafts; the 50,000 objects exhibited there were advertised as 'typical manifestations of the skill and versatility of the Italian race.' Numerous similar shows held at the regional and provincial level were devoted to glorifying artisan existence.[. . .]

It cannot be shown whether such displays actually afforded spectators a measure of ideological reassurance that industrial modernization threatening the livelihood of the small producer and the autonomy and spontaneity of the individual was indeed being forestalled. For the numerous visitors, especially in small towns, many of whom were themselves of recent rural extraction, these shows were nevertheless a major cultural event.[. . .] For the profascist ethnographer Emma Bona, the 'most agreeable aspect' of the thirty major provincial and regional shows organized by the OND from 1930 to 1940 was the 'passionate attendance' of the 'people,' who within the context of the shows themselves repeatedly explained to the collectors the meaning and use of certain artifacts and the traditions associated with them.

The OND was at its most inventive when stage-managing the annual municipal festivals and patron saints' days. Frequently the local organizing committees joined the OND. Otherwise, where festivals played a particularly important role in civic life, as in Naples and Rome, the provincial boards themselves took complete charge of the manifestations, developing them on a new and more splendid basis. With the backing of the OND and frequently with the support of local chambers of commerce, which viewed the festivals as optimum means of boosting tourist trade, additional funds were channeled into the annual celebrations to such an extent that their preparation took on the semblance of small-scale public works projects. By the mid-thirties, all of the major cities were celebrating several resplendent festivals including neighborhood festivals, which were frequently invested with municipal pomp.[. . .]

Festivities were choreographed to involve the greatest possible civic participation. The central event – usually a procession – was truly spectacular, complete with displays of cult figures, costumed peasants, caparisoned horses and oxen, allegorical floats, or, as in Venice and the other seaside towns, regattas with illuminated boats. Numerous side events served to generate even more activity. Thus the Barbary races customary in many towns were updated in the form of cycling events, gymnastics contests, and soccer matches. The committees also sponsored contests for decorated booths, window displays, and for the ornamentation of candles. The public was further encouraged to take part in the re-enactments of local legends that frequently commemorated either a heroic defense against or a miraculous rescue from a 'hereditary enemy'.[. . .]

The OND not only respected the religious origin and nature of popular festivals and patron saints' days, but even fostered the religious fanaticism that sometimes characterized such manifestations. In areas of socialist and republican penetration especially, organizers readily capitalized on the divisions that had arisen between Catholic belief and a powerful anticlericalism, exploiting popular religiosity with the recognition that veneration for the traditional cult might be transferred to the new fascist order. This purpose was explicit in the fascist embellishment on the festival of Noiantri in the artisan neighborhood of Trastevere in Rome. The celebration, originally a day-long event organized around the transfer of the Holy Image of the Madonna del Carmine to the church of San Crisogono, honoured the neighborhood's protectoress, while at the same time marking the proud industriousness that distinguished this district on the right bank of the Tiber from other areas of Rome. In the late nineteenth century, this essentially religious characterization of the community's identity had gradually been superseded by a more secular consciousness; in the three decades after Rome became the capital, the procession had fallen into disuse. It was revived, and then only in a minimal way, in 1900, apparently to satisfy devout women parishioners – the men, that day, republican and intransigently anticlerical, withdrew to drink outside the nearby walls of the city. As socialist sentiment mounted in the neighborhood, competing processions were organized; one in 1905, beginning in Piazza Mastai and celebrating the taking of the Bastille, led to a pitched battle between priests and socialists from the nearby Aurora Club. Members of the Giordano Bruno and Tavani Arquati societies joined the counterdemonstration in 1907, drowning out the processional hymns with the Workers' Anthem.

The neighborhood had put up such a strong resistance to the entrance of the *squadristi* in Rome in 1922 that fascist authorities subsequently were particularly solicitous of its pacification and welfare. The decision to organize a cycle of civic ceremonies alongside the original religious ceremonial was thus supported by Mussolini himself, who in 1927 personally authorized the use of special police funds for the purpose. After 1927, the day-long festivity was transformed into a week-long midsummer festival in which Catholic ritual was fused with fascist ceremonial forms. The neighborhood fascist club, 'Duilio Guardabassi,' counseled by a local festival committee formed of merchants and fascist notables, was naturally concerned to find a 'type' of festival organization acceptable to this refractory community. Accordingly, the new festivity had none of the pagan religiosity of the Palermitan Festival of Santa Rosalia, or the pandemonium of the Neapolitan Piedigrotta. Nor did it have the chaotic merrymaking of the Roman Saint John's Day, which was reorganized under the presidency of the Dopolavoro of the Urbe's 'Righetto' Santamaria 'to show off, to invent the unthinkable, to exaggerate beyond all bounds in order to impress the public.' The Festival of Noiantri still referred to the traditions of the neighborhood; among the major events were a commercial fair to revitalize the depressed artisan economy, a light show, plays in dialect, music, songs, 'healthy and jocund visits' to the many local taverns, the posing of wreaths at a neighborhood monument in honor of the Sharpshooters (Bersaglieri) of Sciara-Sciat, and commemorations of Trastevere's own poet Belli, of 'Er Pittor de Trastevere' Bartolomeo Pinelli, and, of course, of the local fascist 'martyr' Guardabassi. The unifying note was nevertheless religious, from the opening processions and high mass attended by the city's most eminent officials to the fifty-foot-long banner that, draped over the archway entrance, declared in local dialect that the neighborhood was now under the beneficent dual guardianship of the Madonna and the Duce:

Trastevere, Trastevere	Trastevere, Trastevere
Brilli de nôva luce	Shining with new light
Ciaì la Madonna e'r Duce	The Madonna and the Duce
Che vejono su te.	Keep you in their sight

More commonly, the fusion of Catholic ritual and secular celebration was achieved in the ceremonial forms themselves. In the ritual processions, side by side with the cult figures, candelabra, sarcophagi, and fronds might be found - if not the blackshirts - children outfitted in the uniforms of the Balilla, portrait effigies of the Duce, and the processional band playing 'Giovinezza.'[. . .]

The revival of carnival festivities was particularly appropriate in the austere depression years. The frenzied atmosphere of carnival time appears to have been deliberately stimulated by the local festival committees, so as to provide - as was true in mass spectator sports - a public catharsis in organized chaos.[. . .] In keeping with carnival traditions, the OND had abandoned its strictures against public dancing in the *dopolavoro* in 1931; masked balls were authorized, it was affirmed, for the 'sole purpose of providing *dopolavoristi* and their families with the proper amount of diversion.' The public feasts, which by custom had marked pre-Lenten rites, appear to have been celebrated with unusual gusto - and not a little self-consciousness as to their original social functions. At Verona in 1932 the traditional Bacchanal of the Gnoccho, which ended with the public cooking of gnocchi, was further celebrated by the town's Dopolavoro Corridoni with a special free repast for 300 of its impoverished citizens.[. . .]

The overwhelmingly local and regional nature of these manifestations reinforcing, at least in appearance, the solidarity and self-consciousness of specific communities, in some respects conflicted with the essentially national orientation of the fascist regime. Encouragement of popular identification with the state, the nation, or race was - no matter how ancient the resurrected ceremony - hardly to be found in a 'revival of traditions' based on regional or local distinctiveness. Regionalism itself, in its historical and political connotations, was associated with the divisions that had obstructed the Risorgimento. Moreover, in the eyes of many nationalists, it was synonymous with the democratic federalist programs of the postunification period, or worse, the proposals for decentralization advanced by socialists and *populari* in the postwar years. Fascism, as Bodrero emphasized, had 'no intention of re-evoking or stimulating regionalism of this kind.' Purified of any inherited political significance, however, the regional ethnocentrism fostered by the 'return to traditions,' parochial and chauvinistic as it was, offered to the regime a partially acceptable surrogate for national allegiance, one infinitely preferable to class identification or what Bodrero dismissed as the 'pernicious particularism of age-old political rivalries.'

Fascist ethnographers and cultural organizers nevertheless attempted to extract from the myriad local customs some national or quasi-national overtones: the popular esthetic sense displayed in folk costumes; the religious fervor of patron saints' days; the crèche, pointedly contrasted with the Christmas tree of the 'barbaric' North; the celebration of the Epiphany appropriately nationalized as the Befana Fascista. Beyond this, unity was molded out of the diversity of regional customs by numerous national shows.

The marriage of the heir to the throne, Humbert of Savoy, to the Belgian Princess Maria José in January 1930 was, although not a specifically fascist ceremony, seized on as a moment to develop a truly national festivity. The vast costume procession, 'sponosored' by the head of government, was as if designed to evoke a new, yet semifeudal national hierarchy, with the fascist dignitaries, led by Turati (vassals to the royal dynasty), heading up a two-mile-long nuptial cortège composed of 300 contingents of lavishly costumed provincials. As they passed beneath the reviewing stand in Piazza Quirinale, where the royal couple was ensconced beside the crowned heads of Europe, the peasant groups paid homage by depositing 'gifts of the land': sheaves of grain, floral wreaths, baskets of fruit. Propitiary rites for the couple were then celebrated according to the local customs of the regional delegations: by some with candle-lit parades, by others with the release of augury doves, or with group dances or choral recitations of marriage songs. Combining as they did traditional peasant costumes, the military regalia of the House of Savoy, and the sober fascist uniforms, the images of the ceremony – among the most publicized national events before the Ethiopian campaign – suggested that for a brief instant the full fusion of popular customs, dynastic traditions, and fascist ritual had been achieved.

As the most spontaneous of activities organized by the regime, at least in their actual conduct, the revived festivities constituted a sphere where popular acceptance, but also rejection and even subversion, might be most freely displayed. Fascist accounts natually emphasized the wholeheartedness of the people's response to the 'return to traditions,' and certain manifestations – as, for example, the *dopolavoro* INA's prize-winning Saint John's Day float for 1930 showing the *Urdopolavoristi* Adam and Eve astride a mastodon – certainly displayed a creatively popular element in the highly manipulated *cultura dopolavoristica*. Whether the regime would have tolerated the translation of such self-irony into political satire seems most doubtful, however; the preparation of festivities was certainly far too well policed to allow the kind of pornographic exuberance displayed by the mid-eighteenth-century Neapolitan *popolino* in priapic images on masques and floats, an impulse that appalled public authorities and genteel society but was quite uncontrollable because of the breakdown of guild authority and Bourbon absolutism. Nevertheless, fascist festivities were the occasion for protests of sorts: some passive in the form of the withdrawal of participation that the police noted in Turin in the late thirties; some more overt in the 'savage brutality of peasant bombardments' that, according to public officials in Pavia, had disrupted the distribution of grapes at the annual festival in 1933. This particular popular 'invention,' whose main target was the assembled officialdom in the reviewing stand, obviously subverted the original fascist purpose behind the event: to consume peaceably and in a celebratory way the excess grape production that was ruining farmers by driving down market prices. But the very act of grape throwing was itself ritualized and so mediated through the festival form that it was completely cut off from any effective organized resistance to fascism. As such it could hardly be characterized as in any way prepolitical, but rather primitively childish, an act of insubordination within a structure that had been substantially accepted by the participants.

The politics of diversion

Perhaps the most striking aspect of the content of the *cultura dopolavoristica* as it emerged during the thirties was the absence of any overt political appeals. Organization, more commonly than not, substituted for a positive cultural policy, whereas activity – however trivial – served to compensate for the lack of explicit or consistent political direction. From this perspective, the *cultura dopolavoristica* might be understood better as a policy of diversion from political and social concerns than as a cultural program designed to impart fascist principles. [. . .]

Until the Ethiopian campaign there was no discussion of the content of a fascist popular art within OND circles. Beginning in May 1935, however, the editors of *Gente nostra*, recognizing the need to recall the masses from the fantasy world of sentimental comedies into the real world of national struggle, opened its columns to debate on cinema and theater. The contributions it received might best be characterized as the ingenuous proclamations of an exhilarated younger generation of intellectuals, inspired with the belief that enthusiasm alone could generate a new fascist culture. Contributors called for a 'new mass theater,' whose main protagonists, rather than being 'the central focus of action,' as in the traditional form, would serve as simple vehicles for the story line. Film directors similarly were admonished to produce truly popular epics:

> Photogenic women, 'vamps,' and 'sex appeal,' they belong to a different kind of film, the kind produced purely for diversion. We shall use the sunburnt faces of our peasants, of our workers, the healthy faces of our mothers.
>
> Let us encourage productions that examine labor in the fields and workshops; let us make a film that is closer to us and to the time we live in; with the people and for the people we shall give life to a new fascist film.

By the spring of 1936 the proper thematic for a truly epic film was declared to be the 'New Empire.' Neither sentimental nor exotic, it would illustrate how fascism's 'proletarian' ideal of colonial acquisition differed fundamentally from the anachronistic French and English notion of the 'white man's burden.'

Gente nostra itself was used for the first time during the Ethiopian campaign as an organ for overt government political propaganda. Before then, occasional articles had dealt with colonialism – focusing, however, not on its political aspects, but rather on the pulchritude of native women and the exoticism of primitive customs. When the Sanctions were imposed on Italy in November 1935, political cartoons suddenly appeared in *Gente nostra*, adopting an appropriately populist imagery to convey fascist aims to a mass public that had hitherto been left ignorant of high politics. Italian war aims were couched in readily comprehensible terms: Italy was a proletarian nation, impoverished by the gluttony of plutocratic nations; these plutocracies, it was explained, had denied Italy its rightful place in the sun, despite the centuries of civilization, scarcity of natural resources, and abundant population that made it far more deserving. More specifically, who were the plutocracies? Grinning cowboys, dwarfish gendarmes, or Colonel Blimps, the latter caricatured as tight-fisted, high-handed tourists, picking their way through

Italian ruins with disdainful condescension for a people reduced by its poverty to a servile status. What were Italy's intentions? Propaganda evoked a misplaced altruism. Italy, it would appear, was bent on a civilizing mission: The Negus had enslaved a Christian population that, starving and brutalized, eagerly awaited liberation. The gallantry of Italy's youth was fired by the picture of the exotic and oppressed Ethiopian maiden calling for deliverance. Once liberated and subjected to the ministrations of Italian culture and technology, Ethiopia was destined to become a fertile land of prosperous settlers and happy natives, whereas Italy, its imperialist ambitions finally satisfied, would hold out a better life for its citizens. War-the ultimate diversionary strategy-lent itself well to the conventions of the diversionary tale.

Once the campaign was concluded, the debate over the content of fascist popular culture disappeared together with the political cartoons from the pages of *Gente nostra*. Thereafter, the magazine occasionally would feature short stories referring explicitly to patriotic themes; and peasants or soldiers-rarely workers-appeared as protagonists. But, although the protagonists changed, the underlying values did not. The same petty bourgeois aspirations found as basic themes in earlier works were imputed to their more plebeian subjects. Film directors and authors continued to subscribe to accepted conventions, embellishing political themes with sentimentalism, rather than seeking to evoke a detached identification with the principles of fascism or with the new national collectivity.

That fascist low culture was essentially diversionary is not after all surprising. The full ideological assimilation of the popular classes into a new national consensus, which-as envisaged by fascist planners in the twenties-involved moral elevation, popular education, and vocational instruction, was in fact precluded by the very structure of the regime's cultural institutions. No amount of directives stipulating the content of a new 'national' culture could be effective when the agencies of culture themselves, by reinforcing existing economic and social barriers, prevented their implementation. Youthful intellectuals, inspired during the Ethiopian campaign by their renewed faith in fascism's revolutionary possibilities, were no more successful than jaded OND functionaries: When seeking to apply the precepts of 'reach out to the people' to the cultural domain, they too were frustrated by bureaucratic structures that, staffed by low-level cultural organizers, systematically segregated the intellectual elites from a mass public.

If not the unifying national culture aspired to by the younger generation, the *cultura dopolavoristica* nonetheless performed significant functions in legitimizing fascist rule. Although lacking the fundamental authenticity of 'popular culture,' fascist low culture did appropriate petty bourgeois ideological motifs, popular ritual forms, and, if only momentarily during the mid-thirties, a populist language with potential appeal to industrial workers. In this sense the *cultura dopolavoristica* mediated between 'popular culture' and official ideology; it was responsive to-and at least partially an expression of-its popular audience, even while incorporating popular themes and forms as elements of official ideology. What had been essentially autonomous expressions of individual or group aspirations or prejudices were in this way transformed into cultural manifestations that were acceptable to, and to a certain extent supportive of, the dominant ideology.

The ideological inconsistency and slight political content of the *cultura dopolavoristica* perhaps belied its capacity to influence popular opinion. Cultural autarchy was unquestionably most complete at the lower levels of the society; ideological defenses were consequently weak. With the 'coordination' of popular cultural institutions, workers were deprived of autonomous means of political expression and opportunities for contact with intellectuals on a more or less equal footing. They were cut off from the alternative sources of information available to the cultured elites through the foreign media and from the critical debates that were tolerated by the regime within intellectual circles. The petty bourgeois functionaries staffing the regime's cultural agencies were thus able to exercise a virtually uncontested authority over popular cultural manifestations. Susceptibility to the stultifying conformity they fostered varied, with workers with prior political experience proving most resistant. The petty bourgeois, that is, younger workers, and especially the peasants, whose previous contact with national political life had been highly sporadic, were far more impressionable. For an often ill-educated public, whose first introduction to national cultural and political events was mediated by fascist agencies, the terms of discourse were inevitably set by official ideology.

The fundamental eclecticism of *dopolavoro* pastimes, although an advantage in attracting a socially diversified audience, proved in the end highly disadvantageous in sustaining its support. As an essentially unstable cultural amalgam, fascist ideology required a monopoly if it was to retain its authority and credibility. Censorship to a certain degree protected it from the competition of more coherent ideological forms. The *cultura dopolavoristica*, however, contained within itself certain insoluble contradictions. The social attitudes it fostered – passivity, ignorance, individualism, traditionalism, evasion – were appropriate as long as the government's overriding concern was to ensure normality. They were compatible with bursts of uncritical enthusiasm, as evidenced at the time of the Ethiopian campaign. However, when the regime in the late thirties sought to sustain mobilization with a firmer identification with fascist principles, these same attitudes proved counterproductive: 'A salubrious institution,' as the *dopolavoro* was described by a former fascist, the journalist Emilio Radius, 'yet a dangerous one for a regime seeking to mold the Italian people into a population of warriors.'

Index